Red Revolution 2020 and Beyond

Strategic Challenges to Resolve Naxalism

Red Revolution 2020 and Beyond

Strategic Challenges to Resolve Naxalism

V K Ahluwalia

B L O O M S B U R Y
NEW DELHI • LONDON • OXFORD • NEW YORK • SYDNEY

BLOOMSBURY INDIA
Bloomsbury Publishing India Pvt. Ltd
Second Floor, LSC Building No. 4, DDA Complex, Pocket C – 6 & 7,
Vasant Kunj, New Delhi 110070

BLOOMSBURY, BLOOMSBURY INDIA and the Diana logo are
trademarks of Bloomsbury Publishing Plc

First published in India 2013
This edition published 2013

ISBN: 978-93-82951-28-5
2 4 6 8 10 9 7 5 3 1

Printed and bound in India by Replika Press Pvt Ltd

Dedicated to
the numerous civilians
and soldiers, who lost their lives due
to left-wing extremist
violence in India.

Contents

List of Tables, Figures and Appendices

Tables

Figures

APPENDICES

Foreword

It is always a pleasure to write the foreword for a well crafted book on a subject of vital topical importance.

"Naxalism" is the Indian nomenclature for classic Maoism, as enunciated by Mao Dzedong in China and crafted more specifically for an Asian milieu, rather than the classical Europe-oriented Communism of Karl Marx and V I Lenin. It has to be understood by Indian policy makers that Indian Naxalism is an entirely homegrown problem, whose remedy too has to be entirely homegrown.

Paradoxically, whereas Indian Naxalites make no secret of their objective to overthrow constitutional democracy in India by armed struggle, yet unlike India's other insurgents in Jammu and Kashmir, and the North East, Naxalites cannot be truly considered (at least not yet) as separatists, seeking to dismember the country at the behest of foreign powers and covert agencies. However, by their geographical location in the core heartland of India, the Naxalites of the "Red Corridor" states stretching from the Nepal border to the dry forests of central and south-central India, present very attractive strategic targets for seduction and subversion by foreign-funded separatism, especially from neighbouring countries.

Governments at the central and state levels, along with the police and administrative machinery, as also Central police and para-military forces, particularly those at the cutting edge, require to understand that socio-political action, and politico-security campaigning, have to be the basic operational philosophy and way of life, for securing the nation against the violence of Naxalism which is spreading in the tribal dominated heartlands of India. Let there be no mistake or doubts, that Naxalism, with its complexities and as yet unknown variations, complexities and mutations is the *major future threat* to national security. It can cripple the nation, unless adequate steps to arrest the slide are taken in time.

The Indian Army has always been the last resort of the nation, and has extensive experience of counter-insurgency and counter-terrorism against various opponents, but their exposure as on date against Naxalite opponents has been restricted. The contents of the book should provide sufficient food for thought for the thinking soldier and even more important, to his counterparts in civil administration at all levels. If the book is read by the political class as well, so much the better.

The author, Lt Gen VK Ahlwalia, seeks to place before a wider audience, his personal expertise and wide experience in this complex and sensitive task. He has made an earnest endeavour to answer the questions that he had set for himself – from the fundamental issues to the complex conflict scenarios. While drawing useful deductions from the past insurgency campaigns, he has aptly analysed the relevance of a few of those lessons in resolving Naxalism. The key strategic challenges, the strategic options available to the Naxals and the urban perspective plans of the Naxalites amply underscore the magnitude of the problem that needs to be addressed on priority. The author has written a scholarly and vividly descriptive book, which I commend alike to the professional, the intellectual, as also the general reader.

General Shankar Roychowdhury, PVSM
Former Chief of Army Staff, Indian Army (1994–97)
Former Member of Parliament, Rajya Sabha

Preface

It was around 11.30 am on April 6, 2010, during the tea break in the Army Commanders' Conference at Kashmir House, New Delhi, when I saw the TV screen displaying the breaking news: "Naxals ambush CRPF column in Dantewada, and kill 73 personnel (later increased to 76)." As it surely was the deadliest and bloodiest-ever attack on the security forces – with the largest killing in one single incident – it generated serious discussion not only among the security forces but also in the entire country. Even before I could absorb the shocking news, by evening teatime the same day, the ticker read, "Army Commander, Central Command, already in Delhi to make presentation on Naxalism." This served as an epiphany to me. While the challenge always existed, I could foresee the magnitude and enormity of the problem that India will face in the coming decade and beyond. For next two days, I encountered the frequently appearing news items saying that the army, with my headquarters as the controlling organization, was likely to be moved into the areas affected by Naxalite movement. This was not true. It was a mere speculation by the media, though the subject was under discussion at the TV shows. Nevertheless, it surely set us thinking more seriously about the ominous nature of the problem, its potential to snow ball, and the possibility of it acquiring a critical mass. This was the second major attack by the Naxalites within 50 days, the earlier one being the attack at the camp of Eastern Frontier Rifles at Silda in West Midnapore (West Bengal), on February 15, 2010, in which 24 personnel were killed. A few more major attacks took place in May and June 2010 in Chhattisgarh and Odisha.

While I was quite aware of the problem of Naxalism prevailing in some of the states of the country due to various incidents of violence and increase in their intensity, the seriousness of the movement dawned on me only in early 2006, when I took over as Director General of Military Training at the army headquarters (HQ). During this period, the army nominated a few more regimental training centers to train additional personnel of the central police forces, now called Central Armed Police Forces (CAPF), as an endeavor to build their capacity and capability to counter Naxalism in an effective manner. Subsequently, I took over as the Army Commander of the Central Army on March 1, 2010, with most of the states critically affected by the Naxalism – Jharkhand, Chhattisgarh, Bihar, and Odisha – in its area of responsibility. This assessment is essentially based on the geographical spread, strength of the Naxals' cadre, and the intensity of violence. As mandated charter of my duties, I visited these states and interacted with various functionaries of the government, the media, the NGOs, and the locals of the affected areas. These interactions, along with the visits to remote places and attending numerous discussions on the subject, formed the basis of my understanding of the root causes and the ground realities of Naxalism.

The first half of the 20th century was characterized predominantly by the inter-state wars. However, after the end of World War II in 1945, there was a progressive increase in intra-state conflicts, because of ethnic, religious, caste, and region-based differences. A large number of these conflicts, which accounted for enormous deaths and destruction the world over, were in the form of various insurgencies. Likewise, India too has been a witness to myriad threats, which have a direct impact on the internal security of the country. These include terrorism, insurgency, rise of religious fundamentalist organizations, communal conflicts, ethnic and caste-based conflicts, fake currency rackets, cyber crimes, drug trafficking, illegal migration and resultant demographic inversion, and left-wing extremism (LWE). Today, insurgency is at the center stage of the security concerns of India. The situation in Jammu and Kashmir (J&K), and the northeastern states has been witness to separatist activities. Naxalism, which began as an agrarian movement, has taken the shape of a revolutionary movement. The peasants' uprising of 1967 at Naxalbari was a turning point in the history of LWE. Naxalism has further accentuated the agenda with its alarming levels of proliferation into a large number of states. It would have a definite adverse effect on the rapidly developing political, economic, social, technological, and military strength of India. How did we arrive at such a critical state? Who is responsible for this? We as a country, its citizens, the political parties, the successive governments in power – at both the center and the states for the past four decades – and the other elements of national influence are all responsible for the movement having reached such disturbing levels. The responsibility has to be shared pretty widely!

It is important to clarify that the terms Naxals, Naxalites, and Naxalism have been frequently used in the book because of its better understanding among the masses. It actually refers to the activities of the Communist Party of India (Maoist), also called CPI (Maoist). It was formed because of the merger of the Maoist Communist Centre of India (MCCI) and the CPI (Marxist-Leninist), "CPI (ML) People's War" (popularly known as PWG). The activities of the CPI (Maoist) account for more than 95% of the Naxal-initiated acts and killings.

Unfortunately, we, in India, do not expose our children, studying in high schools and colleges, to even the rudiments of national security and its impact on various facets of the country's overall well being viz its unity, integrity, and development. With the rapidly changing nature of threats and the security environment the world over, sub-conventional threats will be far more relevant to the national security than ever before. The youth of the country will experience the impact of "these very real threats" in the foreseeable future. This book attempts to give an insight into a conflict that has affected a large segment of India's population, in its heartland, and the likely future scenarios. This further prompted me to delve deeper into the nerves of the affected masses with the aim of understanding their sensitivities, unrealized aspirations, and offer possible solutions, which could be scripted into an institutionalized memory in the form of a book. It would also be possible to add my experiences of serving in the intense counter-insurgency operational environment of the northeastern states and J&K. My wife and both my sons were keen that I share my experiences and thought process on a subject so vital to the country's security. It is one of the significant ways in which a veteran can share his experiences with the next generation, and make a humble contribution towards strategizing the national initiatives for conflict resolution.

Any meaningful analysis of the problem of this magnitude requires accurate statistical data, correct recording of various incidents, and understanding of the ground realities. Although the data pertaining to Naxalism is available in the open domain, there are wide variations in the statistics being reflected at different web sites. A fair amount of data was obtained from the annual reports of various ministries and state governments, from their web sites. During 2010–2012, I addressed numerous training establishments – both the armed forces and civil – with participants having varied levels of intellect and grasp of the ongoing conflict. My interaction with the students and participants, "helped me to develop various ideas and solutions" which have been included in the book. During 2011, the first-ever army formation was inducted for training in the Naxal-affected areas of Chhattisgarh, amid strong protests and bandhs from the rebels. This event was given wide coverage by the media. This necessitated my frequent visits to some of the most sensitive areas of the state, including my stay at the training camp and personalized interactions with the locals, to understand the ground realities. I had the benefit of compiling the data and discussing various facets of Naxalism with Ranjan Prabhu, Brijesh Pandey, AIS Dhillon, BB Parida, PV Ramana, SN Handa, B Vijay Kumar, Poshuk, Vardaan, PP Prakash and Michael St John. I deeply appreciate their support and positive contributions at various stages of the book. I am also grateful to Suresh Gopal, Jyoti Mehrotra, Raj B Prasad and the staff of Bloomsbury Publications, and the Amity University for their tacit support. I owe my gratitude to all those who have been directly or indirectly associated with me and had made a lasting impact on my thoughts on Naxalism, and internal security of the country.

This book aims at comprehensively analyzing the genesis of Naxalism, its ideology, strategic aims, and the strategy for conflict resolution. This book is divided into 10 chapters. Chapters 1 and 2 shed light on the landmark events that define the face of the Naxalite's revolution and further discuss the inequality and socio-economic conditions that foster and propel the revolution. Chapters 3 to 5 further build a deeper understanding of the Naxal's ideology, the impact of bloody years of violence, and analyze the strategic options available to them in the future. Simultaneously, useful lessons, as relevant in the Indian context, are drawn from a study of the some of the past insurgency campaigns. In Chapters 6, 7 and 8, an examination of the strategy for conflict resolution, and the strategic challenges faced by the country, amply highlight the enormity of the problem. After having studied Naxalism from various perspectives and presenting all the relevant facts, Chapters 9 and 10 crystal gaze into the scenario 2020 and beyond, and analyze the urban perspective plan of the Naxals. In addition, drawing from the overall appreciation of the threats, various facets of perception management, conflict resolution and a possible way ahead is proposed. As sub-conventional threats will perhaps be far more relevant to India's internal security in the years ahead – for a number of reasons – the political class, civil servants, uniformed personnel, and the academic community needs to comprehend the problem holistically, and then give serious consideration to taking proactive measures to mitigate the threats.

This book contains professional perspectives gathered as a result of numerous interactions with various experts, field experiences, and from my personal notes on the subject. The opinions expressed and the recommendations made are entirely my own. These do not represent the views of any government organization, the Indian Army, or the Amity University.

V K Ahluwalia

Introduction

India faces a large number of external and internal security challenges due to its geo-strategic location, size, population, demographic profile, and the prevalent politico-socio-economic conditions in the country. Besides long international borders and coastline, it has a number of island territories, an exclusive economic zone, off-shore assets and sea lanes of communications to protect. The external challenges will continue to persist primarily due to the unresolved boundary disputes with Pakistan in the west and China in the north. With the ongoing low-intensity conflicts in Jammu and Kashmir and the northeastern states, she is faced with the looming internal security challenge from the Naxalites. Left-wing extremism (LWE) is an extremist ideology propagating violent struggle to achieve a classless society. There are a number of organizations in India that promote extreme left-wing ideology, and therefore LWE is an umbrella word to describe their activities. Although the impact of Naxalism has been observed in a large number of states, the states that prominently stand out are Chhattisgarh, Jharkhand, Bihar, Odisha, Andhra Pradesh, parts of Maharashtra, and West Bengal. The frequency and intensity of violence had continued to increase progressively with effect from 2001 to 2010, in particular.

Robert M. William Jr. mentions in his book, *The Wars Within*, that the 20th century has been the bloodiest century in the history of the globe. Although estimates vary widely, the tale of death and destruction is monumental.[1] More than 70 civil wars have occurred around the world since 1945, claiming approximately 20 million lives and displacing more than 67 million people.[2] These conflicts are the greatest threat to the ascent of developing nations that account for nearly 75% of the world's economically and socially backward population. Due to globalization, there has been a huge demand for the scarce natural resources, and institutions the world over are looking to grab a piece of this fast-diminishing resource. This heightened race has led to a large-scale mining and extraction of natural wealth, resulting in significant displacement and social exploitation of the natives of such areas. In the Indian context, globalization is seen as a threat by a large number of ethnic groups and communities, particularly the tribal people living in the remote and inaccessible areas. It, therefore, adds a new dimension to their perceived struggle to protect their self identity. They are fighting to bring about social, economic and political inclusion.

In spite of being located in one of the most unstable regions of the world – with myriad internal and external threats – India has been able to achieve and maintain impressive economic growth rates. Notwithstanding this, some of these threats endanger the internal peace and security of a nation "whose religious, ethnic and cultural diversity has to a large extent provided a platform to many, for so many years to push for secessionist or revolutionary movements within."[3] These so-called revolutionaries have realized that many of India's adversaries will enthusiastically support their struggles or movements ideologically, economically, and politically. Besides an adverse effect on the security and growth story, such threats would gradually erode the secular, sovereign, and democratic system of the country.

Among all the internal armed conflicts in India, the Naxalite problem at present is the greatest threat to India's internal security. To analyze the extent and nature of this threat, one must comprehensively understand its genesis and the historical realities from a multidisciplinary perspective. There are a number of questions that need to be answered, from the very fundamental issues to the complex conflict scenario.

- What are the aims and objectives, strengths and vulnerabilities, the ground realities, and the center of gravity of the Naxalites' struggle?
- What are the dynamics and its drivers, actors and their interests, and various forces at work? How does it affect the security and the economic growth of the country?
- How are tribal societies – the worst affected – coping with the conflict in their midst? What should be done to protect their interests?
- What is likely to be the future of the conflict in "2020 and beyond?" Will it penetrate into the urban areas and industrial hubs of the country, as planned by the Naxals?
- What are the areas of concern and strategic challenges to combat Naxalism?
- Are the current national strategies and policies of the government adequate to deal with the ongoing conflict? If not, what are the ways to resolve the conflict?

The LWE has been operating in parts of the country for a few decades. Consequent to the merger, the CPI (Maoist) became the major LWE outfit responsible for most incidents of violence and killing of civilians and the SF. Naxalism is a generic word used to describe the activities carried out by a group of activists forming part of various organizations functioning primarily under the Maoist ideology in a number of states in India. The Naxal activists use this ideology to garner ground-level support from the oppressed masses. Though revolutionary in its basic idea, over the past few years, it has slowly hinged more on extreme violence against the state machinery to achieve its aim of overthrowing the sovereign Indian state.

According to their "Urban Perspective Plan", the Naxals are also making inroads into the important cities and industrial hubs of the country due to the discontent among the urban population with high level of corruption at all levels and ineffectiveness of the administrative machinery. This discontent has manifested itself in large-scale support for various movements in the recent years. Though these movements are peaceful at present, they may become a cause of security concern in the future, if corrective measures are not put in place soon. The Naxal revolutionaries wish to establish their stronghold in the cities, something that is the part of their objectives and ideology, to exploit some of these mass movements.[4] In consonance with their aim, the Naxals have also made concerted efforts to penetrate and generate a support base among the youth in the educational institutions. This needs to be noted and suitable pro-active measures initiated to prevent the spread to urban areas.

I am of the firm belief that leaders must look ahead into the future, with a view to understanding the scenarios that are likely to come forth. To do so, we should analyze in detail the thought process of the insurgents and their leaders. Therefore, an effort has been made to examine in detail two of their most important documents – "Strategy and Tactics of the Indian Revolution (STIR)" and "Urban Perspective Plan (UPP)" – which highlight their ideology, rationale, the strategy, and tactics to be adopted to carry forward the movement in the future. Although the world's political, economic, and security scenario is changing at a rapid pace, and it is difficult to foresee more accurately into the distant future, an effort has been made to look at the likely future scenarios. This would enable the policy makers to formulate their strategies for the future, rather than resorting to crisis management. I have done some crystal gazing to put down my thoughts on the "Scenario 2020 and beyond", for both rural and urban Naxalism; and made recommendations towards formulation of national strategy.

Notes

1. Robin M. Williams Jr., "The Wars Within: The People and States in conflict", (New Delhi: Manas Publications, 2004), xii.
2. Paul Collier and Nicholas Sambanis, "Understanding Civil War: Evidence and Analysis" (Washington, DC: The World Bank, 2005), xiii, accessed February 24, 2012, http://books.google.co.in/books?id=yNTQ-BDLPxIC&printsec=frontcover&source=gbs_ge_summary_r&cad=0#v=onepage&q&f=false.

3. Brahma Chellany, "Regional Security Challenges: Indian State in Asia", in *Security Politics in Asia and Europe*, ed. Wilhelm Hofmeister (Singapore: Konrad-Adenauer-Stiftung, 2010), 158–166.
4. Makrand Gadgil, "Security Concerns over Naxalite Arrests in Urban Maharashtra", *Livemint*, accessed December 12, 2011, http://www.livemint.com/2011/05/24003819/Security-concerns-over-Naxalit.html. (The new strategy focuses on a six-stage approach called SAARRC – Survey, Awareness, Agitation, Recruitment, Resistance and Control. They have completed the first stage of survey, i.e. identifying the target groups, potential areas of discontent and flash points in urban areas. Now they are in the process of implementing the second, third, and fourth stages of their strategy. In fact, the Maoist's documents, Strategy and Tactics of the Indian Revolution and Urban Perspective Plan cover their thought process in a detailed manner.)

Chapter 1

Defining Moments of Naxalism

In March and April 2012, the Naxalites had, in a repetition of their earlier tactics, abducted two Italians and a Member of the Legislative Assembly (MLA), in two separate incidents, in Odisha, and, the district collector (highest civil bureaucrat of a district) of Sukma, in Chhattisgarh.[1] All hostages had returned home safely, but only after the two state governments struck deals with the respective rebel leadership. In addition, even as their spatial spread has been steadily on the rise since 2001, fatalities – of civilians in particular – from Naxal violence and the destruction of infrastructure had also touched high levels – peaking in 2009 and 2010. The country was shocked by the cruel tactics of the Naxals in January 2013. Following the encounter of the Security Forces (SF) with the Naxals on January 7, 2013, in the Karmatiya forests of Latehar district in Jharkhand, the bodies of a few slain CRPF personnel were found to be booby trapped with improvised explosive devices (IEDs). Further, as if that was not enough, they employed the most inhuman and brutal tactics: they placed 2.5 kg of explosives inside the stomach of one of the martyred soldiers.[2] In response to the mounting criticism, the Naxals have also accused the SF of not following any "rules of war"; and hence, they would go beyond the rules.[3] In an audacious and dreadful ambush, in broad day light, on May 25, 2013, the Naxals killed 28 people including prominent political leaders like N.K. Patel, and Mahendra Karma – the founder of the two major anti-Maoist movements in Chhattisgarh – and security personnel near Darbha Ghat in Bastar district. Earlier also, the Naxals had attacked the convoys of Chandrababu Naidu, the then Chief Minister (CM) of Andhra Pradesh in October 2003 and Buddhadeb Bhattacharjee, the then CM of West Bengal in November 2008, both in their respective home states. They both had survived the attempts on their lives. The country continues to witness such bloody attacks by the rebels in the areas critically affected by the Naxalism. The local population remains the worst affected, as there have been a few instances when innocent civilians have also been killed during operations by the SF.[4]

While discussing the fragile internal security environment, Kautilya – the known revolutionary thinker, writer and a shrewd political leader – comes to mind.

> "*There are various kinds of dangers*
> *That which is of external origins and internal abetment*
> *That which is of internal origins and external abetment*
> *That which is of external origins and external abetment*
> *That which is of internal origins and internal abetment*
> *Of all the above kinds of dangers, internal dangers should be got rid of first*
> *For they are the internal troubles, like the fear from a lurking snake*
> *Those are more serious than external troubles.*"
>
> – Kautilya (350 BC–283 BC)

Kautilya is traditionally known as the author of the "Arthashastra," meaning "Scriptures of Wealth," written around 2350 years ago. During this period, Chandragupta Maurya extended and consolidated his empire with the help of Kautilya. Considering the then prevailing state of splintered kingdoms and unstable environment, and to ensure comprehensive protection of all its vital interests, he accorded higher priority to tackling internal threats. If the internal situation of the nation remains weak, it has, among others, a direct adverse impact on sense of security among the people, and an equally undesirable blow on political, social, and economic growth of the country.

Whenever people have faced food insecurity, poverty, unemployment, exploitation, political oppression, the affected classes have generally revolted against the authoritarian regimes. Historically, such revolts have predominantly manifested in armed rebellions, because violence is a method of being visible to the state. Years of social discrimination, economic exploitation and landlessness in India, both pre- and post-independence, had made conditions ripe for the communist ideologies to take root. These were further encouraged by the successful revolutions taking place elsewhere in the world, notably China. A deeper insight into the Indian history suggests that both before and after independence, there have been classic uprisings of the tribal groups and the poor farmers in the vast stretches of Bengal, Bihar, Bastar, Chota Nagpur, and Andhra Pradesh against the British and feudal landlords. The current Naxalite or the Maoist movement has been active in India since 1967. It was against the backdrop of sheer exploitation, injustice, and poverty that Naxalism started as an agrarian rebellion by the Santhal tribes of Naxalbari village in West Bengal in 1967.[5] The agrarian revolution against the ruling class subsequently morphed into an insurgency in the 1980s with the rise of the People's War Group and Maoist Communist Centre India (MCCI). When the CPI (Marxist Leninist) People's War, popularly known as the PWG, and MCCI merged to form the Communist Party of India (Maoist) on September 21, 2004, their military wings also merged to form the Peoples's Liberation Guerilla Army (PLGA). This gave a near pan-India orientation to "Naxalism", which takes its names from Naxalbari, the birth place of the commencement of agrarian movement of "Land for Tillers". To get a clearer picture of the Naxalite movement, a brief historical perspective has been traced giving the important landmarks – a journey that had its fair share of "ups and downs."

Peasant Uprisings

There have been many revolts by the peasants and tribal groups against authoritarian regimes, land lords, money lenders, and petty government officials on account of agriculture-cum-land–related policies, exploitation, social discrimination, and forced cultural changes. Prominent among them were Ho, Munda, Kol, or Santhal uprisings. While some of these uprisings did achieve partial success, none of them could acquire any unique identity relating to a specific cause or the nature of uprising. A case in point is the uprising led by Birsa Munda in Bihar in 1899, in Chaibasa and Chota Nagpur region. It was during these days that he started propagating, though in a vague way, the concept of an independent Munda Raj.[6] For the ruling classes, it was simply an audacious rebellion by the tribal people against the British authority. Those were indeed the classic uprisings of the Adivasis[7] and poor people from Bengal, Bihar, and Chota Nagpur regions. Although, they rose against issues like exploitation, economic deprivation, and social discrimination, the British rulers managed to suppress them, thanks to the efforts of the armed forces and the active backing rendered by the Hindu and Muslim zamindars.[8]

Indigo revolt

With expansion of the British power, indigo planting became increasingly commercially profitable due to the demand for blue dye in Europe. The indigo planters, mostly Europeans, made concerted efforts to make money as they mercilessly persuaded the peasants to plant indigo instead of rice, tobacco and other crops. The farmers were unprotected from the brutal planters, who resorted to mortgage or destruction of their property, if they were unwilling to obey them. As per the Act of 1833, the planters were granted a free hand to pursue their agendas. Even the zamindars, moneylenders, and other influential people continued to support the British planters. Due to injustice and severe oppression unleashed on them, the farmers resorted to revolt, which began from Nadia. After the Indian War of Independence in 1857, the discontent continued to grow among the farmers. In February–March 1859, the farmers refused to sow a single seedling of the indigo plant. With common causes of sufferings at the hands of the planters, the resolve of the farmers – across their religious affiliations – grew stronger. They stood together and revolted. Most importantly, it was a revolt of both the major religious groups of farmers in Bengal. What is of great significance is that a farmer, Haji Molla of Nischindipur, said that he would "rather beg than sow indigo."[9] Prominently, Nadia, Pabna, Khulna, Malda, Dacca, 24 Parganas, Burdwan, Murshidabad and adjoining areas were affected by the revolt. Refer Figure 1.1 (p. 5).

Bhumkal rebellion

The state of Chhattisgarh was carved out of Madhya Pradesh on November 1, 2000, as the 26th state of India. It is the ninth largest state in India, with a population density of 154 and 189, as per census 2001 and 2011, respectively. The state is extremely rich in natural resources especially minerals and forests. In fact, 90% of India's iron ore, considered the best in the world, is found in Chhattisgarh alone.[10] It is also home to a large tribal population amounting to 31.8% of its total population.[11] Since the late 18th century and through the 19th century, Chhattisgarh has witnessed several tribal rebellions/movements. These tribal movements like the Halba rebellion (1774–79), Paralkot rebellion (1825), Tarapur rebellion (1842–54), Maria rebellion (1842–63), Bastar Revolt for Independence (1856–57), Koi Revolt (1859), Muria rebellion (1876), and the Bhumkal Movement (1910) remained focused on asserting their traditional rights on the local resources, lands, and forests. Refer Figure 1.2 (p. 5). The tribal groups often rallied around the issues of traditional culture and the tribal way of life, and protested against the perceived exploitative system of governance. It also shows that the tribal groups have rebellious instincts, primarily because of the inequality, injustice, illiteracy and lack of opportunities. They also felt that they were subjected to an unjust political, economic, and social order, first by the British and thereafter by the successive governments of independent India. Bastar's tribal groups consist of Gonds (subgroups include the Marias, Murias, Abhujmarias, Dhurwas, Dorlas, etc.) and non-Gonds. Marias attracted attention for their "Ghotul" system of community interaction among the younger generation.[12]

Of all the previous-mentioned rebellions, the most widespread, known, and important movement was the Bhumkal rebellion of 1910. It is considered to be the largest tribal rebellion of its times in Bastar.[13] Out

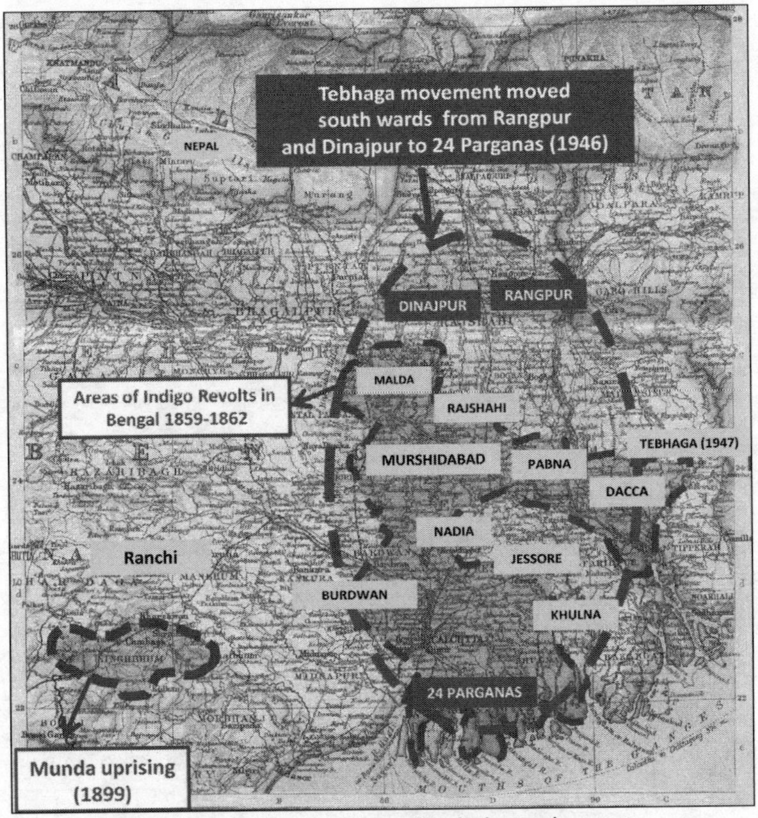

Figure 1.1: Major Uprisings Pre-independence (Pre-independence map of undivided Bengal)

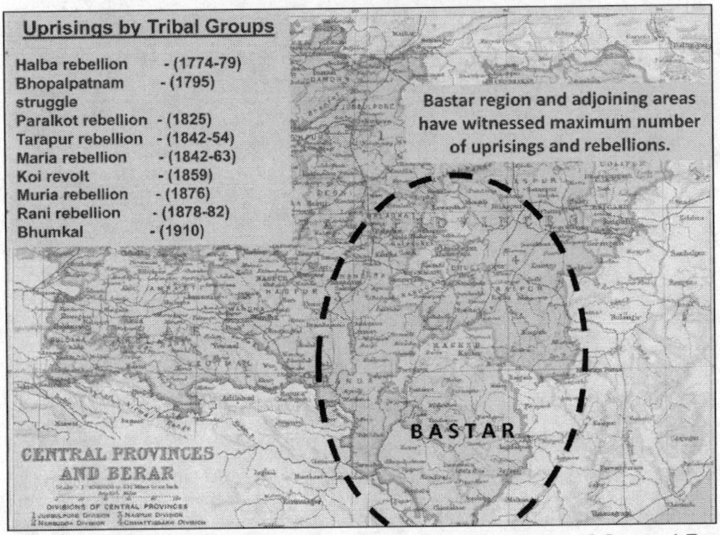

Figure 1.2: Uprisings by Tribal Groups: Bastar Region (Map of Central Provinces)

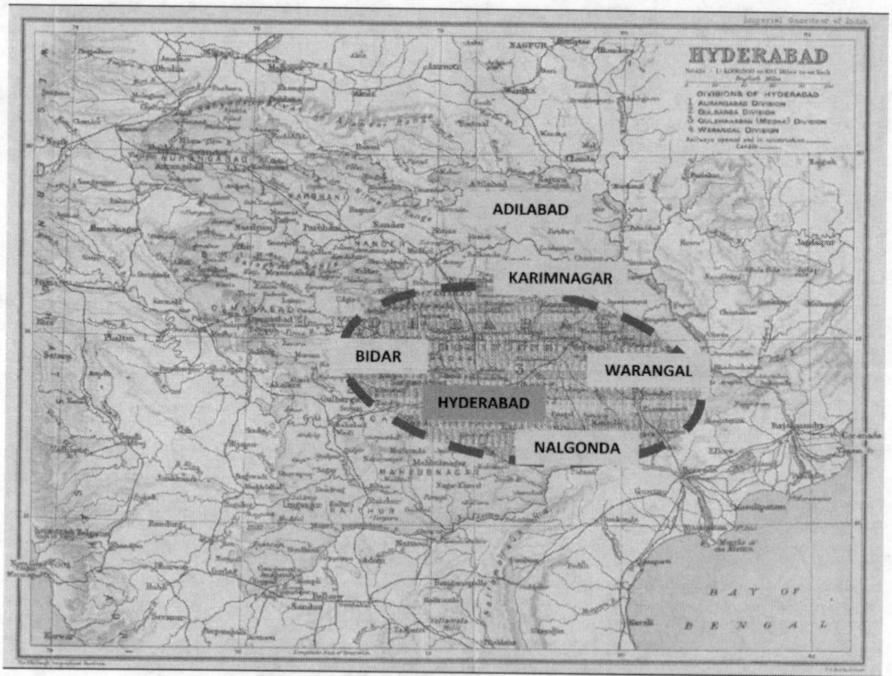

Pre-Independence Map of Hyderabad

Figure 1.3: Telangana Armed Struggle (1946–1951)

Source: http://www.google.co.in/imgres=http://sagarsrivastavagd.blogspot.com

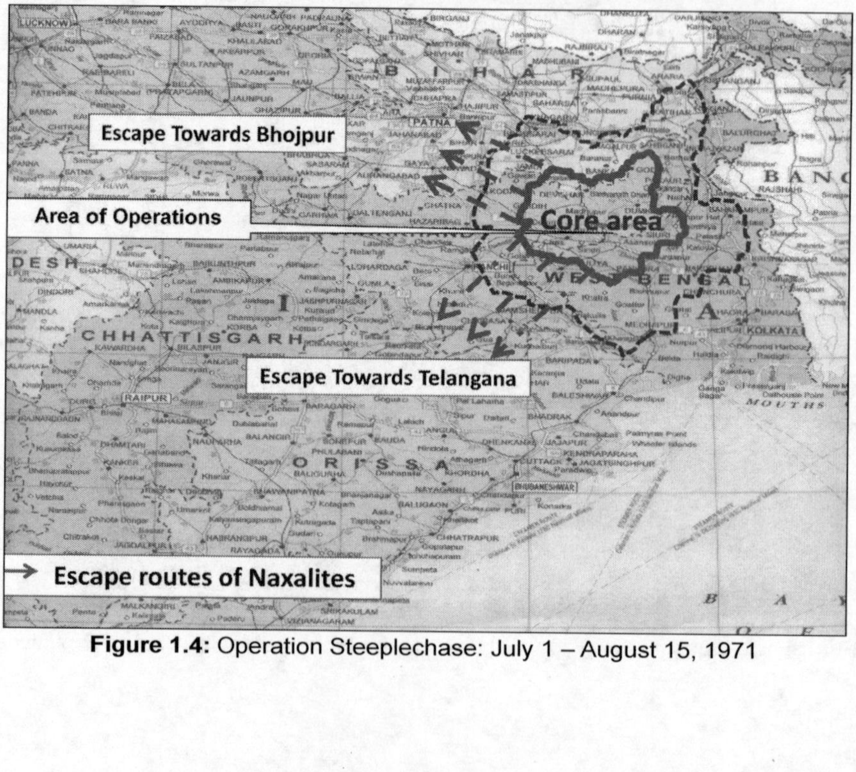

Figure 1.4: Operation Steeplechase: July 1 – August 15, 1971

of the 84 parganas of the Bastar district, 46 were affected by the rebellion. This rebellion continued the struggle for preserving and defending the traditional tribal rights and their way of life. The main reasons for this rebellion were exploitation of natural resources and an attempt to subvert the traditional customs and culture of the tribes due to migration of outsiders, mostly businesspersons, traders, and government officials in the wake of growing capitalist commercial activities. In 1908, the British declared the forests to be reserved forests. Subsequently, the contractors from outside were given rights to take timber and wood for railway sleepers. This deprived the tribes of their main source of livelihood. It was a typical case where the British did not seem to care for the welfare of the tribes. Introduction of the British system of education and schools were seen as an attempt to surreptitiously subvert their traditions and culture. This, coupled with exploitation by the government officials and the brutality of the police, culminated into the Bhumkal Uprising.

Tebhaga movement

The literal meaning of *Tebhaga* is "two–third" – it was a demand of the land tillers (sharecroppers) of Bengal to get two-third share of the produce of crops, as against the prevalent practice of half of the produce. Although the draft bill was prepared, it never became an act primarily due to the pressure of the powerful landowners, who were required to lose their share and get only one-third. Thus, when the farmers saw that their demands were not likely to fructify, in the spirit of Tebhaga, they intensified their struggle from 1946. The catchword that went around was, "We want Tebhaga. We will give our lives but not our crop."[14] The movement spread from Rangpur and Dinajpur in the north to 24 Parganas in the south, wherein the farmers forcibly took two-thirds of the harvested crop. Out of the 19 districts of Bengal, the most intensely hit areas were Dinajpur, Rangpur, Jalpaiguri, Khulna, Mymensingh, Jessore and 24 Parganas. It resulted in clashes between the farmers and the landowners. Jyoti Basu, the patriarch of the CPI (M), called the movement as the proudest movement in the history of farmer's movement in West Bengal. The demand of the movement was for enactment of a law for increasing the share of the Adiyars and the Bargadars, who tilled the lands of the landlords and who constituted 41% of the farmers in 1940, from half to two-third.[15] Refer Figure 1.1 (p. 5).

Telangana armed struggle

The communists, from the very beginning, directed the Telangana peasants' armed struggle. It was also called the "Vetti Chakiri" movement.

It was a communist-led peasant rebellion against the feudal lords of the Telangana region, and later against the princely state of Hyderabad, between the period 1946 and 1951. The Communist Party of India (CPI) had led the rebellion. The peasants launched their struggle on economic issues against forced labor, illegal extractions, and unauthorized evictions, against the feudal lords of the region. The revolt started in 1946 in the Nalgonda district against the feudal lords and quickly spread to Warangal and Bidar districts in around 4,000 villages. Peasant farmers and laborers revolted against the local feudal landlords (*jagirdars* and *deshmukhs*).[16] They virtually ruled over all the communities in the village, managed tax collection (revenues), and owned almost all the land in that area. The Nizam had little control over these regions barring the capital Hyderabad. Chakali Ilamma,[17] belonging to a low-caste Rajaka caste, had revolted against zamindar named Ramachandra Reddy, who had tried to forcibly take away her four acres of land. Her revolt inspired many to join the movement. The initial modest aims of the uprising were to do away with the illegal and excessive exploitation meted out by these feudal lords in the name of bonded labor. The most vociferous demand was for writing off all debts of the peasants that were manipulated by the feudal lords and moneylenders. The Telangana armed struggle (1946–51) was much more broad based and had no parallel in Indian history since the Sepoy Mutiny of 1857.[18] Refer Figure 1.3 (p. 6). After independence, certain amount of land reforms did take place in the affected areas; as a result, the movement subsided.

Naxalbari and Beyond

1967 – Naxalbari

Naxalbari has been discussed separately, as it has a special place in the history of the LWE. Naxalbari, a part of Darjeeling district, became famous for being the site for initiating the left-wing poor peasants' uprising in May 1967, which had begun with the "land to tiller" slogan. The incident was triggered in Naxalbari when the police opened fire on a group of villagers, who were demanding their right to the crops. Charu Majumdar, along with other prominent members, had led the uprising effectively. The Naxalbari uprising was termed as the "first authentic Maoist phenomenon in India" by the leaders of the revolution. The uprising had received wide support from the Chinese Communist regime, as also coverage in the media. Within a few days, July 5, 1967, edition of People's Daily carried an article entitled "Spring Thunder over India", which said, "A peal of spring thunder has crashed over the land of India." The Chinese people joyfully applauded this revolutionary storm of the Indian peasants in the Darjeeling area, as do all the Marxist-Leninists and revolutionary people of the world." Naxalbari movement saw the emergence of strong senior leaders with full faith in hard-core ideology, which was supported by a large number of middle-level activists in the form of students and educated people of the society. The initial phase of Naxalism saw the rise of great ideologues, and even today, majority of the Naxals are still following the ideological line. Charu Mazumdar had set 1975 as the target of liberating the entire country.[19]

The revolt was primarily in the area of three police stations – Naxalbari, Kharibari, and Phansidewa. As per census report of 1961, about 65% of the population of these three police stations was scheduled caste (SC) and scheduled tribes (ST), who worked as agricultural labor or in mines, forests, and tea plantations. A small percentage owned small land holdings. The majority cultivated on agency basis (baghchash). The baghchashis were exploited by the jotedars (landlords). When the Land Reforms Act was passed in 1955,[20] the jotedars started transfers of land to bypass the provisions of the Act. The Santhals, armed with bows and arrows, forcibly occupied the lands, lifted stocks of hoarded rice, and killed an inspector of police. After this, there was a major deployment of police forces by the state government. Consequent to several operations, the movement was crushed. Though not many people were killed in these clashes, this uprising was hailed as "the single spark which can start a prairie fire."[21] The uprising received wide support from the Communist regime in China. However, the West Bengal government was able to bring the situation under control within 72 days.

Thereafter, a formal meeting of the Communist revolutionaries from various states was held in November 1967. It finally resulted in the formation of the All India Coordination Committee for the Communist Revolutionists (AICCCR) in May 1968, with the basic ideology of protracted armed struggle and non-participation in the democratic process. Contrary to the views of predominant section of the AICCCR, Kanhai Chatterjee had maintained that armed struggle and annihilation of the class enemy should be carried out only after building the mass base.

April 22, 1969, the birth centenary of Lenin, turned out to be a historical day – the AICCCR split resulting in the formation of CPI (Marxist-Leninist) CPI (ML), under the leadership of Charu Majumdar. During this period, P. Nagi Reddy group formed the Revolutionary Communist Committee in Hyderabad, another faction that splintered from the AICCCR. While the members of the CPI (ML) party widely supported the ideology of a protracted people's war against the ruling class, the "revisionist",[22] the CPI (Marxist) had embraced the parliamentary path to socialism. Difference in the perception of ideology led to another split on October 20, 1969. Dakshin Desh Group, which was formed by Kanhai Chaterjee, split from CPI (M) on the issue of Maoist versus Marxist ideology. He reorganized the Dakshin Desh Group to form the Maoist Communist Centre (MCC) on October 20, 1969. Thereafter, the MCC, which already had its influence in West Bengal, further expanded its activities towards Bihar. Due to the ongoing rift among the lower and the upper castes in Bihar, the party established itself in Bihar in a quicker period. In January 2003, another significant merger took place between the MCC and the Punjab-based Revolutionary Communist Centre of India (Maoist), led by Shamsher Singh Sheri. The unified organization was renamed Maoist Communist Centre of India or the MCCI.[23]

Srikakulum Armed Struggle

Srikakulum lies in the northeastern coastal portion of Andhra Pradesh, bordering Odisha. It is a hilly-cum-forest area in the Eastern Ghats, inhabited predominantly by the landless girijans or tribes, who were exploited by the sahukars (moneylenders). While the movement in Srikakulum is known to have started as early as 1961, it remained a low-key affair until the Naxalbari uprising in May 1967. The Naxalbari uprising was a turning point in the history of armed struggle from which the people of Bihar, Uttar Pradesh, and Andhra Pradesh drew great inspiration. October 31, 1967, was a landmark in the history of the armed rebellion of Srikakulum, as the landlords, during a clash with the girijans, shot dead two tribal persons. This infuriated the tribal people, who fought against the landlords. Around the same time, based on a decision taken by the AICCCR, guerrilla squads (dalams) were formed to organize armed struggle with a view to seize their land, property and to annihilate the class enemies. During the two years (1968 to 1970), the Revolutionary Communist Committee of Andhra Pradesh, led by T. Nagi Reddy, and the Srikakulum movement brought under their control large areas of the northern districts of Telangana, and Srikakulum. Based on a strong response from the state government, by July 1970, a large number of police personnel and leaders of the uprising were killed.

West Bengal and Bihar

The two districts of Bengal that have contributed significantly to the struggle of the tribal groups and the farmers were Midnapur bordering Bihar and Odisha, and Birbhum. Midnapur, which has a sizeable tribal population of Santhals, Oraons, and Lodhas, had witnessed an organized movement in the Debra and Gopibhallapur police stations. The majority of them were landless laborers. A small proportion owned small plots of land or cultivated the jotedar's land as *Bargadars*.[24] After the

Naxalbari uprising in 1967, a section of CPI (M) workers in Midnapur started propagating the extremist line.[25] They supported the kisans and bargadars and worked for a movement against the jotedars. During the period 1968–1970, in similar incidents, the affected people of the Mushahari block of Muzaffarpur district of Bihar, in particular, resisted the might of the powerful landlords. This had a phenomenal effect on the other villagers in the adjoining areas.

Charu Majumdar[26] had led the Naxalbari movement effectively. In addition, having written his ideological-political thoughts in the "Eight Historic Documents", in 1965–1967, he was recognized as the undisputed leader of the Naxalite movement. The untiring efforts of Charu Majumdar and Kanu Sanyal, and the success of the Naxalbari uprising saw the mushrooming of other Maoist organizations and spread of the movement into a number of other states. After the success of Operation Steeple Chase, the joint operation in July-August 1971, Charu Majumdar was arrested the following year on July 16, 1972, from Calcutta (Kolkata). He reportedly died in police custody (Lal Bazar lock-up) after a brief illness on July 28, 1972, because of which the leadership of the CPI (ML) virtually collapsed and the party started breaking into a number of factions. The period 1972–1980 saw a large number of splits and mergers, particularly the CPI (ML). This period is also referred to as the period of decline of the Naxalite movement due to splintering of the group into smaller factions. The Naxalites were divided into 40 odd factions, based on differences in the perception of leaders regarding the objectives to be achieved and the methodology to be adopted to carry forward the movement.

Some of the defining moments of Naxalism – between 1967 and 2012 – have been covered briefly. By the middle of 1970s, stray incidents of looting of arms and killings of "class enemies" had continued to progressively increase. There were approximately 4,000 incidents of Naxal violence during 1970-1971. Concerted police operations were launched. Finally, these culminated in "Operation Steeple Chase", a joint Army-PMF-Police operation from July 1, 1971 to August 15, 1971. Refer the map of Operation Steeplechase at Figure 1.4 (p. 6).[27] In this, the Army provided the outer cordon for joint operations, to seal the routes of entry and exit. The CRPF provided the inner cordon, and the state police moved into the affected areas. As there was not enough organized resistance, the movement was brought under control within 45 days. The operation was generally successful in containing the first agrarian armed rebellion in India, even as some of the surviving die-hard Naxals escaped into the neighbouring areas of Bhojpur of Bihar and Telangana forest areas of Andhra Pradesh.[28] It led to decline in the movement from 1971 to 1980.

The second phase refers to the period 1980–2004, during which Kondapalli Seetharamaiah (Andhra Pradesh) broke away from the CPI (ML) and went ahead to form the People's War Group (PWG) in April 1980. During the period 1980-2004, various factions worked on improving their organizations, mass base and frontal entities. The Party Unity (PU) group attempted to bring unity among all the splinters of CPI (ML). In August 1998, CPI (ML) Party Unity, which was based in Bihar, merged with CPI (ML) People's War Group, and came to be known as CPI (ML) People's War. In the 1980s, there was a second surge of the left wing violence due to formation of PWG. When the Andhra Pradesh police started conducting sustained anti-naxal operations, the cadres shifted into the secure bases in areas bordering Maharashtra, undivided Madhya Pradesh and Odisha.

CPI (Maoist) Phase

According to their document, "Party Programme", the ideology affirms its commitment to "protracted armed struggle" to undermine and to seize power from the state. Two important documents of the Maoist called the "The Party Programme" and "Strategy and Tactics of the Indian Revolution" are important milestones in the manifestation of clear-cut goals of the group. It also resulted in the formation of the PGA or the Peoples Guerrilla Army in 2000.[29] The present day ideology and strategy of the left-wing extremists flow from their merger of the line of thought of the MCCI and the PWG. It aims at the establishment of a Compact Revolutionary Zone (CRZ) stretching from Nepal to Andhra Pradesh and beyond, while continuing its pursuit of *creation of a people's democracy through seizure of power via a protracted armed struggle, armed struggle being central to its scheme of things.*[30] If we analyze the party's ideology critically, it sends a dangerous signal. It has serious implications for the country, primarily because the stated aim of the party is to overthrow the government, by protracted armed struggle against the state. It is literally a war against the state. In the case of Philippines insurgency, Seachon writes, "Armed revolution was regarded as the only way to overthrow the United States-sponsored government, free the people from their oppression, and institute a people's democratic revolution."[31]

During this phase, the newly formed People's Liberation Guerrilla Army (PLGA), began carrying out bold, mass attacks against armed police posts, armories and jails in strength, in far-flung areas. The aim was to loot weapons, ammunition, instil fear, tie down the security forces (SF) on protective/defensive mode in wide spread areas and then proceed to create liberated zones. The spatial growth of Naxalism, over the years, has been dramatic. From just 9 states and 53 districts in 2001, it is estimated to have affected, to varying degrees, some 212 districts in almost 15 states during 2009-2010. Another authentic study gave the figures as 223 districts.[32] With an overall decline in the incidents of violence and killings in 2011-2012, there has been some improvement in the situation on the ground.

There are a number of organizations in India that propagate extreme left-wing ideology,[33] and therefore, the LWE is an umbrella word to describe their activities. In spite of the unification of ultra-left groups, conservative estimates put the present number of the LWE outfits in India at 39.[34] Naxalism, on the other hand, refers to the activities of the CPI (Maoist), which today accounts for more than 90% of the total LWE incidents and 95% of the resultant killings.[35]

Notes

1. Ghosh Avijit, "Reds aiming at high value targets", say analysts,' *Times of India*, April 26, 2012.
2. VK Ahluwalia, "Reds use brutal tactics to create fear psychosis", *Times of India*, January 19, 2013.
3. Mohua Chatterjee, "Reds will repeat tactics of using jawans' bodies as booby traps", *The Times of India*, February 11, 2013.
4. Times News Network, "Bastar furious over 'encounter' that killed 3 kids", *The Times of India*, May 20, 2013. (Cases in point being the reported controversial killings by the SF in Sarkeguda (Bijapur district) on June 29, 2012 and the killing of civilians including children at Edasmetta (Bijapur district) on May 17, 2013.)
5. The Santhals are the largest tribal community in India, who live mainly in the states of Jharkhand, West Bengal, Bihar, Odisha, and Assam. There is also a significant Santhal minority in the neighboring country, Bangladesh, and a small population in Nepal.
6. "People's Democracy", *Times Today*, accessed on August 14, 2012, http://thetimestoday.blogspot.in/2010/07/munda-rebellion-birsa-munda.html.
7. Adivasi is an umbrella term for a heterogeneous set of ethnic and tribal groups claimed to be the aboriginal population of India. They consist of substantial indigenous minority of the population of India.
8. T.R. Jain, Mukesh Trehan, Indian Economy, V K Publications, 2007, 130-131. In this system, one or more persons, known as the Zamindar, own the whole village or the entire land of the village. A **Zamindar** or **zemindar**, was an aristocrat, typically hereditary, who held enormous tracts of land and ruled over and taxed the people. Over a period of time, they took princely and royal titles. During the colonial period, Zamindar would collect all taxes on his lands and then hand over the collected taxes to the British authorities (keeping a portion for himself). The system was legally abolished after India attained independence.
9. "Indigo Rebellion: The International Encyclopedia of Rebellion and Protests", http://www.blackwellreference.com/public/tocnode?id, and "Modern Indian History", www.kooladdict.com/modern-indian-history/

indigo-revolt. Indigo is a color named after the purple dye derived from the plant –was used for dyeing the textiles in England. The biggest indigo concern was established in Nadia-Jessore-Khulna.

10. Government of Chhattisgarh Web site, accessed February 08, 2012, www.cg.gov.in.
11. Ministry of Tribal Affairs, GoI – Annual Report 2010-11.
12. For more details, see "Ghotul system of Chhattisgarh tribals", Travelspedia, accessed November 21, 2012, http://travelspedia.com/South-Asia/India/Chattisgarh/8889.html.
13. Lingo Mudyal Pen, "Bhumkal Bastar", accessed August 14, 2012, http://bhumkal.blogspot.in/.
    H.L. Shukla, Batar ka Mukti Sangram, Madhya Pradesh Hindi Grantha Academy, Bhopal 1995 (The 150 year history of protests and rebellion in Bastar culminated in the Bhumkal rebellion of 1910).
14. Prakash Singh, "The Naxalite Movement in India" (New Delhi: Rupa Publications India, 2006).
15. "Jyoti Basu Memoirs, So Far As I can Remember", Chapter VII, Tebhaga Movement, accessed December 12, 2011, http://jyotibasumemoirs.wordpress.com/page/2/.
16. Carolline M. Elliot, "Decline of a Patrimonial Regime: The Telangana Rebellion in India 1946", accessed December 12, 2011, http://www.scribd.com/doc/15377979/Decline-of-a-Patrimonial-Regime-The-Telengana-Rebellion-in-India-194651.
17. "Demand for Installing Chakali Ilamma's Statue", *The Hindu* (Chennai, India), November 1, 2010, accessed February 16, 2012, http://www.hindu.com/2010/11/01/stories/2010110160410300.htm.
18. Prakash Singh, "The Naxalite Movement in India" (New Delhi: Rupa Publications India, 2006), 5.
19. Nayak Girdhari, "Neo-Naxal Challenge: Issues and Options" (New Delhi: Pentagon Security International, 2011), 19.
20. The Land Reform Act, 1955, promulgated among other things a ceiling on holding of land by families. This sought to bring about equitable distribution of cultivable land among the economically poor and downtrodden class.
21. Venkitesh Ramakrishnan, "A Peal of Spring Thunder has Crashed over the Land of India", *Frontline* 22 (October 21, 2005), Editorial published in *The People's Daily*, China on 5 July 1967.
22. In the late 19th century, *revisionism* was used to describe democratic socialist writers such as Eduard Bernstein and Jean Jaurès, who sought to revise Karl Marx's ideas about the transition to socialism and claimed that a revolution through force was not necessary to achieve a socialist society.
23. "Maoist Communist Centre", accessed February 10, 2012, http://en.wikipedia.org/wiki/ Maoist Communist_Centre_of_India#cite_note-2.
24. The West Bengal Act 2 of 1950 defines a bargadar as meaning a person who, under the system generally known as Adhi, Barga, or Bhag, cultivates the land of another person on condition of delivering a share of the produce of such land to that other person.
25. Prakash Singh, "The Naxalite Movement in India" (New Delhi: Rupa Publications India, 2006), 59.

26. Charu Mazumdar, or more popularly known as CM, was born in a Zamindari family of Siliguri in 1918. In 1937-38, he dropped out of college and became a Congress worker. After a few years, he quit the Congress and joined the CPI, working in the peasant front. In 1964-65, he was sick and devoted time to studying and writing about communism and Mao's thought. It was here that he developed his ideas, which were recorded in his writings and speeches of 1965-67 – subsequently known as the "Historic Eight Documents." These formed the political-ideological basis for the emergence of the Naxalbari movement.
27. VK Ahluwalia, "Bloodiest Years of Naxal Violence: Strategic Challenges", Defence and Security Alert, November 2012, 12-17. Parts of this article have been cited in this book.
28. Nayak Girdhari, "Neo-Naxal Challenge: Issues and Options" (New Delhi: Pentagon Security International, 2011), 1.
29. Perhaps in response to a government decision to launch coordinated action against the Naxalites by police forces of the various Indian states affected by Maoist violence, the PWG formed the PGA, its military wing in December 2000 by reorganizing its guerrilla force.
30. Press statement issued by the CPI (Maoist) immediately after their official declaration of merger on 14 October 2004 concluded, "the countryside and the protracted people's war will remain as the center of gravity of the party's work while urban work will be complimentary to it."
31. Art Ryan L. Seachon, "Insurgencies in History: A Blueprint for Future Strategy", *OG 5 Digest*, October-December 2004: 16(1/5).
32. A study commissioned by Bureau of Police Research And Development, conducted by Centre For Development and Peace Studies, Guwahati.
33. Ministry of Home Affairs (MHA). " ... The CPI (Maoist) continues to remain the most dominant among the various LWE groups, accounting for more than 90 percent of the total LWE incidents and 95 percent of the resultant killings", *MHA Annual Report 2011-12. 29.*
34. Nayak Girdhari, "Neo-Naxal Challenge: Issues and Options" (New Delhi: Pentagon Security International, 2011), 5. (He also mentions that CPI (Maoist) as being responsible for 91% deaths in the country).
35. Ministry of Home Affairs (MHA). *MHA Annual Report 2011-12*, 29.

Chapter 2

Inequality Persists

We think sometimes that poverty is only being hungry, naked and homeless. The poverty of being unwanted, unloved and uncared for is the greatest poverty. We must start in our own homes to remedy this kind of poverty.

– Mother Teresa

In this chapter, I was keen to bring out the "socio-economic conditions" of the people in the Naxal-affected areas. However, while compiling the statistical data, it became evident that while the poverty indices have declined over the years, the inequality in distribution of wealth, resources and opportunities continue to persist. In some cases, the gap between the rich and the poor has widened further. This is a ground reality. Therefore, the title of the chapter was changed to "Inequality Persists", instead. Stieglitz, Nobel laureate and author of "Price of Inequality", succinctly summarized his own argument in an online column, "Inequality leads to lower growth and less efficiency. Lack of opportunity means that its most valuable asset – its people – is not being fully used."[1] Thus, inequality has a direct impact on the social cohesion of a country. This Chapter has two distinct parts; first, the prevailing inequality in human development indices and basic amenities; and second; the prominent underlying causes of Naxalism.

According to the preliminary survey of the 68th National Sample Survey Organization (NSSO), "Rising poor – rich divide shows that the growth has not trickled down – the poorest 10% living in the villages spend, on an average, 15 times less than the top 10% living in the cities."[2] It also showed some other details pertaining to the rich and the poor. Similarly, Kanti Bajpai writes that India has the second worst record in the world, with 43% of its children suffering from malnutrition. Countries like Bangladesh, Nepal, Niger, Burundi, etc., have achieved better records in some of the human development indicators.[3] India remains home to the largest number of undernourished people in the world: 217 million as of 2012.[4] Considering the fact that India is one of the fastest growing economies of the world, some of these statistics and achievements confuse the mind – why does such a huge divide persist between the rich and the poor? Which are the specific areas that are affected by low social, psychological, and human development indicators, and the likely reasons thereof? Are these areas of deprivation, social exploitation, and discontent confined to difficult and remote forested areas only?

Rich Land Poor People – The Conundrum

The areas affected by Naxalism are among the poorest, the remotest, the most backward areas, which are poorly connected by rail and other forms of surface communication in India, but are rich in terms of mineral wealth and natural resources. As aptly remarked by a statesman, it is a case of "rich land but poor people". This is true not only for the states afflicted by Naxalism in India, but also for many such areas or countries in the world, which are rich in natural resources but have been exploited unscrupulously by the state or a group of individuals or an individual, e.g. Congo, Sudan, Nigeria, etc.

If we look at forest cover in our country, the Naxal-affected states account for 40% to 45% of the total cover [refer Figure 2.1 (p. 18)]. Similarly, these areas are extremely rich in mineral wealth, possessing almost all type of minerals listed in the periodic tables [refer Figure 2.2 (p. 18)]. Although it has not been possible to quantify the total value of the mineral wealth, including the reserves, it suffices to say that the mineral wealth adds to India's richness in an enormous way. With the availability of such huge natural resources, conflicts between communities or between the community and the state take place. The higher the stake, the greater is the intensity of the conflict, highest being when the issue at stake is unconditional domination.[5]

It is important to analyze the relative deprivation and exploitation of the people, particularly with reference to the human development indicators and the compensatory benefits given to the tribal and poor people on account of giving away their lands for mining, industries, special economic zones (SEZs), and creation of dams. What started purely as a revolt against unjust practices by the feudal landlords is today a movement sweeping across a large part of the country. It is evident that certain parts of central India are the worst affected.

According to a study chaired by D Bandhopadhyay, Expert Group of Planning Commission, poverty alone does not drive a man to violence, it is the prevalence of social discrimination, exploitation, denial of justice, and poverty that does. While people may be able to withstand extreme hardship and poverty, they will not bear injustice and discrimination in the present age. After independence, the poor people of the

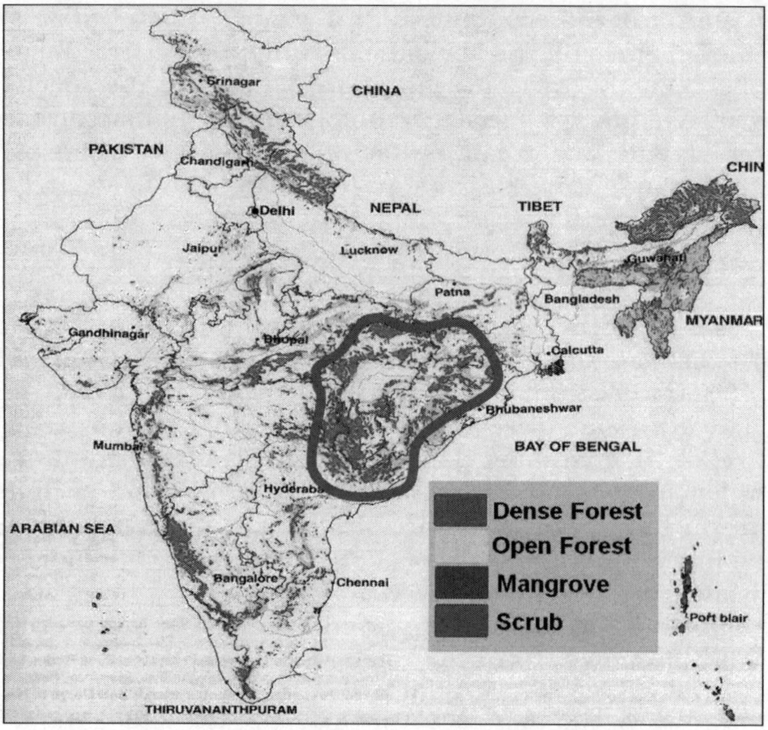

Figure 2.1: Forest Cover in Naxal-Affected Areas

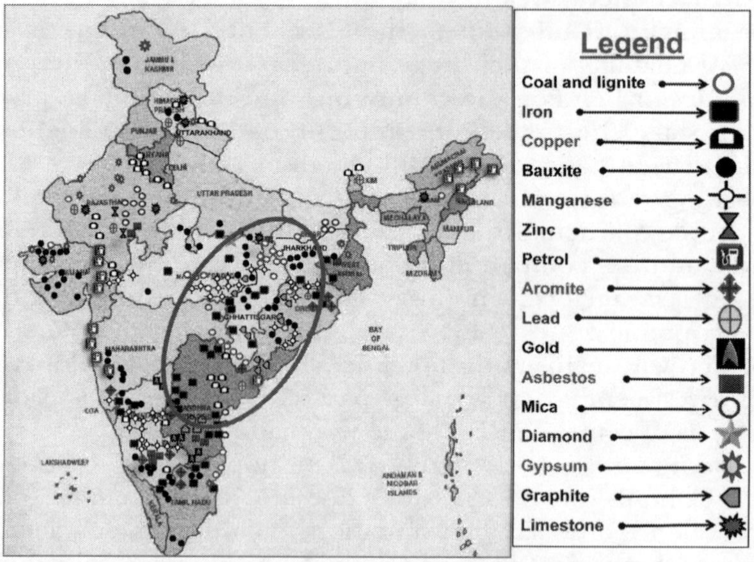

Figure 2.2: Mineral Wealth in Naxal-Affected Areas
Source: Hindustan Times, 09 Oct. 2011, http://www.leadthecompetition.in/

country felt that the democracy would reduce the existing inequality, improve their quality of life, and uplift the socio-economic fabric. Non-implementation of land reforms laws, outdated forest laws, corrupt and repressive administration made the situation worse for the lower class, especially the tribes, in these regions. Irrespective of the political parties in power, the country has witnessed numerous cases of unbridled corruption and lack of public accountability. These factors coupled with illegal and uncontrolled mining activities, clearances of forest for timber, dams, and industries lead to large-scale displacements of indigenous tribes, without any meaningful rehabilitation programs. The Maoist had strongly opposed the formation of the 300 SEZs, announcing these zones as "de facto foreign enclaves", thus enabling companies to grab prime agricultural lands.[6]

Impact of displacements

According to a study by D. Bandhopadhyay, Chairman of the Expert Group of Planning Commission, on "Development Issues to deal with Causes of Discontent, Unrest and Extremism", the villagers in the Naxal-dominated areas lost confidence in successive governments because 55 million of the rural population was displaced between 1951 and 2005. This was because of development projects coupled with the apathy of the successive governments towards the rural population. Concept of development has varying perceptions with different categories of people – industrialists, government officials, local poor people, mining contractors, forest officials and Naxalites. Sometime in December 2011, I had addressed the middle level and senior functionaries of an industrial organization on the "Leadership Challenges". During the teatime, I got involved in a discussion with a senior representative of the corporate about Naxalism. He lamented that the government, the people, social activists, and civil government functionaries do not seem to understand that acquisition of land and development should go hand in hand, for the region to grow and to develop. I asked him, much to his discomfort, what kind of a role they had played, as a leading business house, to uplift the quality of life of the local population, resettlement of displaced people, empowerment of youth with job-related skills and job opportunities, and towards the environment. I had already known the answer even before I asked him. It is equally true of the PSUs. It boils down to the fact that, barring an odd business house, majority of them have only exploited the local populace and the natural resources – *jal, jungle, jamin, and khanij* (water, forests, land, and mineral wealth, respectively), to maximize profits, without contributing much to the local population (society) and the environment.

The affected people in LWE-affected states have developed dislike towards development due to large-scale displacement of people, sometimes more than once, without ensuring proper compensation, resettlement, and rehabilitation. Rehabilitation programs, if any, were also not effectively implemented leading to further discontent. All this has had a profound negative impact on the socio-economic conditions of these areas. In most of these cases, the tribal population was the worst affected. What does displacement mean to the poor people – they have to suffer the consequences of economic dislocation, food insecurity, jobs, shelter and social disruption, among other. In addition, it may take years to overcome the "emotional and psychological trauma", borne out of unjust treatment. These sentiments were fully exploited by the Naxal leaders to propagate the plight of the people at the hands of the government.

Tribal Population – The Worst Affected

Despite the critical leadership and ideological guidance provided by the committed ideologues from urban areas, Naxalism today largely remains a tribal phenomenon, along with dalits, deprived lower class/ caste people, poor farmers, and unemployed rural youth. India's tribal population, with almost 533 tribes, constitutes some 8.2% of India's overall population. They primarily inhabit India's forest tracts. A study of the geographical distribution of this population presents some interesting insights.[7] Seventy six percent of our ST population resides in the forested tracts of central and peninsular India. A mere 11% to 12% of India's tribal population resides in the forests of the northeast. The tribal population, as percentage of the state's population, is high in the states affected by Naxalism: Chhattisgarh (31.8%), Jharkhand (26.3%), Odisha (22.2%), Madhya Pradesh (20.3 %), Andhra Pradesh (6.7%), Maharashtra (8.9%), and West Bengal (5.5%).[8] The SC population, on the other hand, constitutes 19.9% of India's overall population. Interestingly, nearly 74% of India's SC population lives in the following 10 states: Uttar Pradesh, West Bengal, Bihar, Tamil Nadu, Andhra Pradesh, Madhya Pradesh, Maharashtra, Rajasthan, Karnataka, and Kerala. Some of these states are also affected by Naxal activities. There are a large number of de-notified tribes in the country, whose nation-wide survey is yet to be conducted.[9]

The forest cover has been cleared for large-scale mining and other projects from a large number of states, more importantly, the Naxal-affected areas.[10] Large-scale mining and clearing of forest for hydroelectric projects have left a large percentage of the tribal population and poor people from rural areas landless in their own land. It means loss of livelihood. These initiatives, including land acquisition, should actually have been taken only after satisfying ourselves with social audit, psychological impact, and economic safeguards. The lack of political will to enforce land reforms in the post-independence era was the primary cause of the first Naxal upsurge in India in 1967. The basic cause of the uprising – *the glaring lack of land reforms* – has still not been addressed in India. In spite of having a large number of protective legislations, land alienation in the tribal population is very high.[11] It has been observed that in most of the states with Fifth Schedule districts,[12] a good number of claims of the tribal people have not been disposed off favorably. A report of the Government of India (GoI) on the subject does require an urgent corrective action.[13]

In comparison with the national average of 27%,[14] about 48% of India's ST population is below the poverty line. The tribal population, in particular, has remained marginalized, with not many representatives fighting for their cause. A small number of political leaders, though present, have apparently not contributed significantly for the tribal's cause. It is this, which has forced India's forest tribes to take up arms and seek redress through violent means. The lack of political mobility among the central Indian tribes and the apathy of the state administrative machinery have ceded this strategic space to the extremist organizations. This, in sum, is the basis of the escalating tribal insurgency, which is being coordinated, controlled, and augmented by the Naxalites in central and peninsular India. The movement is suitably aided by its inaccessible and forested terrain that favors guerrilla warfare, a favorite tactics among the insurgent groups. In the case of Bihar, it is a conflict between the upper and the lower castes, because the tribal population is just 0.92% of its total population. Of late, there has been some increase in cases of inter-caste conflicts and organized crime in the erstwhile MCCI's areas of influence, in the guise of Naxalism.

Human Development Indicators – An Analysis

During my visits to the Naxal-affected areas and interaction with the local populace, I did pay particular attention to the security situation, socio-psychological conditions, the availability of basic amenities, and employment opportunities available to the people. For any nation, human development indicators are a function of economic growth, social policy, education, life expectancy, and poverty reduction measures at the macro level. Thus, these indicators, in true sense, manifest the levels of social and economic conditions of the society. Besides exploitation and lack of justice delivery mechanism at the grass roots, data analyses of these indicators tend to present a clear picture regarding the ground conditions of various social groups. Thus, it is easy to assimilate the reasons for the higher levels of Naxalism in some areas of the country in comparison with others.

Lack of some of the basic needs and facilities do acquire serious dimension among the affected people to fight for their rights. These pronounced disparities have an unbearable effect on the psyche of the affected population and a cause of their resentment. Some of the indicators of major concern in these areas which have led to lower social and economic development of these groups are poverty, education, unemployment, asset ownership, health, and sanitation. Principally, the data has been obtained from the document, "India Human Development Report, 2011" and annual reports of various ministries. While the statistics quoted may be of the period 2007 to 2010, based on their authentic publications, the latest figures may be a shade better. However, these statistics portray the general trend of the human development indicators.

Poverty

Poverty is the parent of revolution.

– Aristotle (384 BC – 322 BC)

Poverty constitutes the greatest source of misery and degradation in life. The incidence of poverty in India came down from about 55% in 1973-74 to 27% in 2004-05.[15] Across all the social groups, the incidence of poverty among the dalits and the tribal population is much more pronounced. The percentage of dalits and tribal population below poverty line in rural areas was 36.8 and 47.7, respectively, in comparison with an average of 27% for the nation. In rural India, the incidence of poverty among the tribal population in Odisha is 76%, which is much lower than the national average. Similarly, the incidence of poverty among the dalits is the highest in Bihar (64%), followed by Jharkhand (58%), Uttarakhand (54%), and Odisha (50%). The rate of decline of rural poverty during 1994-2004 was also lower (4.3%) among the tribal population in comparison to 9% in the case of the other communities.[16] It is evident that neither the state's intervention nor the market liberalization policies have registered the desired impact on alleviation of poverty.[17] The poverty level in various states of our country is given at Figure 2.3.

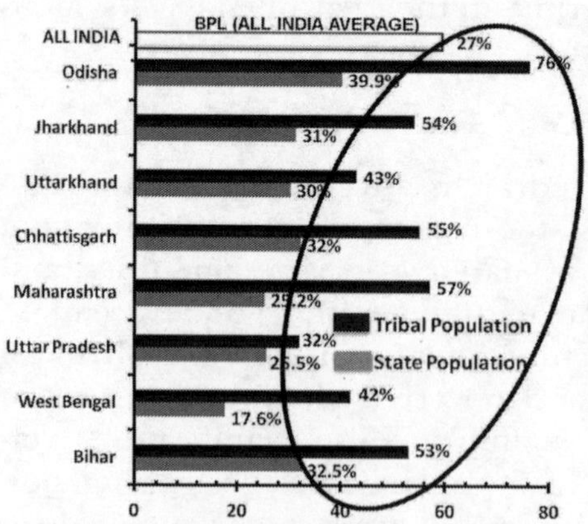

Figure 2.3: Percentage of Tribal Population BPL in Rural Naxal-Affected States

Source: Annual Report 2010-11, Ministry of Tribal Affairs, GoI, Table 6.3, 26.

It can be observed that the BPL percentage of Naxal-affected states is much lower than the national average of 27.

Asset ownership

Considering the fact that nearly 70% of India's population lives in the rural areas, where land continues to remain an emotional issue – it enables the people to generate income and remain engaged in dignified employment. I do distinctly remember, as a young boy in the late 1950s, that my grandparents were most emotional and possessive of their land holding – it gave them a great sense of overall security (food security), economic advantage, and prestige in the village. Even today, land continues to provide similar multi-faceted support. In both rural and urban India, there is hardly any change in the extent of inequality in the ownership of assets between 1991–92 and 2003–04.[18] In fact, the distribution of assets of which land accounts for nearly 60% is extremely unequal, with the top 5% of households owning 38% of the total assets as against only 13% being held by the bottom 60% of the households. This indicates a definite concentration of wealth in the hands of a few. This is also corroborated by the incidence of landlessness, which is higher among the dalits and tribal groups than among other communities. On a comparative scale, 10% of the dalits (at the ground level, the actual percentage would be much higher) are landless and 77% are near landless, while for those excluding the dalits and tribals, the percentages are 4.8 and 63, respectively.[19]

Though the tribal population had a much better land holding than the dalits at the time of independence, the incidence of landlessness has grown faster in their case because of large-scale displacement and occupation of their land by the non-tribal immigrants to their area. Even those who own land, not all are able to cultivate it because a large portion of tribal land is unfit for cultivation. Regarding the rest, lack of resources like modern cultivation means, non-availability of micro-credit does not permit its profitable cultivation. Only 26% of the land owned by the tribal groups is irrigated in comparison with 53% of other communities.[20] As no worthwhile cash crops are grown in these regions, the income from the produce is barely enough for sustenance. Consequently, in a few areas, poppy and cannabis cultivation has become a means of livelihood of the people, as well as a source of generating funds by the Naxalites.

Employment opportunities

According to the *HDI Report 2011*, the growth rate of employment has clearly not been commensurate with the GDP growth. As compared to the period 1993 to 2000 when the growth rate of employment was 0.66, the growth rate for the period 2000 to 2008 has been only 1.27 suggesting only a marginal rise, despite considerable acceleration in GDP. This indicates a significant fall in elasticity of employment with respect to the output.[21] Employment opportunities have a very important role to play in human resource management, empowerment, and enhancement of human capabilities. It not only ensures economic security, but also promotes general participation in the society and economy. It is necessary for promotion of health and education that are the pre-requisites for poverty alleviation.

High unemployment rates, given in percentages of their population, in the five Naxal-affected states of Andhra Pradesh (8.2 rural and 13.6 urban), Chhattisgarh (5.8 rural and 19.9 urban), Jharkhand (10.5 rural and 13.4 urban), Odisha (6.4 rural and 24.0 urban), and Madhya Pradesh (9.0 rural and 12.5 urban) are partly indicative of frustration and anger among the people. The unemployment rates of the tribal population are also the highest in the country, much higher than the national average of 7.5 for rural, and 10.0 for urban areas.[22] These areas also account for about 42% of the ST population of the country. High unemployment finally manifests in higher incidents of Naxal violence. Such statistics reinforce the need to initiate steps to improve the employment opportunities – perhaps the biggest challenge to the country – for the ST, SC and the poor people. The fruits of growth should be inclusive, sustainable, and should reach the grass roots to make a difference in lives of the poor people.

Food insecurity

While both the dalits and tribal groups suffer from acute food deficiency, the tribal population faces it far more than the other segments of society. As per Human Development Report 2011, there is not a single state with a Hunger Index below 9.9 (considered moderate), the best performing state being Punjab with a Hunger Index of 13.63.[23] It is pertinent to note that the states affected by Naxalism rank at the bottom of the pile in the Hunger Index. Nearly 71.6% of tribal households in these states are food deficit for two to three months.[24] The incidence of starvation deaths, characteristic of extreme impoverishment, is the highest in the tribal areas. A comparison of a few of the Indian states and the sub-Saharan nation of the Democratic Republic of Congo (DRC), which has close to the same population and a similar Multi-dimensional Poverty Index,[25] shows that nutritional deprivation, arguably the most fundamental facet of poverty, in a few states exceeds that in the Democratic Republic of Congo.[26] Lack of employment opportunities and food insecurity causes a great amount of dissatisfaction among the affected population.

Health and education

It is an acknowledged fact that LWE-affected regions have poor social infrastructure, mainly in areas of education and healthcare. The health care facilities require much greater attention. The total expenditure on health care (both private and public) by India as a percentage of its GDP stood at 4.2% in 2007.[27] As per GoI Report 2008, the infant mortality rate, indicative of the reach of primary health care, is as high as 84.2 per thousand in the case of tribal population and 82 per thousand in the case of dalits in comparison with 61.8 in the case of others. Majority of the tribal population is settled in the LWE-affected areas. As per data from National Family Health Survey (NFHS III), the disparity is also reflected in the high morbidity, low level of immunization, high level of malnutrition among women, and vaccination coverage in these communities.

India has guaranteed the right to free and compulsory education for all children between the ages of 6 and 14 years, through the Right to Education Act.[28] Although the literacy rate in India is below the desired level, it is slowly, over the past decade or so, on its way to a steady increase. In the states most affected by Maoist violence, there is a trend of convergence on the national average as far as literacy rates of ST are concerned. The same is the case with literacy rates of SC where the national average is 60.5%.[29] Still overall, approximately 40% of the tribal and lower-caste population is illiterate in absolute terms, which leaves them vulnerable to exploitation. It can also be argued that to some extent the rise in education levels in rural India in comparison with those a decade back has led to greater awareness about individual and community rights. This awareness has resulted in greater expectations from the state in matters of governance and administration. As per Ministry of Tribal Affairs, Annual Report 2009-2010, comparison of the literacy levels of the tribal population and all-class composition in the Naxal-affected states, in comparison to the national average, is given at Figure 2.4.

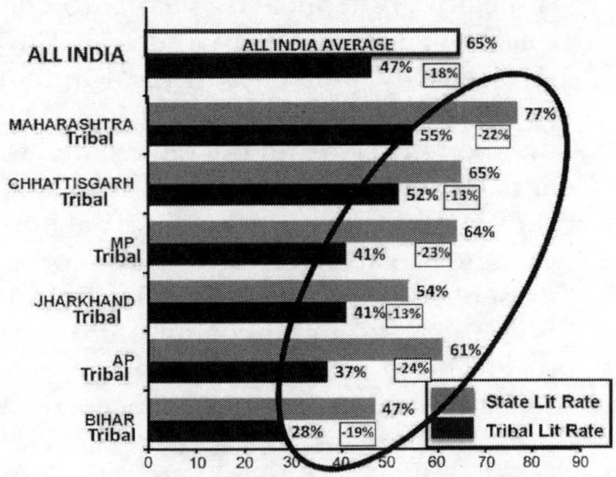

Figure 2.4: Literacy Rate

Source: Ministry of Tribal Affairs: Annual Report 2009-10.

Lack of Social Infrastructure

Economic and social infrastructures have to complement each other to uplift the conditions of the masses. Therefore, there is a need to provide social infrastructure like housing, power, telephony, sanitation, and roads connectivity that can give economic growth a human face. Availability of infrastructure is a positive requirement for developmental process. It has been generally observed that the states with higher index of infrastructure[30] also have the lower head count ratio of poverty, suggesting that development – both economic and social – is a means of poverty alleviation.

- Housing is a basic physical need of every individual, as it provides a sense of identity, safety, and security to an individual and his family. While only around half of the SC and one-third of the ST population in rural areas reside in permanent houses, the statistical figures of the Naxal-affected states are much lower. The situation regarding access to drinking water, sanitation, and wastewater outlet also reveal wide disparities and unsatisfactory conditions.[31]
- Electrification of rural areas, though a most difficult goal to achieve due to varied terrain conditions and requirement of support infrastructure, is most rewarding in terms of the socio-economic multiplier effects it has on the human development arena. It holds the key to greater agricultural productivity, improvement in delivery of health and education, access to communications, and improved quality of life. As compared to 96% of urban India having access to electricity, only 66% of rural India has access to it, which is well below the national average of 75%.[32] Here again, there is a large gap between the rich and the poor states, with poor states being the ones afflicted by Naxalism. As per Figure 2.5 (p. 27) (November 2006), showing the electrification in rural households, it has been observed that the Naxal-affected rural areas were among the worst affected (in most of these areas, availability of electricity was under 25%).
- With the revolution in communications and the society marching on to the information superhighway, reliable communication creates social networking and enhances economic opportunities, besides providing means to keep social ties between migrants and their families alive. Telephone Regulatory Authority of India (TRAI) in its 2008 report[33] has observed that "if a country has one percent more mobile subscribers than another, than its GDP per capita will be about US$ 200 higher." Telephone density has increased at a very impressive pace over time, from 26% in 2008 to 66% in 2010. However, a look at the telephone density of the Naxal-affected states

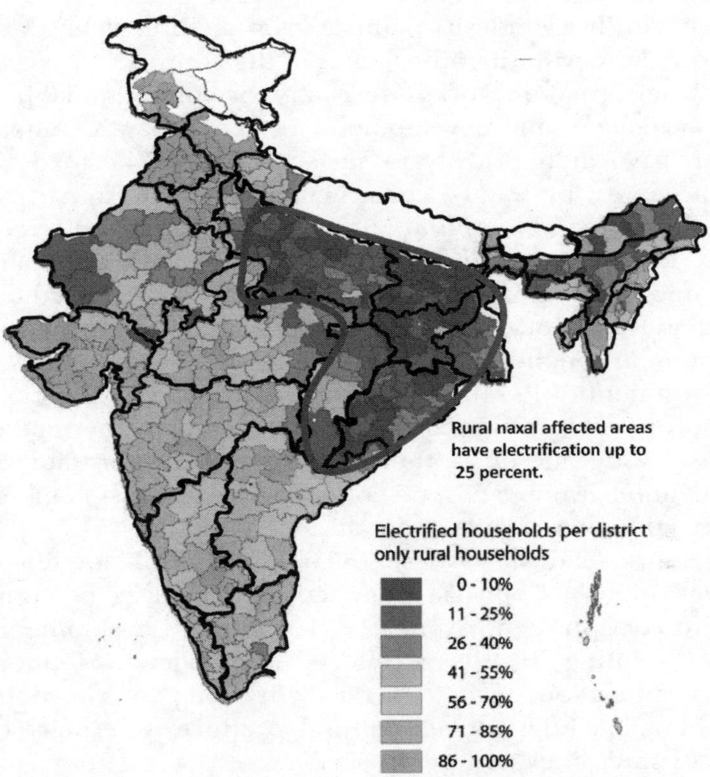

Figure 2.5: Electrification of Rural Households per District
Source: Centre for Energy Policy and Economics (CEPE) Working Paper No. 51 (Nov. 2006)

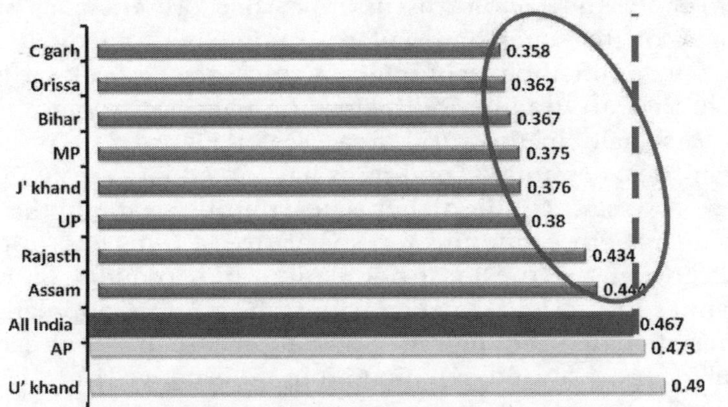

Figure 2.6: All India HDI
Source: India Human Development Report 2011 by IAMR Planning Commission, Government of India

(except Andhra Pradesh) paints a grim picture, when the statistics are compared with the other states of the country.[34]

- An efficient road network is necessary for both national integration and socio-economic development. In the Malayan campaign, the British gave high priority to surface connectivity to develop the remote areas, by way of constructing roads and airstrips. India's road network of 3.3 million kilometers is the second largest in the world. Rural and other roads account for maximum share of the road network at 2.65 million kilometers. A study carried out by the International Food Policy Research Institute on linkages between government expenditure and poverty in rural India has revealed that an investment of Rs. 10 million in roads uplifts 1,650 people above the poverty line. In spite of substantial growth in the road coverage in the past decade or so, there still exist wide inter-state variations. The national average of road connectivity is 81.2 kilometers per 100 square kilometer of area. States like Chhattisgarh (54.7), Jharkhand (14.8), and Madhya Pradesh (53.6) are quite below the national average in terms of road connectivity. The lack of connectivity, therefore, cripples the overall socio-economic development of these states, resulting in adverse effects on public distribution system (PDS), education, medical services, training for vocational skills, marketing facilities for agricultural produce, veterinary cover for animals, and other vital public services.

Human Development Index (HDI)

The socio-economic factors discussed earlier present a clear trend. The poorest of the states have failed to implement adequate reforms or policies to uplift their economically and socially backward classes. As a result, they are trailing well below the national average regarding all HDIs, especially in the rural areas. Refer Figure 2.6 (p. 27). This disparity in socio-economic conditions has forced large-scale migration from these poor states to the richer states, putting strain on the existing infrastructure (both economic and social) there. This has, in the past, led to dissent among the local population and frequent outbursts of anger manifesting itself in violence against the migrant population. This has further alienated the migrant population, which was already living a life of abject poverty and exploitation in their native lands, leading to simmering discontent. Mao Zedong had said that people are the water in which the fish (meaning guerrillas) swim. The alienated population of the rural areas were, thus, the most gullible to support the movement of the Naxals. Having seen the social and human development indicators of the LWE-affected states and compared with the ground realities, it is evident that, over the years and irrespective of the political parties in power, the fruits of growth have not really reached the poor people. Looking at the spread of Naxalism, it stands out that the Naxal-affected areas are not only confined to difficult hilly and forested areas alone, but also cover large contiguous tracts in the plains as well. Such areas include the fertile lowland plain south of the Himalayas, such as Bihar and eastern Uttar Pradesh, and fertile lands in Telangana region.

Prominent Underlying Causes

Many countries, the world over, have confronted insurgencies in the past. The nature and causes of each insurgency are different and these do not remain static. Based on the politico-socio-economic conditions, and the structural problems in society, the causes of discontent are varied; however, poverty, unemployment, underdevelopment, and inadequate governance are among the main causes of such movements. The insurgencies continue to be dynamic as they adapt to the rapidly changing fault-lines and environments quickly.

Displacement of tribal population

India is home to second largest tribal population of the world, second only to Africa. Historically, the governments, both pre- and post-independence have neglected or failed to penetrate the difficult terrains, i.e. the dense forest tribal tracts or the rugged hilly regions of the northeast and parts of central India. Consequently, efforts to provide surface connectivity, basic amenities to the people and to carry out developmental works were not taken up, based on some unconvincing reasons like preservation of the identity and culture of the tribal people. Thus, the tribal population, for long, has lived in a state of isolation, insulated from the fruits of globalization, liberalization, economic growth, and development. It is not that industries have not penetrated these areas, but the policies of the successive governments, have generally not supported the welfare of the tribal population and the local inhabitants. These areas are the richest in mineral deposits: 85% of India's coal reserves are in Chhattisgarh, Jharkhand, Andhra Pradesh, West Bengal, and Odisha. These areas also have huge deposits of iron ore and bauxite. Industrialization, therefore, has brought about violent clashes in the Naxal-affected areas. Disorganized economic policies by the state governments and the politician-criminal-contractor nexus, in some cases, have allowed exploitation of the vast mineral and natural resources of these regions with impunity, and total disregard of the rights and sensitivities of the tribal population in the region. *A large number of mega hydroelectric projects, smaller dams, mines, and now the establishment of SEZs have led to the large-scale displacement of tribal population.*[35] Available estimates of people displaced by large and medium dams in India show that the 140 dams for which such figures are available have displaced over 16 to 38 million people.[36] It is estimated that only 25% people displaced in India have been resettled. Absence of any credible rehabilitation programs resulted in the victims joining the rebels en mass.

In the past three decades, Deshpande writes that 92,000 villages have been destroyed from the map of India, as the land has been acquired for industrialization, mining, creation of water reservoirs for dams, etc.[37] PSUs and state sponsored projects also account for a large number of displacements. Arundhati Roy discusses the issue of displacement of people and its impact in her essay, "The Greater Common Good: Human Cost of Dams"[38] Another report of the Working Group on Human Rights in India and the UN states that 60 to 65 million people have been displaced in India since independence, due to ostensible development projects. India has the highest number of people displaced annually due to such projects in the world.[39] In addition to giving up traditional crops (*bewar*) or shifting cultivation (*Baiga*), the primitive tribal group of Chhattisgarh has been repeatedly facing displacement from their home and forest-dependant livelihood over the years, a few more than 12 times, as more areas are being notified as reserve forest in the state. In addition, 15 out of 19 villages are still to be dislocated.[40] Kujur reiterates that the people that were displaced due to the construction of the Hirakud dam in the 1950s were neither fully rehabilitated nor their complete compensation paid.[41] Similarly, the Machkund and Balimela hydroelectric power stations were constructed in the 1940s and 1970s, respectively. The Balimela water reservoir has a catchment area of approximately 4910 sq kilometers, which resulted in displacing people of 69 villages, and cutting off 151 villages. Some of the villages, on displacement due to construction of water reservoirs, do not have access to a road, due to creation of huge water reservoirs and catchment areas, in an extremely difficult terrain. Hundreds of people are still living on tiny islands within the dam area, which are being referred to as the 'cut off areas'. With hardly any signs of governance, a few of such remote areas in Malkangiri districts are also home to large-scale Naxal activities. It was in the same Balimela reservoir- in Malkangiri district- that the Naxals had ambushed and killed 35 greyhounds of Andhra Police, on June 29, 2008. Repeated displacement of such large number of people, without proper resettlement and rehabilitation plan, is a major cause of Naxalism.

The Supreme Court of India ruled that Naxalism was a result of an oversight of constitutional provisions relating to administration of schedule areas and tribes of the country.[42] Essentially, these constitutional provisions, with the help of plethora of judgments by the apex court, provide guarantee to indigenous people on the right over their land they live in and its produce. It is difficult to digest, but it is true that there is a little understanding of tribal areas and their society, as they are extremely heterogeneous in terms of their ethos, language, culture, food, etc. Additionally, there is a wrong perception among many of us, that the tribal societies have no democratic culture.[43] The administration must use innovative means to facilitate sustained dialogue between the tribal and non-tribal societies on one hand, and between the government and tribal societies on the other hand. By bridging the communication gap, the process of building trust between the state and the tribal population would commence and their aspirations would start receiving due attention.

Inability to enforce land reforms

In his paper, "Land Reforms in India: Issues and Challenges", Manpreet Sethi discusses the prevalence of "semi-feudal agrarian system" at length. British East India Company changed India's traditional land use and landownership patterns to ease the acquisition of land at low prices for mines, plantations, and other enterprises. The introduction of the institution of private property delegitimized the community ownership systems of tribal societies. Moreover, with the introduction of the land tax under the Permanent Settlement Act 1793,[44] the British popularized the zamindari system at the cost of the *jajmani*[45] relationship that the landless shared with the landowning class. Owing to these developments in a changing social and economic landscape, India, at independence, inherited a semi-feudal agrarian system. The ownership and control of land were highly concentrated in the hands of a small group of landlords and intermediaries, whose main intention was to extract maximum rent from tenants. Under this arrangement, the sharecropper or the tenant farmer had little economic motivation to develop farmland for increased production.

India's initial five-year plans allocated substantial budgetary amounts for the implementation of land reforms. A degree of success was even registered in certain regions and states, especially with regard to issues such as the abolition of intermediaries, protection to tenants, rationalization of different tenure systems, and the imposition of ceilings on landholdings.[46] However, bureaucratic inefficiency and political apathy resulted in the fact that between 1950 and 1980, only 5% of landless population had received land from the state, and the state could manage to distribute only 28% of arable land in its possession, sharply in contrast with China, where both the figures are 90%. Even in the case of Japan, allotment of land to the landless and distribution of arable land is 81% and 41% respectively.[47] Rammohan observes, "Regrettably, only three states had implemented the land ceiling laws, legislated by all the states by 1955.These were the states of Jammu & Kashmir, West Bengal and Kerala...."[48]

Most studies indicate that inequalities have increased, rather than decreased. The number of landless laborers has risen, while the wealthiest 10% of the population monopolizes more land now than in 1951.[49] Stakes of the landed elite, feudal landlords, and their powerful connection with the political-bureaucratic system have blocked meaningful land reforms and/or their earnest implementation. Forty percent of rural households have no land or less than half an acre of land. The estimated number of landless rural families in the country is 1.30 to 1.80 crores.[50] The number of small and marginal operational holdings has been increasing steadily over the years. While the economy is at present growing at a rate of about 5% to 9%, agriculture that provides employment to 58% of the country's workforce is growing at less than 3%. The share of agriculture as part of the GDP has in fact fallen by 3.7% since 2000.[51] This is correctly seen as signifying rising economic disparities between the agricultural and non-agricultural sectors of the economy. Land as a basis of livelihood for subsistence, survival, social justice, and human dignity has largely been lost sight of. This failure, inadequacy, or injustice of state mechanisms and institutions has created space for Naxal activities. In a few cases, the Naxals moved in and forcibly took over land, belonging to the landlords or the government, and handed over to the landless. The Naxals have had even greater success with respect to government land. Large tracts of government-held land were reportedly allotted to the landless. There was a steep rise in the popularity of the Naxals and their leaders. This is exactly what Mao Zedong had done in the 1930s in China, to emerge as a popular leader.

Looking at the course of events dispassionately, the state governments should have taken the initiative to legally transfer land to the landless, as per the provisions of the Land Ceiling laws. This was not to be. Most of the state governments can solve such problems by legalizing the transfer of land from the landlords or awarding of title deeds of the government land to the landless of the land occupied by them, as it is within the powers of the government to do so. The state governments should sincerely carry out survey and build up the database of land records afresh, but it is feared that it may tantamount to legalizing the activities of the Naxals.[52] Judicious and bold policy making, and effective implementation on the ground would perhaps be the answer to the problem.

Forest lands

The forests provide the people their consumption needs – fuel and firewood, medicines, food and drink, implements and housing materials.

However, over the years, large areas of forest lands have been diverted for mining, setting up of hydroelectric projects, irrigation schemes, and SEZs.[53] These diversions by the government in most cases have not been done with proper social audit of the likely consequences. There has been no involvement of the stakeholders (i.e., the tribal groups of the region) in the decision-making process, through their panchayats and gram sabhas. Thus, most of these projects have resulted in curtailing the rights of the tribal community on their own land, which have had adverse effect on the ecology of the regions. ST and other Traditional Forest Dwellers (Recognition of Forest Rights) Act, 2006, seeks to recognize and vest the forest rights, and occupation in forest land in forest dwelling ST and other traditional forest dwellers, who have been residing in such forests for generations but whose rights could not be recorded. This act, if implemented, would provide the requisite relief to a large segment of affected population.

Pending implementation of the act, the Naxals have taken the initiative to encourage and assist the adivasis to occupy the forestlands. It has taken place in some parts of Andhra Pradesh, Chhattisgarh, the Vidarbha[54] region of Maharashtra, Odisha, and Jharkhand. In fact, much of it is not fresh occupation but reassertion of traditional rights declared by the law to be illegal. The government's statistics show that 39% of what is called forest encroachment in the whole country has taken place in the region mentioned earlier.[55] Prior to 1980, various state governments would, off and on, acknowledge this fact by regularizing the occupation; thereby, giving back what has been unilaterally taken away. But the Forest Conservation Act, 1980,[56] put an end to such regularization, and put the forest dwellers perpetually on the brink of eviction from their own habitat. This enabled the Naxals to step into the vacuum to espouse the popular cause and secure popular support.

Poor governance

In the urban areas, the people get to interact with the government officials to project their problems and to see for themselves the multifaceted functioning of the officials, though not efficient enough. On the other hand, in most of the areas critically affected by Naxalism, there is little or no governance at all, with the writ of the Indian state not existing or not effective enough in such remote rural areas. Civil administrations, police, revenue department, and the judicial institutions have a rather tenuous presence, as government officials do not find it remunerative to visit these areas. The perception of the local populace about the state is based on their interaction with the forest guards, police, petty officials, and low-level educational staff, who are less than motivated and committed to support and protect the people. Nor are they accountable to anyone. On the contrary, the same officials exploit the poor people by buying their forest produce or goods at low prices or by making them do menial jobs. The exploited people become frustrated with the state.

The prime minister had noted at the chief ministers' meet of Naxal-affected states on July 14, 2010, "Without adequate and reasonably efficient staff, it would be difficult to implement any strategy or programme for these areas." The problem of "adequate and reasonably efficient staff" is far more intractable, as the state governments, it appears, do not have the will and the capacities to overcome entrenched structural obstacles. Grants, allocations, and schemes announced by the state therefore are hardly ever implemented in time; out of Rs. 5,858 crore allocated to insurgency-affected districts in 2007 for development schemes, more than Rs. 2,700 crore were not spent at all. Those officials, who do have to stay in these areas, are obliged to pay "taxes", and those projects which do get executed, have to divert a set percentage of funds as "levy" to the Naxalites.[57] Some of these shortcomings have allowed the rebels to run parallel governments in such areas. The practice of holding "Jan Adalats", land distribution, construction of irrigation facilities and tax collection by the Naxal cadres indicates the absence of the governance system by the state in some of the areas. It also reveals the reach, the writ, and popularity of the Naxals, who have gained the trust of the tribal population and rural folks, who see them more efficient and effective in dispensing social justice than the government machinery itself.[58] Union Rural Development Minister realized the inadequacy in the prevalent system when he suggested that, in addition to government's initiative of two-pronged strategy of development and security, there is a need to strengthen the political process and justice to the tribal community.[59]

Marginalization of tribes

It has been observed that the ST have little representation in the decision making process (whatever little part they have, is purely regional and has limited national status). This has not allowed them to develop a meaningful stake in the democratic system. This lack of political empowerment is reflected in the clear development differential between the ST and other communities. Guha highlights the wide gap in the development indices like literacy rate, BPL, school dropouts, safe water availability, access to doctor, and immunization.[60]

Many Naxal-affected districts are marked by a high proportion of dalit population, especially in Bihar, where they have been taking an active part in the left-wing insurgency, as part of the former MCC. While the dalit angst has been partially addressed due to the superior political mobilization of the SC, it is the political marginalization of the ST that has forced them to resort to violence and let the left-wing extremists espouse their cause. Therefore, the ST-Naxal nexus is a cause of worry and concern for the nation's security.

Livelihood

A large number of tribal groups are involved in such labor where there is no discernible employer, and thus they come under the purview of self-employment. Since the Naxals are in any case not bothered whether or not there is a law governing the right they are espousing, they have intervened and determined fair wage rates in their perception in most of the labor processes in their areas of influence. The rebels have secured increases in the rate of payment for the picking of tendu leaves, which is used for rolling beedies (local cigarettes with tendu leaves), in the forest areas of Andhra Pradesh, Chhattisgarh, Odisha, Maharashtra, and Jharkhand. This was a very major source of exploitation of adivasi labor, which the Naxals have been able to put an effective end to in a few areas. The exploitation was so severe that the rates have, over the years, increased up to fifty times what the tendu patta contractors used to pay before the Naxals stepped in.[61] This is something that should have been done by the state. To do so, the state officials have to know the ground realities, the difficulties of the people, and then rectify such glaring anomalies in the system. It is, therefore, necessary for the state to provide for Minimum Support Price (MSP) for all types of minor minerals and forest produce. There is also a need to institutionalize the procurement system to be more efficient and effective.

It may be recalled that the Forest Rights Act (2006) decrees that the state governments must grant community rights to the tribal groups by which they will have the right to collect and sell forest produce. This will ensure more wages for the tribal groups as they can sell directly to the trader or the contractor and get better price. However, probably not wanting to lose their monopoly or revenue share, Supriya Sharma feels that the state governments have yet to fully implement the act in letter and spirit.[62] Mendha Lekha, village in Gadchiroli district, has become the first village in the country to formally receive the community forest rights, to be given transit passbooks to harvest and to sell bamboos.[63] This has not been appreciated by the Naxals, as the village panchayats are being empowered. They fear that they would lose their control on the population in the long-term perspective. Other states also need to emulate the example of Mendha Lekha. Unequal pay among sexes is also another common point of discontent, though this is also protected under the law.[64] Traditional rights also give right over common property in tribal areas. Enjoyment of common property resources as a traditional right by cattle-herds, fishing communities, toddy toppers, and stone workers has become vulnerable due to the appropriation of these resources by the dominant sections of society. This is an area where there is, in general, no legislative protection at all of traditional rights, though some states have framed some policies to address the same. The Naxals have taken advantage of this situation and have "ensured" protection of this right in areas where they are active.[65] The government should consider legislative protection of an umbrella nature; or else writ of the Naxals will continue to run large. There has been good news on this score – the government has decided to amend the forest laws to give the tribal groups bigger share in the minor forest produce trade.[66] Rammohan offers a solution by way of dividing the forests into sections of ten villages and establishment of Tribal Advisory Council in each section to organize the collection of forest produce and lease with mining companies.[67]

Cash crops

The Naxal-affected areas do not have any meaningful cash crops, in comparison with other parts of the country. Majority of tribal people are landless. They are exploited by the landlords and the business community. It is one of the reasons for the tribal people to indulge in drug cultivation and trade to sustain themselves, with much lesser effort. It also helps the rebels to generate revenue for their party's tasks. "*In Afghanistan, the Taliban are known to have funded their operations through opium trade. Taliban commanders on the village level have expanded their activities related to drugs, extortion and charging protection fees to running heroin refineries, and engaging in kidnapping and other smuggling schemes. As insurgent commanders become more deeply tied to criminal activity, it will become more difficult for the coalition of foreign forces in Afghanistan to defeat them.*"[68] The latter part, as stated about Afghanistan, is an area of great concern to India as well. If not checked, we are likely to face a near similar situation in the future in the LWE-affected areas. Some of the prominent areas of poppy cultivation are Ghagra area of Gumla district in Jharkhand, and in parts of Kishanganj and Purnia districts in Bihar.[69] In fact, there are many more LWE-affected areas involved in cultivation of poppy and cannabis, and drug trade.

Social discrimination

The fight against the social discrimination is perhaps the most significant issue used by the Naxals to carry forward their movement. Discrimination on grounds of caste, sex, religion, etc., is barred by the Constitution in Articles 14 to 17. Positive enactments for penalizing discrimination have been legislated in the case of the SC and ST. The SC & ST (Prevention of Atrocities) Act, 1989, is not merely a penal law. It envisages the setting up of an elaborate system for prevention of such atrocities. The law has, however, been seen as merely a penal law – its full potential has not been implemented by the administration, on the ground. Thus, social discrimination of these people continues to remain as one of the root causes of support for the movement. Naxals themselves have a dismal record of exploitation of the poor people and their children, in particular. As reported on a number of occasions, they have been indulging in sex abuse, recruitment of child soldiers, use of innocent civilians as human shields, and killing innocent civilians to terrorize them.

Notes

1. Joseph E Stiglitz, Nobel laureate and author of "Price of Inequality", www.nytimes.com/2012/.../the-price-of-inequality.
2. Nilin Sethi, "Rising Poor-Rich Divide Shows Growth Hasn't Trickled Down", *The Times of India*, August 02, 2012. Some of these figures remained contested on various counts.
3. Kanti Bajpai, "Parliament Fiddles While India Burns", *The Times of India*, September 15, 2012.
4. Rukmini Srinivasan, "At 217m, India Houses Largest No. of Malnourished", *The Times of India*, October 10, 2012.
5. Robin M. Williams Jr., "The Wars Within, Peoples and States in Conflict" (New Delhi: Manas Publication, 2004), 92.
6. K. Srinivas Reddy, "Maoist to Resist Formation of SEZs", *The Hindu*, February 21, 2007.
7. Table 2A.1, Appendix to "India Human Development Report 2011", p. 253. Tribal population as 8.2% is as per Census 2001.
8. Ministry of Tribal Affairs: Annual Report 2009-10.
9. Aarti Dhar, "De-notified tribes to get better deal in 12th Plan", *The Hindu*, December 19, 2012. Over 200 communities were identified by the British as the "criminal tribes" under the Criminal Tribes Act 1871. The Act was annulled after Independence and the communities identified were referred to as de-notified, nomadic and semi-nomadic tribes.
10. As per "Indian State of Forest Report 2009", the loss of forest cover in square km since 2005 is as follows: Chhattisgarh, 108; Madhya Pradesh, 28; Jharkhand, 5; Odisha, 27; and Andhra Pradesh, 48.
11. *Source*: Table 4.5, "Report of Committee on State Agrarian Relations and the Unfinished Task in Land Reforms", Commission by Ministry of Rural Development, GOI, 2009.
12. Essentially, The Fifth Schedule is a historic guarantee to indigenous people on the right over the land they live in. The Fifth Schedule of the Constitution of India deals with administration and control of scheduled areas and ST in these areas. The Fifth Schedule covers tribal areas in 9 states of India, namely, Andhra Pradesh, Jharkhand, Gujarat, Himachal Pradesh, Maharashtra, Madhya Pradesh, Chhattisgarh, Odisha, and Rajasthan.
13. Ministry of Rural Development, GoI. "Report of the Committee on State Agrarian Relations and the Unfinished Task in Land Reforms Commission,

2009." The report states, "This leads to the conclusion that the present schematic and legal arrangement for the restoration of tribal lands has not been successful on account of a number of factors including the political ramifications of such steps, the ineffective and inefficient revenue machinery and the convergence of interests amongst the political groups, the bureaucracy and the classes alienating the tribal lands. This is mainly attributed to the failure of the state governments to act on behalf of the tribals to a political choice."

14. Rukmini Shrinivasan, "55% of the Country's Population Poor: Report", *The Times of India,* 15 July 2010. "About 645 million people or 55% of India's population is poor as measured by this composite indicator made up of ten markers of education, health and standard of living achievement levels."
15. Data Source – "India Human Development Report, 2011", Table 3.32, p. 114. (However, the figures, as per international standards based on poverty line of US$ 1.25 per person per day, stand at 42% for India.)
16. Data Source – "India Human Development Report, 2011", Table 3.35, p. 116.
17. R. Radhakrishna and Shovan Ray, "Handbook of Poverty in India: Perspectives, Policies, and Programmers" (Oxford University Press, 2005).
18. Asset Ownership (NSS Database, HDI Report 2011) – Bottom 60% households held 14.8% assets which remained more or less unchanged from 1991 through 2003.
19. R. Radhakrishna and Shovan Ray, "Handbook of Poverty in India: Perspectives, Policies, and Programmes" (Oxford University Press, 2005).
20. R. Radhakrishna and Shovan Ray, "Handbook of Poverty in India: Perspectives, Policies, and Programmes" (Oxford University Press, 2005). (Latest figures for 2012 are likely to be better.)
21. Chandrashekar and Jayati Ghosh, "Employment under New Growth Trajectory" (New Delhi: Economic Research Foundation, 2010).
22. Tables 3A.5 and 3A.6. "India HDI Report 2011", pp. 262–263.
23. The India State Hunger Index (ISHI) is a tool to calculate hunger and malnutrition at the regional level in India. It is constructed in the same fashion as the Global Hunger Index (GHI) 2008 and was calculated for 17 states in India, covering more than 95 percent of the population. A score of 9.9 and below is considered moderate on the index. A score of 19.9 and above is considered serious and alarming.
24. R. Radhakrishna and Shovan Ray, "Handbook of Poverty in India: Perspectives, Policies, and Programmes" (Oxford University Press, 2005).
25. Developed by the Oxford Poverty and Human Development Initiative (OPHI) for the United Nations Development Programmes (UNDP) 2010 Human Development Report, the MPI attempts to capture more than just income poverty at the household level.
26. Rukmini Shrinivasan, "55% of the Country's Population Poor: Report", *The Times of India,* 15 July 2010.
27. "Total Heath Expenditure", accessed February 23, 2012, *The Economic Review,* http://www.theindiaeconomyreview.org/Article.aspx?aid=63&mid=4.
28. This is stated as per the 86th Constitution Amendment Act added Article 21A.

29. Table 6A.3, "India Human Development Report 2011", 350.
30. The infrastructure indicators were constructed by the Eleventh Planning Commission. These were agriculture, banking, electricity, transport, communication, health, and civil administration.
31. "Monitorable Targets & Milestones for 2010-11, Infrastructure Sector: Planning Commission".
32. "Human Development Index Report 2011", 391. Also see http://www.cepe.ethz.ch/publications/workingPapers/CEPE_WP51.pdf
33. TRAI, "Measures to Improve Telecom Penetration in India – The Next 100 Million Subscribers", 2008.
34. "Ministry of Telecommunications – Annual Report 2010-11."
35. D. Bandhopadhyay, "Development Challenges in Extremist Affected Areas: Development Issues to Deal with Causes of Discontent, Unrest and Extremism." A report of the Expert Group (New Delhi: Planning Commission, 2008), 48-49.
36. Report submitted by the SANDRP to the World Dams Commission in the year 2000, pp. 104-108.
37. Vinaya Deshpande, "Engage, Don't Encroach", *The Hindu*, June 22, 2012.
38. Arundhati Roy, "The Greater Common Good: Human Cost of Dams", April 1999, accessed on April 22, 2012, http://www.narmada.org/gcg/gcg.html. "...According to a detailed study of 54 large dams done by the Indian Institute of Public Administration, the average number of people displaced by a large dam is 44,182. Admittedly, 54 dams out of 3,300 is not a big enough sample. But... it's all we have... let's err on the side of abundant caution and take an average of just 10,000 people per large dam. 33 million... That is what it works out to... What about those that have been displaced by the thousands of other development projects?'
39. Anahita Mukherjee, "India Uproots Most People for Progress", *The Times of India*, June 04, 2012.
40. Meena Menon, "Forest versus Forest Talk", *The Hindu*, August 05, 2012.
41. Kujur Rajat Kujur, "Underdevelopment and Naxal Movement", *Economic and Political Weekly*, February 18, 2006.
42. Utkarsh Anand, "Naxalism: A Result of an Oversight of Statutes, Says SC", *The Indian Express*, October 03, 2012.
43. Jaideep Hardikar, Special Correspondent, "The Telegraph", during his address at the National Conference at Jamia Milia University, New Delhi, on September 26, 2012.
44. Lord Cornwallis concluded the Permanent Settlement Act 1793. Under this act, the landholders or Zamindars were admitted as the absolute holders of landed property and it fixed the method and limit of payment of revenue to the British East India Company. This act was instrumental in forming an alliance between the Zamindars and the British rulers.
45. "Sociology Guide", accessed on August 17, 2012, 'http://www.sociologyguide.com/rural-sociology/jajmani-system-rural-society.php. The notion of the jajmani system was popularized by colonial ethnography. It tended to conceptualize agrarian social structure in the framework of exchange relations. In its classical construct, different caste groups specialized in specific occupations and exchanged their services through

an elaborate system of division of labor. Though asymmetry in position of various caste groups was recognized, what it emphasized was not inequality in rights over land but the spirit of community.

46. Bengal Land Reform Act, 1955 and Operation Barga [Operation Barga was a land reform movement throughout rural West Bengal for recording the names of sharecroppers (bargadars) while avoiding the time-consuming method of recording through the settlement machinery. It bestowed on the bargadars, the legal protection against eviction by the landlords, and entitled them to the due share of the produce. Operation Barga was launched in 1978 and concluded by the mid-1980s]. Accessed on July 18, 2011, http://www.scribd.com/doc/28335857/Land-Reforms-in-West-Bengal.
47. P.K. Agrawal, "Naxalism: Causes and Cure" (New Delhi: Manas Publications, 2011), 11.
48. E.N. Rammohan, former DG BSF, "The Naxalite Maoist Insurgency in India: The Root Causes and a Possible Solution", *USI* CXLII (July–September 2012): 356.
49. Manpreet Sethi, "Land Reforms in India: Issues and Challenges" (New Delhi: Manas Publications, 2006), 2.
50. Monitorable Targets & Milestones for 2008, Infrastructure Sector: Planning Commission.
51. This is perhaps an indication of lower levels of investment in the agriculture sector, particularly when the percentage workforce of the total population engaged in agriculture is 58 percent. FAO report, accessed on December 12, 2011, http://www.fao.org/fileadmin/templates/ess/documents/food_security_statistics/country_profiles/eng/India_E.pdf accessed (first published on May 05, 2011).
52. D. Bandhopaday, "Development Challenges in Extremist Affected Areas", A report of the Expert Group (New Delhi: Planning Commission, 2008), 45–47.
53. Special Economic Zones (SEZs) – special zones set up by the government to encourage industrial growth where requisite support infrastructure will be set up by the government and the industry will be awarded tax concessions.
54. Vidarbha is the eastern region of Maharashtra state made up of Nagpur, and Amravati.
55. D. Bandhopaday, "Development Challenges in Extremist Affected Areas", A report of the expert group (New Delhi: Planning Commission, 2008), 45–47.
56. In 1980, the Forest (Conservation) Act was enacted for providing a higher level of protection to the forests and to regulate diversion of forest lands for non-forestry purposes. Prior approval of the Central Government being essential for de-reservation of forest lands and/or diversion of forest lands for non-forestry purposes is the main feature of the act. However, it took away the flexibility of the state governments to give away and regularize land holdings of the traditional tribal groups or forest dwellers.
57. Ashutosh Bhardwaj, "Maoist Payment: Essar GM held", *Indian Express*, September 28, 2011.
58. "Maloy Krishna Dhar (Former Joint Director of Intelligence Bureau), accessed February 23, 2012, http://www.sify.com/news/my-secret-wish-is-to-become-a-Naxal-news-national-jegq8jeaegb.htmls.

59. For more details, see "Four Pronged Policy Needed to Tackle Maoism: Jairam", *The Hindu*, September 24, 2012.
60. Ramachandra Guha, "Adivasis, Naxalites and Indian Democracy", *Economic & Political Weekly*, August 11, 2007. (This essay argues that adivasis as a whole have gained least and lost most from six decades of democracy and development in India.)
61. In 1980s, the rates in erstwhile Madhya Pradesh (now Chhattisgarh) were 10 paise per bundle. They have now been increased to 70-80 paise per bundle by the state government. However, there are reports that the Naxalites have bartered a higher rate to the tune of Rs 1.20 in 2011 directly from the contractors in return for safety.
62. Supriya Sharma, "Out of 12,000 Forest Villages in Chhattisgarh, only 250 have been given Community Rights, under the Forest Rights Act (2006)", *Times News Network*, 13 July 2011, accessed February 23, 2012, http://articles.timesofindia.indiatimes.com/2011-06-13/india/29652744_1_tendu-wage-rate-Naxal-control.
63. Special Correspondent, "Bamboo 'revolution' to beat back Maoist", *The Hindu*, September 18, 2012.
64. The Equal Remuneration Act mandates payment of equal wages for men and women for work requiring the same skill and effort.
65. D. Bandhopaday, "Development Challenges in Extremist Affected Areas", A report of the Expert Group (New Delhi: Planning Commision, 2008).
66. Nitin Sethi, "Govt changes forest law for tribals", *The Times of India*, September 09, 2012. Among other initiatives, bamboo has been defined as grass and not a tree.
67. For more details, read E.N. Rammohan, "The Naxalite Maoist Insurgency in India: The Root Causes and a Possible Solution", *USI* CXLII (July–September 2012): 357.
68. Peters Gretcher, "How Opium Profits the Taliban" (US Institute of Peace, 2009).
69. Tusheet Saraf, "Maoists in India", accessed on December 29, 2012,.http://www.civilserviceindia.com/subject/Essay/maoists-in-india.html.

(*Note:* Available authentic statistics have been quoted in the book, primarily to highlight the prevalent trends in availability/distribution of resources, HDI, basic amenities and social infrastructures, in the worst hit Naxal states. The latest statistics could be marginally better.)

Chapter 3

Ideology and External Linkages

We cannot be sure of having something to live for unless we are willing to die for it.

– Ernesto Che Guevara

CENTER OF GRAVITY

During the concluding part of my talk on Naxalism at the Lucknow University in 2011, one of the students asked me, "What, in my view, is the 'center of gravity' of Naxalism?" I threw open the question to the audience. It was an open-ended question, because it did not specify whether it related to the insurgents or the counter-insurgents. However, I guess the question implied, "center of gravity to tackle Naxalism". The answers suggested by them were issues like good governance, the people, Naxals' leadership, ideology, empowerment of people, support of external powers, etc. Majority of them felt that "the people" should be the center of gravity. The thought process of the students on all the answers given was not without logic. To answer the question, there is a need to understand the main driving force behind an insurgency, among other aspects. For the same conflict, will it be different at different phases, places and set of people? If we accept the answer, "the people", then the question arises who drives the people. The leaders drive the people, who in turn are indoctrinated by an "ideology". Really speaking, the ideology drives the movement/revolution. It could also be a combination of the ideology and the leadership. Therefore, it suggests that there are multiple centers of gravity in a complex insurgency environment. The insurgents and the counter-insurgents have to analyze for themselves the power-cum-sensitivity of a particular driver and actual ground conditions to determine the center of gravity. Goswami, an analyst, argues that "popular legitimacy and population support", are the most crucial factors for optimal counter-insurgency outcomes.[1] General Templar, the High Commissioner and Director of Operations in Malaya, had said that "winning the hearts and minds (meaning 'people' as the center of gravity)" – a phrase coined by him – was the most important aspect to win the Malayan Insurgency. David Galula, a French officer, based on his experiences of the Algerian War writes, "The aim of the war is to gain the support of the population rather than control of territory."[2]

One thing that stands out clearly is that both the insurgents and the counter-insurgents require the support of the people to achieve success in their laid down goals. In another case, the SF may find that a particular insurgent leader has an overwhelming influence on all actions in a specific region. Some regions may have a strong ideological base, which can be the driving force to produce more leaders and insurgents. They then propagate the ideology in an effective manner, which sways the population and fuels violence. The immediate requirement may suggest the leader or the ideological base as the "center of gravity" to make progress in the anti-naxal campaign. In the case of the "Shining Path", in Peru, Abimael Guzman had acquired a huge status as the leader of the movement. On September 12, 1992, Peruvian police captured Guzmán and several Shining Path leaders, during a raid in the Surquillo district of Lima. The capture of the rebel leader Guzman – the center of gravity – left a huge leadership vacuum for the Shining Path, resulting in rapid decline of the insurgency. In Indian context, the death of Charu Mazumdar on July 28, 1972, resulted in the decline of the Naxalite movement. Due to sudden vacuum in the leadership of the CPI (ML), the party splintered into a number of factions.

In some cases, more than sustaining the ideology, the insurgents are fully involved in organized crime, drug trafficking, and extortion. The center of gravity in such cases would lie in tackling crime and exposure of the nexus between the insurgents and the crime-mafia. Some of the activities of the Naxals suggest that they are indulging in terrorism, with jargon like class struggle and people's war thrown in to mask it as an insurgency. Although the ideology propagates shunning the democratic process, a large number of Naxal cadres, over-ground workers in particular, have contested elections with support from their party. It is evident that in a complex insurgency environment such as Naxalism that is spread over such a large geographical area and population, there are multiple centers of gravity. Therefore, population alone is not the center of gravity. In a generic and more acceptable form, the "support of the population" *is often a critical requirement and a critical vulnerability. Support of population should therefore be a strategic, operational, and tactical objective of the insurgents and the counter-insurgents.*[3] Kilcullen suggests that center of gravity is "connecting to the general population".[4] In the case of Naxalism too, the "support of the population" remains the top priority. It would, therefore, be prudent to create a secure environment and seriously address the three issues: first, the ideology of Naxals by ensuring good governance, good delivery mechanism, and perception management; second, the Naxal leadership; third, cutting off the supply routes of funds, arms and explosives, both from internal and external linkages.

Ideology

The ideology of the Indian Maoists, which has driven the revolution, owes its origin to the ideological thoughts of Karl Marx, Lenin, and Mao Zedong. In broad terms, Marx brought forth the need to overthrow capitalism, transform socio-economic conditions, and create a classless society by relentless class struggle. Lenin raised the theory and practice of proletarian revolution to a completely new level, as he led the proletariat in seizing and consolidating its political power. He identified the rural masses as the revolutionary class. His revolutionary slogan was "land, bread, peace".[5] Mao Zedong, also called Mao in short, worked on three pillars of his ideology. These were the protracted people's war, revolutionary struggle by the affected people (poor peasants) against the ruling class, and the famous three-stage strategy[6] (Strategic defensive, strategic stalemate and strategic offensive). Mao's thoughts grew out of his experiences of socio-economic and security conditions prevailing in China in the 1930s and 1940s, the pre-revolutionary phase of China. These experiences and the ground conditions formed the basis of the People's War concept, which later became the doctrine of the Red Army and the People's Liberation Army (PLA). Mao also drew from the works of the country's most famous military strategist, the 5th century BC general, Sun Tzu (also called Sun Zi), other theorists and from his personal experience of the "Long March" and peasants' uprising. He created a comprehensive doctrine to wage a revolutionary people's war, incorporating political, economic, and psychological measures, along with protracted armed struggle against a superior enemy.

In India, the Naxalites theory has undergone a major change from "Land to the Tillers" of the early years to the present anti-globalization and anti-economic liberalization. India has witnessed a large number of insurgencies since 1950s. Most of them are "state specific", except for the LWE and Naga insurgencies that had spread to other states. All of them are characterized by protracted armed struggle due to socio-economic exclusion, governance deficit, and lack of political will to find an amicable solution. The merger of the political parties and the two guerilla military wings of the MCCI and the PWG, i.e. People's Liberation Guerilla Army (PLGA) and People's Guerilla Army (PGA) into the unified PLGA, has considerably strengthened the Naxals. Since 2004, the military wings of the Naxals are better organized in terms of their structure, command and control, weapons, training, intelligence, and communication systems. With the merger, the movement acquired a near pan-India character, which started manifesting in planned coordinated attacks, large-scale violence, and killing of innocent civilians. These developments have thrown up several challenges to the state and its systemic tools, especially after the recent success of the Naxalite movement in Nepal. A close look of the map of India and Nepal suggests that the movement extends right from the borders of Nepal to the southern parts of India, though not in one continuous stretch. With Tibet no longer being a buffer from China to India, and China planning to extend the Lhasa rail link and roads into Nepal, the threat has assumed a new dimension.

The Naxals are acutely aware of the inherent weaknesses of the federal structure of the government; large diversity in the society; splintering of political parties; lack of national consensus; rise of regional, caste, and religion-based parties; and government policies being pursued in rural India. These offer them adequate opportunities to strengthen the movement and advance towards a successful armed revolution. The ideologues also realize that without a united party, a people's army and a revolutionary united front, the revolutionary potential of the situation in India cannot be realized fully. Naxalism also poses a serious long-term ideological threat, through its potential to generate a serious rural-urban fault line. This fault line will acquire the proportions of a serious threat once Indian demographic bulge acquires a critical mass because of rising unemployment and socio-economic inequality. Naxalites do not belong to any particular religion or community, but are driven by an ideology. They are largely adivasis, dalits, poor farmers, and marginalized sections of society. Though the basic issues are land reforms, forest rights, resettlement of displaced people, and socio-economic exclusion, it is known that they are actually fighting to overthrow the Indian state and seize political power.[7]

In the perception of the Naxalites, the teeth for suppression to the state is given by the armed forces or the police forces of the country, be it the army, the police, or the paramilitary forces; and thus, it recognizes the need to destroy these forces first, without which only limited success would be achieved. It further appreciates that the Indian revolution would have to pass through two stages. The task of first stage is to change the semi-colonial, semi-feudal society into an independent new democratic society, based on the fundamental contradictions in the Indian society, i.e. the contradiction of the Indian people with imperialism and the contradiction of the broad masses with feudalism. Again, in its continuity, the task of second stage is to establish the socialist system and continuing the revolution, advancing towards communism. For the armed struggle, it advocates setting up of a people's army, which would initially adopt the guerrilla form of warfare to preserve its strength (in the initial part of its formative years when it is not as powerful as the armed and police forces of the state). In opposition of the parliamentary form of government, it puts forth the fact that the method has not benefitted the nation since independence, and therefore stands exposed before the people. Finally, it sees the CPI (Maoist) party as the vanguard of the proletariat class, and supports all other revolutions going on against the ruling class in the world.[8]

In China, it was, in essence, an agrarian revolution that overthrew the landlords and developed a three-phase model of People's Revolutionary War that defeated the Republic of Chiang Kai Shek[9] and ushered in communist rule. The revolution started in the countryside and later overwhelmed the cities. Mao used space to extend the war in time, to drag it on for decades to harass, wear down, and exhaust the enemy (ruling class); to induce war weariness and homesickness; and wear down enemy's will to resist. To mobilize the masses, Mao used political mobility, propaganda, and subversion. The prime aim was to attack the will of the "class enemy" and counter his industrial growth and mobility, with support of the masses. Although the Naxals have also tried to mobilize the masses and undermine the writ of the government, they have not achieved the desired results. Consequently, there has been an apparent shift in their ideology – they aim to organize the people against socio-economic fault-lines rather than attempt to over throw the government.

Organization and Leadership

The CPI (Maoist) is typically organized on the basis of standard communist structure. It has a parallel political and military organization, which functions under the central committee, which is the highest decision-making body within the party. At present, it is assessed that the Naxals have a 19-member Central Committee and a seven member politburo[10] with five regional bureaus. Muppala Lakshmana Rao alias Ganapathi, who replaced Kondappally as the general secretary of the People's War, was elected the general secretary of the CPI (Maoist). The politburo of the party includes Nambala Keshava Rao, the chief of the CMC and one of the main functionary of the central committee. The other brains behind guerrilla warfare are Mallojula Venugopal alias Bhupathi (younger brother of Kishenji), Kishan Da, and Katakam Sudershan.[11]

The key command and control organ of the CPI (Maoist)'s military wing is the Central Military Commission (CMC), which presently has seven members.[12] All armed cadres of the party are constituted under the People's Liberation Guerrilla Army (PLGA), which is guided by the

CMC at its apex. The entire territory under the Naxal influence has been organized into "zones", which more or less coincide with state boundaries. Zones are further divided into "areas", which control the basic unit known as "dalams"[13] – groups of 10 to 30 odd cadres coming from nearby villages. The total hardcore cadre strength is estimated to be between 14,000 and 16,000,[14] but these figures are just a wild guess since there are frequent changes, because of which the movement is generally decentralized and fluid. As per another view, the military formation of the CPI (Maoist) includes estimated 10,000 armed cadres, apart from a huge mass of 1,00,000 people's militia.[15] There are "committees" at zonal and area levels. While the operations are led by the dalam commanders, the organizational chain is neither standard nor sacrosanct; changes are rather frequent. For organization of CPI (Maoist) Central Committee and the regional bureaus at all India level, refer Appendix A.

There are five regional bureaus, which control the zonal military commissions. These, in turn, control the fighting cadres or the dalams (platoon equivalent) and the sangams (over-ground workers). The force is divided into three types: the primary force – platoons (military platoons and protection platoons); secondary force – guerrilla squads [Local Guerrilla Squad (LGS) or Central Guerrilla Squad (CGS) or Special Guerrilla Squad (SGS)]; and the base force or the people's militia. Members of the people's militia are not hardcore well-trained guerrilla fighters, but ordinary men and women such as laborers, peasants, unemployed youth, etc., and are imparted minimum military training. There are prescribed norms for granting membership to the cadres, and that women comprise 40% of the total cadre strength of the Maoists.[16] In comparison to the Nepal's Maoist insurgency, there is some similarity in the organizational structure and the modus-operandi of the rebels.

Effective "Sarkars"

According to the statements issued by arrested top cadres of the Naxal wings, it indicates the presence of an "unarmed wing", which does not indulge in violence and operates as the grassroots political, administrative, justice delivery, and supportive wing of the insurgents. The hierarchical setup of parallel governance and intelligence wings of Naxals in village and tehsil areas are divided into units like "raksha dalam", "janata sarkar", and "area sarkar".[17] According to the reports, a janata sarkar covers 4 to 5 villages and works on the directions of the area sarkar. Area sarkars co-ordinate with zonal committees to spread their network in urban and rural areas. The raksha dalam is responsible for providing security to the members of the janata sarkar. The functioning of the janata sarkar can be compared with the gram panchayat[18] and the area sarkar with the block panchayat. While these "sarkars" carry out the political work of the Naxals, they are ably supported by the parallel military organizations like the "dalams" at area level.

Ninth unity congress

The central committee and the political bureau of the CPI (Maoist) have generally been holding their meetings periodically. The contours of such deliberations pertain to ideology, strategy, resolutions, monitor progress of various programs, conduct self-critical analysis, and issue directions for mid-course corrections, where required. The Ninth Unity Congress of CPI (Maoist) was held in the remote forested areas in one of their guerrilla bases in January-February 2007, after approximately 36 years. Some of the important documents that were presented, deliberated upon, and adopted were "programme of the party, party constitution, strategy and tactics of Indian revolution, urban perspective plan, and political resolution on international and domestic situation."[19] In other words, the conference covered all significant aspects related to further strengthening the revolution. The conference pledged to spread the revolution by broadening the mass base, establishing base areas and liberated guerrilla zones, and moving into semi-urban areas. In addition, the conference confirmed their faith in NDR through agrarian revolution with protracted armed struggle as the path to support the movement in J&K, Manipur, Nagaland, and Assam, and to oppose setting up of SEZs being planned in the country.[20]

Modus operandi

The modus operandi of the Naxal operations can be divided into four distinct parts; namely, military operations, intelligence system, psychological strategy, and procurement and employment of weapon systems. Having studied the guerrilla warfare in detail, they have applied the tactics with resourcefulness against the SF. With known asymmetry in their combat potential, they optimize their strengths – detailed knowledge of terrain, physically tough, highly mobile, expert in minor tactics, minimum logistics requirements, good intelligence system and above all, the commitment to the cause – to conduct attacks with surprise and speed at the weakest point of the SF and other targets. With hit and run as the basic tactics, they achieved expertise in their ability to concentrate large numbers at the point of decision undetected, to disperse after an operation, and thus create an aura of bravery and invincibility. By adopting IED as a prominent attack tool, they avoid direct confrontation with the SF. This backed with effective information gathering systems is a deadly combination.

The operational philosophy of the Naxals suggests that, in the future, with a more responsive organization, better weapon systems, more combat experience, and quality training, they would like to achieve two important milestones. The first would be to transform PLGA into PLA; and second, to graduate to mobile warfare. The stated aim was to strengthen the primary force into cohesive platoons and companies, to provide the nucleus force for swarm type of attacks. With extensive use of IEDs and explosives, they have been attacking the SF establishments and columns to kill personnel, loot arms and ammunition, and destroy the government property. On a number of occasions, they have targeted civilians as well.

The Naxals have a simple but effective intelligence system, predominantly based on human intelligence. In the remote areas, they have a large number of sympathizers and supporters among the population, who utilize women and schoolchildren also to gather intelligence, and to pass on to the appropriate cadres. Tribal loyalties also play a significant role in working for their brethren, the Naxals, who have acquired Robin Hood image by working for the local people and providing them the necessary relief in their routine-cum-emergent requirements, specially medicines, essential stores and ensuring minimum support prices for their goods. With the revolution in media and communication technology, the Naxals have also switched on to mobile phones, internet, and satellite communication facilities, where feasible.

As part of their psychological strategy, they mobilize the masses by motivation or armed coercion, and instigate them to destroy government property. The Naxals take initiatives to develop infrastructure to meet the aspirations of the people. Simultaneously, they aim to deter the government agencies to carry out any developmental works, by killing key personnel or taking them as hostages. In other words, a kind of fear psychosis is created among the stakeholders. They have targeted a large number of economic infrastructures such as bridges, culverts, mobile towers, electric sub-stations, railway tracks and pipelines carrying slurry from the mining areas. In 2011-12, it was reported that they have been using the children and women as human shields in various operations,[21] so that whenever any casualties occur due to firing by the SF or otherwise, the population would be alienated against the government machinery. Such an action would serve their interests the most. It is then possible to exploit the anti-government sentiments of the population to recruit the youth to embrace Naxalism. Overall, they aim to discredit the authority of the state and the SF, and gain moral, and psychological support from the local population.

The Central Technical Committee (CTC) of the Naxals plays a significant role in planning the procurement or acquiring various arms, ammunition, equipment, explosives, IEDs, and communication systems. Small-scale foundries or manufacturing units are tasked to fabricate and manufacture small arms, rocket launchers, explosive devices, IEDs, and booby traps, though crude, to meet the requirements of different categories of force structure. These are supplied to the Naxals, by local manufacturing units in places like Mungher, Jamui, Gumla, Latehar and Dantewada, among others. During one of my visits to Kondagaon and Jagdalpur, I was shown a document of the Maoists, which gave details of their tactics at the platoon level. The document was so similar, in its content, other than use of words like dalams, sanghams, that my first impression was that it appeared to have been compiled by a retired functionary of the army or the CAPF. Possibly, some of the ex-servicemen, living in the affected areas, may have been coerced into preparing their tactical documents, and for imparting training in basic tactics, including handling of IEDs.

Leadership and cadre

The highly affected areas by Naxalism cover Chhattisgarh, Jharkhand, Odisha, Bihar, northern Andhra Pradesh, eastern fringes of Maharashtra, parts of West Bengal and Madhya Pradesh. In all these states except Bihar, the cadres are mostly tribal – poor, and unemployed, with average measly monthly income of Rs. 600 to Rs. 800 for the entire family in mix of cash and kind, and most of the times received only during the working season. On the other hand, the tribal cadres from these regions are normally offered a monthly remuneration of up to Rs. 2,000 and a cut of the extortion money[22] (a princely sum as compared to their legitimate earnings of Rs. 600–800 per month). There are also increasing reports of use of children in the armed wings.[23] The group has traditionally used children to carry out work as couriers or spies. However, of late, there have been credible reports that recruitment and use of children has been institutionalized by creation of "Bal Sangathans" in adjoining areas of western and southern Jharkhand, southern Chhattisgarh, Gadchiroli in Maharashtra, and south western parts of Odisha. Children above the age of 12 years are given training in use of weapons, gathering intelligence, field craft, and use and planting of landmines and IEDs.[24]

As for the leadership, the entire middle-level cadres come from small town graduates and dropouts in their 20s and 30s, hailing from Andhra Pradesh, Bihar, Odisha, and Bengal. Most of these leaders, who came during the early part of the movement in 1960s to 1980s, were fiercely motivated and were ready to sacrifice anything for the cause. Despite the fact that there is no national-level charismatic leader, yet the movement had gained momentum, particularly after the merger. The common thread that runs through such a huge population and land mass to give impetus to the movement is abject poverty, exploitation, trust deficit with the government, and food security – meaning job for the people. While the senior leadership comprises hard-core ideologues, who continue to propagate the Maoist ideology; of late, it appears that the middle-level leaders' belief in the ideology is moderate to low. They are not hard-core in their thoughts and propagation of ideology. The Naxals – more prominently in the erstwhile areas of MCCI – have also taken to organized crime and extortion, to make easy money. One of the main causes of concern to the Naxals is that the ideology has started to deviate from its original path.

Compact revolutionary zone (CRZ)

The Naxals have been keen to establish a CRZ or a Red Corridor stretching from Nepal in the north to the southern tip of India.[25] This will encompass the dalit-cum-tribal areas of Bihar and Uttar Pradesh, and predominantly the tribal-cum-backward areas of Madhya Pradesh, Jharkhand, Odisha, Chhattisgarh, Andhra Pradesh, Maharashtra, Karnataka, and Kerala. This is in accordance with their strategy to make bases in rural areas, and ensure – through violence or threat of use of violence – that the state administrative machinery is left defunct and the writ of the state does not run. It would thus give them operational space to function with impunity. These bases allow them to regroup, train, and expand their activities, thus increasing their power and influence into the neighboring areas. Thick jungles, contiguous tribal belts, characterize the CRZ, and vast underdeveloped regions spread across the country, including the area of Abhujmadh in the Dandkaranya region (90,000 sq km). Refer Figure 3.1.

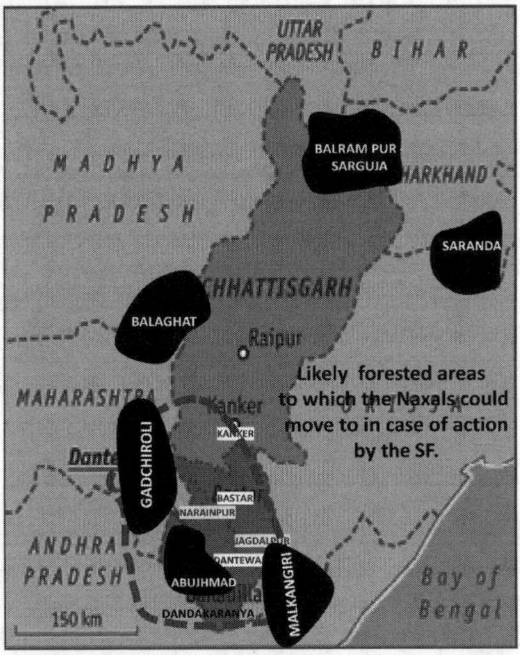

Figure 3.1: Dandakaranya Special Zone and Safe Sanctuaries

The Abhujmadh area has extremely thick jungles spread over an area of about 4000 sq km and inhabited by various tribes with nearly 20,000 tribal families living in 237 villages in a most primitive manner with virtually no basic amenities. Till date, after some recent efforts, this area remains only partially surveyed.[26] With limited presence of the state in this region, the only organizational presence is that of Baba Amte in Chandrapur and Gadchiroli areas in Maharashtra and the Rama Krishna Mission in Chhattisgarh.[27] Thus, the Naxals have taken advantage of the void in state control, and have established large-scale presence in the Dandkaranya region. Most of their safe sanctuaries, training areas and strategic base camps are located in these regions. Refer Figure 3.1.

Funds and Weaponry

In their strategy of spatial expansion, Naxals are deeply concerned about the mineral rich areas of Jharkhand, Odisha and Chhattisgarh. They would ensure effective control of these areas to prevent unhindered exploitation of the natural resources by outsiders, and in return leverage financial benefit for themselves. They openly extort large sums of money from mining companies, transportation of slurry and private industries (steel, power, cement, alloys, chemicals, etc.) in the area in return for safe passage of men and materials of the companies. They also extort money from the transporters, forest contractors and development agencies. As per reports the development funds meant for Naxal-affected states ultimately goes into the coffers of the ultras through the contractors engaged by the authorities for executing developmental works.[28] The labor of public sector undertakings (PSUs) and a large number of industries in this area are generally under control of the Naxals. They have penetrated most of the labor unions to retain control on the activities of the industries or mining activities. This gives them great advantage in terms of controlling production, transportation of raw material and finished products, thus retaining the ability to generate finances for the organization.

The Maoists total revenue from extortion, drug cultivation, and racketeering was estimated to be 25 billion rupees ($ 552 million) in 2010.[29] As per some other estimates, the Naxals annual extortion industry is nearly Rs. 1,200 crores. The generation of this whopping amount is from a number of sources including extortion, drug trafficking, levy paid by contractors, forest officials, hobnobbing with multinational corporations, politicians, bank robberies, and industrialists controlling the mineral rich areas. In fact, the bulk of the financing is through drug trafficking. Reports available with the Central Economic Intelligence Bureau (CEIB) has indicated that close to Rs. 1,000 crores is contributed by this illegal activity alone. In fact, satellite images available with the government have revealed a massive increase in cultivation of poppy and cannabis in Naxal-dominated areas.[30] The availability of this large amount of funds not only assists in building of military strength through procurement of weapons, but also helps in increasing their support base by disbursing aid and loans. Lately, there have been admissions from arrested top leaders that a good part of the funds is now being utilized for hiring good lawyers to fight court cases against their jailed associates.[31] The aspect that is of concern is the nature of management of this fund. Apart from funding the day-to-day functions, including buying weaponry and such like equipment, the Naxals also maintain reserve fund which can sustain their movement for over one year in their fight at full scale.[32] Due to the control of the Naxals, funds allotted to panchayats also are diverted for meeting the requirements of the rebels.

As far as weapons are concerned, a large part has been stolen from armories of state and central police forces, as also from slain police personnel. It has been estimated that close to 2,500 weapons and lakhs of rounds of ammunition have been snatched away by the ultras during the last decade (*The Hindu,* December 5, 2010). During the raid at Nayagarh in Odisha alone, in 2008, the Naxals had taken away weapons of the SF (LMGs, AK series of rifles, SLRs, etc.), in excess of 1,000 along with a huge quantity of ammunition. There are numerous such attacks or raids on police/SF posts and jails, from where a large number of weapons have been taken away by the Naxalites. In my view, the actual figures are much more than 2,500 weapons, as reported. Of late, there have been credible reports that the Naxalites are procuring weapons from external sources like China.[33] Suspected links among the PLA (Manipur)[34] and the proximity of Cox' bazaar (infamously renowned for gunrunning)[35] has helped the Naxalites smuggle in a large proportion of arms and weaponry into its areas. See Figure 3.2. The weapon systems are being made available more as a commercial activity than as part of an ideological support. Some private firms have also been assisting the rebel groups with imported hi-tech gear.[36]

With the number of SF being inducted into the Naxal-affected areas, the Naxals have been resorting to stand off attacks using landmines. This expertise in the use of landmines and IEDs[37] has reportedly been gained through the LTTE connections.[38] Most of the explosives for use as landmines or IEDs are however stolen by them from the mining companies, which use these explosives for blasting purposes. The electronic detonators are so small that very large numbers can be concealed effectively and transported safely, without being intercepted by the police. Most of these activities are helped by porous borders, corrupt law enforcement officials, limited safeguards for "hawala"[39] transactions, inept policing and politician-criminal nexus, which allows

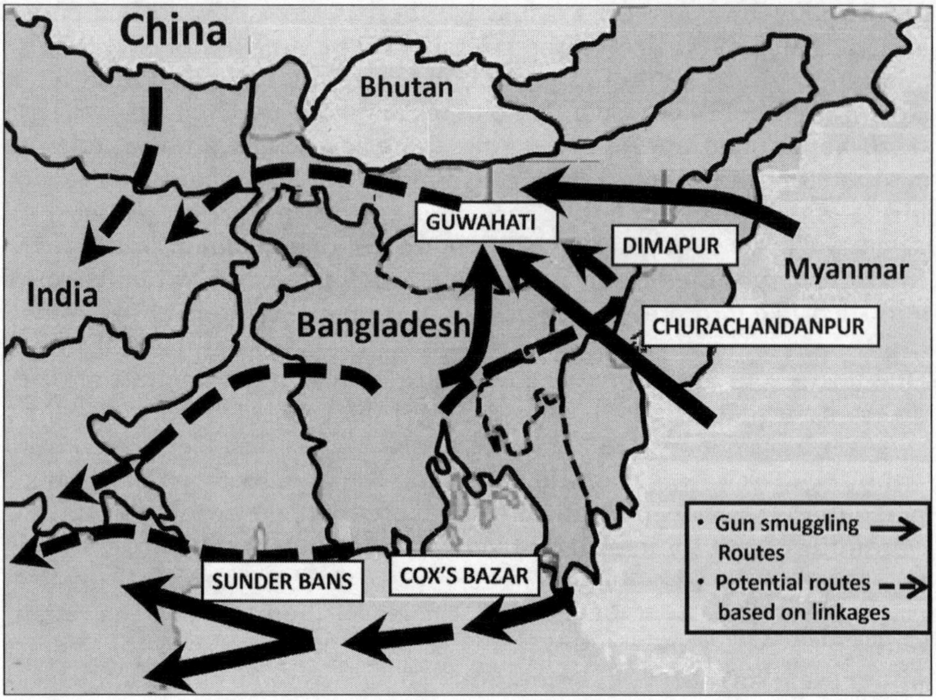

Figure 3.2: The Great Northeast Arms Bazar

for freedom of space for criminal elements to operate with impunity. It is these illegal networks of criminals, which are used by the Naxals to carry on with their armed struggle through drug trafficking, arms trade, and illegal financial transactions.

External Linkages

Drivers

Intelligence reports and captured literature from camps and bases have revealed that the Naxals have established linkages with many other groups within and outside India, to sustain their movement. Major drivers – to sustain the movement – are propaganda/ideology, weapon systems, training, finances, drugs, linkages with other militant organizations and external powers. There are a number of enthusiastic agencies in India's neighbourhood willing to provide support to the movement.

External powers and linkages

The Naxal organizations, on many occasions, have openly supported the actions and causes of the J&K terrorist groups. With the tightening of the security at the border in J&K, and the ISI establishing their bases in Nepal and Bangladesh,[40] the J&K terrorist organizations could make use of these bases to enter India through the strongholds of the Naxals, and reach their target areas in J&K or in the rest of the country. For example, the Lashkar-e-Taiba terrorists, who carried out the attack on the American Center at Kolkata in 2001, had escaped to Jharkhand and taken refuge in a LWE sympathizer's house in Ranchi. In return, the J&K terrorist organizations could possibly provide with other forms of support – finances, weapon systems, communication equipment, and training in explosive devices – to the LWE groups.

During the meeting of the chief minister on May 5, 2012, the union home minister had announced that the Naxals have made inroads into/ established links with ultras in Assam, Arunachal Pradesh, Manipur, and other states in the northeast. With the near collapse of insurgencies in the northeastern states, they are trying to secure a toehold in the northeastern region by striking deals with rump outfits.[41] In addition, they are reportedly targeting victims of ethnic riots and floods. During their campaign in the tea belts of Assam, they have been exhibiting footage of some Hindi films on Maoist ideology and their fight for liberation of the oppressed in order to motivate them to join their outfit. The Assam Police arrested Aklanta Rabha alias Mahesh, a CPI (Maoist) CMC member and chief of the party's north-east operations and his aide Suraj Rabha, a top-ranking arms trainer of Maoists in Jharkhand, at Guwahati on April 26, 2013. Mahesh was the main facilitator for Maoists' gun-running and served as a conduit for procuring sophisticated arms from across the border. One of their aims has been to maintain strong presence along the supply route of weapons. The CPI (Maoist) has established links with militant groups of the northeast like Kamtapur Liberation Origination (KLO), *United Liberation Front of Assam* (ULFA), Nationalist Socialist Council of Nagaland (NSCN) (IM), and People's Liberation Army (PLA) of Manipur. In addition, there are reports and evidence to suggest that the LWE cadres have linkages with militant organizations like Telangana Rashtriya Samiti, which is spearheading the separatist movement in Telangana, and even with other groups operating in Karnataka, Tamil Nadu, and Kerala.

In September 2012, sophisticated M16 rifles, the primary weapon of the US Armed Forces and other modern arms and ammunition were recovered from Jharkhand.[42] It seems to show that the northeast arms supply route to the LWE is active and functional. The direct routes from Cox Bazar to the coast of Odisha, Andhra Pradesh, and to the Sunderbans is also a distinct possibility to supply lethal weapons. Manoharan, an analyst, firmly believes that because of extensive linkages with both state and non-state actors within and without India, the LWE fails to strictly qualify as an "indigenous" movement. The actors with which the Naxals have linkages, include Maoists of Nepal, militant groups operating in the northeastern India, anti-India terror groups based in Pakistan, and organizations like Coordinating Committee of Maoist Parties and Organizations of South Asia (CCOMPOSA), Friends of Indian Revolution (FOIR), International Conference of Marxist-Leninist Parties and Organizations (ICMLPO), and International Communist Movement (ICM).[43]

The Communist Party of China (CPC) has been a known sympathizer since the early days of the Naxalbari uprising in 1967, wherein national dailies of China had carried editorials glorifying the armed struggle. Although the relations between the Chinese Communists and the Indian Naxals had strained in the later years (after the death of Mao in 1976) owing to various reasons including ideological differences, these have apparently been revived. Repeated recoveries of Chinese-made arms and radio sets from Naxal cadres seems to confirm the linkage. Some of the arrested Maoists have revealed the existence of supply chain from China.[44] Subramanian Swamy, an expert, says that the Maoists are one of the proxies the Chinese use in India to take care of their anti-Indian agenda.[45] The contours of cooperation between the Chinese Communists and Indian Maoists appear fairly large, given the revival of support, linkages, supply of weapons and equipment. The comments from scholars in China (Professor Shi Hongyuan of the Chinese Academy of Social Sciences, *Contemporary World Socialism Issues*, and No. 1/2009 issue) seem to suggest that China may be comfortable to see the CPI (Maoist) gaining power by contesting elections.[46] With modern means of communications, Naxals have established linkages with external powers, militant organizations within India and abroad, to sustain, and thereafter to further strengthen the movement.

Notes

1. Namrata Goswami, "Counter-Insurgency Best Practices: Applicability to Northeast India", *Small Wars Journal*, Journal Article, December 06, 2012.
2. Galula, David, "Counterinsurgency Warfare: Theory and Practice", Westport, Connecticut: Praeger Security International, 1964, 54-56.
3. Jonathan P. Klug and School of Advanced Military Studies. "Behind the Mosaic: Insurgent Centers of Gravity and Counterinsurgency" (Fort Leavenworth, KS: US Army Command and General Staff College, 2012).
4. David J. Kilcullen, "Counterinsurgency", Oxford University Press, 2010.
5. R.K. Gupta, "The Crimson Agenda: Maoist Protest and Terror" (New Delhi: Wordsmith, 2004), 21.
6. *Strategic Defensive:* Essential features are: hit and run, stretch enemy's operational and logistical resources, carry out swift tactical offensives with local numerical superiority at the point of decision, widen mass base by ideological indoctrination, establish secure bases in inaccessible areas, and recruit fresh cadres for the revolution.

Strategic Stalemate: Salient features are: marked increase in the primary force and its organizational structure, ability to marshal a larger force for a prolonged battle of attrition at a place of tactical advantage, attack on government officials and thus neutralizing their developmental activities in the rural areas, making inroads into semi urban and urban areas. Simultaneously, ideological indoctrination, widening mass base and cadre strength must continue to build a conventional force.

Strategic Offensive: The force assumes the dimensions of a conventional force in its organization, structure, command and control, weaponry, training, surveillance, communications, intelligence, firepower, mobility including air assets. The force is capable of limited positional warfare and manoeuvre warfare to match the state forces, with the support of the masses. Mao had achieved this capability of strategic offensive in China's civil war.

7. In his reply to the debate in the Lok Sabha on Dantewada massacre, the Home Minister Mr. P.C. Chidambaram said, "let us not have any illusion about the goal of the Naxals... their goal is to seize political power and their method (to achieve this) is armed liberation... the PLGA will soon become the People's Liberation Army... they call this war and the state their enemy."
8. For more details, see CPI (Maoist) Party Programme.
9. Chiang Kai-shek (1887–1975) was a political and military leader of 20th century China. The Communists (CCP) defeated the Nationalists in 1949, forcing Chiang's government to retreat to Taiwan. Chiang ruled the island as the self-appointed President of the Republic of China until his death in 1975.
10. P.V. Ramana, "Measures to Deal with Left-Wing Extremism/Naxalism", In *IDSA Occasional Paper No. 20,* Annexure 3 (New Delhi: Institute for Defence Studies and Analyses, 2011), 61.
11. Yatish Yadav, "Paramilitary Forces Prepare List of Eight Most Wanted Maoists", *The Sunday Guardian,* Oct 09, 2011. (Lately, as per Ramana, the CMC has Nimbala, T. Tirupathi, Misir Besra, Deo Kumar Singh @ Arvindji Ranjit Bose @ Kanchan Dor, etc.)
12. P.V. Ramana, "Measures to Deal with Left-Wing Extremism/Naxalism", In *IDSA Occasional Paper No. 20,* Annexure 3 (New Delhi: Institute for Defence Studies and Analyses, 2011), 62.
13. "Sangams and Dalams": Both are Telugu words, which provide the teeth to the Naxals. Dalams are the front line of the entire Naxal force, which carry out the offensive and sabotage actions against the SF, the police, government functionaries, and state infrastructures. These forces are the well trained and equipped with the available weapons and equipment. They are organized in companies, platoons, and special action teams/sub-teams, akin to regular forces. The Sangam are the over ground workers, who carry out numerous other tasks to assist the rebels.
14. Philip Bowring in his article "The Maoist Who Menace India", *New York Times,* April 17, 2006, quoting a RAW official which puts the figure to 20,000.
15. A study commissioned by Bureau of Police Research and Development, conducted and compiled by Center for Development and Peace Studies, Guwahati.
16. For an insightful account, read P.V. Ramana, "Growth of the CPI (Maoist)",

In *Naxal Violence: The Threat Within*, eds. G. Kanwal and D.C. Katoch (New Delhi: KW Publishers, 2012), 103.
17. Ashutosh Bhardwaj, "Unarmed Wings Help Naxals Urban Spread", *The Indian Express*, October 10, 2011.
18. Gram panchayats are local self-governments at the village- or small town-level in India. As of 2002, there were about 265,000 gram panchayats in India. The gram panchayat is the foundation of the Panchayat System. A gram panchayat can be set up in villages with minimum population of 300. Sometimes two or more villages are clubbed together to form group-gram panchayat when the population of the individual villages is less than 300.
19. Maoist Documents, CPI-Maoist on the 9th Congress, January-February 2007, SATP, accessed December 21, 2011, http://www.satp.org/satporgtp/countries/india/maoist/documents/papers/19feb07.htm.
20. Maoist Documents. Accessed December 21, 2011, http://www.satp.org/satporgtp/countries/india/maoist/documents/papers/19feb07.htm.
21. Sandeep Joshi, "MHA Concerned Over Maoist Acquiring Modern Weapons", *The Hindu*, September 06, 2012.
22. Sunial Sonkar, "Maoists Offering Salary to Cadres, Unemployed Youth Attracted", *Naxal Terror Watch*, March 28, 2010, accessed January 07, 2012, http://naxalwatch.blogspot.com/2010/03/maoists-offering-salary-to-cadres.html.
23. This aspect of recruitment of children into the Naxals' force was confirmed to me during my field visits and informal interaction with the local population in the Naxal affected areas.
24. The UN in its annual report on use of children in armed conflicts has expressed concern on the use of child soldiers in Chhattisgarh by the Maoist. "Maoists Recruiting, Indoctrinating Children: UN", *The Times of India*, June 20, 2012.
25. R.K. Gupta, "The Crimson Agenda: Maoist Protest and Terror" (New Delhi: Wordsmith, 2004), 29.
26. "Efforts Are on Through the Help of ISRO to Carry Out GIS Mapping of the Areas", *The Indian Express*, October 28, 2011.
27. Arundhati Roy, "Gandhi but With Guns", *The Guardian*, March 27, 2010, accessed February 23, 2012, http://www.guardian.co.uk/books/2010/mar/27/arundhati-roy-india-tribal-maoists-1.
28. "Corporate Houses under Maoist Funding Shadow", *The Pioneer*, September 29, 2011.
29. Prem Mahadevan, "The Maoist Insurgency in India: Between Crime and Resolution", *Small Wars and Insurgencies* 23, No. 2 (2012): 205.
30. "MHA: Freeze Maoist Finances", *The Asian Age*, September 26, 2011.
31. "MHA: Freeze Maoist Finances", *The Asian Age*, September 26, 2011.
32. Jawaid Sohail, "*The Naxalite Movement in India: Origin and Failure of the Maoist Revolutionary Strategy in West Bengal, 1967–1971*" (New Delhi: Associated Publishing House, 1979), 37.
33. "China Providing Rocket Propelled Grenades to Maoist", *Rashtriya Sahara*, October 13, 2011.
34. "NE-Maoist – J&K Mega Rebel Plan Revealed", *The Asian Age*, October 08, 2011.

35. Vijay Sakhuja, "Bangladesh – Of Terrorists, Gun Runners and Pirates", *IPCS*, May 06, 2003, accessed May 06, 2003, www.ipcs.org.
36. Sanjay Ojha, "Firm Helps Reds Import Hi-Tech Gear", *The Times of India*, March 31, 2013.
37. The ambush and killing 76 CRPF men on 6 April 2010 is an indicator of the expertise in tactical use of IEDs.
38. "LTTE Training New Groups of Maoists?" *The Asian Age*, October 11, 2011.
39. Hawala is an informal value transfer system – a parallel or alternative remittance system that exists or operates outside of, or parallel to, traditional banking or financial channels, which are mostly in illegal form.
40. Under Sheikh Hasina's government, India has got unprecedented cooperation from Bangladesh on security issues – uprooting training camps and disrupting network of northeast insurgents and other militants operating from its territory.
41. Ajit Kumar Singh, "Maoists Look at North-East", *Pioneer*, November 5, 2011.
42. Sandeep Joshi, "MHA Concerned Over MHA Acquiring Modern Weapons", *The Hindu*, September 06, 2012.
43. For more details, see N. Manoharan, "No More 'Indigenous': External Linkages of Left Wing Extremism", Article 1508, *CLAWS*, July 17, 2010.
44. Das Madhuparna, "Arrested Maoists Reveal a Supply Chain From China", *Indian Express*, December 8, 2010.
45. Subrahmaniam Swamy, "China: Dimensions of Threats to India", Talk at Vivekananda International Foundation, January 29, 2010.
46. Anoop A.J. (Researcher, VIF), "China – Naxalite Linkages: Gauging its Dimensions", accessed on April 21, 2011, see more at: http://www.vifindia.org/article/2011/march/25/China-Naxalite-linkages-Gauging-its-dimensions#sthash.q2EFf7Ca.dpuf.

Chapter 4

Relevance of Past Insurgency Campaigns

Unique Character of Insurgencies

The world has suffered a number of insurgencies and intra-state conflicts during the twentieth century, majority of them were post-World War II. Although the list of insurgency campaigns runs into hundreds, some of the prominent countries that were involved in them since 1940s are China, Malaya (now Malaysia), Kenya, Cyprus, Rhodesia, Oman, Muscat, Greece, Northern Ireland, Philippines, Peru, Guatemala, Vietnam, Sri Lanka, Nepal, Afghanistan, Iraq, Pakistan and India. Based on their experiences, a number of think tank organizations and experts on counter-insurgency have documented their thoughts on various campaigns and the reasons for their success or failure. Coupled with this, while making remarkable observations and identifying the critical elements of each counter-insurgency campaign, they have made recommendations, some of which are still relevant to help resolve complex conflicts of contemporary times.

Being a student of history, I have always felt that it is good to analyze some of the old insurgency campaigns. It is not with the aim of blind replication or applying those logics in the present day conditions, which could be dangerous, but with the aim of studying the overall situation, events, incidents, strategic challenges, decisions taken, rationale to adopt a particular course of action, and to examine the outcome of such decisions. Case studies per se should not be the sole guiding factor to resolve present/future conflicts. In other words, there is also a need to analyze all the important events, incidents, after-action reports that are compiled by observers and people on the ground. As insurgencies are complex in nature, a researcher must systematically collect, collate, analyze, and, where possible, quantify the information for feeding into a decision matrix table. A few lessons from old campaigns can be selectively applied to meet the new emerging situations.

National Reconciliation Law and peace negotiations, paved the way for conflict resolution in Guatemala (1960–1996). As brought out by SGM Herbert A. Friedman in his accounts, "There were just three successful cases where a legitimate government in power had beaten back a communist insurgency. These were in the Philippines, Greece, and Malaya. In Philippines, the victory against the HUKs was achieved by the land reforms; in Greece by tightening the borders and not allowing the guerillas to slip into Albania for refuge and resupply; and in Malaya by separating the insurgents from the population and letting them starve in the jungle."[1] Though Friedman has put it rather simplistically; neither is there any single prescription to resolve such insurgencies nor are such "lessons drawn" transferrable.

Human dimension

> *We know it's the human factor, and not material resources, which decide the outcome of war. That is why our people's war, led by Ho Chi Minh, was on such a large scale. It took in the whole population.*[2]
>
> – General Vo Nguyen Giap

Most theorists of the insurgency and counter-insurgency campaigns have categorically emphasized that the center of gravity in an insurgency environment remains the "support of the people". The causes, aims, approach, and techniques of tackling different counter-insurgency campaigns vary on the basis of a number of factors. However, there are certain lessons from a successful campaign, particularly the human aspects that are equally applicable in the contemporary conflicts. Therefore, the human dimension aspect has not changed, be it related to developmental, cultural, environmental, or security issues. The core leadership qualities, therefore, do not really change, though the tools have changed over the years. Every insurgency has its unique and peculiar set of conditions, which have to be examined in detail to find a workable solution. Therefore, both the successful guerilla campaigns and the successful counter-insurgency campaigns have been analyzed to draw some useful lessons, as applicable to the Indian environment.

Chinese Revolution (1927–1949)

The Chinese Revolution, mostly referred to as a Civil War (1927–49), was a war fought between the Kuomintang (KMT or Chinese Nationalist Party), the governing party of the Republic of China, and the Communist Party of China (CPC) (also known as CCP – Chinese Communist Party), for the control of China. The war eventually led to China's division into two Chinas, Republic of China (ROC) and People's Republic of China (PRC). Although the revolution ended on October 1, 1949, with the founding of the PRC, the tensions continued to persist. Even today, the conflict continues in the form of military threats, and political and economic pressures exerted by the PRC, particularly over the political status of Taiwan.

The aim of looking at the "Chinese Revolution" is to briefly underscore the condition of the masses, the infighting among various parties, internal security conditions, emergence of Mao Zedong as the undisputed leader, building a mass base, and the growth of the Red Army. The Civil War in China from 1927 to 1949 was a result of the fall of the monarchical system in 1912. Without a structured form of government, the country was in a chaos.[3] The war began in April 1927 and ended when major active battles ceased in 1949-1950. The war represented an ideological split between the nationalists KMT and the communist Chinese Communist Party (CCP), which was led by Mao Zedong. Mao experimented with rural land reforms and recruited troops for the communist military, known as the Red Army. Working with the Red Army, Mao developed new guerrilla warfare tactics that drew the KMT forces deep into the hostile countryside, where they were harassed by peasants and destroyed by the Red Army. In a few similar cases in India, but at a much lower level, the Naxalites drew the SF deep into the hinterland, an area controlled by them, and then struck with speed and surprise to cause maximum casualties.

Mao began the 12,500 km (8,000 miles) long march to the west and north China, which was completed in 370 days.[4] He had already orchestrated the long march from October 1934 to October 1935 to raise the esteem and prestige of the communists.[5] During the long march, Mao could connect better with the local population, as a result he and his supporters gained power and prestige. From 1935 to 1949, some of the principles followed by Mao to strengthen the revolution were "simple administration, reduce bureaucracy, send intellectuals to the villages, reduce rents, oppose landlords oppressive activities, cooperative agriculture, etc."[6] Mao Tse-Tung gained control of China in 1949. Thus, began a new era in Chinese politics – the communist era.

Analysis of Mao's success

There are many factors as to why Chiang Kai-shek lost control of China. The main factor was the Japanese invasion of China beginning in 1937, known as the second Sino-Japanese War.[7] The world was under severe economic depression[8] during the period of the Civil War in China. This had a devastating effect on the economy of China, which at that time was already in a poor state. Coupled with severe economic problems and a raging civil war, the conditions were ripe in China for a mass revolution. The major contributing factors to the success were:

- The Japanese invasion of China in 1937 was the turning point in the period of Chinese history. The KMT had to fight on two fronts simultaneously – a conventional war with the Japanese forces and a guerilla war with the communists, who took on the KMT at every opportune moment, though temporarily aligned with them to fight the Japanese. While the KMT was busy fighting the Japanese military, the CCP was building in strength and number.[9] The casualties of the KMT were close to 3.2[10] million out of an approximate strength of 5.7 million troops.[11] This weakening of the KMT forces made it easier for the communists to battle them when the civil war resumed at the end of the Sino-Japanese war.
- Support from the peasants was an important factor because peasants made up a large amount of the Chinese population (75% to 80%) and Mao realized that in order to get into power he would need a lot of mass support. He made strict rules within the Red Army which ensured that the personnel of the army were courteous in their dealings with the peasant masses. He also put in place the land reforms, wherein the land held by the landlords was forcibly seized and given to the landless. The already impoverished and exploited peasant masses suddenly saw a messiah among them and wholeheartedly supported Mao and his forces, during the revolution.
- As part of the instrument of surrender in 1945, all Japanese forces excluding the ones in Manchuria were asked to surrender to the forces of Chang Kai-Shek. [12] This allowed Mao to send his forces into Manchuria, take over most of the Japanese military hardware surrendered to the Soviets, and arm it. These arms and hardware were later mastered by the communists through the help of defecting KMT forces and were used against the KMT in the civil war.
- During the 8,000 miles long march, Mao gained unchallenged command of the Communist Party, and won the support of the local population. In addition, the marchers' legendary discipline increased party prestige and the movement grew rapidly.[13]
- The ruling KMT forces were led by Chiang Kai-Shek, who was found wanting in his leadership capabilities. His regime was plagued by bureaucratic inefficiency and corruption. In addition, his "Scorched Earth" policy, which dictated burning of farmland, destruction of bridges and dams to flood the land to stall the advancing Japanese Army, further alienated the peasant class, who lost a lot of land and produce, thus creating conditions of abject poverty and food insecurity. Mao's land reforms policy to snatch away the land from the landlords was carried out in a brutal manner, but the communists became popular with the local population.

It is more than evident that the Naxalites in India do not enjoy most of the advantages, as Mao Zedong and his party did during the pre-revolutionary phase of China, from 1927 to 1949. Contrary to the Red Army's courteous and compassionate behavior with the masses, the Naxals have killed a large number of innocent civilians, terming them as police informers. In addition to destruction of social and economic infrastructures, they have targeted a passenger train – Gyaneshwari express, in which 148 people were killed on May 28, 2010. With such nefarious actions in the long term, the Naxals would alienate the support of the population. Communist China had a charismatic and popular leader, who enjoyed overwhelming support of the masses. This is not true in the case of the Naxals.

Malayan Insurgency (1948–1960)

Malaya is a rich country, with large forest cover, extensive rubber plantations, and is the largest producer of tin. The communist fanatic Chin Peng led the Malayan Communist Party (MCP). The Malayan Emergency was a guerrilla war fought primarily between the Commonwealth Armed Forces and the Malayan National Liberation Army (MNLA), the military arm of the MCP from 1948 to 1960. MCP adopted a multi-ethnic outlook by attempting to recruit Malays, Chinese, and Indians, the three major ethnic groups in Malaya, but by the end of World War II (1939–45), it had ended up as a mainly Chinese party.[14] The Malayan Emergency was the colonial government's term for the conflict. Although the British post World War II had a huge hands on experience in counter-insurgency operations in Kenya, Cyprus, Muscat and Oman, Malayan Emergency was a unique case of success. The campaign was a mixed strategy encompassing civil, police, military and psychological warfare programs.[15]

Causes of conflict

The Japanese invasion in 1941 and subsequent withdrawal at the end of World War II left the Malayan economy disrupted. Problems included unemployment, low wages, scarce and expensive food. There was considerable labor unrest and a large number of strikes occurred between 1946 and 1948. In the transition from wartime to peace, food shortages in Malaya led to public riots, workers' strikes, and demonstrations for higher wages. The MCP involved itself in these causes, and came into conflict with the British Military Administration.[16] On June 16, 1948, the first overt act of the war took place when three European plantation managers were killed at Sungai Siput, Perak. The British administration, finding it difficult to control the situation, declared a state of emergency.

It blamed the troubles on the communists. The emergency caught the MCP off guard.[17] The British did not achieve much success in the initial stages from 1948 to 1950, till the arrival of General Sir Harold Briggs in April 1950.[18] In the early stages of the conflict, the guerrillas envisioned establishing "liberated areas" from which the government forces had been driven, and the MNLA control established. They were unsuccessful, however, in establishing any such areas. This was primarily because they did not have much support base between the original Malayan and the Indian communities there.

British response

The initial government strategy was primarily to guard important economic targets such as mines and plantation estates. Subsequently, General Sir Harold Briggs, the British Army's Director of Operations in Malaya, developed an overall strategy known as the Briggs Plan. Briggs maintained that the Malayan Emergency was a political campaign. Its central tenet was that the best way to defeat such an insurgency was to cut the insurgents off from their supporters among the population. While providing safe and secure environment to the population, the aim was also to get steady flow of information from all sources. The most important aspect of it was the policy involving creation of new settlements. This involved forced relocation of some 500,000 rural Malayans (about 10% of Malaya's population), including 400,000 Chinese, from squatter communities on the fringes of the forests into well-guarded camps called 'New Villages'. In most cases, these villages were constructed and fortified. The purpose of this was to keep both the inhabitants in and the guerrillas away. Though the people resented this at first; however, the availability of better civic amenities in these settlements soon turned out appealing to them. They were given money and ownership of the land they lived on. Isolating a population, which might be sympathetic to guerrillas, was a counter-insurgency technique, which the British had used before, notably against the Boer Commandos in the Second Boer War (1899–1902). However, in Malaya, the operation was conducted in a more humane and efficient manner.

Killing of Sir Gurney, the British High Commissioner in Malaya on October 6, 1951, brought into sharp focus the need to fight the insurgency with a multi-pronged strategy, encompassing political, social, legal, tight governance, development, and public perception management. General Sir Gerald Templar succeeded Sir Gurney. He reorganized the intelligence system, training and military structures, and imposed restrictions on the movement of the population and their daily needs. While the MNLA bolstered the supply network from the

"Min Yuen",[19] General Templar initiated the process of "Peace Talks" as part of the psychological operations. With the independence of Malaya on August 31, 1957, the insurrection lost its rationale as a war of colonial liberation.

Analysis of Malaysia's success

The Malayan counter-insurgency campaign is a perfect example of how focused social and economic development combined with a strong political will and visionary leadership can lead to putting down any insurgency whose root cause normally is discontent. The primary emphasis was on breaking the guerrillas' links to their popular base, imaginative exploitation of surrendered insurgents, use of police jungle squads, and food denial operations.[20] Security operations, intelligence organizations, development activities and perception management were placed under one authority, which ensured seamless coordination and execution on the ground.

Some of the major reasons for the success were as follows:

- Emergency operations were divided into three main phases, based on the ground situation.[21] Although the initial phases aimed at providing a safe and secure environment, little success was achieved towards the overall plan during Phase 1 of the operation.
  - Phase 1, "counter terror in 1948-49": Basically, area sweeps, large-scale detentions, search operations, rapid buildup of SF were the main stay of this phase. (The operations did not achieve success due to lack of intelligence, and inadequate coordination among various agencies including the police, military and the intelligence organizations).
  - Phase 2, "clear and hold in 1950–52": During this phase, the focus remained on clearing certain areas and holding them with adequate forces. Simultaneously, development of the area was initiated and projects implemented on the ground.
  - Phase 3, "optimization from 1952–60": By February 1952, General Templar had already arrived. Having analyzed the situation on the ground, he coined the phrase "Winning the Hearts and Minds" of the people.[22] He focused on the administration, intelligence, relocation, and resettlement of the population into "410 New Villages". By 1954, the insurgency was clearly on the wane; the remainder period was spent on mopping up operations.[23] (Based on his experience, research and study of various experts, Nanavatty brings out the "emphasis" of different instruments of power at various stages of counter-insurgency.)[24]

- The British administration was quick to realize the need to maintain a balanced approach to the problem in Malaya. From the outset, they opted for a balanced civil/police/military response to the problem, rather than having only security-centric focus. The police played a predominant role. The police strength was increased manifold. It relied more on the use of civil arm rather than on the military. Strict measures like population control through issue of identity cards, food control of ethnic Chinese squatter settlements, and food denial were carried out to break the links between the insurgents and the locals. While conducting various operations, it was ensured that there was minimum inconvenience to the local population. The judiciary and the administration continued to function at the grassroots providing the much-needed governance even during critical periods. The approach was to carry out strict security measures with a human face and within the ambit of law and good governance.
- In order to synergise the political, social and economic development efforts, and security operations, a central command authority was considered most essential. Rather than creating a separate counter-insurgency chain of command, the colonial administration then managed the campaign through a British style committee system, which essentially followed the existing civil administrative structure at each level but was at the same time linked closely with the military and police setup. The high commissioner/director of operations had four main components; namely police commissioner, security forces commander, defence secretary and civil administration. With a single individual appointed to direct the entire campaign, the British were able to focus on critical issues to achieve optimum results.
- To a large degree, the success of the Malayan counter-insurgency operations is credited to the Briggs Plan.[25] By isolating this population in the "new villages", the British were able to stem the critical flow of material, information, and recruits from peasants to communist guerrillas. Simultaneously, surface connectivity was improved to the remote areas to complete development projects.
- The British administration saw intelligence as crucial to the success of the operations in Malaya at that time. He was of the view that Malaya was a war of intelligence and that communism could not be beaten by troops alone.[26] Intelligence operations received a huge boost in the Malayan campaign. Human intelligence was given the highest priority to know the real situation on the ground. They also established a national-level intelligence school to train personnel. With innovative interventions, defections were induced among the insurgents. These defectors finally became the key source of intelligence and facilitated meaningful forms of psychological

warfare. To operate and penetrate into the largely ethnic Chinese insurgent group, special linguistic training was provided to the operatives. The campaign will also be remembered for highly published reward for surrender program, imaginative exploitation of surrendered insurgents and food denial to the insurgents.[27] 'Information Services Department' was effective to conduct psychological war. Leaflet campaign and loud speakers, mounted on vehicles and aircrafts, countered the rebels' propaganda in a befitting manner.

- General Templar took a large number of hard-hitting decisions and measures that affected the local population in many ways. A major rural development program was undertaken to provide the much-needed succor to the locals and it helped shape their perception about the administration. The British were successful in getting the support of the local population not only in Malaya, but also in Kenya, where the support of the native Kenyans emerged as the lynchpin in the successful prosecution of the struggle against the Mau Mau.[28]

Tripura Counter-Insurgency

The insurgency in Tripura was a classical case of illegal migration from erstwhile East Pakistan (later Bangladesh), which resulted in demographic inversion, ethnic divide, economic neglect and abject poverty. The insurgency that grew gradually in 1970s was controlled – though not fully resolved – after a number of years, due to the successful counter-insurgency campaign led by the visionary leadership and creative multi-dimensional and multi-pronged response. Tripura scripted a story of triumph[29] over insurgency and conflict resolution. However, as a precautionary measure, disturbed area act has been further extended in some of the sensitive and vulnerable areas of Tripura.[30]

Genesis

Before independence, Tripura was a princely state that acceded to the Indian Union on October 15, 1949. Partition in 1947 left Tripura isolated, as it lost rail connectivity with the rest of India.[31] It had an enormous impact on the economy, trade, education, and employment opportunities. Tripura's tribal majority population also underwent a sea change because of unhindered migration from East Pakistan and subsequently from Bangladesh. The indigenous tribal people, who accounted for 95% of the population of Tripura in 1931 census, was reduced to just 31% at the time of 1991 census.[32] Insurgency started as a protest movement primarily against this foreign influx.

The insurgency remained low key from 1990 to 1995, but grew in extent and magnitude from 1996 to 2004.[33] The insurgency progressed and expanded mainly due to the rugged and harsh terrain that favored the guerrilla tactics adopted by the outfits and the proximity of Bangladesh, whose porous borders provided extensive safe havens to the militants. The terrorist activities continued for some 45 years, peaking by 2000.[34] Besides killing of civilians and SF, large-scale violence disrupted civic life and communications, and led to the closure of many educational and financial institutions, threatening the authority of the state.

State response

The state government evolved a strategic plan aimed at long-term conflict resolution through a multi-dimensional approach to the problem. The plan aimed at first controlling the security situation through sustained counter-insurgency operations. These operations were ably supported by psychological operations, media, and perception management initiatives and various confidence-building measures. Once the security situation became conducive for the civil administration to function, time was not wasted and immediate action plan was put into place to implement development plans, civic action programs by the SF, and political reforms.[35] As per Chakraborty, the situation was brought under control, with minimal casualties to civilians and the SF.[36] The state had started with a number of peace initiatives in the hope of ending the insurgency. Persistent efforts by the government to bring back the militants into the national mainstream finally paid off in 2006 when a number of the militants surrendered.[37]

Analysis of Tripura's success

The development model of the state government of Tripura was the adoption of policies that benefit the "poorest of poor", and makes people active participants of the development process.[38] Some of the major reasons for the success are as enumerated below:

- The government constituted a well-conceived, coordinated counter-insurgency campaign with clear-cut objectives. It first aimed at swift area domination including effectively sealing the porous borders with Bangladesh. The state built up the capacity of its own police forces to take on the insurgents. The state, along with the central paramilitary forces, took on the insurgents with complete co-ordination and co-operation. Special Police Officers (tribal population included) were inducted and channeled into operations. This proved to be valuable in terms of gathering intelligence and keeping a tab on the activities and movement of the insurgents, collaborators, and over-ground workers.[39] Involvement of the local police meant good knowledge of the terrain and the rebels. Strict monitoring of operations of the SF along with sensitization of the forces on human rights issues ensured that there were no major complaints against the police forces.[40] This created a favorable picture in the minds of the citizens about the police forces.

- The Tripura government gave high priority to manage 856 km of porous border with Bangladesh. The state police and central PMF (now called CAPF) were strengthened, and the border was secured with barbed wire fencing along with flood lighting. Resultantly, there was progressive decline in the rate of infiltration. The Tripura police played a pivotal role in the counter-insurgency grid.[41]
- Tripura's slogan, "*forest for environment and environment for livelihood*", and provision of "Patta" to 1.2 lakhs families remained popular with the local population.[42] As part of its effort to find a lasting solution to militancy, the state government has economically rehabilitated 1,285 tribal guerrillas since 1998.[43]
- A sustained and well-planned psychological operation was mounted to correct the average tribal person's perception of the state and the nation. It aimed at inducing confidence and credibility of the state's intentions. A large number of open sessions were conducted on behalf of the state at numerous locations, mostly involving the youth. Electronic and print media, art groups, intellectuals, and interactive seminars carried forward these messages of the government that shaped the perception of the common person especially in the insurgency hot beds. It also focused on provision of jobs to tribal population, especially to family members of victims of violence, attractive rehabilitation packages consisting of monetary benefits, and vocational training to enhance job-related skills to increase chances of employment.
- Improvement of the security situation was promptly capitalized upon by quickly reaching out to the citizens through implementation of viable development plans and effective governance. Great emphasis was laid on development of infrastructure like road connectivity, rail and air connectivity, power, and telecommunications.[44] The state government

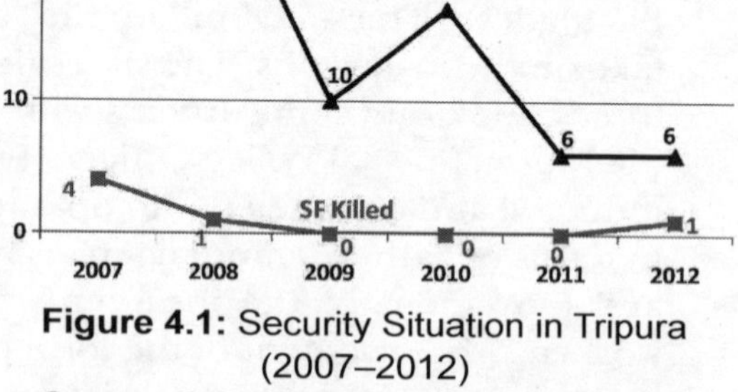

Figure 4.1: Security Situation in Tripura (2007–2012)
Source: GoI website and compiled data.

immediately established its writ in the areas vacated by insurgents through an efficient administration. Micro-democratic institutions like autonomous development councils, gram panchayat, and village councils were strengthened and legitimized without pandering to petty political issues; thereby, demonstrating strong political will. These institutions turned into vibrant local governance modules, which brought all communities, especially the tribal people into the development stream, bringing about substantial empowerment and a sense of fulfillment.

Tripura's success story provides a number of useful lessons to emulate. Improvement in the security situation is clearly visible in Figure 4.1.

Andhra Pradesh Success Story

Origin

In April 1980, Kondappally Seetharamaiah managed to unite some splintered groups in the region under one banner – CPI (ML) Peoples War or more commonly known as PWG. It was perhaps the first party to profess guerrilla warfare as the tactics of the armed struggle, and hence setup an armed outfit at local levels, which later transformed into the People's Guerrilla Army (PGA) in the year 2000. Throughout the 1980s and the 1990s, the violence in the state continued to increase unabated, largely due to the vacillating approach of the state government towards the PWG. Political conflict between the two main parties in the state at that time was deftly leveraged by the PWG to enhance its mass base and combat potential. Both these parties used politics of collusion with the PWG to come to power or perpetuate their power in the state.[45] In the decades prior to its merger in 2004 with the MCCI, the PWG had killed more than 4,000 persons including innocent civilians and security forces and destroyed property. By 1985, the violence especially the ambushes and landmine incidents against the police had reached a level, which could no longer be ignored by the state government. The kidnapping of a group of IAS officers and their subsequent release in return for jailed cadres of the PWG was the turning point in 1987,[46] that prompted the government to finally setup the 'Greyhounds', a special anti-naxal 'elite' force trained in guerrilla tactics in 1989. The state rose to the occasion to tackle Naxalism. It developed a model counter-insurgency campaign, which helped it to reign in the terror network created by the PWG and considerably reduced the violence levels in the state from 320 fatalities in Naxal related incidents in 2005 to just 10 in 2011.[47]

Marwah correctly observes that the state government was taken by surprise when the Naxals presented "an eleven – points charter of demand, including land reforms and creation of a separate state of Telangana."[48] By a continuous dialogue, the aspirations of the rebels can be known and assessed, well in advance. Notwithstanding this, the development initiatives brought about a significant decline in the violence levels in the state and the police managed to eliminate a large number of PWG/CPI (Maoist) cadres.[49]

Analysis of success

Some of the major reasons of success, including police actions, are:

- It was rightly understood that if the policy makers are themselves divided over an issue, the issue can never be resolved. From 1995 onwards, in particular, the state governments continued with the approved policy, realizing its potent effectiveness. Thus, petty politics was generally not allowed to circumvent the gains made by the administration and the security forces.
- A separate wing under the General Administration Department was created to co-ordinate and oversee the implementation of Remote and Interior Areas Development (RIAD) program along with a host of other socio-economic plans. Some of the notable programs implemented in the state are:
  - — **Rajiv Arogya Shri:** A low cost health insurance program for rural population below poverty line (white cardholders). This insurance program pays the entire cost of medical treatment and any necessary surgery to a maximum of Rs. 2,00,000.[50]
  - — **Pavala Vaddi Scheme:** A program that provides loans at 3 percent per annum interest rate, designed to encourage small-scale businesses and entrepreneurship primarily targeted at rural women.[51] Coupled with this, INDIRAAMMA Illu (Integrated Novel Development in Rural Areas and Model Municipal Areas) is a program for construction of heavily subsidized housing for the rural poor.
  - — **Mahatma Gandhi National Rural Employment Guarantee Act (MGNREGA)**: The State made concerted efforts to implement MGNREGA. Information Technology-enabled implementation of the act (documentation and online audit) and independent social audit of various works and its effects on the rural areas and the population has achieved good results.
  - — **Jala Yagnam:** A program to irrigate 1,00,00,000 acres of land through construction of major, medium and minor irrigation projects. It helped Andhra Pradesh make significant progress in areas of sustainable agriculture by making wastelands cultivable.[52]
  - — **Other state sponsored subsidies:** A host of many other state

sponsored subsidies like free electricity, scholarships, free emergency ambulances and increase in minimum support price for rice helped the poor to improve their socio-economic standing in the last decade.

Successive governments in power in Andhra Pradesh have taken steps towards implementation of land reforms – by using information technology enabled enterprises to computerize the land revenue records to efficiently settle title deeds – and distribution of government and forestland.[53]

Innovative force and employment

It was rightly visualized by the state leadership including the police authorities that in order to fight the PWG cadres in their home turf, a force offensive in mindset and trained in guerrilla tactics would be needed. This led to the raising of an independent and elite commando force known as the "Greyhounds" in 1989. Some of the measures brought out during the national security capsule at the Indian Police Academy, Hyderabad, on May 10,2011, are:

- All new police inductees have to spend their first four years of service in these greyhound units before getting their transfer to the district police establishments. Meritorious service with the greyhound units was made a mandatory requirement to get accelerated promotions and additional commando pay as incentive.
- The Greyhounds Training School was revamped and new training courses and methodologies introduced, along with suitable training facilities set up at each greyhound's unit location for imparting refresher training.
- The concept of keeping one administration and security duties company, and one training company at all times in the battalion HQ was strictly implemented. Most importantly, the remaining six companies were deployed as three joint operating bases (JOBs) consisting of two companies each. Experience proved that a single company deployment was not giving optimum operational results in the Naxal affected regions.
- The greyhounds units reported to the Special DIG HQ-in-Charge for Naxal-affected region, overlapping several adjacent districts. They did not report to or work under the district police set up. Their operations were supplemented by adequate technical intelligence teams, which could intercept any wireless transmission.
- A Special Intelligence Branch (SIB) was setup in 1990. This agency was separated from the Police HQ and was made to report independently to the CM's Office. The agency was tasked only to

track Naxal movement, and thus was highly effective in anti-naxal operations. It shared its intelligence laterally with the greyhounds, thus integrating actionable intelligence with surgical strike capability, both within and outside the state.[54]

Andhra Pradesh formulated and implemented a comprehensive surrender and rehabilitation policy. The surrendered Naxals are now eligible for a monthly stipend of Rs. 2,000 each for a maximum period of 36 months and an immediate grant of Rs. 1.5 lakh. The Naxals are also given free legal service after the surrender.[55]

Lessons from campaigns

Popular support was found to be an important contributor to insurgency outcomes. However, ***tangible support****—the ability of insurgents to replenish and obtain personnel, material financing, intelligence and sanctuary—was found to be even more important than popular support.*

– Keys to Successful Counterinsurgency Campaigns Explored (RAND Corporation)

A study of the campaigns suggests that the "support of the people" and "cutting off tangible support" remain central to winning a counter-insurgency campaign. A number of lessons are relevant to the ongoing internal armed conflicts in India. It also brings forth two significant issues; first, the lessons learnt, and second, the fundamental principles of the counter-insurgency campaigns.

Lessons in brief are as follows:

- Strong political will and visionary leadership are required to confront the situation boldly. Principally, insurgencies are based on political and ideological issues, necessitating the use of civil arm, police, and military, in that order of priority. In a highly insecure environment where the military wing of the insurgents is fully organized, military along with the police has a predominant role, in the initial stages, to create a secure situation for development to progress.
- Establishment of a central authority – with the principle of civilian supremacy – to ensure seamless coordination, integration, and "unity of effort". Getting the government on the ground implies understanding the ground realities and implementing policies on the ground: focused social and economic development, allotment of land to the landless, relocation and resettlement of the displaced, jobs to victims of violence, and creation of employment opportunities. Therefore, there is a need to analyze the actual problems of the population, region wise, and address them based on assessed priorities.
- Success hinges on good governance: improve the delivery mechanism

on the ground, availability of basic amenities, improve connectivity, and empower the rural economy. The IT-enabled implementation will help effectively monitor the progress of various welfare schemes.

- An effective national-level intelligence network is vital for internal security. While over-reliance on technical intelligence could be disastrous, traditional human intelligence should be accorded the highest priority.
- Security operations should be conducted with a humane face, and strictly within the ambit of law. Security operations require quality training, actionable intelligence, and good leadership to succeed. Isolating the insurgents from their dependencies – popular support, resource control by cutting off the supply of essential items to the insurgents – will weaken the Naxals.
- Improvement in surface and telephonic connectivity, along with other infrastructure, will help empower the rural economy faster. In addition, empower rural areas by initiating special programs, e.g., Remote and Interior Areas Development (RIAD) programme in Andhra Pradesh and Rural Development Programme in Malayan Campaign.
- Special drive to recruit youth in military, police, public sector undertakings, government services, and the industry at large, will wean away the youth from the Naxals.
- Development and security initiatives should be supported by psychological operations (PSYOPS), media, perception management, and confidence-building measures. "Peace talks" should be included as part of the PSYOPS, e.g. Malayan Campaign. Open sessions could be conducted with the affected population to brief the real intentions of the Naxals and the state.
- Reward scheme for the surrendered insurgents and imaginative exploitation.

Fundamental principles of counter-insurgency campaign that emerge are: the primacy of political purpose, unity of effort and comprehensive national plan (CNP), understanding human terrain, neutralize the ideology and their (insurgents) organizations, exploit insurgents' vulnerabilities, gain people's support and mobilize them, operations in accordance with law of the land, integrate intelligence, perception management, deny external support, and maintain flexibility to carry out mid-course correction.

Notes

1. SGM Herbert A Friedman (Ret.), "Psychological Warfare of the Malayan Emergency, 1948–1960", *The Falling Leaf*, 189: 7.

2. Paddy Colligan And G. Dunkel, "Celebrating 100th Birthday Of Vietnam's Hero General Giap", *Workers World* September 2, 2011.
3. Jennifer Lynn Cucchisi, "The Causes and Effects of the Chinese Civil War, 1927–1949" (Master's Thesis, Seton Hall University, New Jersey, 2002), 1.
4. Chunhou, Vaughan Zhang, and C. Edwin, "Mao Zedong as Poet and Revolutionary Leader: Social and Historical Perspectives" (Maryland: Lexington books, 2002), 65.
5. Edwin Pak-wah Leung, "Historical Dictionary of Revolutionary China, 1839–1976" (New York: Greenwood Press, 1992), 236.
6. "The Victory of the Communist Chinese Revolution, 1927–1949", accessed October 01, 2012, ocw.mit.edu/courses/history/21h-001..revolution.../lecture12.pdf..
7. Jennifer Lynn Cucchisi, "The Causes and Effects of the Chinese Civil War, 1927–1949" (Master's Thesis, Seton Hall University, New Jersey, 2002), 2.
8. The **Great Depression** was a severe worldwide economic depression in the decade preceding World War II. The timing of the Great Depression varied across nations, but in most countries, it started in about 1929 and lasted until the late 1930s or early 1940s.
9. Jennifer Lynn Cucchisi, "The Causes and Effects of the Chinese Civil War, 1927–1949" (Master's Thesis, Seton Hall University, New Jersey, 2002), 21.
10. Hsu Long-hsuen, and Chang Ming-kai, "History of the Sino-Japanese War (1937–1945)" (Taipei: Chung Wu Publishing, 1972).
11. Horner David Murray, "The Second World War", Volume 1, *The Pacific* (Routledge, Taylor & Francis, 2003), 14–15.
12. Robert A. Pape, "Why Japan Surrendered", *International Security* 18, No. 2 (Autumn, 1993): 154.
13. BBC Online Network. Accessed December 12, 2011, http://news.bbc.co.uk/hi/english/static/special_report/1999/09/99/china_50/long.htm.
14. Cheah Boon Kheng, Red Star Over Malaya – Resistance and Social Conflict During and After the Japanese Occupation of Malaya, 1941–46, 133. The author is a professor at the History Department, National University of Singapore in Kent Ridge, Singapore.
15. R.W. Kromer, "The Malayan Emergency in Retrospect: Organization of a Successful Counterinsurgency Effort", a 1972 RAND study.
16. Cheah Boon Kheng, "The Communist Insurgency in Malaysia, 1948-90: Contesting the Nation-State and Social Change", *New Zealand Journal of Asian Studies* 11, No. 1 (June 2009).
17. Ibid.
18. R.W. Kromer, "The Malayan Emergency in Retrospect: Organization of a Successful Counterinsurgency Effort", a 1972 RAND study.
19. Min Yuen was a civilian organization, which provided the MNLA with supplies and information.
20. Robert W. Komer, "The Malayan Emergency in Retrospect", In *RAND Report* (Rand Corporation, 1972), R-957.
21. RUSI Analysis (28 November 2009), "Analysis Commentary, Extracting Counter insurgency lessons: The Malayan Engagement and Afghanistan", http://www.rusi.org/analysis/commentary/ref:C4B14E068758F1/#.UGqcX5htgrk, accessed on October 02, 2012.

22. Noor R. Ampseller, "Hearts and Minds: Malayan Campaign Re-evaluated", *Defence Viewpoint*, October 02, 2012.
23. R.W. Kromer, "The Malayan Emergency in Retrospect: Organization of a Successful Counterinsurgency Effort", a 1972 RAND study.
24. Rostum K. Nanavatty, "Internal Armed Conflict in India, Forging a Joint Civil- Military Approach" (New Delhi, Pentagon Press, 2013), 19.
    - Initially, counter-insurgency lays stress on military success – the destruction of the insurgent – and winning the support of the people.
    - Subsequently, there was a subtle shift in emphasis to a people-centric approach – mobilizing the people; according primacy to the political aspects of the campaign; adopting a "comprehensive" approach; and ensuring legitimacy.
    - Latterly, the stress on making the indigenous government and its forces primarily responsible for counter-insurgency once again highlights preoccupation with interventionist counter-insurgency operations in support of a host country.
25. Malayan Communist Party. Accessed October 03, 2012, http://en.wikipedia.org/wiki/Malayan_Communist_Party.
26. Bruce Hoffman and Jennifer Morrison Taw, "A Strategic Framework for Countering Terrorism and Insurgency", *RAND Note*, 1992, 79.
27. R.W. Kromer, "The Malayan Emergency in Retrospect: Organization of a Successful Counterinsurgency Effort", a 1972 RAND study.
28. Bruce Hoffman and Jennifer Morrison Taw, "A Strategic Framework for Countering Terrorism and Insurgency", *RAND Note*, 1992, 38.
29. For more details, read DN Sahaya, Governor Tripura (2003–2009), "How Tripura Overcame Insurgency", *The Hindu*, September 16, 2011.
30. "Disturbed Areas Act in Tripura Extended for 6 Months", *The North east Today*, March 14, 2012.
31. Sushanta Talukdar, "Infrastructure Development Apace", *The Hindu*, September 30, 2012.
32. Accessed December 27, 2010, www.satp.org/tripura/background/index.html.
33. D.N. Sahaya, Governor Tripura (2003–2009), "How Tripura Overcame Insurgency", *The Hindu*, September 16, 2011.
34. Sujit Chakraborty, "No Leeway Any More for Militants", *The Hindu*, September 30, 2012.
35. For more details, read D.N. Sahaya, "How Tripura Overcame Insurgency", September 16, 2011.
36. Sujit Chakraborty, "No Leeway Any More for Militants", *The Hindu*, September 30, 2012.
37. D.N. Sahaya, Governor Tripura (2003–2009), "How Tripura Overcame Insurgency", *The Hindu*, September 16, 2011.
38. Sushanta Talukdar, "Tripura Looks Ahead", *The Hindu*, September 30, 2012.
39. D.N. Sahaya, Governor Tripura (2003–2009), "How Tripura Overcame Insurgency", *The Hindu*, September 16, 2011.
40. Ibid.
41. Statement of Chief Minister, Manik Sarkar, at the CMs Conference in New Delhi on August 18, 2009.

42. Sushanta Talukdar, "Tripura Looks Ahead", *The Hindu*, September 30, 2012.
43. Sujit Chakraborty, "No Leeway Any More for Militants", *The Hindu*, September 30, 2012.
44. For more details, read Sushanta Talukdar, "Infrastructure Development Apace", *The Hindu*, September 30, 2012.
45. Koratala Satyanarayana (1923–2006) was a communist leader tom Andhra Pradesh. In 1997, as the then State-level General Secretary of the CPI (M), deposing before the *Advocates Committee*, stated, "In our experience, the political parties that have been in power in the state for the last three or four decades have been trying to utilise or use services of these extremist groups, either to come to power or to perpetuate their power."
46. "Kidnapping the State Authority", http://umasudhir.wordpress.com/2010/09/03/kidnapping-the-states-authority
47. www.satp.org accessed on December 30, 2011.
48. Ved Marwah, "India in Turmoil", Rupa, 2009, 150.
49. Ibid.
50. Rajiv Aarogyasri Scheme, "Aarogyasri Health Care Trust", https://www.aarogyasri.org/ASRI/FrontServlet?request.
51. For more details, Pavala Vadi scheme, accessed via http://andhrabank.in/english/Pavala.aspx.
52. Goginei Ram (2011), Austin, TX USA. "Jalayagnam in Andhra Pradesh, India", Jalayagnam.org. Accessed on December 29, 2011.
53. "Land Title Deeds Disburses to 1.65 Lakh ST Families in Andhra Pradesh", *Jagran Post*, October 17, 2012.
54. N. Kiran Kumar Reddy's (2011) address at the CM's Conference on Internal Security held at New Delhi on 01 February 2011 via http://cm.ap.gov.in/01feb11speech.asp, accessed on February 24, 2012.
55. "Government Approves Surrender Policy for Naxals", *The Indian Express*, 7 September 2009 accessed via http://www.indianexpress.com/news/govt-approves-surrender-policy-for-Naxals/514017/ on December 30, 2011.

Chapter 5

The Bloodiest Years

Deadliest Attacks

The level and intensity of Naxal violence had increased manifold since 2001, and peaked around 2009 and 2010, also called the "Bloodiest Years". While discussing a few important attacks during the bloodiest years of Naxal violence, the aim would be to briefly highlight their tactics, nature of targets selected and aims, and the modus-operandi. It also discusses the impact of the violence on security and economy of the country. During the period 2001 to 2004, while the PWG and the MCCI were busy discussing the modalities for the merger of the two parties, they continued to plan and prepare for major attacks and raids on jails, police stations, and armories.

It was the night of February 7, 2004 when approximately 300 extremists of the PWG attacked Koraput town, the district headquarter in Odisha. They came in trucks, jeeps, and motor cycles, after having taken precautions to block the three main entry roads into the town. They overwhelmed the town with speed in a well-planned operation, and are believed to have looted over 528 weapons. During the six-hour operation, they looted the district armory and five police stations, and attacked the Koraput jail, the superintendent of police (SP) office, and the Odisha's State Armed Police battalion.[1] While they attacked five police stations, an unbelievable feat, they got their biggest catch from the district armory, without any meaningful resistance. It was a meticulously planned, deftly executed operation, in which they divided themselves into different groups, to tackle the jail and the armory simultaneously.

Another ghastly incident that shocked the country was the "water ambush" on June 29, 2008, in which the Naxals displayed their professional ability, when they attacked a motor launch carrying 66 personnel across the Balimela reservoir, on Sileru River, in the Malkangiri district. Figure 5.1 (p. 81) shows the Balimela reservoir. Most of the targeted persons were the greyhound commandos. The

Naxals were continuously monitoring the movement profile of the SF personnel. As per reports, the state police had apparently booked the motor launch, in advance, for the force personnel to return after their combing operation in the remote areas of Malkangiri district. The rebels correctly guessed that the motor launch was booked for the greyhounds. They were fully aware of the strength and the intended movement of the commandos. It is learnt that the rebels positioned themselves at three different places on either side of the reservoir, with major weight of their presence at the hilltop inside the reservoir, so as not to miss their target. The insurgents opened heavy volume of fire with AK47s, LMGs, and even rocket launchers on the motor launch ferrying the commandos, from the hillock. Some of the commandos did get on their feet to return the fire, but the fire of the rebels was accurate and devastating. Due to the melee that ensued, the boat capsized. It resulted in 35 commandos being killed. It took a number of days to retrieve the bodies of the troops.[2]

The Naxals showed their professional presence to the world, by taking on the greyhounds who were credited with a large number of successful operations against the Naxals. As it was known to be a sensitive and high threat area, infested with the rebels, the margin for error in such high threat areas is razor thin. The incident also sharply highlighted a few weaknesses in the overall system of planning of the entire operation, acquisition of intelligence about the Naxals, method of securing the selected routes of travel, leakage of plans of movement, and allowing the entire force to travel on one motor launch. The tri-junction of the border areas of Odisha, Andhra Pradesh and Chhattisgarh remained active with large-scale violence by the Naxals. The area has three important rivers; Sileru and Saberi rivers separating Malkangiri from Andhra Pradesh and Chhattisgarh respectively, and the inter-state river Mahendrataneya between Odisha and Andhra Pradesh.[3] Secrecy, surprise and mobility being the main tactics and strength of the Naxals, they went on to raise a boat wing to facilitate faster movement of their cadres and weapons, across the water bodies.[4]

April 6, 2010 would always haunt the nation due to the deadliest attack by the Naxals on the CRPF column at Chintalnar, in Dantewada district, in which 75 CRPF personnel and one policeman were killed.[5] Refer Figure 5.2 (p. 81). The Naxals had carried out detailed reconnaissance over a period to ascertain the strength of the "area domination patrol", its movement profile, routes, timings, relative positions of various weapons carrying groups and the weaknesses thereof. Based on the intelligence gathered, it led to meticulous planning, preparations and rehearsals before the final blow was delivered in the early hours of the morning. Having analyzed the routes of reinforcements in advance, they planted

Figure 5.1: Balimela Reservoir*Source:* Google Earth

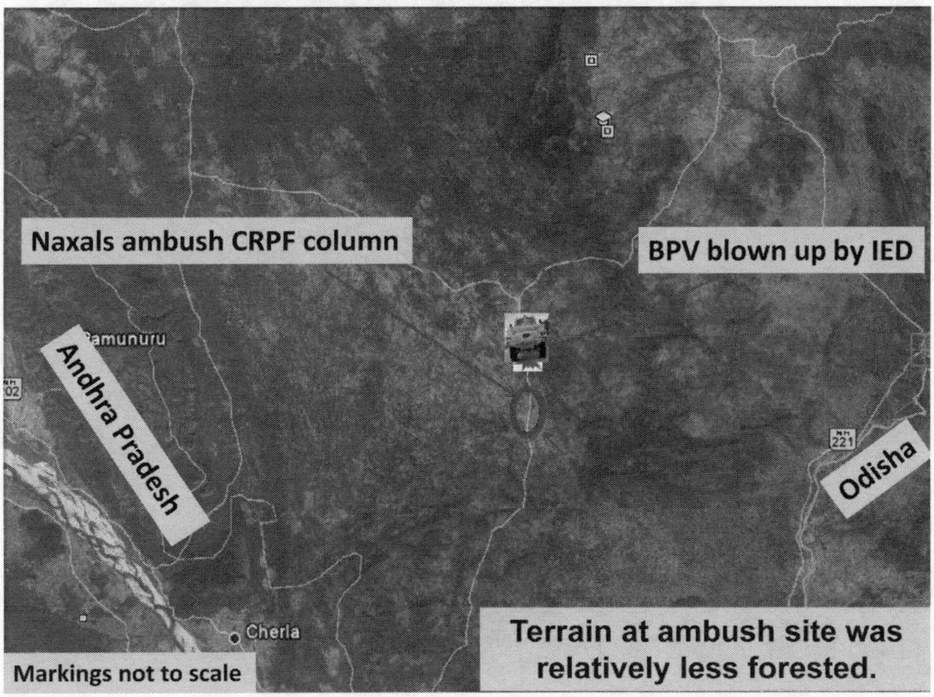

Figure 5.2: Ambush at Chintalnar, April 6, 2010

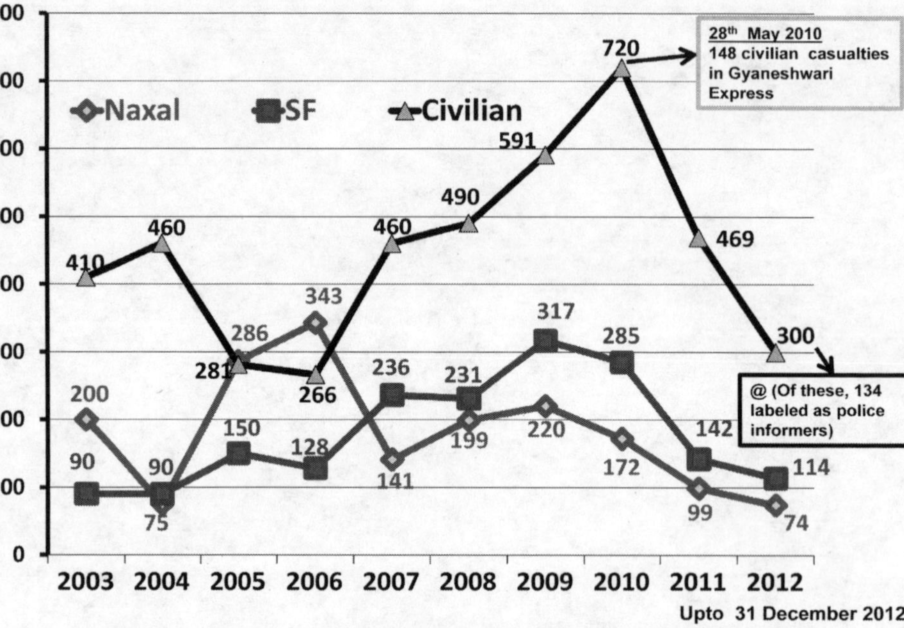

Figure 5.3: Casualties: Violence in LWE Affected Areas, 2003–2012
Source: http://mha.nic.in/pdfs/nm_stat_nv-161012.pdf, and SATP Database

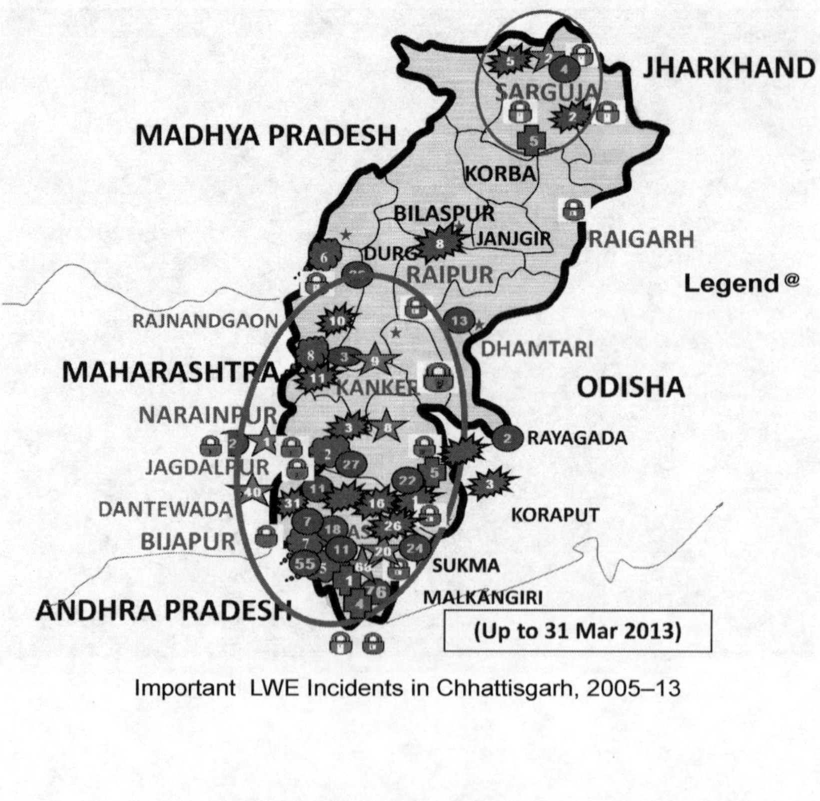

Important LWE Incidents in Chhattisgarh, 2005–13

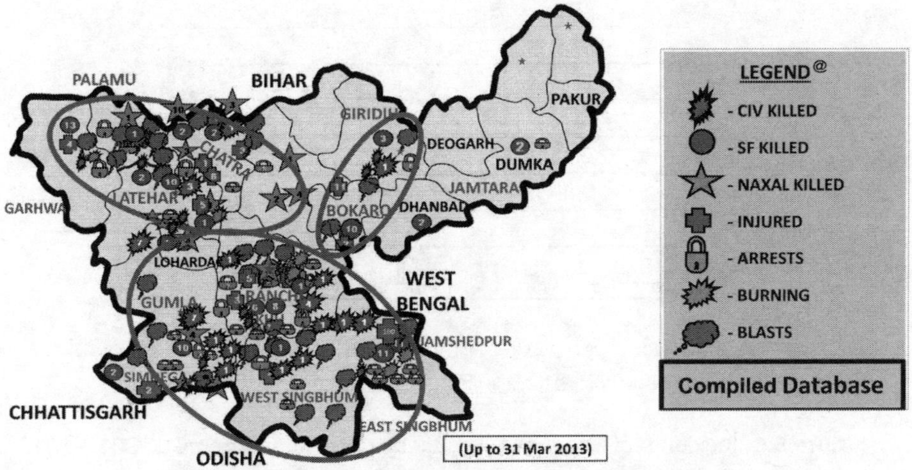

Important LWE Incidents in Jharkhand, 2005–13

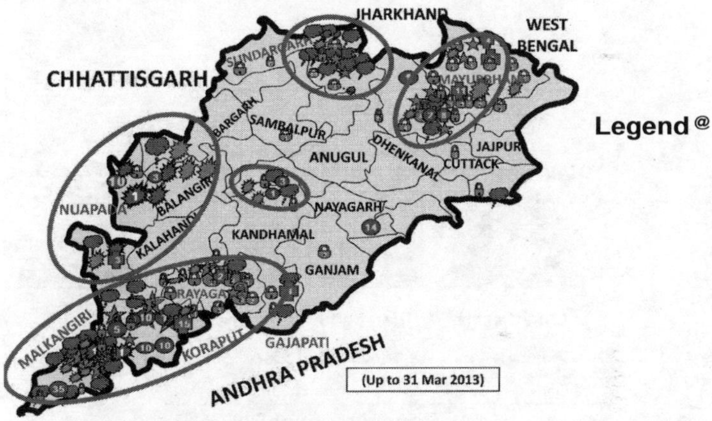

Important LWE Incidents in Odisha, 2005–13

Figure 5.4: Important LWE Incidents

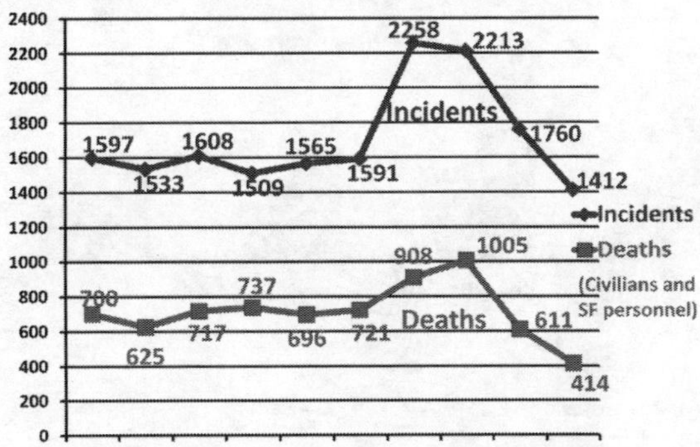

Figure 5.5: Naxal Violence in India: 2003–2012

Source: GoI, SATP website and compiled data.

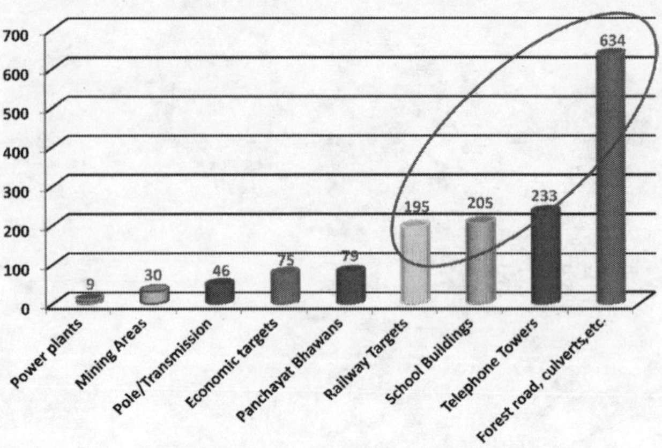

Figure 5.6: Incidents of Economic Targets by Left Wing Extremists: 2007–2012
Source: Satp.org, and http://mha.nic.in/pdfs/nm_stat_nv-161012.pdf, accessed on April 4, 2013.

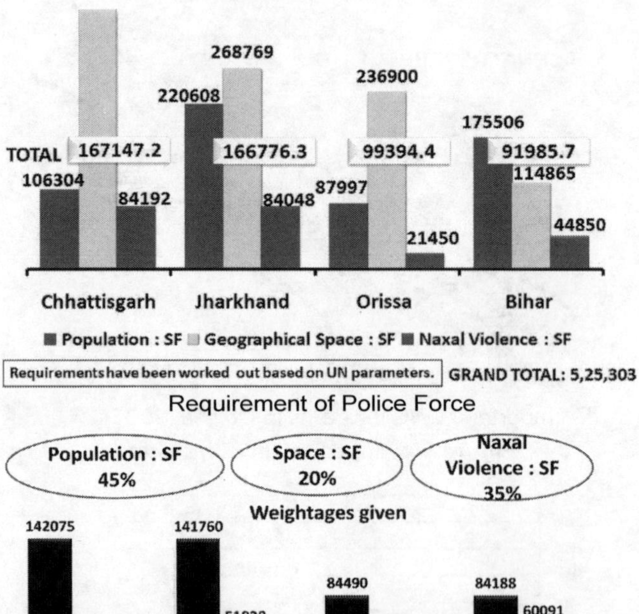

Requirement of Police Force

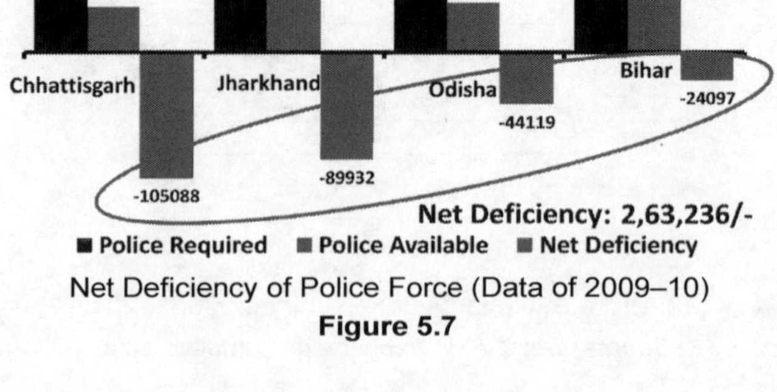

Net Deficiency of Police Force (Data of 2009–10)

Figure 5.7

IEDs and blew up the bulletproof vehicle (BPV) that had moved up with troops from the other company, for rescue tasks. The Naxals carried away a huge cache of weapons and ammunition. Mekala covers some of the significant features of the operation, and "one-man enquiry report" that gives the details regarding "planning for operations, training, leadership and operational discipline".[6]

A study of some of the raids or attacks by the Naxals on police stations, prisons, armories, and columns of SF suggests that they studied their intended targets in detail, obtained maximum intelligence from their network of sources, and executed the operation boldly. The violence continued with the bloody attacks on the Dantewada jail (2007),[7] the killing of Jharkhand Mukti Morcha (JMM) MP Shri Sunil Mahato at Jamshedpur (2007), and the attack on Rani Bodli Post in Dantewada district (2007). Besides operational issues, these attacks underscored the sensitivities and weaknesses at the bi-junctions and tri-junctions of the LWE-affected states. More importantly, it brought to focus the importance of leadership of the SF, at both the planning and the execution levels. Consequently, there has been some improvement in the standard of training, weaponry, surveillance, and communication systems of the CAPF.

Successful operations by SF – The SF too have conducted a number of successful operations against the Naxals, but more importantly from 2011 onwards. Elusive Maoist top leader Koteswar Rao alias Kishenji, a Maoist politburo and CMC member, was killed in a well planned operation by the joint forces at Burisole forest in West Midnapore district of West Bengal on November 24, 2011. Similarly, the deputy leader of the Odisha's Maoist party was killed by the police in an encounter in Karanjadua forest in Gajapati district on March 11, 2013.[8] Gadchiroli police shot dead eight Naxals near Bhatpur village on the Maharashtra and Chhattisgarh border on April 4, 2013. The greyhounds and the CRPF killed nine Maoists in the Kanchala forest astride Andhra Pradesh and Chhattisgarh border on April 15, 2013. It is evident that the Naxals are focusing on the sensitive inter-state boundaries. Likewise, a number of their leaders including Kobad Ghandy have been arrested.

Analysis of Violence

An analysis of Naxals' strategy, tactics, and violence would not only give out the criticality, the degree of effect in various areas, and the trends, but it would also help analyze the strategic options available to the Naxals. It would then be possible to formulate a broad strategy to resolve the conflict.

On March 13, 2006, the Union Home Minister highlighted the "14 Point Policy" of the Union government to deal with Naxalism (refer

Appendix B for the detailed analysis).[9] Apparently, most of the issues correctly spelt out in the policy pertaining to governance, development, empowerment, collective approach to security on inter-state boundaries, special focus on socio-economic developmental programs, and psychological reassurance-cum-perception management were not pursued with vigor, both by the center and the states, to ensure their implementation on the ground.

Naxalism continued to spread geographically to more areas, with progressive increase in the intensity of its activities from 2001 onwards. The spatial spread increased from 51 districts in 2001 to 165 in 2005 and 212 in 2010.[11] What are the reasons for the same? It is primarily based on two important reasons; lack of political will and lack of a comprehensive national strategy and plan. It resulted in gross under estimation of the Maoist's threat by the country, coupled with weak response from the states and central governments. While the vacuum continued to prevail in governance, administration and security machinery of the government, the Naxals quickly occupied the territorial and social space in the remote areas. While they achieved successes in various operations, the CAPF and police forces suffered huge reverses during the initial period from 2004 to 2010.

The dichotomy

Despite high-intensity insurgency, insecure environment and violence that disrupted educational, health, and financial institutions; communications; development of infrastructure, which compromised the authority of the state, the state and central governments regarded the violence predominantly as a law and order problem till around 2004. This view of the policy makers resulted in the union government leaving it to the states to solve the issues, law and order being a state subject under the Indian Constitution. However, due to country's vast diversity, regional politics and interests of individuals continued to play a greater role than national interest, at the state level. Therefore, each state followed its own policy for containment of the Naxal activities ranging from appeasement/no action to un-coordinated police actions. The merger had allowed the CPI (Maoist) to have an operational space spanning a large number of states, but the problem was dealt with in a piecemeal manner by all the states without inter-state coordination. This helped the Naxals effectively escape the police dragnet by moving into neighboring states, when the heat was turned on by one state, e.g. police action on PWG by Andhra Pradesh resulted in their cadres escaping into the neighbouring states of Chhattisgarh, Odisha, and Maharashtra, where they got safe sanctuaries due to inaction by the authorities there.

The difficult terrain and remoteness of the region also facilitated uninterrupted growth of the Naxals. Thus, during the initial formative years of the CPI (Maoist), it got the much-needed breathing space for organizing and equipping its cadres to take on the SF. The Naxals managed to create a safe corridor – not continuous though – where the writ of the authorities did not run, thus giving success to its strategy of first establishing the so-called liberated zone and secure bases, before it commences its move towards the semi-urban or urban locations of the country. At the national level, the problem was not as visible as it should have been; thus, no serious effort was made to resolve the conflict. It is not surprising therefore, that, by 2006, Naxal violence had pushed the cross-border terror in Kashmir to second place. The comparative statistics in the Table 5.1 are indicative of the levels of violence perpetuated by the Naxals. As can be seen, the number of deaths due to Naxal violence is considerably more than that in J&K insurgency (Table 5.1). It is indicative of both the spread of the violence and the level of expertise gained by the Naxals.[12] Some of the deductions from an analysis of major Naxal-related incidents for the period from 2003 till date merits serious consideration to initiate corrective measures. See Figure 5.3, p. 82, and also refer Appendix C for graphical annotation of major Naxal-related violence and incidents.

Table 5.1: Comparative Violence Profile, 2006–10[10]

Category	*Persons Killed*	
	Naxal Related Violence	*J&K Insurgency*
Civilians	2,237	661
Security Forces	1,297	511
Naxals/Militants	1,200	1,880
Total	4,734	3,052

Categorization of Naxal-affected areas

A detailed analysis of Naxal violence was carried out on the basis of statistical data pertaining to number of incidents, civilians/SF personnel/Naxals killed, number injured, arrests, blasts, etc. It clearly shows the areas that are critically/moderately/marginally affected by Naxalism. Categorization of the areas with specific names of places has been covered in Chapter 10. Maps of Chhattisgarh, Jharkhand and Odisha, duly updated up to March 31, 2013, are given in Figure 5.4 (p. 82-83), to highlight the critical areas.

High rate of casualties

According to available data, it is evident that the violence has always caused large casualties among the innocent civilians. The Naxals have been carrying out brutal repression against the civilians by branding them as police informers or class enemies. The Naxals have also accused the SF of not following any "rules of war".[13] The attack on the Gyaneshwari Express on May 28, 2010, indicates that terrorism has been masked conveniently by the ideology of armed struggle by the masses. As per the MHA report, the Naxalites have killed 5,467 civilians and destroyed 281 schools from 2001 to 2011 and that the ultras do not want the tribal groups to join the main stream through education. The civilian casualties have been high since 2003 and have consistently maintained very high figures until 2010,which cannot be ignored.

The merger of MCCI and PWG, and their military wings into PLGA, gave an impetus to the movement to grow in strength, resulting in a steady increase in Naxal violence, and casualties to the SF, in particular. During this period, the government also started inducting a large number of forces into the Naxal affected areas, without ensuring the basic requisites of an anti-insurgency operational capability. Thus, the SF provided a large target to the Naxals, which led to a large number of casualties. Resultantly, from 2007 onwards, there was a reversal in attrition ratio wherein the SF suffered more casualties than the Naxals until 2010.[14] Thereafter, the SF turned the tide in their favor from 2011 onwards. Refer Figure 5.5 (p. 83).

Besides the significance of human intelligence, there are four important points that come to my mind. First, there is a huge difference between routine policing and counter-insurgency operations. Such operations require committed and motivated junior leadership to operate on the ground along with their troops. Second, it must be understood that there is no substitute to carrying out role-oriented training of troops, along with their leaders, so that all ranks are fully integrated as homogenous sub-units/units to operate in the Naxal-affected areas. This also means that the troops must be fully trained and equipped to perform in an intense counter-insurgency environment. Third, while giving priority to the intelligence system, traditional human intelligence would require much greater attention. Over dependence on technical intelligence alone could be risky. Fourth, to gain "Human Intelligence (HUMINT)", the SF have to make special efforts to win the hearts and minds of the locals. The SF have to be innovative to exhibit genuine concerns for the affected people, in both their thoughts and actions on the ground.

Trends

The terrain in the affected areas is difficult and thickly forested. It also provides rebels the ability to make full use of Mao's guerrilla strategy and tactics – hit and run, prolong the struggle to gain time, create an aura of invincibility and utilize space to disperse and deny a target – which have been the preferred method of the Naxals in their attacks on the SF. Administrative boundaries of the states – cutting across this kind of inaccessible terrain – allow them to carry out trans- border activities, to escape the SF dragnet. That is why we see the largest number of Naxal related incidents close to the bi-junctions and tri-junctions of the affected states. In addition, there has been a departure in the Naxal methodology of operating in the last decade or so. They, along with the mafia, are resorting to strong-arm tactics for large-scale extortion and other illegal activities to fund their movement. This has to a large extent been possible due to the availability of large natural resources like minerals, which have attracted huge investments by the government and private corporations into the area. Mining operations, along with the industries and socio-economic developmental projects, have provided the rebels with quick access to easy sources of funds, wherein they extort "protection" money from these corporations and contractors, to let them function in peace.

The Naxal incidents point to a definite change in trends as far as the methodology of violence is concerned. In the northern areas, like Bihar, Jharkhand, West Bengal, and northern Odisha, the Naxals have mostly resorted to sabotage activities like blowing up of railway tracks and stations, destruction of plant equipment and communication towers, and attack on isolated police posts. Jharkhand also accounted for a large number of cases of extortion, incidents of IED attacks, kidnapping, and killing of civilians. In the southern areas (southern Chhattisgarh, southern and southwestern Odisha, eastern Maharashtra), the Naxals have resorted to attacks on moving columns of SF, attack on posts, and huge IED attacks. Standoff attacks using IEDs has been a recent trend and is fast becoming the lynchpin method of attack by them in all the affected regions. This is mostly due to the improved response of the SF to guerrilla style attacks; thereby, forcing the Naxals to adopt the strategy of standoff attacks, during which they are least vulnerable.

A close look at the two charts of "Naxal violence" and "incidents and casualty analysis" (Figures 5.3 and 5.5, pp. 82-83), suggests two important aspects. First, there has been a progressive increase in casualties of SF personnel from 2004 onwards till 2009. By then, the PLGA had fully honed their skills in guerrilla warfare and the SF was still in the process of capacity and capability building. The net result was that, between 2004 and 2012, the SF suffered the highest number of casualties (317) in 2009 and the second highest in 2010. The number of civilians killed was also among the highest during these two years. However, by 2011 and 2012 the SF had become reasonably proficient in anti-naxal operations. They reversed the trend of casualties in favor of the SF, so essential to bolster their motivation and morale.

Having not achieved the desired success in controlling certain specific areas, there has been a change in the ideological thoughts of the Naxals. Post-2004, they have increased their armed violence and killings, with a view to show the state in a poor light and, at the same time, create fear psychosis, gain moral ascendency and invincibility in the eyes of the local population. The Naxals have increasingly resorted to kidnappings, using civilians as human shields and firing on helicopters.[15] Also, there was a marked increase in the criminal activities and extortions in Jharkhand, Bihar, Chhattisgarh, and Odisha. During various elections, they have not only provided support to a number of political candidates, but also fielded candidates to contest elections. In order to control the local governance, the Naxals had fielded more than 50 candidates for elections to panchayats in Malkangiri and Koraput (Odisha) in February 2012.[16]

The brutal attack in Karkatiya forests in the Latehar district killing 10 personnel of the SF on January 7, 2013, is a grim reminder of their potential.[17] Emboldened by the dreadful attack on the convoy of the Congress party on May 25, 2013, in the Bastar region (28 killed), the Naxals – close to the general election 2014 – are likely to increase attacks on soft targets including political leaders. In a counter- insurgency role, the CAPF would be required to carry out, among others, tasks such as resource control, population's movement control, area domination, cordon and search, search and destroy, etc. Generally, the CAPF have a defensive mindset due to their primary role of policing, mostly protection, and law and order related duties. The nominated counter-insurgency force requires a re-orientation of their role from defensive to a "role oriented offensive mindset", to bring about substantial effectiveness in counter-insurgency operations. The actions of SF should be based on actionable intelligence, and must aim to prevent loss of innocent civilian lives and minimize collateral damage, lest we create more Naxals due to alienation of population.

IED attacks

According to the reports, huge unbelievable quantity of imported ammonium nitrate, the preferred ingredient for making bombs, goes missing from Indian ports.[18] Adequate explosives and electric detonators are available in the Naxal-affected areas for mining purposes. There has been a progressive increase in the IED attacks against the troop carrying vehicles of SF, as part of the change in their tactics. Statistical analysis of IED attacks pertaining to the type of explosives used (high or low explosive), activating mechanism (anti-handling, command, delay type), locations (public place, forest area, government property, road side), and the target of attack (public, railways, SF, VIP, government property), for period 2009 to 2012, clearly highlight their expertise and thought process. Explosives or IED attacks have caused more than 60% of the total casualties to the SF.

In 65% cases, command-type mechanism was used, which also ensures that the Naxals are least vulnerable. They have been extremely innovative in use of IEDs. The huge quantity of explosives – being used in the IEDs – have made mine protected vehicles look redundant. They have innovatively placed IEDs in the trees, and in some cases detonated a large number of them simultaneously, to take on targets at different places. The casualties apart, stress and fear psychosis sets in the minds of troops to carry out their routine tasks. Having seen some of the most barbaric methods of using the IEDs by the Naxals, I feel that the SF and the civil administration together are required to urgently put in place, both passive and active counter – IED measures to minimize their own casualties, if not eliminate them completely. To minimize the casualties, some of these measures are given at Appendix D. Clay Wilson gives more details in "Improvised explosive devices (IEDs) in Iraq and Afghanistan: Effects and Countermeasures".[19]

Impact on Security and Economy

Impact on security

The Naxals have continued to indulge in significant violence and killing of civilians and SF, which affects "human security" adversely. The local populace is the worst affected because of physical, psychological, economic and social insecurity. They lead their lives in an environment of fear, stress and uncertainty, which also results in trauma and mental disorders. Such an insecure and volatile environment causes conflict between various cultures and societies, based on the attitude and stance of each community towards Naxalism as a movement.

The Naxals have links with transnational drug and weapon smuggling mafias, and also links with other militant organizations like the Lashkar-e-Taiba, Nepal's Maoists, PLA (Myanmar), militant groups operating in the northeast, anti-India terror group based in Pakistan, Bangladesh and organizations like CCOMPOSA, FOIR, etc. In addition, India is located at the crossroads of the Golden Crescent and the Golden Triangle – the bulk drug-producing and trafficking regions in the world. These linkages could pose a potent threat to the national security. The strategic rail and road arteries of the country, to the Siliguri corridor and to the northeast, pass through the Naxal-affected areas, which if blocked, at a critical time, could cause huge operational, logistical, and administrative difficulties, not only to the armed forces but also to the civil administration in the northeast. Due to the insecure environment prevailing in the region – people do not want to even travel in trains passing through certain passages, for the fear of "rail tracks being destroyed or rail blockages". The Naxals have continued to extort money from the contractors, industries, mining areas, and governmental organizations; levy local taxes on contractors and local population to amass their funds. A few of their activities suggest that they seem to enjoy the patronage of the political leaders. Besides the over-ground workers participating in the elections, the Naxals have also supported certain political parties during the elections. It is evident because some of the Naxal-affected areas have been achieving a polling percentage of more than 55% to 65%, which is much higher than the average in those states. A case in point is the high polling percentages for assembly elections in Bihar, Jharkhand, and eastern UP between 2009 and 2012.

Due to political compulsions, the mandate and role of the police, the state police forces are not permitted to pursue the insurgents across state boundaries, due to which significant cases of violence occur on or in the proximity of the inter-state boundaries. There is no institutionalized mechanism put in place to address such security-related issues at the inter-state boundaries. Thus, these areas continue to remain sensitive, because the insurgents are able to take full advantage of the lacunae in our system of functioning between the states. The success achieved by the Naxals in various operations against the SF, economic targets, and government infrastructure, gives them psychological and moral ascendency in public perception. It also depicts the states' control and their legitimacy in a poor light. The threat to urban areas has been discussed in detail separately. A fragile internal security environment poses serious challenge to India's rise as a great power. Nanavatty makes an apt comment regarding the impact of the internal armed conflict on the national will and morale.[20] In the long term perspective, the intangibles must be given their due importance to further build on "Nationalism".

Impact on economy

Most of the mineral resources, especially coal, iron ore, bauxite, tin and manganese are available in abundance in the Naxal-affected areas, as a result of which, besides the mining industry, a large number of alloy, steel, cement and power plants of the country are located here. These areas also have approximately 40% to 45% of the forest cover of the country. As the area has an insecure environment due to persistent threat from the Naxals, there is a great amount of uncertainty and loss of confidence among the corporate houses and the industry to invest in these areas. The Naxals have also been targeting the economic structures such as railway tracks, oil pipelines, electric substations and transformers, mobile towers, culverts, and bridges (refer Figure 5.6, p. 84). These have significant adverse impact on the economic development of the region. Frequent boycotts and blocks on the rail and road arteries have an undesirable effect on the economic activity, because of which the foreign and home-grown MNCs have not been investing in these areas. In addition, the transportation of the minerals and the slurry is adversely affected due to road and rail blockages. A large number of cases of extortion and kidnapping have been reported from Jharkhand, Chhattisgarh, and Odisha, which instills fear among the industry and contractors. It has also been observed that the resources allocated for social and economic development of the region or the state's assets are often diverted towards security requirements. In other words, the socio-economic development projects continue to remain neglected.

There are numerous examples where the industrial-cum-mining mega projects have got substantially delayed or did not make any headway because of government procedures, decision-making, or the industries not taking actions to look after the interests of the local population. Most industrial projects have been stalled over land acquisition issues, accusations of corruption, environmental violations, and a popular backlash against the industry. There has also been unfettered mining that has affected the livelihoods of locals, who have not benefitted from these projects. Major hurdles to land acquisition are born out of the country's flawed colonial Land Acquisition Act, 1894, which empowers the state and its associated agencies to acquire land by using the public purpose clause even in the case of private companies. Inadequacy or lack of compensation remains the single biggest reason for resentful opposition to land acquisition, resulting in trust deficit. Rehabilitation and resettlement is another area of serious concern.[21] Mega infrastructural projects require interaction, and clearances, from multi-ministerial, government, financial agencies, PSUs, and private organizations, which is rather time consuming. There is, therefore, an urgent need to have a robust single window decision-making body to clear various bottlenecks, in compliance with the law, existing rules, and, more importantly, within a laid down period. Yet, as land acquisition is a state subject, this statutory body could facilitate and coordinate expeditious clearance of the infrastructural projects. As reported by the media on a number of occasions, some of the mega projects of Jindal, Essars, Tata, Mittals, Aditya Birla, POSCO, etc., have been delayed because of protests by displaced locals, stalled mining approvals, land acquisitions, and delays in environmental clearances, among other reasons.[22] In some cases, the delays have been attributed to uncontrolled violence and insecure environment. It is also true that some of the established industries have not participated in the economic-cum-environmental development of the area. They have not contributed towards the well-being of the society and the environment, as part of their CSR. The industry also needs to take action in terms of empowerment of youth with job-related skills, provision of employment to the locals, resettlement, and rehabilitation of displaced people, which has not been visible. In the long-term perspective, the industry must understand that their growth and prosperity depends upon the well being and progress of the region, its people, conservation of the environment and sustainable development. They must play their full part to support the people to make the region secure and economically prosperous.

Security Matrix

Strengths, weaknesses, opportunities and threats (SWOT) analysis

From the security perspective, the endeavor of the state must be to control the growing menace of Naxalism by application of the CAPF and the state police. To do so, the requirement is to carry out SWOT analysis, examine the dimensions of the Naxal threat and exploit their weaknesses; as also to arrive at an optimum force required for combating Naxalism. The salient issues of SWOT analysis are as given below:

Strengths	*Weaknesses*	*Opportunities*	*Threats*
• Commitment and the will • Elusive and mobile • Knowledge of terrain • Support of population • Expert in minor tactics • Aura of bravery and hardy • Innovative communications • Secure bases • Minimum logistics • Simple but effective intelligence system • Effective front organizations	• Funds, weapons, and leadership • Fear of betrayal and infighting • No elaborate logistic bases • Non-tribal people, non-farmers are not fully supportive • Huge age difference between the leaders and the Naxals • Vulnerable to psychological warfare and backlash of population • Deviation in ideology, shrinking recruitment base • Inadequate progress in urban areas • Loss of leaders	• Create mass support • Secure bases in inaccessible areas • Subvert population/ fence sitters • Move to urban areas • Penetrate labor/ industrial workers unions/slums/ghettos • Links with external powers and militants • Subvert government organizations and essential services sector • Further, enlarge the front organization • Motivate recruitment into cadre	• Denial of operational space • Denial of external support • Change of political objectives • National consensus & strategy • Perception management by state • Effects of "Insurgency fatigue" • Crossing of threshold could result in army's deployment

Police-population ratios

The police-population ratio (police persons per 100,000 population) in India is rather low (1.33 per 1,000) in comparison to some of the countries affected by insurgency or terrorism.[24] The details of police-population ratio (policepersons per 1,00,000 population) of India and some of the other countries of the world are given at Table 5.2.

Table 5.2

Foreign Countries		*India*	
N Ireland *	175	All India Average*	133
Turkey *	238	Bihar	62
Thailand *	335	Jharkhand	139
Greece *	426	Chhattisgarh	164
Sri Lanka *	172	Odisha	108
Italy	559	Andhra Pradesh	128
USA	315	Uttar Pradesh	76
Spain	312	West Bengal	93
UK	235	UN Recommended	222

Note: UN Recommends 2.22 per 1,000.
* Countries affected by insurgency/terrorism.

Requirement of police forces

The requirement of police force, in an insurgency environment, is a direct function of three important factors, namely – total population, total geographical space, and strength of the Naxal cadre, the intensity and frequency of violence. Although the United Nations has suggested certain parameters to calculate the ideal requirement of police force, as given below, the calculations and weight-ages have been done based on the lessons learnt and experiences of counter- insurgency operations in the Indian context.

- Police to population ratio.[25]
- Police to space ratio. [26]
- Police to Naxal ratio.[27]

The requirement of policepersons to Naxal ratio has been worked out taking into account the advantages the Naxals enjoy over the SF due to their familiarity of the terrain, local intelligence and guerrilla tactics adopted. Each of these ratios independently affect the numbers of police persons required; however, each factor, be it the population, the space or the number of Naxals are extremely intertwined with each other. Therefore, by allocating suitable weightages (percent) to each of these ratios out of a total of 100, the optimum requirement of police force has been arrived at, as given in the Figure 5.7 (p. 84).[28] The ratio of weight-ages would actually depend on the prevailing conditions on the ground, in each region.

This requirement is by no means meager. A look at the present manning levels given in graphs would indicate that the deficit is quite huge, and therefore requires immediate attention to surmount the problem. One of the ways to do it is by providing employment opportunities to the locals by organizing large number of recruitment rallies in the affected areas. This will achieve the twin purposes of creating employment opportunities in the backward districts to wean away the youth from the Naxals, and at the same time overcome the deficiency in the police force. However, it is easier said than done – the states and the center put together do not have the capacity and the infrastructure to train such large numbers in a short period. In the instant case, only four naxal-affected states have been taken into consideration to highlight the gross deficiency in the police forces. Hence, it is necessary to build up the capacity of the infrastructure at all levels to be able to achieve the desired level of force structure.

Quality force

While carrying out considerable amount of recruitment into the CAPF, as is being done by the center to supplement the effort of the states, the envisaged insurgency/violence level in the future must be kept in mind, because a few years later, the insurgencies would be controlled to an acceptable level. At that point, the requirement of the force would be much less. Thus, unplanned large-scale recruitment could drive a deep wedge in the finances of the state governments later. Hence, a balanced approach must be undertaken in this regard. In addition, the aim should be to improve the capability of the CAPF, rather than numbers alone (quality versus quantity). Capability of force refers to effective junior leadership, high proficiency in training, equipment profile, weapon systems, mobility, and reliable communication system. In addition to the junior leadership, the most important requirement in a counter-insurgency environment is an effective intelligence network, to fight a well-trained Naxal guerrilla.

Judicial system

Police alone cannot improve the security scenario. For police to be effective in its mandated role, the judicial system – its organization, staff, procedures, communication facilities, revenue records of land, and data – should be fully in place to achieve optimum results. The judiciary also has to be strengthened to speedily dispose off judicial cases related to

Naxal violence. The availability of "judges per 1,00,000" in India is very low in comparison to other countries: USA 11, Sweden 13, China 17, Belgium 23, Germany 25, Slovenia 39, India 1.02. However, as seen in the statistics, one would immediately realize the actual reasons for the large number of cases pending before our courts. It is common knowledge that with poverty, unemployment and non- accountability, corruption is a natural fallout. Judicial system is virtually nonexistent in the remote areas – police, trials, prosecution, justice and prisons are ineffective- as a result of which the Naxals provide swift justice in "jan adalats" or "janathana sarkar" (people's court).[29] Therefore, it is imperative that a responsive judicial system with specific focus on the Naxal-affected regions be setup to carry out speedy disposal of legal cases, otherwise "jan adalats" by the Naxals would continue to be held in the future too. Gram panchayats and gram sabhas should also be empowered to settle petty disputes, including land cases.

Salwa Judum

The Chhattisgarh government had initiated an irregular civilian force, called "Salwa Judum" to protect the people. "Salwa Judum" meaning "Peace March", or "Purification Hunt"[30] in Gondi language, was a people's resistance movement started by Mahendra Karma, the leader of the opposition in the legislative assembly of the Chhattisgarh government. Having survived earlier attempts on his life, he was killed by the Naxals, in a brutal manner in the Bastar region on May 25, 2013. The state legalized the movement through the Chhattisgarh Police Act, 2007, wherein the Salwa Judum cadres were designated as special police officers (SPOs). With a view to protect the people, the state government armed them lightly and provided them a monthly honorarium. Thereafter, the Salwa Judum increasingly formed part of the state government's anti-Naxal policy. Since the time of its inception, a few Salwa Judum members have been accused of looting houses, burning down villages, and causing displacement of thousands of tribal people. The Supreme Court in 2007 appointed the National Human Rights Commission of India (NHRC), an autonomous statutory body of the government, to investigate the activities of the Salwa Judum. The NHRC report substantiated the government-sponsored arming of civilians. However, on July 5, 2011, the Supreme Court while hearing a petition filed by Nandini Sundar against the Chhattisgarh government passed a judgment prohibiting the recruitment of tribal youth as SPOs in the Salwa Judum.[31] In passing the order, it categorically observed that the appointment of tribal youth as SPOs, who are barely literate, and armed with firearms, had endangered and will necessarily endanger the human rights of others in society. The Chhattisgarh government has since disarmed and disbanded the cadres that formed part of Salwa Judum, and has begun the process of absorbing them into the state police forces, to protect them from a possible backlash from the Naxals.

Assessment

The modus operandi of the Salwa Judum activists was simple. Apart from holding relatively large meetings, releasing anti-naxal posters and pamphlets, and maintaining vigil at the local level, the campaign aimed at population's movement control through herding of tribal groups and villagers into makeshift camps funded by the state. The cadres – belonging to the movement and in some cases the government forces –provided these camps with the protection. However, they also became hotbeds of human rights abuses. To move villagers into these camps and as a method of retribution against villages, which were seen as pro-Naxal, it is widely alleged that the Salwa Judum cadres forcibly evicted and in some cases burned down a large number of villages, leading to displacement of more than 3,00,000 tribal people. Since the formation of the Salwa Judum, more than 800 people have lost their lives, 98 among them being the SPOs themselves. Salwa Judum cadres were supposed to be the "guides, spotters, and translators", as also the source of intelligence. They were, contrary to the instructions, armed and were involved in fierce combat roles – in anti-naxal operations – without any formal training. It led to swift retribution by the Naxals against the Salwa Judum cadres. This turned into a kind of a conflict between two groups, in which the end losers were the innocent tribal people of the region. This happened because the Salwa Judum cadres were neither adequately trained in the legal aspects of operating in insurgency conditions nor educated on aspects of human rights. There were no safeguards or limitations placed on the number of SPOs, which could be appointed, their qualifications, and suitability for the job. As a result, the movement, which was supposed to protect and defend the rights of the tribal groups, itself became to be seen as the oppressor due to the creation of a conflict situation between the Naxals and the Salwa Judum. The violence by and between the Naxals and Salwa Judum had created fear psychosis, uncertainty and helplessness among the local populace.

It has been seen by experience[32] that creation of some of the civil resistance movements or committees and appointment of the SPOs have given a boost to anti-insurgency movements, notably in some parts of J&K. The Chhattisgarh government too had notable success, in the initial stages, due to the Salwa Judum in its anti-Naxal operations, since the cadres were locals who not only knew the terrain but also could recognize Naxal cadres. They were the valuable assets in the field of intelligence. However, the use of these cadres in offensive operations gave them a misplaced sense of power, which they allegedly used to perpetuate excesses against the local population. Thus, it is imperative that the mandate of such groups is not only clearly spelt out, but also enforced by the authorities. Suitable eligibility conditions, command and control structures and institutional conduct of training must be put in place before such cadres are appointed, and armed as the SPOs.

> *It seemed that rebellion must have an unassailable base, something guarded not merely from attack, but from the fear of it.*
>
> – T.E. Lawrence, *Seven Pillars of Wisdom* (1922)

Notes

1. "Naxalites Attack Koraput Town, Loot Police Stations", *The Times of India*, February 07, 2004.
2. Amarnath K. Menon, "A Deadly Ambush", *India Today*, July 03, 2008.
3. Kujur Rajat Kumar, "Violent Revolution: The Naxal War Zone in Odisha", *IPCS*, July 08, 2008.
4. Ibid.
5. V.K. Ahluwalia, "Bloodiest years of Naxal violence : strategic challenges", Defence and Security Alert, November 2012, 12-17. Parts of the article have been cited in this book.
6. Dilip Kumar Mekala, "Few Lessons Learnt, Revisiting the Horrors of Chintalnar Massacre", http://forceindia.net/FewLessonsLearnt.aspx, Force magazine.
7. Rajat Kujur, a well-known expert on Naxalism, wrote in his article, "Dantewada Jailbreak: Strategic Accomplishment of Naxal Designs" that "This is a classic case of Naxal attack, where something 'next to impossible' was made to look so simple that one cannot but admire the Naxals."
8. Sandeep Mishra and Hrusikesh Mohanty, "Top Maoist deputy killed in Odisha", *The Times of India*, March 12, 2013.
9. In fact, immediately after the home minister's announcement, there were two major incidents of violence that shook the states of Odisha and Chhattisgarh. The Naxals attacked Odisha's state armed police camp in the Gajapati district on March 24, 2006 (looted arms and freed 40 prisoners), and the second attack at the relief camp at Errabore in Dantewada district, on July 27, 2006, killing 25 people, injuring 80 others, and kidnapped more than 20 people. Both the attacks were well planned, with 500 to 800 Maoists in the attacking force.
10. "Naxals Surge Ahead: The Nation under Siege", Martyrs' Memorial Research Institute (MMRI) and *MHA Annual Report 2007-08*, June 29, 2011.
11. The SF got back at the Naxals from 2011 onwards, as a result there was a decline in the Naxal-affected areas.
12. High levels of SF casualties indicate the expertise gained by the Naxals in the conduct of guerrilla warfare. The Naxals are better organized in their command and control structures, recruitment, training, weapons, and intelligence gathering and communication facilities.

13. Mohua Chatterjee, "Reds will Repeat Tactics of using Jawans' Bodies as Booby Traps", *The Times of India,* February 11, 2013.
14. The CAPF were not proficient enough to adapt to the intense CI environment, where the insurgents were fully trained in guerrilla warfare tactics. Particularly in 2006-07, the CAPF were neither fully equipped nor trained and oriented to the new operational role. However, subsequently, the combat potential of the CAPF improved manifold and their results showed a marked improvement.
15. Jaideep Hardikar, "Maoist Art that Downed Chopper Chilling Drill in Old Manual", *The Telegraph,* January 22, 2013. As per the booklet, "*Jung Ke Hunar* (The Art of War)", a copy of which was found by the SF in Chhattisgarh's Abujh Madh forests in 2012, the rebels prepared themselves for almost a decade to train their cadres on how to bring down helicopters, using even an ordinary weapons like 303 rifles. The Naxals had prepared the manual in 2003.
16. Pranab Dhal Samanta, "Alarm Bells: Maoists 'Win' 30 Blocks in Orissa Panchayat Polls", *Indian Express,* February 16, 2012. All their nominees have been elected unopposed after the Maoists warned local people against nominating any other candidate. The Maoists have taken control of about 30 blocks in these two districts. It has caused some concern as a large number of social welfare schemes and their funds are controlled by the panchayats.
17. Anumeha Yadav, "Belly bomb sewn into soldier's body", *The Hindu,* January 11, 2013. Subsequently, a belly bomb (a pressure activated IED) was also sewn inside the dead soldier's body, perhaps to blow up the medical staff and hospital premises during the post-mortem procedures.
18. Deeptiman Tiwari, "3.5 Tonnes of Ammonium Nitrate Untraceable Each Year: Spillage at Ports Continues; Only I Kg Required for a Bomb", *The Times of India,* August 6, 2012.
19. Clay Wilson, "Countering Improvised Explosive Devices", accessed on April 5, 2013, http://www.nato.int/cps/en/natolive/topics_72809.htm and "Improvised Explosive Devices (IEDs) in Iraq and Afghanistan: Effects and Countermeasures".
20. Rostum K. Nanavatty, "Internal Armed Conflict in India, Forging a Joint Civil-Military Approach" (New Delhi, Pentagon Press, 2013), 11. "Internal armed conflicts can have a debilitating effect on the self confidence and self esteem of a nation. It can undermine national will and morale: both constituents of national power."
21. For an insightful account, see "Mega Project Development: Issues in Land Acquisition" a report presented at seminar organized by the Center for Politics and Governance, New Delhi, compiled by Observer Research Foundation, January 20, 2010.
22. Ramprastha Primera, "Orissa Industrial Dream Mired In Delays", *Indian Express,* October 29, 2012.
23. http://nitawriter.wordpress.com/2007/08/20/poor-people-to-police-ratio/, accessed on September 07, 2012 and wiki/Police_Service_of_Northern_Ireland.
24. "Poor Police to People Ratio Forces Common Man to Fend for Himself", August 20, 2010, accessed September 07, 2012, http://nitawriter.wordpress.

com/2007/08/20/poor-people-to-police-ratio/ and latest details of India given in “Police Strength, Expenditure and Infrastructure”, http://ncrb.nic.in/ciiprevious/data/cd-CII2004/cii-2004/CHAP17.pdf.

25. Normal Police Population is 2.2 per 1000 as per UN standards and 13 to 25 per 1000 for Counter Insurgency areas. The recommended ratio for Naxal affected areas is 13 per 1000 for critically affected states.
26. Ideal ratios vary from less than 1 to 7-8 SF per square km. Recommended is 3 per square km in critical districts and 2 per square km for other Naxal affected areas.
27. Ratios vary from 20 to 60 per terrorist based on intensity of engagement. Ideally, over 30 police personnel per terrorist would provide the tipping edge.
28. As the Naxal movement will be controlled in a few years, the states must plan to make up deficiency by about 20 percent (i.e. recruit 52647) for 4 states, as calculated, over next five years. It would help to augment the force to an affordable level to meet Indian security environment, and not necessarily the parameters given by the UN.
29. During my meeting with the senior functionaries of the Jharkhand government in 2010 and 2011, and to my query on Naxal violence in the state, they briefly explained the circumstances under which not only the youth, but also the entire family used to join the Naxals as the best choice available. In addition, they explained the system of ‘internal and external ‘adalats by the Naxals, to dispense justice. External adalats (meaning courts of justice in rural areas, but covering a larger span) oversee the functioning of the internal (village/local) adalat for its effectiveness, failing which punitive actions are taken against the internal adalats.
30. Ved Marwah, “India in Turmoil”, Rupa, 2009, 152.
31. Hearing plea against Salwa Judum, SC says, “State cannot Arm Civilians to Kill”, *Indian Express*, April 1, 2008.
32. Kavita Suri, “Village Defence Committees by Kashmiri Women”, first published on 25 Feb 2005. Accessed via http://www.sawf.org/newedit/edit02212005/kashmir.asp on 21 Jan 2012. Also, the author while serving in operational areas in Poonch, Rajouri and Akhnoor, south of the Pir Panjal Ranges, in 1992, and 1996-98, had observed the effectiveness of the concept of Village Defence Committee (VDC). They were reasonably effective, especially in Doda, Udhampur, Reasi, Poonch & Rajouri.

Chapter 6

Strategic Options for Naxalites

One of the distinctive features of the Naxalite movement is that they have committed themselves to documenting their thoughts on ideology, strategy and the art of war. It is evident that they have not only studied the thoughts of Karl Marx, Lenin and Mao Tse-Tung, but have also analyzed various guerrilla campaigns of China, Peru, Vietnam, Philippines, Turkey, etc. In this chapter, Maoists' document, "Strategy and Tactics of the Indian Revolution (STIR)",[1] has been analyzed along with strategic options available to them.

Strategy and Tactics: Maoists' Document[2]

One of their most important documents, "STIR" – said to be a blue print of the Naxals' strategy for the ensuing years and a roadmap for their revolution – has been examined in detail for two major reasons. First, the aim is to understand the psyche and thought process of the Naxals; and second, to assess the document and compare with the existing ground realities; and, more importantly, to broadly recommend actions to be taken at various levels to resolve the conflict. Therefore, analysis of the document has been divided into three parts. The first part gives the thought process, the strategy and tactics of the Naxals to give the movement a meaningful direction. The second part critically analyzes the document from a holistic perspective, and throws light on the relevance of the envisaged revolution in the contemporary times. The third part examines the strategic options available to them, and the likely future scenarios, to formulate a "national strategy" to combat Naxalism.

Naxal's view

Although five draft documents were prepared by the Maoists after a series of intense discussions over a prolonged period, this document (STIR) is the synthesis of all the important policies, perceptions and experiences of the two parties (MCCI and PWG). It is a voluminous document – with 13 chapters – that covers strategy and tactics in two different parts. It has political and intellectual overtones, and indicates a protracted armed struggle, suitably modified for the Indian conditions. The political and military strategy is based on three broad factors, which include a detailed and objective analysis of (a) the class character of the Indian society; (b) the character of the Indian state; and (c) an in-depth analysis of the uneven, economic, political, social, and cultural developments in the country. Based on their analysis, they have worked out the strategy and tactics to carry their movement forward. It categorically states that while the strategy of the Indian Revolution would remain the same throughout the country, it underscores the need for different tactics to be followed in different regions at any given time, due to the uneven economic, political, social, and cultural developments in the country and a host of other related factors. This is an important aspect that needs to be taken note of by the government, so that its counter-strategy/grand strategy is also formulated at the national level, with different sub-strategies/ tactics to meet the developmental-cum-security requirements, specific to a particular area/region.

An in-depth analysis of the uneven economic, political, social, and cultural developments in the country by the Naxals has been undertaken to formulate appropriate strategy and tactics and, thus, successfully exploit the existing fault lines. The aim of this political strategy is to unite all the native forces against imperialism, feudalism, and comprador bureaucratic capitalism, while the military strategy aims at establishing revolutionary "Base Areas", first in the countryside, where the state is relatively weak, the terrain is favorable, and then gradually moving towards the cities. Discussing the four major contradictions of the Indian society and the state, it finally suggests that the most serious contradiction (principal contradiction) is the one between feudalism and the masses, and this is the main obstacle to economic and social development of Indian society. It therefore aims to exploit these major prevailing weaknesses in the remote and backward areas of the country, as also spearhead the NDR.

Having carried out the SWOT analysis of the character of the Indian state and its armed forces/SF, it correctly deduces that it would not be possible to stage a simultaneous revolution – an armed insurrection – throughout the country. The document clearly highlights the weaknesses of the SF in the rural-cum-remote areas in comparison to the cities. Hence, the vast countryside would be the most suitable for the revolutionary people's army to strike at the enemy (SF). Therefore, the Naxals would establish guerrilla zones in these areas, develop them into strategic base areas, that are strong, self-sufficient to sustain revolutionary operations, before targeting the urban areas to capture power countrywide. The fact that there are liberated zones has been acknowledged by the government, is the first step towards rectification of the problem.[3] It is interesting to note that the document has discussed the following aspects in some detail:

- To give accurate direction and momentum to the Indian revolution, there is a need to understand the relations among the 'Party, the People's Army, and United Front (the three magic bands)', and further build these institutions. Therefore, top priority should be given to building the mass base, people's army and establishing base areas in the targeted areas.
- The basic principles of the strategy and tactics of the PLGA for various contingencies have been amply highlighted in the document. One of them states, "*We must mobilize the people to support our armed forces enthusiastically and to fight the enemy together with them. The people are the eyes and ears of the army; they feed and keep our soldiers. It is they who help the army in sabotage and in battle. The people are the water and our army the fish.*"

Assessment

Kautilya, the famous statesman-cum-politico-military strategist of 320 BC had said, "A strong enemy can be overcome by the union of large numbers, just as grass through its collectiveness wards off erosion caused by heavy rainfall." Having observed the activities of the Naxals over the last few decades, it is clear that the ideology of Mao Tse-Tung has inspired them considerably, to formulate the said document. However, it appears that the above-mentioned words of Kautilya too have had some influence on the formulation of the said document.

Clearly, the document (STIR) combines the ideologies of the MCCI and PWG, and has been formulated after a series of intellectual deliberations. The strategy and tactics discussed in the document have been evolved from the basic tenets of Maoism (of Mao Tse-Tung), Marxism, and Leninism. Apparently, a few changes have been made to adapt it to the Indian conditions. The Maoists have failed to understand that the theory that was adopted by Mao in 1930s cannot be replicated in the current scenario due to vast differences in the global world order between the 1930s and the present day. This misconception has been adequately reflected in its document, the "Party Programme", where it opposes the liberalization of the economy and globalization, referring to them as methods for imperialist forces to control the capital wealth of the world.

In the contemporary environment, the Maoist's ideology is regressive and out of tune with the times. After Mao's death in 1976, even China has not persisted with Mao's ideology; instead, they too have changed with the global dynamic reality. There are serious inadequacies in the ideological and conceptual framework of the Indian Maoist document, STIR, primarily due to the vast differences in the geo-politico-socio-economic-security environment that had prevailed in China during the pre-revolutionary phase and the contemporary situation in India.

Dichotomy: Blind replication

The CPI (Maoist) has carried out demographic mapping of India to identify and exploit the weaknesses in the Indian system of governance. They have correctly identified some of the existing inequalities and inadequacies in the country at large, so as to align their strategy with the aspirations of the masses. Therefore, implementation of land reforms; forest rights; land acquisition policy for industrial-cum-mining purposes; basic amenities; resettlement and rehabilitation policies for displaced people should be addressed at the earliest. The MHA's Annual Report 2010-11 (Chapter II) states that the left-wing extremists operate in vacuum created by the functional inadequacies of field-level governance structures. The annual reports of various ministries have given details of the holistic plans and allotment of funds for tribal welfare, security, development, and governance-related works in the LWE-affected areas. Despite such a large number of schemes and allotments of funds, the results on the ground are not commensurate with the resources made available.[4] Time bound implementation and audit of schemes and reforms at the grass roots would be the key to successful management of the conflict.

The said document states that the path followed by the Chinese revolution is also relevant for semi-colonial and semi-feudal India due to basic similarities between India and pre-revolutionary China. This is considered the most important aspect that determines their political and military strategy and tactics. The Naxals' branding of India as being "semi-colonial" does not hold good in view of the current political, economic, and social status enjoyed by the country among the comity of nations in the new world order. The commitment of the central and state governments, despite a few differences in their perception to tackle Naxalism, to ensure development and to improve the security environment have been underestimated, if not grossly ignored. It is likely that the Naxal leadership has deliberately presented a feeble picture of the state, as a part of their propaganda strategy, to woo the masses and to galvanize agrarian support in the rural areas. It probably tries to take advantage of the literate/semi-literate people who would be able to read the document, but may not have the analytical skills to see through their ulterior motives and larger agenda. It is this literate and semi-literate class, which would constitute their front organizations and leadership in rural areas, respectively. The Maoist's document is somewhat incoherent in content and spirit, since it does not assign due significance to the might of the state, which manifests itself in the form of the largest functional democracy, vibrant economy, dynamic fiscal and monetary policies, along with strong armed forces and police forces. It is however correct that a large number of welfare programs and schemes have not been implemented on the ground, as the benefits could not reach the poor people.

Leadership and insurgency fatigue

Leadership is an extremely important requirement to lead an insurgency. Mao Zedong, General Giap, Fidel Castro, Jomo Kenyata, Charu Mazumdar and Prabhakaran were well known leaders, who enjoyed popular support and provided a momentous direction to their movements. At present, the Naxals do not have any such charismatic leader at the national level to carry forward their movement. The other flaw in the Naxal's document is that the timelines for various stages of strategy have neither been appreciated nor spelt out, thereby indicating a desire to pursue an open-ended revolution, without giving any time lines and objectives to be achieved. To that extent, the desired end state remains ambiguous and directionless. While Mao categorically stated that time is no constraint in a protracted people's war, the value of time in the contemporary world scenario is starkly different. A prolonged campaign can lose its original direction and momentum, thus losing the purity of ideology. In addition, in a long drawn protracted conflict, "Insurgency Fatigue", which manifests in different forms and at different stages, is an extremely important factor, having a telling effect on all the stakeholders. Insurgency fatigue affects the local population the most, as the civilians are often caught between the insurgents and the counter-insurgents. The local population and the SF, in that order, are the worst sufferers, as they become tired and fatigued to live in an uncertain environment. Generally, long drawn insurgency campaigns start moving towards organized crime, settling personal scores, subversion, sabotage, and terrorism. Some of these tendencies are already visible in the north-eastern states' insurgencies and Naxal-related incidents.

The document has apparently ignored the vulnerabilities of the movement and the related contingencies. Interestingly, the document does not highlight anything pertaining to organizational structure, hierarchy, command and control, source of funding, procurements, logistics, and other administrative issues that support the ideology, strategy, and tactics being propagated. These issues have probably been deliberately omitted in this document. This reinforces the fact that the Naxals realize and understand that their organization, tactics, funding, procurement, and logistics are illegal, and therefore cannot be revealed, lest the state targets them. There is no ambiguity in their thought process regarding elections; it clearly rejects any participation in elections since its stated strategy is to seize power through a protracted peoples' war. However, contrary to their belief, they have continued to sponsor/ support select candidates for the elections in various states and the local governing bodies.

The rebels had understood long ago that a considerable part of the Indian Army would inevitably be deployed in Kashmir and the northeastern states of the country; hence, it will be difficult for the state to mobilize the army against the revolutionary war. It is true that the army has not been employed for a number of other important reasons, including the one mentioned in the document.

Strategic stages

The document states that the protracted people's war will pass through the three strategic stages: strategic defensive, strategic stalemate, and strategic offensive.[5] It is based on their experience of revolutions in China, Vietnam, and a few other countries. In theory, the concept of three strategic stages may sound logical. However, it has a serious flaw, because the Naxals have apparently applied this concept based on their experience of the armed conflict in China, with the Japanese forces (1937–1945) and between the nationalists and the communists in the pre-revolutionary phase in the 1930s and 1940s. Over the last 70–80 years, there has been a marked change in the system of governance, the prevailing security environment and economic growth, improvement in the human development indices and developmental initiatives. In addition, the Naxals have not fully analyzed and appreciated the strength of the armed forces, the CAPF, and state police forces of the country in comparison to the conditions prevailing during China's pre-revolutionary phase. It would be extremely difficult for them, if not impossible, to achieve the second and third strategic stages. This notwithstanding, they have correctly appreciated the revolution to be in a phase of self-defense, as stated in the document. Thus, at present, it perceives itself to be weaker than the might of the state, and therefore would continue to resort to guerrilla tactics in the near and foreseeable future. At the same time, they will try to carry out all the possible actions to increase their power, both political and military, to gain parity or even ascendancy over the government machinery in selected areas. Nayak has merit when he states, "Contrary to popular perception, it is not all about guerrilla warfare but about revolutionary politics, which accounts for 70 percent of the strategy. Revolutionary politics is a combination of information warfare and political warfare. More than armed fighting, they use propaganda."[6]

Guerrilla warfare and changed tactics

Mao and Che Guevara are the acknowledged masters of guerrilla warfare. An analysis of the military strategy and tactics, given in the document, shows that the Naxals have studied in detail, the guerrilla warfare documents and campaigns of various countries, more prominently of China's revolutionary war. They have been more innovative and dynamic to change their tactics. While adopting hit and run tactics and IED attacks, they have tried to avoid direct and prolonged confrontation with the SF. As per their tactics, they have carried out a swift and surprise attack on the SF only after allowing their columns to move out of their operating bases to a far distance, much out of the "reinforcement and logistics support" of the operating bases. In certain cases, due to extremely difficult terrain with dense forest cover, poor weather conditions, and greater distances from the communication facilities, including mobile towers, it is not possible for troops to communicate effectively with their bases. Considering some of these constraints, the Naxals have also been able to target the reinforcing columns of SF, by way of IED attacks and springing multiple ambushes simultaneously, thus causing casualties to the troops and taking away their weapons and ammunition. Refer Figure 6.1. Such tactics give the Naxals major advantage of causing large-scale casualties to the SF in a single incident, while maintaining low vulnerability to their own-armed cadres. In so doing, they achieve psychological advantage, moral ascendency among the Naxal cadres, as also recognition and better credibility among the masses.

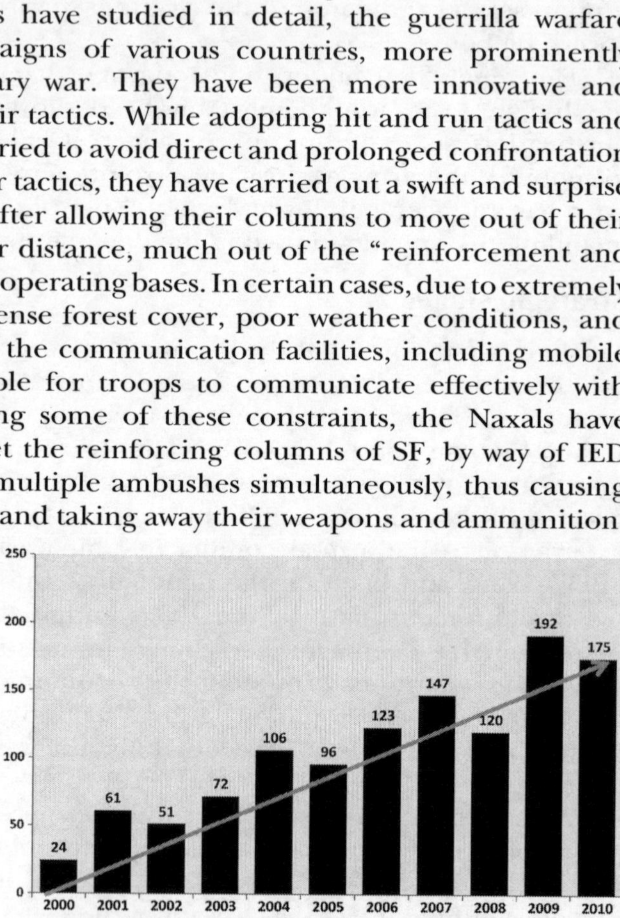

Figure 6.1: IED Incidents in Naxal Affected Areas, 2000–2010
Source: National Bomb Data Centre.

Among other lessons, it would be expedient for the SF to understand the importance of "fighting a guerrilla better than a guerrilla", i.e. do not fight a guerrilla in a conventional manner, bound by standard operating procedures. The SF should be highly mobile, flexible, and be capable of undertaking sustained operations for five to seven days. Besides organizing intense operation-oriented training of the SF and their ability to operate in small teams, the success would lie in obtaining timely and accurate information, failsafe communications, and good junior leadership. The junior leaders must remain pro-active, dynamic, and innovative to operate in such unconventional situations. The SF must also understand the psychological impact of counter-insurgency operations on civilian population. Invariably, as such operations cause considerable inconvenience and hardships to the local population, the junior leaders and the troops must be fully sensitized of the problem and the remedial measures to minimize the hardship to the local population. The SF, in coordination with the civil administration, must continue to support and respect the people, by genuinely looking after their interests.

Naxals have come to realize that information gathering systems are the backbone of any counter-insurgency operation, and have sought to effectively implement the maxim "*kill one, terrorize ten thousand*", to terrify anyone indulging in such activities.[7] The Naxals used the most brutal and inhuman tactics during the Latehar incident in January 2013, among other. They may have achieved their short-term goal of achieving control over the population, but they would lose out the support of the people – the center of gravity – in the long term. On the other hand, the Naxals too have alleged that the attack by the SF on the Maoists did not follow "any rules of the war". They have categorically stated that they would continue to use brutal tactics.[8]

The Naxals have continued to use abduction as a tool to force the government to meet some of their demands, as also to show their presence and visibility at all levels. In reply to a starred question in Lok Sabha on November 22, 2011, the Minister of State for Home Affairs stated that the Naxals had abducted a total of 1,554 people in Chhattisgarh, Jharkhand, Odisha, West Bengal, Andhra Pradesh, Bihar, Maharashtra, Uttar Pradesh, and other states between January 1, 2008, and November 14, 2011. Of them, 489 were abducted from Chhattisgarh, 463 from Jharkhand, and 137 from Odisha. Overall, 328 persons were killed by them. In the recent past, there has been a change in the tactics of the rebels; i.e., to kidnap selected, high profile targets, including foreigners, to achieve greater publicity, propaganda, and visibility not only at the national level but also at the international level. Therefore, it would be expedient to analyze the places of kidnapping incidents, killings thereof, the motive of abduction (termed as police informer or contractor not paying local levies to the rebels or settling personal scores), the duration of abduction, and any other statistics, which suggest a particular pattern/

trend. Thereafter, work out a strategy to contain and to minimize such kidnappings, if not eliminate altogether.

One of the recent reported phenomena in their tactics has been to use children, women, and innocent civilians as human shields to protect themselves from the SF.[9] They have adopted this tactic in situations where they are relatively weak in combat and have a larger interest to prevent the SF from making inroads into certain specific areas to retain their control on the population and the place. At times, it could be to protect an important leader, who may have been encircled in an area. During operations with the Naxals, it should be the earnest endeavor of the SF – though difficult to achieve in an uncertain and intense environment – to ensure that no innocent lives are lost, and that collateral damage is minimized, if not totally avoided. The rebels have trained themselves to fire at the helicopters – IAF and BSF helicopters were fired upon in January and April 2013 respectively in the same general area – to cause casualties and to deter them from operating in the Naxal dominated areas.

While I was commanding the brigade in 2002, it reminds me of an incident in J&K, where the militants had fired small arms weapons and lobbed a grenade at the last vehicle of a commander's convoy and killed one soldier and injured two seriously. As the troops had identified the cluster of houses from where the militants had fired on the convoy, a group of civilians prevented them from entering the premises. Resultantly, the army could neither fire towards the houses nor pursue the fleeing militants, primarily to avoid any casualties to the civilians. It is a practical problem on the ground. While we expect our troops to be immune to their emotional and psychological pressures, particularly when their colleagues have been killed, it is difficult to control such situations. It requires training and leadership of exceptional quality to control the troops in such a charged atmosphere, so that no innocent civilians' lives are lost, while dealing with the terrorists. Under such circumstances, a high level of personal and collective emotional stability and stress handling capability is required by the troops operating in counter-insurgency environment. In an ambiguous and in an uncertain environment, particularly at night, identification of insurgents and civilians does pose a major problem, resulting in casualties to civilians. "In extreme instances, frustration arising from the identification problem can result in counter-insurgency troops committing excesses, such as what happened at My Lai, Vietnam, in 1968, at Haditha, Iraq, in 2005, or at Accomarca, Peru, in 1985."[10] Having known the tactics of the Naxals, in the Indian context, we have to devise ways and means to prevent loss of civilian lives, particularly at night and in the hours of poor visibility. It means the troops must be provided illumination facilities and be equipped with modern night vision surveillance devices, which can distinguish a person holding a weapon from the unarmed men and women, as also their movement profile to distinguish hostile actions. UAVs could provide some information, but it has to be interpreted with great care. In addition, SOPs need to be formulated covering various sensitive contingencies that involve civilians. The troops have to be mentally conditioned and psychologically indoctrinated for situations in counter-insurgency operations, for which there is no alternative to structured "quality training".

Strategic Options for Naxalites

Having seen the strategy and tactics of the Naxals, it is assessed that they could have the following strategic options[11] in the future:

- **Option I:** Raise the ante, go for more spectacular offensive activities in the critically and moderately affected areas, and progressively expand to urban and semi-urban areas. Also, take actions to bridge the 'strategic gap' between the northern and southern areas of Naxal operations.[12] Refer "Major Naxal related incidents" at Appendix C.
- **Option II:** Lower the ante with intermittent attacks, until forced by the SF to react. Utilize the time to rest, refit, recoup and reorganize the party, including establishing linkages with the militants of the Northeast and seeking support of the external powers. Simultaneously, organize recruitment of fresh cadres.
- **Option III:** It is a multi-pronged approach to emerge stronger.
  - To work towards widening the mass base to other parts of the country, more importantly to the northeast, other strategic urban areas and industrial hubs; and hence spread the Naxal ideology nationwide. While doing this, they would attempt to keep the pressure on police forces, relieve pressure on their traditional strongholds, but would ensure that it is below the threshold of armed forces employment.
  - Selectively allow pro-naxal candidates to participate in democratic process and influence the polity in their favour.
  - Reach out to 'sympathetic' external powers to get support in propagating their ideology, funding of activities, provisioning of arms and equipment for the PLGA, to subsequently transform into the PLA.
  - While seeking support in global forums for their cause to gain greater visibility, progressively expand into semi-urban and urban areas. (Over the last two decades, urban centers have already borne the brunt of numerous terror attacks in India.)

- **Option IV:** It may change the thrust of the insurgency in a different direction.
  - On suffering reverses with the SF and unable to sustain operations, some factions of the Naxals could break up into smaller but more violent insurgent-cum-terrorist organizations in select base areas (areas which are secure and the Naxals still enjoy the popular support), to continue with criminal activities, extortion, drug trade, to make easy money.
  - Simultaneously, a few hard-core ideologues may continue to hold certain islands of resistance to keep the movement alive, both in the rural and urban areas.

Evaluation of options

Though the Naxals have a plethora of options before them to carry on with their revolution, they are severely limited by their present organizational strength, lack of charismatic and popular leader, the actions being undertaken by the government, at both the central and the state levels, and poor support to the cause by the urban middle class.

- **Option I:** This would require a strong and highly trained armed force having a distinctly stable and professional command and control structure with the right amount of financial muscle, firepower, intelligence, communication and logistics backup. This is not available to the PLGA in 2012-2013. They have suffered huge set back in losing a large number of their leaders – either killed in operations or arrested by the police. In addition, there are differences on ideological-cum-leadership issues, due to which the Naxals are on their back foot. Coupled with the proactive stance of the government at present, it is unlikely that they would be able to take this option in the near future.
- **Option II:** To keep the masses appeased with their revolutionary ideas and not lose momentum, this option, as the only option in isolation, is not likely to be exercised in the present circumstances. However, it may be used region wise, based on casualties suffered by the Naxals in prolonged operations, poor state of arms and ammunition, low morale; so as to rest, recoup, recruit fresh members, train, and manage financial support for continuing violence at an opportune moment. This period may also be utilized to establish rapport with the local population in new areas, to seek secure bases and external support. On balance, it may also form part of a combination with other options.
- **Option III:** This is the most likely option (despite certain recent

reverses), which is already being played by the Naxals, with minor variations.

- Being acutely aware of their weaknesses, the Naxals are likely to take up this path to allow it a greater degree of ideological flexibility and operational freedom.
- Though the Naxals are averse to participating in the election process as a result of their rejection of the parliamentary system, they may resort to fielding pro-naxal candidates, to gain entry into the national or state level polity with a view to either subvert the system or to influence key policies at the appropriate levels. This option again is not likely to be exercised as a standalone method since it reverses their basic stance of resorting to armed struggle to seize political power.
- The Indian Republic is a strong and vibrant democracy with one of the fastest growing economies in the world. It has highly capable and apolitical armed forces and central police forces, which have repeatedly proved themselves to the task of countering both internal and external threats. In such a scenario, it would not be possible for the Naxals to exhaust the state – even partially – through armed struggle on its own without the tacit support of external powers that see us as their adversary. Though at present, there is no concrete evidence of any institutionalized direct support from external forces as is the case with J&K or the North East, the Naxals have established links with a large number of militant organizations, both within and outside the country. It would be naïve on our part to underestimate the analytical prowess of our adversaries in realizing the potency of Naxalism as a weapon against the nation state. Therefore, a natural course of action for the Naxal leadership will be to look outside the boundaries of the countries for support of all forms, to further strengthen and sustain their revolution.
- Economic growth brings about rapid urbanization; the same is true of India as well. The Naxals have perhaps understood that the real power of the state, therefore, lies in the urban areas/industrial hubs, and so does the discontent, due to lack of foresight and planning to cater for such high trajectory growth. It has resulted in a severe lack of basic infrastructure and amenities in these areas. Therefore, they are likely to adopt the option of progressively expanding into semi-urban/urban areas/industrial hubs to gain momentum for their revolution, as these areas may not only provide them with the mass base, but may also provide the logistics and financial support. They

are making efforts to penetrate some of the industrial areas around Dhanbad, Bokaro, and Rourkela in Jharkhand and Odisha respectively, around National Capital Region (NCR) and in the western corridor along Pune-Nashik-Surat. The front organizations have been espousing their cause from the urban and semi-urban areas. Attacks on soft targets including political leaders may increase in the future.

- **Option IV:** This option could be exercised when the Naxals have suffered huge losses, and they are not getting adequate volunteer recruits into their cadres. They could turn on to criminal-cum-terrorist activities, kidnapping of prominent officials, and drug trade for their survival. However, the selected areas could be mining-cum-industrial areas close to the bi-junctions and the tri-junctions of the affected states. According to a study, some of top guerrilla/terrorist groups in the world have transformed into transnational criminal organizations, who were more interested in profits than politics. It gives examples of such groups of Kosovo, Colombia, Spain, Sri Lanka, Turkey, and Lebanon, who were engaged in narcotics and drug trafficking and other crimes to pursue their agendas.[13]

Future Scenario

Considering the SWOT analysis, the present scenario, and the direction in which the revolution of the Naxals is heading, it is assessed that the Naxals may adopt any one or a combination of the various options, in the immediate future, and in the long term.

- **For period 2013 to 2020:** The central and state governments are alive to the problem, because of which a number of socio-economic-security schemes and reforms have been planned, and resources allocated. So far, the results are not commensurate with the resources made available, due to a number of reasons. It is optimistically assumed that there will be progressive improvement in the situation in rural areas in the future. However, pro-active measures to prevent spread of Naxalism to urban areas and the industrial hubs have not been initiated with the seriousness they deserve. Therefore, the options available to the Naxals, in the order of priority, could be Option III and Option II. The priorities could change depending on the prevailing ground situation. This combination would allow them to enhance their mass base, financial and intellectual base, get moral and material support from sympathetic external powers, progressively make inroads into semi urban/urban areas/industrial hubs, and keep the CAPF and the state police forces engaged. It would provide them the time to improve their combat capability – by keeping the threshold of violence under a limit – thereby, preventing deployment of the armed forces (the army in particular). The Naxals would wait for the correct opportunity (political instability/overwhelming mass support) to undertake offensive actions, and penetrate the urban areas or negotiate and participate in the democratic process. The government would do well to take pro-active measures and remain extra vigilant during the run up to the general elections in 2014, to prevent escalation of Naxal violence, failing which rebels could start re-emerging stronger. The Naxals are aware that the "General Elections of 2014" would give them adequate opportunities to increase their visibility, at both national and international levels. However, with the shrinking 'traditional strong hold areas' and elimination of Naxal leaders, we could expect a progressive increase in surrenders by the rebels, to join the main stream. The government should be fully prepared to provide them security and an acceptable resettlement package. Genuine concern to resettle them would help restore the confidence of the local population and investors at large.

- **Period 2020 and beyond:** It is difficult to crystal gaze beyond 2020 with much accuracy, due to rapid changes in the environment. However, the situation would clearly depend on the success achieved by the government and all other stakeholders upto 2020. It is quite likely that the results of the government's initiatives would be visible by about 2020. Therefore, initially, it could be Option II, but subsequently, Option IV may be predominant. Option IV is already in place, in some form or the other, because the rebels are indulging in organized crime, extortion and acts of terrorism in the guise of Naxalism. With synergized application of all elements of national power for the next 8 to 10 years, the Naxals may be left only with one option, i.e. Option IV, accompanied with the Naxals selectively accepting the democratic process to contest in elections. A few hard-core ideologues may continue to hold certain islands of resistance to keep the movement alive, both in the rural and urban areas. If suitable pro-active actions are not taken, urban areas may witness an increase in activities of the Naxals – with vastly different manifestations in comparison to the rural insurgency.

Notes

1. The joint central committee of the PWG and MCCI, before their final merger in September 2004, conceived the document titled "Strategy and Tactics of the Indian Revolution (STIR)". Five draft documents were prepared after a series of intense discussions over a long period.
2. Parts of the strategic essay, by V.K. Ahluwalia, "Strategy and Tactics of the Indian Maoists: An Analysis", Strategic Analysis, IDSA, September- October 2012, have been cited in this book.

3. Jairam Ramesh, "Reds Call Shots in Liberated Zones", *The Times of India*, December, 2011. The minister in his address to the media while on a trip to review projects in Saranda (West Singhbhum District) remarked that there are zones in west Jharkhand and south Chhattisgarh where the writ of the state does not run. "In the heart of the country, these two places are liberated zones. Our officers – be it deputy commissioners, block development officers or anganwadi workers and health employees – don't venture into these places of Jharkhand and Chhattisgarh. The public distribution system is not working", said the rural development minister.
4. Funds such as special infrastructure scheme(SIS), security-related expenditure (SRE), central assistance to civilian victims, integrated action plan (IAP), road requirement plan, fortified police stations scheme, civic action programs, backward regions grant funds (BRGF), and hostel and ashram fund have been made available.
The Annual Report 2010-11, Ministry of Tribal Affairs, GoI, gives details of the restructured 20 points programme 2006, programmes for development of 'particularly vulnerable tribal groups', vocational skills training and allotment of funds (Annexures 6D, 7A, 11A,12A).
5. Essential features of the three strategic stages have been covered in Chapter 3. However, as the insurgents grow in strength, they aim to transform their forces to regular armies, capable of fighting the regular forces of the government in conventional battles. A few cases in point are Mao's fight against the nationalist forces (KMT) in China, Ho Chi Minh and his forces against the French (defeat of the French forces at Dien Bien Phu is well known), and later against the Americans in Vietnam. Even LTTE under Prabhakaran had created a powerful force to fight against the Sri Lankan regular forces, though the end results in this case were different.
6. Giridhar Nayak, national dialogue, "The Naxalism Problem, Issues, Challenges and Alternative Approaches", organised by the Institute of Peace and Conflict Studies (IPCS), March 2012.
7. While terming terrorism as a negative weapon, Che Guevara had said that it (terrorism) could turn people against the revolutionary movement itself.
8. Mohua Chatterjee, "Reds will Repeat Tactics of using Jawans Bodies as Booby-Traps", *Times of India*, February 11, 2013.
9. Sandeep Joshi, "Abandon Operations if Maoists Use Human Shields, Security Forces Told", *The Hindu*, July 07, 2012.
10. Joe Quinn, Mario A. Fumerton, "Counterinsurgency from Below: The Afghan Local Police in Theoretical and Comparative Perspective", November 2010.
11. The strategic options have been discussed to sensitize the policy makers, to take appropriate pro-active measures to resolve the conflict.
12. The northern areas refer to Bihar, Jharkhand, south western West Bengal, northern Odisha, Eastern UP and adjoining eastern MP. The southern areas comprise Chhattisgarh, southern and western Odisha, eastern fringes of Maharashtra, northern Andhra Pradesh.There is a wide strategic gap between the two areas of Naxal operations.
13. For more details, Chris Dishman, "Terrorism, Crime, and Transformation", Studies in Conflict & Terrorism, U.S. Commission on National Security, Arlington, Virginia, USA.

Chapter 7

Strategy for Conflict Resolution

"All men can see these tactics whereby I conquer, but what none can see is the strategy out of which victory is evolved."

– Sun Tzu[1]

The aim of this chapter is to briefly analyze LWE against the backdrop of the bigger picture – broad security scenario, threats to India's security, and the processes involved to formulate a national security strategy. Whenever we discuss about strategy, one of the most prominent name that comes to mind is the famous military strategist, the 5th century BC general, Sun Tzu, who said, '*...to fight and conquer in all your battles is not supreme excellence; supreme excellence consists of breaking the enemy's resistance without fighting.*' The ultimate aim should, therefore, be to achieve a strategic situation that gives an overwhelming advantage over the opponent or his designs. The concept is equally true for the counter-insurgency campaigns, albeit with certain modifications. Strategy is derived from the Greek word *strategia,* meaning the "office of general, command, general ship," which in essence suggests that a general sees the bigger picture at the theatre level. He makes an overall plan to achieve his strategic goals and objectives to achieve a decisive victory; i.e., finally win the campaign or the war. To defeat the "Naxal Challenge," it would be all about gaining a position of advantage over the insurgents by correctly applying country's resources and strengths to exploit their weaknesses, and to develop the affected regions.

As there is always an element of uncertainty about the future of complex conflicts like Naxalism, strategy is more about a set of strategic choices than adhering to a fixed plan. Therefore, strategy aims to achieve a pre-selected goal or objective of immense significance, by optimum marshalling and employment of all available resources. To do so, there is a requirement to assess the overall situation and to analyze various strategic options. At the national level, strategy is the art of controlling and utilizing the resources of a nation.[2] Therefore, politico-socio-economic objectives and scarce national resources are allocated according to the considered priorities given in the national strategy/plan. It should seek to shape the environment, by being pro-active. In India, we are generally known to be reactive in our approach – the buzz word is 'crisis management.' As a nation, we should have appreciated the challenges posed by the Naxals almost three decades ago – in early 1980s – to take suitable pro-active measures to resolve the conflict.

National strategy should be derived from the end state that a nation is trying to achieve, by choosing the most suitable course of action. National strategy consists of the sub-strategies: political, economic, social, perception management, environmental, cultural and security. While constructing these sub-strategies, the risk factors must be taken into account to bridge the gap between the end state and the means-cum-resources available to implement the plans. Professor Richard Yarger provides a succinct summary of the US Army's preferred strategic framework that "strategy is all about how (ways or concepts) leaders will use the power (means or resources) available to the state to exercise control over sets of circumstances and geographic locations to achieve objectives (ends) that support state interests." Finkelstein sums up with an equation: Strategy = Ends + Ways + Means.[3] To put it simply, strategy is the matching of means to ends by particular ways. As such, good strategy is fundamentally comprehensive. The strategist must have a wide-ranging vision of what else is happening in the environment, and a higher-resolution grasp of the potential interconnected "ripple" effects of various policy choices.[4]

Conflict Resolution

Conceptually, conflict resolution refers to finding ways, methods, and processes with a view to facilitate peaceful ending of a conflict. Therefore, a wide range of methods and processes are available for addressing a conflict, including but not limited to dialogue, negotiation, mediation, confidence building and diplomacy. Conflict resolution, in the initial stages, may involve conflict management, in which two or more parties continue the conflict, but adopt less-than-severe violence or extreme tactics, as a result that they reach a conciliatory agreement on a few contentious issues. Often, even the most professional armies of the world recommend that while commencing an offensive operation against a well-prepared enemy, the selection of the initial objective to capture should be such that it guarantees 100% success. There is a rationale behind this – it has a great effect on the morale of own troops to maintain the tempo of operations thereafter. Simultaneously, initial adverse effects in operations weigh heavy on the minds of enemy commanders and troops alike. In our context, Naxals are not our enemies – they are the citizens of the country. Therefore, the endeavor should be to "first resolve the less contentious issues that are achievable in a shorter period". In this case, it would be a win-win situation for both the parties, i.e. insurgents and counter-insurgents. If the main cause of the conflict is addressed either partially or fully, then the conflict is likely to be resolved, but may take more time to achieve the desired end state.

Conflict resolution, therefore, begins with comprehension of the problem: what does it involve, identification of the key strategic challenges, and formulation of a national strategy to combat Naxalism. The observations of Dr. Mockaitis are apt, "The insurgencies do not conclude with a clear cut victory by any one side."[5] Going by the lessons of some of the successful counter-insurgency campaigns, in the contemporary times, we should not expect insurgencies to end in a clear and decisive manner. The pockets of resistance from the hard-core ideologues and the fear of insurgency resurfacing cannot be ruled out. In Afghanistan, the US may actually withdraw bulk of its forces by 2014, as per their announced plan, yet the conflict may remain far from being managed for a smooth transition. Having faded away in 2002-03, the Taliban have re-emerged as a reckonable force. Resultantly, there has been a progressive increase in the casualties of the Afghan National Security Forces, due to violence since 2012. Besides Afghanistan, the Taliban will pose a serious regional security threat to the neighboring countries. A number of questions are being raised about the future of Afghanistan, after 2014. While India has successfully resolved the insurgencies in Mizoram and Punjab, it could only control it to an acceptable level in Andhra Pradesh and Tripura.

Conflict resolution process

Naxalism is a multi-faceted problem of national dimension and needs to be resolved through strategic orientation at the apex level of governance. Strategic orientation begins with the acceptance of the necessity for such a focus, as also the grave consequences of the lack of it. To counter the Naxals efficiently and effectively, there is a need to design the grand strategy for conflict resolution incorporating all the strengths of strategic vision, strategic leadership and strategic thinking. There are distinctive but overlapping phases in the process of resolution of conflict of such a magnitude. The phases must be designed to manage the conflict, make the environment secure, restore the faith of the people and then move on to conflict resolution. Though, classically the phases need to be applied sequentially, the phases may overlap or be addressed in a non-linear manner, depending upon the conflict specific scenario. These phases should concurrently be supported by a series of other organized activities aimed at strengthening the demoralized population and society, and weakening the Naxals.

The important components and the steps involved in resolving an internal armed conflict like Naxalism, are as follows:

- Assessment of overall situation to understand and assimilate the geo-strategic environment, economic environment, threats, challenges, envisaged scenario 2020 and beyond, and on-ground translation of national goals and objectives.
- Establishing strategic intent, national aims and interests, and national security objectives.
- Analysis of Naxals and own strategic options, listing them in the order of priority and evaluating the best course of action available to the government in light of the most dangerous course adopted by the Naxals.
- Formulation of counter-Naxal strategy, by migrating through the steps such as review of the key strategic challenges, followed by evolution of strategies. This part has two distinct aspects; i.e. first, formulation of the grand strategy, and second, formulation of sub-strategies that spell out the specific tasks to various elements of national power like the ministries, different components of central and state governments, public and private institutions, industry, NGOs, CAPF and the military. At present, there is no such known formal document to spell out the responsibilities, so that each organization can prepare itself for the assigned tasks.
- Implementation of strategies by considering the tangible as well as intangible measures such as implementation of security-cum-development action plans, perception management, resource allocation, psychological impact, and interventions for mid-course corrections.
- Evaluation of strategies and control mechanism is a must for the government to retain the initiative, and to ensure isolation of the Naxals. This could be best done by setting the benchmarks for measurement of performances. Implementation of plans on ground – in the Naxal-affected states – remain the biggest challenge.

National Vision

National vision foresees the overall aspirations of its people and the nation in a long-term perspective. Essentially, a vision must be forward looking, holistic, and balanced, reflecting and reconciling the multiplicity of interests and challenges existing in any society. A vision is multi-faceted process building on participation and active commitment of leading stakeholders.[6] The vision must be enduring and credible[7]; it must be audacious yet attainable. Before looking at the scope of the vision, there is definite requirement to know the overall situation and the challenges involved in the long term. The scope of national vision would be to attain security to include physical, political, social, economic, environmental, psychological, and cultural security against both internal and external threats. This would entail well being of citizens, and elimination of all forms of vulnerabilities and discrimination; thereby creating an environment where the nation prospers through the development. It must provide adequate employment opportunities, and promote awareness of our rich spiritual and cultural heritage. This would enable our country to take advantage of the youth bulge and unprecedented opportunities being presented to it by globalization, to ultimately realize its full potential of development.

Broadly, national core values, national aim, national interests, and national objectives are the "ends" that have to be achieved; the "means" is the national power at the disposal of a nation. Preamble of Constitution of India – most meaningfully constructed – would be the basis of our national core values. Core values provide the basis for a nation's existence. Ahimsa (non-violence), sovereignty in all aspects, democracy to flourish, secularism, peace and harmony with in, with neighbors and with rest of the world, care for environment, Athithi Devo Bhava (belief that guest is like a god) and Vasudhaiv Kutumbakam (whole world is a single family) are recommended to be listed as national core values.

National aim emerges from the core values. It is focused at achieving and safeguarding the core values, retaining and reinforcing the basic structure of polity and governance, ensuring territorial integrity, promoting the social, economic, technological, cultural and military strengths under the prevailing regional and global strategic scenario. A recommended national aim could be as follows:

> *India to emerge as a strong united democratic nation, politically stable, with buoyant economy and resolute social, cultural, technological and military strength, and a secure internal and external environment, developing as a major power in Asia and the world; and enjoying a place of power and pride in the emerging world order of the 21st Century.*

National interests are those "key areas" of "national endeavors" that are aimed at achieving national aim and ultimately realizing the national vision. Rukmani Gupta, while discussing China's national interests, sub divides them into two parts as "core interests" and "national interests". She explains the core interests as, "A clear expansion of core national interests is seen as part of a policy from which there can be no retreat, or even a policy of 'strategic offensive' by some scholars in China."[8]

On national interests, she says, "Most Chinese scholars and leaders refer to national interest as comprising of political, economic, security and, more recently, cultural interests."[9] The recommended national interests of India could be national sovereignty, unity and integrity of the country, democratic and secular polity, economic development and inclusive growth, energy security, and a secure internal and external environment. It would also include social and economic justice, amicable neighborhood and favorable world order, and preservation as well as promotion of national core values.

National security

National security is the ability of a nation to protect and promote its national values, pursue its national interests and aspirations under all conditions and threats. Threats to national security may affect any aspect of a nation's life, ranging from its territorial integrity and internal cohesion to its economy, political structures and institutions, diplomacy, national leadership, national character, morale, and so on. The armed forces and the CAPF of India have a vital role to play in addressing some of these threats. As per Dr. Manmohan Singh's speech at the IDSA from Indian perspective, "*Our security policy in the emerging global order must be based on three pillars. First, strengthen India economically. Second, to have adequate defense capability making optimal use of modern science and technology.... Finally, develop partnerships in the strategic, economic and technological spheres, to enlarge our policy choices and developmental options.*"[10]

Security Scenario 2020

At the highest level, national interests consist of the underpinnings for sound grand strategy. The only vital national security interest is survival of the state with an acceptable degree of independence, ensuring that the territorial integrity, traditional life styles, fundamental institutions, values and honor are intact.

The geo-political-strategic-economic factors are likely to influence the security environment in the scenario 2020 and beyond. The future world order is likely to be bi-polar, followed by a polycentric configuration with its center of gravity shifting increasingly to Asia, which will include seven out of the ten largest economies and six nuclear weapon states. Therefore, 21st century will be the 'Century of Asia' for a number of reasons. Lately, the American foreign policy has articulated their grand strategy, reiterating their focus on "Asia Pivot". In his first visit after being elected for the second term in November 2012, President Obama visited three countries of South East Asia, including Myanmar. It does reiterate the resolve of the US to look at this region even more seriously.

Unfettered pace and magnitude of economic growth and military strength of China have already challenged the existing geo-political arrangements, and the balance of power in the world. China's modernization of her armed forces, and development of infrastructure in the Tibet and Xinjian, in terms of roads, rail, airfields, logistics bases, power and telecommunications, have added another dimension to the security concerns of India.[11] China's road and rail links with Pakistan, Nepal and Myanmar, along with her policy of "String of Pearls" may pose a serious challenge to India's security, unless adequate measures are taken to resolve the boundary dispute in an amicable manner, and simultaneously strengthen and modernize her armed forces. A large number of countries are increasing their defence expenditures in Asia to improve their conventional and non-conventional weapon capabilities. Coupled with this, they are indulging in militarization and development of offensive capabilities in nuclear, space, cyber, and information warfare domains. These are likely to result in clash of interests, while new geo-strategic alignments would continue to take place.

Geo-politically, while India's territorial disputes with the neighboring countries are likely to persist, the region will continue to remain unstable due to fragile polity, conflicts and high intensity of violence. At the same time, India's location in the "Arc of Instability" increases the non-conventional threats such as proxy war, insurgency, terrorism, illegal migration, drug trafficking, demographic changes due to migration, ethnic-cum-religious conflicts, fake currency, and piracy in the high seas and so on. Religious extremism coupled with radical politics will continue to complicate the internal security scenario in the sub - continent. Another significant factor is the youth bulge. With a huge youth bulge in India (460 million aged between 13 and 35 years),[12] high unemployment, hyper-urbanization, along with other contributory factors, it continues to remain at a high risk of conflict.

Rising dependence on energy imports will make India increasingly vulnerable economically, as well as diplomatically. The world is likely to see an increase in conflict due to scarcity of resources – energy, water, minerals, and food – and intense competition to get them. Indian Ocean adds another dimension: its geo-strategic importance and vast economic wealth lends itself to be a source of conflict. In addition, there will be an increasing use of "soft power" as a strategic tool in the future. The revolutions of rising expectations will continue to persist. Therefore, non-conventional security threats will pose the biggest challenge in the future. Given the current trend, public opinion – both domestic and international, and the media will be increasingly important forces in international affairs.

National security interests

India's national security objectives are derived from the need to protect her national security interests, and those core values whose violation would have adverse implications for our sovereignty and national security. Some of the broad recommended national security objectives could be the following:

- Defense of national territory over land, sea, air, and space, encompassing among others, the inviolability of our land borders, island territories, offshore assets, and maritime trade routes.
- To secure an internal environment, whereby our nation state is secured against any threat to its unity, integrity, or progress on the basis of religion, language, ethnicity, or socio-economic conflicts.
- To promote harmonious relationships with countries in our neighborhood, and be able to exercise a correct degree of influence, in tune with our national interests.
- To secure our environment from threats of cyber crimes, social web sites, and networks, which instigate internal disorders.
- To be able to effectively contribute towards regional and international peace and stability, and possess an effective capability to assist/ prevent destabilization of our immediate neighborhood, that could have adverse security implications for the country.

Formulation of Strategy

Considering India's rapid growth, it is viewed upon by the world as an important stabilizing factor in the envisaged balance of power. For India, this implies that while maintaining productive relationships with existing power centers of the world, it will have to capitalize on opportunities to build on its strengths, and minimize its vulnerabilities. India has to maintain the strategic flexibility and walk a pragmatic path in the new world order. Thus, there is an urgent need to comprehend the changing security dynamics of the country, and to construct a national strategy for conflict resolution.

Comprehensive national plan (CNP)

> *The reason most people never reach their goals is that they don't define them, or ever seriously consider them as believable or achievable. Winners can tell you where they are going, what they plan to do along the way, and who will be sharing the adventure with them.*
>
> – Denis E. Waitley
> (*American motivational speaker and writer*)

The process commences with the formulation of the grand strategy and sub-strategies. Thereafter, the sub- strategies become the start point for various ministries and departments to put together their policies for immediate, medium and long-term efforts, contributing to the achievement of national goals and objectives. While preparing the plans, there is a need to analyze the cross-term effects on the plans of other stakeholders. These plans must then be presented and discussed in detail at the apex level by the designated coordination committee. The coordinated plan would then be released as the CNP.

To ensure implementation of plans on the ground, two important principles should be given due consideration. First, while strategy and policy formulation should be centralized, execution of the plans needs to be decentralized to provide necessary authority and flexibility to functionaries on the ground, albeit with certain checks and balances. Second, the strategy and CNP, duly prioritized, should essentially include "timelines for various phases and accountability factors". Thereafter, a firm hand would be required to deal with the defaulters.

Notes

1. Sun Tzu, Chapter 6, "The Art of War". Sun Tzu, 5th century BC, was a Chinese general, military strategist and an author.
2. Edward Mead Earl. *Makers of Modern Strategy: Military Thought from Machiavelli to Hitler* (New Delhi: Natraj Publishers).
3. David M. Finkelstein, "China's National Military Strategy", Accessed on March 12, 2013, http://www.rand.org/content/dam/rand/pubs/conf_proceedings/CF145/CF145.chap7.pdf, "The U.S. Army War College utilizes a simple but powerful formula to express what a strategy is and what its critical component parts consist of: Strategy = Ends + Ways + Means." (It refers to goals and objectives + methods + resources available, to be utilized.)
4. Douglas Borer, Michael Freeman, and Steve Twing, "Strategy," In *Gangs and Guerilla: Ideas from Counterinsurgency and Counterterrorism*, eds. Michael Freeman and Hy Rothstein (California, US: Naval Postgraduate School, 2011).
5. Thomas R. Mockaitis, "Resolving Insurgencies", Strategic Studies Institute (SSI), June 17, 2011.
6. "National Vision Matters: Lessons of Success", worldbank.org/cdf, accessed Oct. 21, 2012, http://www.idea.int/publications/nvm/upload/nationalvisionsmatter_english.pdf. (It also mentions that the national vision is the key to bridge the gap between the short term and long term.)
7. As elucidated by the book on the Strategic Management Process published by the College of Defence Management, the vision must endure changes in government and leadership, and to be credible it must have the perception of high probability of success. Accessed October 31, 2012, http://www.managementstudyguide.com/strategic-management-process.htm.
8. Rukmani Gupta, "China's National Interests: Exploring the Domestic Discourse", *Strategic Analysis* 36 (September–October 2012): 811.

9. Ibid., 806.
10. Prime Minister's address on the 40th Anniversary of IDSA, accessed on January 12, 2013, http://pib.nic.in/newsite/erelease.aspx?relid=13232.
11. The PLA is in the process of major transformation of their armed forces, a process that had commenced with the four modernizations in 1979 and it is expected to complete by 2020–2025. There has been a persistent increase in her defense budget every year. It has been steadily building up infrastructure in Tibet Autonomous Region (TAR). It has also been carrying out capacity building of the Pakistani forces as a counterweight to India. As per reports, China has a fairly large presence of its troops/personnel in Pakistan Occupied Kashmir (POK) in general area of Gilgit and Skardu, which is detrimental to overall security interests of India. Over 600 border transgressions by China have reportedly taken place along the 4057 km long LAC in the past three years, with a relatively deep incursion in Depsang Bulge area – well planned and coordinated – in mid April, 2013. However, the tension was diffused by diplomatic means. On the other hand, Pakistan, as a part of its foreign policy, has been supporting insurgencies/proxy war in India since independence in 1947. This coupled with rise of religious fundamentalism and instability in India's neighborhood has only added to our external and internal threats. The terrorist attacks in the country have exposed the vulnerability of our vast and open borders /coastline to sub-conventional threats from external sources.
12. Purie Aroon, Editor's page, *Indian Today*, October, 2011. (Youth bulge issues have been covered in detail earlier.)

Chapter 8

Circles of Concern – Strategic Challenges

Strategic planning is worthless – unless there is first a strategic vision.
– John Naisbitt

Protracted involvement with the conflict-ridden regions such as J&K, northeastern states, and the LWE-affected states in general, and intimate interaction with the functionaries at the senior and the grass roots during my visits to Chhattisgarh, Jharkhand, Odisha, Bihar and Madhya Pradesh, made it possible for me to assess the key strategic challenges for conflict resolution. Given the progressive increase in the spatial spread, casualties, and destruction of infrastructure in the Naxal affected areas, the statistics are too large to be ignored by anyone. Instead, it warrants a serious look. Thomas Jefferson, the American founding father and principal author of the United States Declaration of Independence (1776), said, "*The care of human life and happiness, and not their destruction, is the first and only legitimate object of good government.*" The governments, both at the center and in the states, have a great role to ensure the safety and security of their people. A brief examination of the key strategic challenges faced by other counter-insurgency campaigns would facilitate better understanding of the problem.

Experience of other counter-insurgency campaigns

Purely from the counter-insurgency strategy point of view, it would be worthwhile to briefly see the US experience in Afghanistan and Iraq. The "US counter-insurgency guide" identified three components of an effective counter-insurgency (COIN) campaign: security, economic development and information operations. These three components had to be integrated through a political strategy providing a "framework of political reconciliation, genuine reforms, popular mobilization and governmental capacity building around which all other programs and activities are organized."[1] Though on the face of it, the three components looked impressive, their effective implementation on the ground to reach the grass roots remained a million-dollar question. Sure enough, it did not achieve the desired results within the stipulated period!

With huge experience of quelling insurgencies in Malaya (present Malaysia), Kenya, Muscat, Oman and Cyprus, the Great Britain had adopted the "political/military strategy"[2] for resolution of the conflict in Northern Ireland. It required coordination among the governmental, judicial, economic, social, and psychological agencies to contain and isolate identifiable resistance. In Philippines, the lack of continuity in the government's counter insurgency policies, which tended to change along with the country's leadership, had also become an obstacle in the total elimination of rebel groups.[3] The state of Jharkhand – critically affected by Naxalism – has had eight governments in the last 12 years. Such frequent changes of governments and key appointments dealing with internal security – at both the center and the states – do affect the country's focus in facing the sub-conventional threats, including Naxalism. It continues to remain one of the functional challenges.

Key Strategic Challenges

Human Dimension: Casualties, Trauma, and Mental Pressures

Since "support of the people" is central to winning a counter-insurgency campaign, a brief overview of the human dimension – with the impact of an insecure and uncertain environment – is vital to understand the strategic challenges. This part of human dimension relates to two important facets: first, the trail of death, destruction, and sufferings over the years; and second, the trauma and mental pressures on the affected population due to an uncertain, insecure, and volatile environment. According to the MHA report, the Naxals have killed 5,467 civilians from 2001 to 2011. Even such large numbers of deaths have not really made a meaningful impact on our national conscience. This is because the targets are not high profile and the areas in question do not attract the media focus. Thus, for lack of the limelight, most of them are forgotten and deprived of any sort of compensation for the loss of life and property. Despite India being a vibrant democracy, experiencing rapid social, political, and economic changes, major portion of the populace in the "critically Naxal-affected regions" is still living in a state of helplessness. When the issues at stake are so basic and the question is of future development of the society, expression of genuine concern through all means and actions of governance become primary steps to conflict resolution. The national strategy must first aim to secure the environment, and bridge the trust deficit by exhibiting genuine concern for the poor people. The positive sentiment generated could then provide the start point to end the cycle of violence and counter-violence brought about by the ongoing conflict. Irrespective of the political dispensation, people would embrace peace, if offered through reliable government hands.

Supported by convincing statistical data, Goepner argues that as a state becomes increasingly weak and failed, the likelihood of insurgency increases. As insurgencies and the associated trauma intensify, the rate of mental disorder among the population will also increase.[4] There are a large number of examples in the world, where the population has suffered due to political violence, insurgencies, and conflicts due to regional and ethnic discrimination. The exposure to such intense violence and the consequent sufferings normally result in displacement of people, which disrupts the social and economic lives of the affected people. The internal armed conflicts in Nepal, Afghanistan, Pakistan, Sri Lanka, Myanmar and India, over the past few decades, have brought adverse pressures on the social, economic, psychological, and mental lives of the population. Olugbile and Coker have brought out that the Palestinian children have been found to show evidence of increased aggression, and the survivors of the war in northern Kosovo showed evidence of physical and psychological impairment. The victims and survivors of massive traumatic events suffer mental health consequences.[5]

While no such "known detailed analysis" pertaining to the impact of prolonged insurgencies on the local population has been undertaken in India, prima facie, the rationale given is valid and merits due attention. In a prolonged conflict, the local population is the worst sufferer as they are caught between the insurgents and the counter-insurgents. Over and above, the direct impact of insurgency such as human security, trauma and mental pressures, the indirect effects such as loss of opportunities and wiping out of dreams and aspirations of generations, multiplies the sufferings. It is undisputed that the people in India too have suffered in the northeastern states, J&K, and in the other areas affected by the LWE. All the stakeholders have to understand the impact of such adverse effects on the affected population. Therefore, the human dimension remains the most important factor in a counter-insurgency campaign. In India, post-traumatic-stress counseling for people of the affected regions is unheard of. An intense insurgency environment, such as the one prevailing in the Naxal-affected states, is characterized by uncertain, volatile, and complex conditions at the grassroots level. Trauma and mental pressures equally affect not only the local population, but also the personnel of the SF (counter-insurgents). Due to cumulative effect of factors like command and control, leadership, changing social milieu, stress of uncertain and complex operational insurgency environment, there are numerous cases of troops indulging in cases of suicides and fratricides the world over: Afghanistan,[6] J&K, northeastern and LWE-affected states in India.[7] To take corrective measures, it would be appropriate to analyze the overall impact of an insurgency (LWE) environment on the mental and psychological pressures on the local population, the SF, and the insurgents.

Trust deficit

Insurgency is a result of accumulation of a large number of grievances. Until such time these genuine grievances are addressed and the faith of the population in the legislature, judiciary, and the executive is restored, the problem cannot be effectively solved. There is a need to carry out "Human Terrain Mapping (HTM)" to know the local populace, their demographic profile and socio-economic-cultural aspirations, the affiliations and bonding among various groups, and their genuine difficulties. The data so collected merits a comprehensive analysis, data bank created, and disseminated at the appropriate levels for remedial actions, to build the trust with the people. Therefore, the national strategy must necessarily make the environment secure for the people, and address the trust deficit first. Trust deficit is also a direct consequence of governance deficit, which merits top priority.

Wide diversity

One of the biggest challenges to India's internal security is its wide ranging diversity in terms of its huge population base that is exploding day by day; varied demographic profile with a large number of religions, languages, dialects, castes, cultures, customs, and beliefs; and strong regional affiliations. Given India's pluralistic and secular structure, it has often witnessed a large number of inter-ethnic, inter-religion, and inter-regional tensions and conflicts. Perhaps, it was some of these diversities that led our ancestors to choose a federal system of governance. Though the concept of federal structure was correct in those times, today we face huge decision-making dilemmas due to coalition politics at the center and emergence of strong and influential regional parties at the state level. In addition, over the years, sub-conventional threats have increased manifold, some of which are instigated, overtly or covertly, by inimical organizations operating from India's neighborhood. Due to the country's diversity, one of the most important challenges could be her unity and integrity itself, for which the leaders must rise above petty partisan issues.

Political will and national consensus

Resolution of the conflict such as the LWE – involves many states, multiple agencies and multi-disciplinary initiatives – requires building the national consensus. Really speaking, political will and national consensus bear a close relationship between the two. Without political will and consensus, all endeavors would become non-starters. Hence, both these aspects have been discussed together. One of the biggest challenges facing our country to combat Naxalism is the lack of synergy at the apex level, lack of political will and resultantly lack of national consensus on the methodology of combating it. Besides the adverse effects of the multi-party coalitions at the center, this is partly a direct consequence of the federal structure in general and the center-state relations in India, which promulgates that the management of law and order is a state subject. The differences in interests, ideologies, political leanings and agendas between the center and the states have led to non-uniform policies like the conduct of anti-naxal operations, requirement of establishing unified control headquarters, surrender and rehabilitation policy, uniformity in the "hostage policy", implementation of land reforms and resettlement of displaced people. Disparities in implementation of even vital security, economic and social measures across the Naxal-affected states have resulted into an ambiguous approach towards resolving the conflict. It requires synergized effort and seamless coordination among various states to implement the multi-faceted programs, including security related initiatives. The states do not have adequate resources, the force structure, training and administrative infrastructure, requisite overall intelligence picture including at the international level; and the ability to coordinate various activities at the inter-state boundaries.

A recent case in point is the National Counter Terrorism Centre (NCTC), for which the government issued an executive order on February 3, 2012, to start the functioning of the NCTC. Several states opposed the move on the ground that it infringed on the rights of the states and the federal principle.[8] The states represented that they were not taken on board while taking decision on an important subject like NCTC. The objections of the states are justified, but there is lack of urgency to resolve the issue. India, which has been subjected to numerous terrorists' attacks over the years and continues to remain on the "hit list" of the organizations operating within the country and its neighborhood, there is no ambiguity about the definitive need to have an effective organization such as NCTC at the national level. To support the argument further, consequent to the execution of Mohammad Ajmal Kasab, the lone survivor of the terrorist squad responsible for the killing of 166 people in an attack on Mumbai on November 26, 2008, the terrorist organizations from Pakistan warned that they would strike in India to avenge his hanging by India. Similar threats were issued consequent to the execution of Afzal Guru – convict in the December 2001 attack on the Indian Parliament – on February 9, 2013. Individually, even the states understand that without a nodal agency, they will continue to suffer at the hands of terrorists, whose weapon of attack is 'speed, surprise, violence and publicity'. Notwithstanding the threats, the states saw it as a compromise with the edifice of their authority and sought to challenge the manner in which the entire effort was maneuvered. It is also true that a counter-terrorism strategy cannot succeed without close and continuous coordination between the center and the states.[9] Therefore, this impasse on issues such as NCTC must be resolved with a sense of urgency, in the interest of national security. The political complexities and the growing distrust between the center and the states do weaken our fight against terrorism and insurgency much to the delight of Naxals. The dictum, "a chain is as strong as its weakest link", is true of the center-states relationship. Given such constraints at the national level, achievement of a national consensus and formulation of national strategy are major challenges before the nation today. During the presidential election debate on October 16, 2012, President Obama stated that for him national security was not a "party political issue".[10] National security, therefore, must remain much above petty party politics, individual agendas or vote bank politics, lest we pay a heavy price at the end of the day.

Jal, Jangal, Jamin and Khanij (water, forest, land and minerals)

A number of core issues that have led to the growth of Naxalism have their roots in the discriminatory, outdated and poorly framed legislations like the ones on land reforms, land acquisition, resettlement and rehabilitation, mining and forests. The tribal groups have been demanding their rights on "Jal, Jangal, Jamin and Khanij" (water, forest, land and minerals). This fact has been known since decades, yet there has not been any appreciable urgency and effort to re-frame and introduce "pro-people and pro-poor" legislations, and to genuinely implement the existing ones on the ground, in letter and spirit. What is clearly visible is the lack of urgency to empower the exploited people, thereby denying them their right to survival with dignity.

Any serious commitment for resolution of the LWE hinges on the implementation of four most significant challenges, viz., legislation relating to land reforms, rights of tribal people over the forestland and its produce, rights of the local population on mining output, and resettlement of the displaced people. Enormity of impact of these aspects could be fathomed from the sheer number of lives affected. The figures of displaced people range from 55 million to 65 millions, of which only limited numbers have been resettled and rehabilitated. In fact, land and forest reforms affect the largest segments of the people. A determined effort to resolve these issues will link the government with the common sense of humanity and plug the existing trust deficit.

Federal structure

The federal structure has to factor in the sea change in the geo-politico-economic-technological-security scenario between 1950s and 2010s. When Dr Ambedkar and his team drafted the Indian constitution, the anti-constitutional activities such as proxy war, terrorism, insurgency and militancy in its various forms, and communal/caste/region based conflicts were not foreseen; hence it did not catch their attention in the manner we view such conflicts in todays times. They, therefore, justifiably focused only on the law and order situation. Consequently, the law and order was enshrined in the constitution as the state responsibility. Moreover, the erstwhile law and order situations did not pose any grave threat to the nation's security, and were, therefore, well within the means and manageable limits of the state police. In the contemporary times, emergence of various forms of sub-conventional threats has assumed new dimensions and started challenging the democratic and constitutional authority of the states. These developments have direct impact on the national security. Naxals, with their stated aim of waging a protracted people's war with a view to seize power, i.e. over throw the government too have manifested into a similar threat against the very framework of the nation's existence. In this context, the dimensions of internal security assume a new perspective altogether.

Unlike the 1950s, multi-party coalitions at the center and the recent emergence of a large number of regional political parties into prominence has exacerbated the problems of arriving at political consensus and decision making even on critical aspects such as national security. This problem of "slow or no decision making" is further compounded when decisions are sought in the backdrop of rapid changes in the geo-politico-strategic scenarios. The revolution in technology, communications and the resultant high awareness levels, deny government the luxury of long gestation periods that conflicts may have traditionally provided, before they could be addressed. Today, cyber space, social networking sites, proliferation and dissemination of information – in terms of real time availability – enable the movements to acquire critical mass within no time. In case of Naxalism, despite the fact that the areas in question were primarily tribal, backward and virtually untouched by technology, yet the increase in the Naxal activities, violence levels, spatial spread, and penetration into new areas indicate the proportions that it can assume, as and when some of these dimensions are brought into play.

If an insurgency is allowed to prolong, the ideology tends to mutate, and actions of the rebels may start manifesting in the form of organized crime, kidnappings, subversion and terrorism. Actually, some of these are already visible in abundance in the Naxal-affected rural areas. Mahadevan concludes, "By building up a predatory financial base through demonstrative use of violence, the insurgency (meaning Naxalism) has adopted features of Mafia-style organized crime."[11] It is, therefore, imperative that the center must take on board all the affected states by discussing salient aspects of threats in detail, their impact on various facets of security, economy, environment, and culture. Thereafter, the center should issue policy directives on the methodology to combat Naxalism to the states, irrespective of their political leanings. A study of a large number of counter-insurgency campaigns suggest that the governments that have not been assertive and resolute enough, have generally not succeeded against the insurgencies. It means that governments that are fragile, soft, inconsistent and pliable are unlikely to resolve a conflict in an effective manner. Some of the most successful counter-insurgency campaigns in the world have had the hands of firm, decisive and resolute leaders, who have implemented their vision on the ground. In the Malayan campaign (1948 to 1960), General Briggs and General Templar had made significant contribution to resolve the conflict successfully. In Indian context, political will, resolute leadership, harmonious center-state relationship and implementation of schemes on the ground is the key to improving the situation. Such dangerous conflicts require dynamic national response, which is difficult to achieve in rift ridden multi-party coalitions for some obvious reasons. Is there, therefore, a case to establish a separate constitutional/statutory body – to work in consonance with the concerned ministry – that is entrusted with the vital national responsibility of internal security – LWE?

Non-inclusive growth

Joseph Stieglitz (2012), nobel prize winning economist, supports this argument when he says in his book "The Price of Inequality" that we are reaching a level of inequality that is "intolerable".[12] Today, we have an economy that has been on a growth trajectory for over a decade and will continue to do so for the next few decades. However, as per statistics, our economic growth has been non-inclusive and has progressively widened the gap between the rich and the poor. This has happened primarily due to improper distribution system and, inefficient utilization of resources. People's welfare can only be ensured if a correct analysis of inadequacies in a region/sub region is carried out and resources are allocated and their utilization monitored. The perception that industrialization always results in "development of the region or inclusive growth of the poor people" would be incorrect. At the same time, high GDP growth does not necessarily mean proportionate reduction in poverty levels. This disparity and the voids due to development, governance, and lack of effective delivery mechanism at the grass roots have made a large section of our society poor, disillusioned, and alienated. It is this population, which is malleable to the extremist ideologies or could be exploited for political gains by inimical elements. The phenomenon of malicious and misleading ideological propaganda of the Naxals can be stemmed only through an all inclusive growth – a key strategic challenge – encompassing economic, social, and political sectors, and filling the vacuum thus created.

Poor implementation and lack of accountability

A large number of welfare schemes along with liberal allotment of funds – forming part of the government's initiatives for alleviating poverty, the root cause of the LWE – have not been implemented on the ground due to unprecedented corruption and lack of accountability. Aptly said, "*Non-performers do not attract punitive measures, high performers have no incentives.*" Scott T. Henson, a noted sociologist, commented on the federal structure and accountability, "*They have a structural accountability problem. They are federally funded, state managed and locally staffed, therefore accountable to no one.*" It is relevant and applicable to our system in equal measure. Although the constraints of the federal structure of the government and the lack of accountability may pose serious challenges to effective implementation of welfare schemes, yet the government has to evolve measures to overcome them and take tough decisions. Empowerment of Panchayati Raj Institutions is one such way to achieve meaningful execution of the government's rural development schemes. On the contrary, 65 representatives of "Panchayati Raj" institutions had reportedly resigned in Malkangiri (Odisha), in April 2013, to protest the apathy to their development needs.

Implementation of constitutional provisions

The Naxal affected areas, which are rich in mineral wealth, forest cover, and water, are susceptible to greed of the large corporate bodies due to weak regulatory framework, inadequate accountability, and unprecedented corruption. The interests of tribal and poor people must, therefore, be protected as per provisions in our constitution. According to the provisions of the Fifth Schedule under Article 244 of the Indian Constitution, the governors have multiple powers pertaining to implementation of any law on the grounds of alienation of tribal people, regulation of land allotment, etc.[13] Therefore, the constitutional provisions must be invoked for implementation of various legislations like PESA Act, Scheduled Tribes and other Traditional Forest Dwellers (Recognition of Forest Right Act), 2006, and Relaxations to Provisions of Forest (Conservation) Act 1980. Generally, the governors have not been invoking their special powers for schedule areas to cancel any actions that are detrimental to the livelihood of tribal groups.[14]

Education and unemployment

Unemployment remains one of the biggest challenges to both the center and the state government, having acquired serious dimension. According to reports, self employed workforce shrunk from 56.4% to 50.7% of the total workforce between 2004-05 and 2009-10. Although the government is making concerted efforts to ensure compulsory education of children, there are a large number of children who remain illiterate or with primary education only. School drop-outs are being recruited in the bal sanghams by the Naxals in large numbers. They have destroyed assets pertaining to educational infrastructure with the multiple aims, one of which appears to be to maintain the number of unaware, uneducated and unemployed youth at lowest levels. While on one hand, such a situation serves to prolong and intensify the conflict, on the other hand, even negative acts such as "recruitment as insurgents" can be portrayed as efforts by Naxals towards providing employment and means of livelihood. Therefore, providing education, training on job-related skills and employment to the large youth population, would continue to remain the biggest challenge to the country. While providing vocational training to the youth, development of entrepreneurship and incorporation of corporate sector to initiate small and medium level enterprises in these areas, should be kept in mind. This will result in in-situ absorption of the youth as well as minimum gestation period in terms of passing on the terminal benefit. The focus should be on the aptitude and willingness to learn various skills, and not on higher educational qualifications. Thus, certain amount of relaxation on educational qualifications would help provide vocational education, and training on job-related skills.

Shift in strategy: Urban Naxalism in different form

A study of the Naxals' documents is clearly suggestive of their intent to expand the scope of the movement to encompass the urban and semi-urban areas. Due to the peculiarities of the urban terrain and unprecedented population explosion, urban insurgency could take a different form in comparison to rural insurgency, and pose a greater challenge to the SF and the civil administration. It could be in the form of attack against soft targets, industrial unrests, organized crimes and acts of terror. Therefore, the central and state governments cannot sit tight and wait for urban movement to manifest. Essentially, the means and mechanisms need to be created pro-actively – for urban areas – so that there is an inbuilt preventive check against any such effort by the Naxals.

Prevent further spread

Naxalism has continued to progressively spread, particularly during the last decade. The Governor of Assam, had cautioned the senior officials of the SF at Guwahati on December 21, 2011 that the Naxals have made silent intrusions into Assam and established links with Manipur's insurgent outfits, the People's Liberation Army (PLA). The number of critical districts have steadily increased from 60 to 78, and in 2011 to 83. The remainder districts, out of 212, fall in the category of moderately and marginally/potentially affected by Naxalism. In addition, a close study of the Naxal related incidents, as given at Appendix C, clearly highlights that there is huge physical gap between the northern group of states (Bihar, Jharkhand and West Bengal) and the southern group (Chhattisgarh, Odisha, eastern Maharashtra, and northern Andhra Pradesh) with respect to the Naxal initiated incidents. It would be a challenge to ensure that the Naxals are not able to link the existing "strategic gap", to prevent them from having a continuous Red Corridor, running from north to south. These need to be taken care of simultaneously by development-cum-security initiatives to prevent further spread in rural areas and eventually to semi-urban/urban areas.

Target money power

For an insurgency to grow in strength and to sustain itself, the game changer is the availability of funds with the insurgent. The Naxals are known for resorting to extortion and coercion for raising funds from contractors involved in development projects, mining industry, people involved in illicit drug cultivation and trafficking, trade or transport unions. There have also been cases of siphoning of government's socio-economic developmental funds such as those allotted to the panchayats or other democratic bodies. Some of these fund generating methods are flourishing because of a dangerous nexus among a few politicians, bureaucrats, industrialists, Naxalites, and criminals. The total revenue from extortion, drug cultivation and racketeering was estimated to be Rs. 25 billion ($ 552 million) in 2010.[15] There may be variations in terms of the estimates of revenue generated by the Naxals, yet it is evident that there is a large-scale flow of funds taking place, enabling procurement of sophisticated weapon systems, equipment, surveillance devices, explosives and payment of salaries to the large cadre strength. An examination of the nature of Naxal related incidents, in Jharkhand, Bihar, Chhattisgarh and Odisha, suggests that the Naxals are also using violence and organized crime to raise funds to support their activities. Two pronged strategy; firstly, to dry up the funding by innovatively targeting the sources of funds; and secondly, to expose the fallacies of the movement by publicizing the criminal linkages, should be incorporated in the comprehensive national plan, including the perception management campaign.

External support

There is no concrete evidence of any direct involvement of any external powers, except a few linkages being established with ultras or militant organizations, and supply of weapon systems and equipment. Is Naxalism an indigenous movement? Manoharan feels otherwise.[16] It must, however, be understood that a movement of this magnitude cannot sustain on its own without any external support, be it in terms of funding, weaponry, training, refuge, or ideological support. A 2010 RAND Corporation study on insurgencies indicates that, without external support and available sanctuaries, no internal insurgency can thrive over a period of 10 years.[17] With revolution in communications and media, social web sites, and influence of globalization, the insurgents are increasingly aware of the status of other insurgencies – their ideology, organizations, literature, techniques, availability and sources of weapon systems and funds – to seek support from external powers. Making deliberate inroads into and establishing links with the ultras in the northeastern states is one of the steps to establish direct links with the foreign powers, among other aims. For India's adversaries, this is perhaps one movement that can provide them with a ready tool with which they can undermine the growing economic, political and military strength of India. Some of the important news items, as quoted, are suggestive of the fact that the Naxals are making desperate efforts to establish direct linkages with foreign powers and militant organizations to receive support in various forms to further spread their influence to urban areas and industrial hubs. By so doing, it would serve the strategic interests of India's adversaries, as, besides slow economic growth, the heartland of the country would remain destabilized. It would also open up one more "front" which would require deployment of a large number of security personnel in the region, for a prolonged duration.

The proximity of the affected areas to the strategic and sensitive Siliguri corridor, and the surface communication links with the northeastern states is well known. Therefore, external powers, inimical to India's national interests, are perhaps monitoring the Naxal situation very closely and would most willingly extend overt support to them, as and when they demand for it. For instance, ISI may adopt a more aggressive posture, by way of providing multi-faceted support to the movement and driving a wedge between the people and the SF, to destabilize the heartland of the country. Further, while opening another front for India's SF, it may spread propaganda to deter the industry, investments and development of infrastructure to hurt India economically.

Front organizations

The front organizations of the Naxals, in both urban and semi-urban areas, are today functioning with impunity, primarily due to liberal legal cover that democratic laws provide to them. These organizations provide significant moral support, espouse Naxals' cause, take up issues related to human rights violations, portray the role of the SF and the police in a negative manner, organize funds, and oppose the government policies on various issues. Media and information technology have primarily facilitated the over-arching reach and influence of these organizations. Some of the front organizations, with the active support of the media, have often succeeded in objectively raising the ante by highlighting the incidents of collateral damage at the hands of SF, the social turmoil caused due to repeated displacement of people, poor living conditions of the population and apathy of the civil administration towards the poor. Since national security is a sensitive subject, the media – without curtailing its freedom of expression – needs to be responsible, fair and objective in their reporting. Is there a case to have a brief formal training program for the local media persons – reporting on the ground realities and the activities of the Naxals/SF in vernacular – to ensure an objective assessment? It is important because such reporting alters the perception of the local population.

Traditional tribal culture

Approximately 8.2% of India's population is tribal, which in absolute figures would be very large. In a number of Naxal-affected areas, the traditional tribal culture is vigorously alive. A case in point is Bastar, where tribal people still have an indigenous way of life. A number of rebellions in the past such as Bhumkal Rebellion of Bastar Region of 1910, were generally seen as an assertion of the traditional tribals' rights on land or forests. However, the fundamental anguish was also against disruption of their culture, their way of life and indigenous languages or local dialects. Therefore, the system of education, medical services and developmental activities must factor in the tribal desire to preserve their culture and language. Perception management campaigns must precisely strategize a correct balance between preservation of traditional culture and development. The government cannot afford to be seen as either attempting to water down or trying to impose different culture on the people. Sustained dialogue with the tribal community would help reduce the existing trust deficit.

Central Counter Insurgency Force (CCIF)

Due to overall inadequacy of police force within the states, a plethora of forces like CAPF (CRPF, BSF, ITBP, SSB, CISF, etc.) and intelligence agencies are operating in the Naxals-affected areas. The organizational structure, the mandated roles, working ethos, leadership, training proficiency, and experience of each force in counter-insurgency environment are quite different from each other. To achieve seamless coordination and synergy among the SF is a daunting task by itself, both within each state and more so at the sensitive bi-junctions and tri-junctions of state boundaries. The Naxals continue to move, at will, across the political boundaries of the state, based on the operations being conducted by the SF in a particular area. The ongoing insurgencies, low-intensity conflicts and threat of terrorism are likely to persist in South Asia in the foreseeable future. Knee jerk reactions, by pushing the police or the CAPF to combat an insurgency or terrorism, would not yield any meaningful results. Counter-insurgency operations require special skills, training, knowledge of 'human terrain map (HTM)', intelligence and effective leadership to be successful. Ideally, in the long-term perspective, the country needs to raise a new force or reorganize the existing force structures of the CAPF and IR battalions, to form a Central Counter Insurgency Force (CCIF) for better management of the internal security environment. CRPF is an excellent force for the maintenance of law and order, and to undertake protection related duties. In an intense counter-insurgency environment, the force should be proficient to fight well-trained and motivated young guerrillas (majority of them are 16 to 25 years old), which requires a force with military ethos, and an effective junior leadership. There is, therefore, a need to create a force that is organized and structured – including intelligence mechanisms – to combat Naxalism or internal armed conflicts. Suitability of force needs to be examined in detail, so that it is effective and yet causes minimum turbulence in restructuring. Quality training infrastructures should be created and force trained to achieve better results on the ground. By creating a force responsible for counter- insurgency operations, the country would have a homogeneous force, which would be more efficient and effective, due to its unambiguous role, its commitment, motivation and greater sense of responsibility. Leadership is one of the most important aspects in a counter-insurgency campaign. This would, however, require a comprehensive analysis at the national level, and if accepted, major reorganization and restructuring effort to make CCIF effective.

Police to population ratios

During the Question Hour on December 04, 2012, the Minister of State for Home, Mr Ramachandran said, "The sanctioned strength of total police force as on January 1, 2011 is 20,64,370 and the actual strength is 15,63,301, with a vacancy of 5,01,069",[18] Without getting involved in further figures, it is evident that there is an overall shortage of police forces and CAPF, as also the weapons, equipment and infrastructure. India has a very low police-to-population ratio. The all India average of police-to-population ratio is approximately 1.33 per 1,000, which is far below the desired level of 2.2 per 1,000, as recommended by the United Nations (UN). As the UN figures are more appropriate for the developed/semi-developed nations, India should at best aim for an affordable augmentation, with greater emphasis on the quality of the force, i.e. improved training and modernization for the envisaged tasks. An examination of the requirement of police force for the critically affected states; namely Chhattisgarh, Jharkhand, Odisha and Bihar reveals that there is an overall requirement of 2,63,236 additional police personnel for these four states. Refer Figure 5.7. These figures have to be examined in conjunction with the strength of the CAPF. Even if the government takes a decision to make up the deficiency of police force by 20% of the total requirement (52,647 police personnel), neither the central government nor the state governments have the capacity to impart quality training to such a large number of recruits to be operationally effective for counter-insurgency operations. Along with this, the judicial system also needs to be more responsive to dispense justice to the tribal and the poor people in remote areas.

Capacity and capability of SF

One of the strategic challenges lies in implementation of police reforms, which has also been directed by the Supreme Court, in the historic judgment on September 22, 2006. Till some time ago, the antiquated laws, methods employed for training and policing, the inherent force characteristics such as age profile, outdated weaponry and equipment, the apathy of the government have denied our CAPF and state police forces to build capabilities for dealing with modern day insurgency and terrorism. Ajai Sahni makes his observations on the state police's inadequacies in discipline, leadership and professional competence.[19] Despite some recent piece meal efforts to improve the conditions, there is a large degree of asymmetry between a modern day insurgent or terrorist, and a trooper of the CAPF and state police forces in terms of the reach, leadership, mobility, surveillance equipment, weaponry, communications, logistics and technological prowess.

Capacity and capability building of the CAPF and the state police forces is a huge challenge. It should essentially aim at strengthening the core competencies based on an integrated system approach. It entails a systematic integration with focus on human resource aspects by structural reconfiguration of organizations, training, leadership, logistics, and technology absorption. General George S. Patton, Jr, a celebrated American General in World War II had mentioned that the most vital quality a soldier can possess is self-confidence. Self-confidence can be achieved, among others, by imparting good quality training to the soldiers. Therefore, due to prevalent inadequacies in the state's police, the state governments would have to rely on the central government for additional trained troops, i.e. CAPF, particularly when the intensity of Naxal violence is high. There is an urgent need to build capacity and capability of SF, at both the center and state level, with the focus on quality rather than on quantity. The conflict would actually get resolved only when the state police is fully involved and committed. As the state police is the most visible symbol of state authority – to maintain public order and to create a secure environment for development process to take place – it must be transformed into an efficient and effective force. Some of the successful models, where the state police have played a predominant role, are the Malayan insurgency, Punjab, Andhra Pradesh and Tripura. It is common knowledge that, given a choice, most police personnel do not want to operate in an intense counter-insurgency operational environment, for a number of reasons. The states could consider the model of Andhra Pradesh and Tripura, where the civil police and the intelligence organization contributed in a significant manner.

Armed forces for anti-naxal operations

Naxal-affected areas have engulfed a large part of the heartland of the country. To counter this, a huge force would be required for a prolonged duration. It is evident by the deployment of the army and the CAPF in approximately 70 districts of the northeastern states and J&K, of both regions put together. According to the provisions of Article 355[20] of the Constitution, the army has been deployed to counter the threats to the internal security of the country in J&K and the Northeast, among other states. Besides analyzing the total force that could be employed for internal security without compromising the operational preparedness of the army/armed forces, it would be essential to declare the area disturbed and invoke Armed Forces Special Powers Act, 1958 (AFSPA), to provide legal protection to the forces operating in the area for their actions during anti-naxal operations. While it is undisputed that security of the people must remain the prime concern of the government, it would be prudent to holistically analyze the impact of declaring the heartland of the country disturbed. First, how does it impact the image, the investment climate and the growth story of the country? Second, what are the effects of prolonged deployment of the armed forces on its operational preparedness and military ethos? Third, would pulling out the army from J&K and/or the north eastern states affect the peace and stability of those areas? What is the optimum force that can be employed and for what duration? Fourth, would army's deployment give the Naxals a psychological edge and a moral victory, signifying government's failure on major issues? Fifth, what would be the command and control structure to ensure seamless coordination and unity of effort in anti-naxal operations? Sixth, what would be the response of the states? In the current strategic environment-cum-complex political scenario, decision making itself would be a major strategic challenge.

There is a cross section of the society that feels that since Naxalism has grown progressively and it continues to grow in strength, it is time that the armed forces in general and the army in particular must step in to halt the spread. I believe that this view fails to fully appreciate the distinctions in the nature of the conflict and the fundamental relationship that is prevalent. Naxals seek to protest against the socio-economic conditions that are prevalent in certain regions of the country, and do not seem to borrow ideology from any political aspiration; though the result of the struggle may eventually change the political fabric of the affected regions. This is different from the reason India has had to deal with armed struggle in J&K or in the northeastern parts of India. Unlike Naxalism, majority of other struggles are state specific/regional in nature, and seek to carve out an independent state for themselves out of India. Further, it may be noted that a crucial distinction between Naxal-affected areas, and other parts of India where the army has been deployed to counter internal armed conflicts is that the latter regions are mostly border provinces and that such armed groups enjoy linkages and direct support from external powers. For instance, most armed groups in J&K train their personnel in Pakistan and are actively supported by the government agencies.

Critical situations

In consonance with the provisions given at Article 355 of the Constitution and based on a comprehensive analysis of the situation, the army must remain prepared for undertaking certain special tasks, with a "clear exit policy". In practical terms, the exit policy would actually be a pipe dream for any force in an insurgency environment. The special tasks could be in terms of an area becoming critical to national security due to Naxal violence or the Naxals taking control of certain important establishments or strategic communication network, etc. What could be the legal provisions for such short duration deployment of the armed forces? Rather than having to declare an area disturbed or invoking the AFSPA, would it be more appropriate for the government to examine the feasibility of giving certain statutory powers to the armed forces whenever they are called out for any counter-insurgency or terrorism-related tasks for a specified period and in a specified area. Of course, certain checks and balances must form part of the package, so that the activities of the armed forces are conducted in a legitimate and controlled manner.

Perception Management

In the ongoing information age, "Perception Management" is widely practiced and has become an increasingly important tool of warfare, to assuage the fears and apprehensions of the population at large. In the past, to achieve near-similar objectives, perception management has been called by different names, such as psychological operations campaign, public information, psychological reassurance, information operations (IO), information and education, propaganda and publicity campaign, confidence-building measures (CBM), etc. Propaganda, as a term, draws objections from various quarters. It is, therefore, important to first understand the term *perception* as defined by the Central Intelligence Agency.[21]

The British and the US military forces, in particular, have years of experience in counter-insurgency operations, having participated in Malaya, Kenya, Muscat, Oman, Vietnam, Iraq and Afghanistan insurgencies. The coalition forces also have gained huge experience in Iraq and Afghanistan. They have written field manuals, training pamphlets, doctrines, and related literature on conduct of counter-insurgency campaigns, primarily based on their experiences either as the colonial power or while operating in a foreign land. The operational philosophy, the attitude, and the mindset of such governments and their troops are likely to be vastly different in comparison to the Indian government dealing with indigenous insurgency situation within the country. While the United States may have hit a number of high-value targets by the drones (predators and reapers) since 2004 on Afghan-Pakistan border, a number of innocent civilians have also been killed in such attacks. As far as the Indian strategy is concerned, it has to keep in mind that Naxalism is an indigenous insurgency, which is in the heartland of the country. Although the hardcore Naxals have been extremely violent, destructive, and brutal in their actions, correct balance would have to be drawn in taking action against them. The brutal and inhuman tactics of the Naxals against the so called, 'police informers' and the Latehar incident (January 2013) are well known. It is difficult to distinguish between a hardcore and a sympathizer/over ground worker and neutral population. Therefore, hard-core Naxals must be identified by the intelligence gathering system, to conduct actionable intelligence based operations against them and their secure bases. The country should not be seen as a soft state against such brutal and barbaric tactics. At the same time, the SF must also operate within the ambit of law. India has excellent examples of terminating insurgencies in Punjab and Mizoram due to appropriate politico-civil-SF intervention. But for one main instance of air strikes in Mizoram in March 1966,[22] India has, in principle, not employed air power or artillery or heavy-caliber weapons in the counter-insurgency operations in J&K, northeastern states, and LWE-affected states. On the other hand, there are a number of instances where Pakistan Air Force has carried out air strikes in an insurgency environment against the Balooch nationalists and Pakistani Taliban, Russia's Air Force against the Chechens, and Sri Lanka's Air Force against the LTTE.

Critical period

A study of the famous five documents of the Naxals, presented in September 2004, and their Urban Perspective Plan, released in 2007, suggests that the Naxals are acutely aware of the prevailing inequality and the widening gap between the rich and the poor. With this in background, the Naxals continue to propagate their ideology regularly and motivate their cadres. They are far ahead of the state in their propaganda compaign. As perception management is one area where the governments – at both the center and at the states level – have not applied themselves to counter the ideology of the Naxals, it has, therefore, been covered in some detail. Considering the overall improvement in the security situation, as has emerged from 2011 onwards, it is perhaps the most critical period that perception management should also play its full part, along with other initiatives of the government. We are already late in doing so. During the Malayan Insurgency, General Templar had said, "*The answer lies not in pouring more soldiers into the jungle, but rests in the hearts and minds of the Malayan people.*" Winning the hearts and minds of the people was also part of the perception management strategy. The US military had effectively used information operations (IO), as they called it, between 1981 and 1991in El Salvador in defeating the communist insurgency.[23]

Wide scope

During the Malayan counter-insurgency campaign (1948–60), the British worked on a detailed perception management and propaganda plan to build trust with the population and to discredit the insurgents. In formulating their strategy towards a political problem, they gave higher priority to human intelligence, to get accurate information about the "people". Perception management requires a vast and unique information database, and highly trained analytical skills to shape an information campaign, which is hard hitting and far reaching.[24] This aspect merits urgent focus to capitalize on the success achieved in the ongoing 'development and security' initiatives of the government.

Generally, the civil administration and security forces consider "conducting civic action programs to win the confidence of the people" is the primary function of perception management. It has a much wider canvass. In the larger context, it must address the people's concerns and apprehensions on "*political, ideological, psychological, social, economic, environmental and cultural*" planes. Perception management – incorporating all the elements of national power – is a major challenge to counter the ideology in a planned manner. Assurances of legitimate political concessions/empowerment, socio-economic inclusion must be conveyed, and implemented, as part of the strategy. Psychological reassurance that their traditional culture, customs and language will not only be preserved, but will also be given further impetus may also be necessary. Perception management has various elements like deception measures, psychological operations, and information gathering and counter-propaganda cells. As perception management has not received due attention in India, two important fundamentals – the principles and the objectives – have also been discussed briefly to facilitate formulation of the strategy.

Principles of perception management

The primary aim of the counter-insurgents is to win the support of the population. In comparison to the Naxals, who propagate that they would fulfill the political, social, economic and cultural aspirations of the people, without actually having to deliver on the ground immediately, the government has to strategize to fight through such a misleading campaign. Calamari and Reveron have noted that, while designing perception management campaign, certain principles[25] must be kept in mind, of which the two important ones are discussed. The *first* principle states that manipulating the opponent's pre-existing belief is easier than presenting false evidence in attempting to change it. The *second* principle relates to the concept of conditioning (i.e. manipulating an opponent's perception by presenting information bit-by-bit, as this is far more effective than doing so all at once). My experiences of counter-insurgency environment suggests that a good perception management campaign should be based on truthfulness, genuine concern for the people, honoring commitments made to maintain credibility of the organization (including resettlement and rehabilitation of displaced people, and surrendered rebels), and acceptance of own inadequacies and weaknesses. The principle, "genuine concern for the people" takes care of a large number of issues to meet the aspirations of the people.

In the 12 years long Malayan Emergency, the British decided to achieve physical isolation of the Chinese minority community from the insurgents. As promised, they ensured that the "new villages" – the new settlements – had better facilities than previous places of their stay. Such actions resulted in establishing the genuineness and credibility of the government's intentions. Such campaigns require meticulous planning, preparations and coordination to ensure that the compiled facts, information and plan of action are in consonance with the overall plan. These principles would hold ground only when the projected plans and socio-economic schemes start fructifying on the ground. Otherwise, a hollow perception management campaign can become counter-productive, can discredit the government, and can put the clock back by a few years.

Objectives

Perception management must bring together various specialties to include public affairs, intelligence, psychological operations, civil military operations, and some MHA/MEA specialities, such as public diplomacy and public information systems. Perception management should also be used as a tool for Information Operations (IO).[26] However, it needs to be suitably modified to suit the counter-insurgency environment, as used by the British in Malayan and Kenyan campaigns. In the Malayan counter-insurgency campaign, Brigg's Plan relied more on the political solution than military. He had used information operations (IO) extensively as a part of it. Although Chatterji mentions about perception management at strategic, operational, and tactical level in a generic insurgency environment, strategic and tactical level has been analyzed in the context of Naxalism.[27]

- **Strategic objectives:** At the strategic level, perception management would involve mostly politico-military objectives of Naxals like the ideology, strategy, higher leadership and external linkages. It would therefore involve targeting the ideology of the Naxals by highlighting various inadequacies, supported by examples of the failed systems, at the international level. The perception management process would have to focus on the merits of democracy and would have to substantiate the fact that the objectives of the Naxals as given out in their documents do not hold good in a democratic country like India. Of course, the existing fault lines pertaining to socio-economic disparities, non-inclusive growth and implementation of reforms have to be addressed, with a sense of urgency. Simultaneously, the MEA, the external intelligence agencies and diplomatic support staff should endeavor to get worldwide support on India's view on the ongoing insurgencies in the country, get the outfits on the banned list, and ensure that suitable sanctions are imposed on the external powers that are supporting the Naxal organizations or any other insurgency in India, materially or otherwise.[28]

- **Tactical objectives:** At the tactical level, the objective of perception management would be to isolate the insurgent from the masses.[29] Isolation refers to political, physical and social isolation, something that the British administration achieved in Malayan counter-insurgency campaign, at strategic and tactical levels. To achieve its objectives, the statistical data, year wise, of destruction of economic and social infrastructure needs to be highlighted. There have been instances where innocent civilians including children have been killed or injured during the counter-naxal operations. While genuine mistakes must be accepted and appropriate actions taken against the defaulters, the victim families must be fully supported to send the correct message to the people. Unfortunately, the commitments made by the government functionaries to provide relief to the victim families are not genuinely pursued to their logical completion.

Be fair and objective

Sometimes, operations by the SF can result into collateral damages in terms of loss of lives and property of innocent population; thereby, further exacerbating the problem of alienation of the local population. The propaganda machinery of the Naxals exploits such incidents. In the absence of a coordinated perception management effort, even some of the losses to lives and property caused due to the Naxal initiated acts also are attributed to the SF. For instance, the statistics of civilians killed and kidnapped due to the Naxal activities has been alarming. 1,554 people were kidnapped from January 01, 2008 to November 14, 2011.[30] The Naxals have been using brutal tactics – to kill civilians, have used innocent civilians as human shields, booby-trapped the bodies of slain soldiers, planted explosives inside the stomach of a martyred trooper and sabotage actions against trains – to create fear psychosis. However, there have been no serious queries from the amnesty organizations or social activists regarding right to life of so many civilians/SF personnel having been killed or kidnapped. Who are responsible for such killings? It is, therefore, imperative that a formal organization is established to take a comprehensive look at all the aspects of perception management, i.e. civic action programs, psychological operations and the counter propaganda; and evolve a national level plan to highlight all essential aspects in a fair and objective manner. The central and state governments must also acknowledge and reconcile with the past mistakes with regard to meeting the aspirations of the local populace, and the excesses committed by the SF. Corrective actions should be initiated to prevent recurrence of incidents resulting in killing of innocent civilians and collateral damages.

Conduct of training in Narayanpur – Perception management

To highlight the positive role that a perception management campaign can achieve, one of the cases in which commanders and troops at different levels worked in unison to dispel the fears and misperception, has been discussed. As the Director General Military Training (DGMT) of the Army in 2006-07, we were required to pursue the cases pertaining to acquisition of the maneuver ranges with the state governments. Chhattisgarh government was prompt in offering an area for maneuver range in the Narayanpur district. With state government's specific approval, the army was instructed to commence training for the troops in the designated areas made available by them. It remained in the news for a number of weeks. However, there was huge resistance and threats from the Naxals for the army to not conduct training in Chhattisgarh, more importantly in the general area of Narayanpur ranges – one of the nerve centers of their activities. In fact, the Naxals had mounted a propaganda campaign against the army training in Narayanpur through distribution of leaflets in the entire area, exhorting soldiers not to fight their own people. Refer Appendix E, for a copy of such a leaflet recovered from Kondagaon in Chhattisgarh. It is a hardhitting document that highlights the thought process of the Naxals, their ideology and the reasons why the Army should not move into the Naxal-affected areas. It took us quite some time to finalize our plans to conduct training in the specified area, as the area was not declared disturbed. The Naxals had been misleading the people by spreading rumors about army's induction for training, which, to my understanding, remained largely uncontested. As part of the perception management, we were keen to dispel the fears of the people, the Naxals and their front organizations, and the media by announcing the purpose of our training, the intentions, and the rationale for choosing Narayanpur. The aim was not to get involved in refuting the misleading campaign of the Naxals, but be transparent of our intentions and purpose of training – to the local populace – in a simple and effective manner.

During my first interaction with the media at Raipur on February 15, 2011, I spoke at length about the genesis, the training objectives of the army, suitability of the terrain for jungle warfare, and that the troops would come for a period of two to three months only and thereafter go back to their permanent locations. The briefing of the media, by me personally, was a part of the perception management and to psychologically reassure the people of our intentions. I was unequivocal in announcing that the army will not conduct any anti-naxal operations. I answered a number of questions raised by the media personnel. Two of them, who appeared to speak for the Naxals, asked me about the "rules of engagement" and how the army personnel could be faced with legal actions in case of an encounter with the Naxals. A number of articles on the subject had appeared in the national dailies and the vernacular press. I was happy with the question, because it gave me an opportunity to clarify our stand and to dispel their fears and apprehensions. First, I informed them that the term rules of engagement looked offensive in its spirit, which is not the aim of the army. Therefore, it should hereafter be called as, "Guidelines for the conduct of training", which itself had a great soothing and reassuring effect on everyone. It did not show any offensive intent or the mandate to conduct anti-naxal operations. As the army's primary objective was training, it did not make sense to be laboring so much on the expression, "the rules of engagement". Thereafter, the media rarely spoke about the rules of engagement and the likely implications.

One of the journalist surmised that I was trying to evade one of his questions. He was insistent, repeatedly, to know as to what the army would do in case the Naxals attack the army personnel or the camp, particularly when the area has not been declared disturbed. This was one question that was under discussion among all the stakeholders for some time, including in the TV shows. To know my response, there was pin drop silence among them. I was categorical in stating my response, in a measured way, lest the media misinterprets my intention. I said, "There is no reason why the Naxals would attack the army, which has been detailed to carry out training exercise with troops, in the specified training area allotted by the state government. However, should the

Naxals still decide to attack the army columns, its vehicles or its training camps, they (Naxals) must understand that the army will take appropriate actions to protect its personnel, equipment and material."Apparently, the message was quite clear and left no doubts.

Consequent to the media interaction, the next day, most of the newspapers carried fair and reasonable stories like, "Naxals are our people", "Zone of conflict will soon become zone of peace", "Army will not conduct any anti-naxal operations", "Army is there to support its people", etc. As expected, there were one or two stories, which conveyed my statement in the negative form. On balance, I was very satisfied with my interaction with the media, the representatives of the front organizations and the people in the Naxal-affected areas. However, the Naxals were apparently not relenting. They again issued leaflets in a large number of areas against army's induction for training. Meanwhile, the local commanders at Raipur (Chhattisgarh) maintained the desired thrust with the media, vernacular press and other stakeholders.

Before dispatching the troops for training, I decided to do a similar exercise with media again, in June 2011. The net result was that the army did its training and won the hearts and minds of the local population, by carrying out joint civic action programs, in consultation with the civil administration. To show our genuine interest, recruitment rallies were organized in the tribal belts, for both recruitment into the regular army and the territorial army. The local commanders took initiative to organize pre-recruitment training to make the locals aware of the standards to be achieved. The army took no time to establish trust and confidence with the local population. When the first brigade left the Naxal-affected area after concluding their training, the locals gave them tearful farewell, which received wide coverage in media. Thereafter, a number of army formations have gone for training into the Narayanpur–Kondagaon area. There have been no attacks on any of army's training camps, vehicles and personnel since our first induction in June 2011. In the final analysis, the entire credit goes to the troops and their leaders, on the ground, who achieved their training objectives, and actually won the hearts and minds of the local population.

> *Nine-tenths of tactics are certain, and taught in books: but the irrational tenth is like the kingfisher flashing across the pool, and that is the test of generals.*
>
> – T.E. Lawrence, *Seven Pillars of Wisdom* (1922)

Notes

1. Thomas R. Mockaitis, "Resolving Insurgencies" (Pennsylvania: Strategic Studies Institute , June 17, 2011) 2.

2. For an insightful account, read Art Ryan L. Seachon, "Insurgencies in History: A Blueprint for Future Strategy", OG 5 Digest, October-December 2004: 16.
3. Ibid.
4. For more details, read Erik Goepner, "An Enduring Argument against Counterinsurgency", *Small Wars Journal*, September 27, 2012.
5. For more details, see O. B. Olugbile and A.O. Coker, "Conflict in the Niger – Delta of Nigeria: An Analysis of the Problem", *African Journal of Traumatic Stress* 1, No. 2 (December 2010): 103-104.
6. Robert Burns, "Suicides among US Troops Top Afghanistan War Dead", *Anchorage Daily News*, June 06, 2012. (Suicides are surging among America's troops in Afghanistan, averaging nearly one a day in 2012 – the fastest pace in the nation's decade of war. The 154 suicides for active – duty troops in the first 155 days of 2012. The military also is struggling with increased sexual assaults, alcohol abuse, domestic violence and other misbehavior.)
7. PTI, "CRPF Jawan Shoots Four Mates", *The Times of India*, December 26, 2012. At least 11 instances of fragging have been reported from paramilitary and army units in various insurgency-affected areas of the country over the last one year.
8. "The Way Out of Counter Terror Impasse", *The Tribune*, March 12, 2012. While the proposed NCTC is certainly not a panacea for all terror-based challenges, its creation will certainly lend teeth to the central law enforcement and intelligence, who are often held hostage to state level politics, as law and order is a state subject. It needs early resolution. (There have been instances when the CMs/representatives of the states do not attend meetings at the center on vital issues like "law and order or on internal security" issues (*Times of India*, April 16, 2013).
9. Ved Marwah, "Counter Terrorism Requires Close Cooperation", *The Tribune*, March 11, 2012. According to GoI's statement, there are as many as 66 terrorist/separatist groups active across the country, including 34 in Manipur alone.
10. For more details, read "An Obama come back", Editorial, *The Hindu*, October 19, 2012.
11. Prem Mahadevan, "The Naxal Insurgency in India: Between Crime and Resolution", *Small Wars and Insurgencies* 23, No. 2 (May 2012): 213.
12. For an insightful account, see Yvonne Roberts, "The Price of Inequality by Joseph Stiglitz", accessed November 15, 2012, http://www.guardian.co.uk/books/2012/jul/13/price-inequality-joseph-stiglitz-review.
13. Article 244 relates to the administration of scheduled areas and tribals areas. It states that the provisions of the Fifth Schedule shall apply to the administration and control of the scheduled area and scheduled tribes in any state other than the states of Assam, Meghalaya, Tripura, and Mizoram which are covered under the Sixth Schedule.... Part A of the Fifth Schedule states that the Governor of the state having scheduled areas shall annually, or whenever so required by the President, make a report to the President regarding the administration of the scheduled areas in the state and the executive powers of the union shall extend to the giving of directions by the state as to the administration of the said areas.... The governor has the power to notify that any particular act of the state will not apply to

the scheduled areas. The governor may make regulation for these areas and may repeal or amend any act of parliament or of the legislature of the state.... No regulation shall be made without consultation with the advisory council or any existing law which is for the time being applicable to the area in the question.

14. For more details, see Subodh Ghildiyal, "Deo: AP Guv Didn't Do Much to Stop Mining", *The Times of India*, July 30, 2012.
15. Prem Mahadevan, "The Naxal Insurgency in India: Between Crime and Resolution", *Small Wars and Insurgencies* 23, No. 2 (May 2012): 205.
16. For more details, see N. Manoharan, "No More 'Indigenous': External Linkages of Left Wing Extremism", Article 1598, CLAWS, July 17, 2010. He feels that because of the linkages of the Naxals with a large number of external militant organizations, Naxalism fails to strictly qualify as an indigenous movement.
17. Ben Connable and Martin C. Libicki, "How Insurgencies End", RAND, Santa Monica, 2010, 34–38.
18. http://www.india.com/topic/vacant-posts.html, accessed on December 29, 2012.
19. Ajai Sahni, "Augmenting Threat Sclerotic Responses", *South Asian Intelligence Review*, Institute of Conflict Management, Issue 6, No. 20, November 26, 2007. While commenting on the professional standard of the police, the intelligence system, he writes, "India remains hopelessly unprepared to deal with terrorism and its consequences."
20. Article 355 in The Constitution Of India 1949: "Duty of the Union to protect States against external aggression and internal disturbance. It shall be the duty of the Union to protect every state against external aggression and internal disturbance and to ensure that the government of every state is carried on in accordance with the provisions of the Constitution."
21. Central Intelligence Agency (CIA), Office of Research and Development. *Misperception Literature Survey* (Princeton, NJ: Mathtech, 1979), 5. (According to the CIA definition, 'perception', the process of forming images of the world, can be thought of as involving two sub-processes. Sensory data is first acquired, then it is organized and analyzed to form a coherent, comprehensive picture. Thus, misperception of the world can arise either from incorrect data or from mal-processing of correct data.)
22. B. Raman, "Counter-insurgency Use of Air Power vs. Use of Air Force", April 08, 2010, accessed on March 21, 2013. http://counter-insurgency-use-of-air-power-vs-use-of-air-force/.
    - On 01 March 1966, the Mizo National Front (MNF) made a declaration of independence, after launching coordinated attacks on the government offices and security forces posts in Mizoram. To dislodge the MNF insurgents, the Indian Air Force carried out airstrikes on Aizawl for limited duration, this being the only instance of India carrying out an airstrike in its own civilian territory.
    - During an operation (Operation Sarp Vinash) against the militants in Suran Kot area (south of the Pir Panjal Ranges in J&K) in May 2003, the army had used a helicopter gunship to bust a bunker of the militants on the top of a ridge (Praveen Swami, *Outlook*, June 2, 2003).
23. Maj Robert J. Molinari, United States Army, "Winning the Minds in Hearts

and Minds: A Systems Approach to Information Operations as part of Counterinsurgency Warfare."

24. S.K. Chatterji, "Perception Management in Conflict Zones", accessed November 11, 2012, http://www.au.af.mil/info - ops/iosphere/10winter/iosphere_win10_chatterji.pdf.
25. Peter Callamari and Derek Reveron, "China's Use of Perception Management", accessed February 12, 2012, http://www.informaworld.com/smpp/content~content=a713830380~db=all.
26. Information Operations (IO) is an extension of the security operations with primary objective of achieving and maintaining information superiority. It provides a competitive edge by way of enabling decision makers to take informed decisions. Accessed on March 02, 2012, http://www.carlisle.army.mil/DIME/documents/jp3_13.pdf. According to JP 3-13 (Information Operations, February 2006.

    Among other, the focus of IO must also be to gain information about the local population, their sensitivities, problems and the areas of their lives that require immediate relief. These requirements differ from region to region and must be holistically looked at from that point of view. HTM should be part of the IO.
27. BrigadierS.K.Chatterji,"PerceptionManagementinConflictZones",accessed November 11, 2012, http://www.au.af.mil/info-ops/iosphere/10winter/iosphere_win10_chatterji.pdf.
28. At present, we do not have any concrete evidence of direct interference of any foreign powers providing support to the Naxals. However, in order to sustain the movement for long, they would look outwards for all types of support in the future. In one of the seminars on Naxalism, one of the speakers continued to refer to the Naxals as enemies. It is incorrect – they are neither separatists nor secessionists. However, they have adopted the most unconstitutional methods to project their demands. Hard core rebels and their leaders must be dealt with firmly.
29. BrigadierS.K.Chatterji,"PerceptionManagementinConflictZones",accessed November 11, 2012, http://www.au.af.mil/info-ops/iosphere/10winter/iosphere_win10_chatterji.pdf.
30. Jitender Prasad Singh, Minister of State for Home, in a reply to a starred question in Parliament on November 22, 2011.

Chapter 9

Rise of the Urban Reds: Whispering Storm

During the course of a presentation on "Naxalism and Ground Realities", to operational-level officers at the Sardar Vallabhbhai National Police Academy, Hyderabad, on May 10, 2011, I gave my assessment of the situation in the critically LWE-affected areas. At the end of such presentations, I always look forward to the "Question and Answer" session for two main reasons; one, whether the participants have found the presentation interesting and educative enough (which generally results in thought provoking comments and questions); two, it is an intellectually stimulating exercise for the audience as well as the speaker. In the above case, one of the participants, a senior officer of the police, said that he did not agree with my assessment of the situation in Jharkhand. I informed the participants that sometimes it is good to have a ringside view of the overall activities of the Naxals, their front organizations, the SF, the state authorities and the media. It helps provide an impartial, objective, and holistic analysis, without looking through the prism of any particular stakeholder. In addition, I informed the participants that I had been observing all the affected areas – not any particular state – purely from the national security perspective. In fact, this is something that every responsible citizen of the country should be concerned about and not just the uniformed personnel.

Having analyzed the number and nature of violent incidents, the killings, destruction of property and infrastructure and extortion incidents over the previous few months, I had appreciated that there was a progressive increase in the activities of the Naxals in western Jharkhand, in particular. Therefore, the areas around – Gumla, Lohardaga, Latehar, Palamu, Garhwa, Hazaribagh, and Chatra of Jharkhand – required greater vigil and focus of the SF to maintain a secure environment. The police officer from Jharkhand had objected to my assessment. He counted out the measures that had been put in place by the state authorities to keep the situation under control. While giving space to his emotional argument, I reiterated the rationale for my analysis, and informed him that the situation in an insurgency environment is generally very dynamic – the insurgents can move away to another place to escape the dragnet of action by the SF. However, I maintained that the situation in western Jharkhand appeared to be relatively more sensitive and less than secure, which could be due to a number of reasons. Besides the lack of political will and a comprehensive plan, the other reasons could be the lack of adequate actions by the SF in the Naxal-affected remote areas or an ineffective intelligence mechanism to conduct the operations. I guess that we parted without really agreeing with each other's point of view. Interestingly, but sadly, I had not even left Hyderabad for Lucknow, my headquarters, when I learnt that the Naxals had blown up the ancestral house of an MP of Jharkhand Mukti Morcha, Kameshwar Baitha in Palamu district in western Jharkhand.[1]

This was immediately followed up by the killing of seven people in the inter-Maoist warfare in Gumla district in Jharkhand. In fact, these two unfortunate incidents within two to three days, and more that followed thereafter, including the Latehar incident in January 2013, vindicated my stand. The fact that Jharkhand has overtaken Chhattisgarh in 2012 in the total killings by the Naxals shows that there has been a shift in their area of focus. Out of the total 409 killings of SF and civilians by the rebels in 2012 (until 15 December 2012), Jharkhand accounts for 160 deaths (39%) in comparison to 107 deaths (24%) in Chhattisgarh. Jharkhand also recorded the highest Naxal violence and deaths in the first quarter of 2013.[2]

It is important to understand that with an objective and fair analysis of the data and the situation, it is possible to foresee the imminent threats, with a reasonable degree of certainty. The leaders must always look at the future scenarios holistically with a view to pre-empt an envisaged threat or at least be forearmed to deal with it. Having analyzed the Naxal's strategy, tactics, violence, and strategic options, and keeping in perspective the plethora of government initiatives, it would be possible to crystal gaze and make an assessment of "Naxalism: 2020 and beyond". The contours of "Scenario 2020" have been analyzed under two separate heads, i.e. "Rural Naxalism" and "Urban Naxalism". In addition, the famous document of the Maoists, the "Urban Perspective Plan", has been analyzed in detail, before making an assessment of urban scenario 2020.

Development and Security

Alarmed by the growing influence and spatial spread of Naxalism, the government launched Operation Green Hunt by the CAPF to improve the security environment in the region. Having failed to achieve its aim, the government started instituting a slew of measures integrating "development and security" in one holistic package, as a well-intentioned step. To appreciate the likely scenario 2020, the essential features of the government's schemes are discussed briefly.

Schemes for LWE-affected states[3]

- Security-related expenditure (SRE) scheme: Under the SRE scheme, funds are provided for meeting the recurring expenditure relating to insurance, training, operational needs of the SF, rehabilitation of LWE cadres who surrender, community policing, etc.
- Special infrastructure scheme: This scheme caters for critical infrastructure gaps pertaining to mobility for the police/SF by upgrading the existing roads/tracks in inaccessible areas, providing secure camping grounds and helipads at strategic locations in interior areas.
- Central assistance to civilian victims: The broad aim of the scheme is to assist families of victims of terrorist, communal and Naxal violence.
- Road requirement plan for LWE-affected areas: This scheme envisages development of 1126 km of national highways and 4,351 km of state roads (total 5477 km) at a cost of Rs. 7,300 crore.
- Scheme of fortified police stations: 400 police stations in nine LWE-affected states at a unit cost of Rs. 2 crore have been sanctioned under this scheme.
- Civic Action Program: Under this scheme, financial grants are sanctioned to the CAPF to undertake civic action in the affected states. This scheme aims to build bridges between the local population and the SF.

Security-related measures

- Modernization of the police force in terms of better weapons and equipment.
- Raising of specialized units on the lines of greyhounds of the Andhra Pradesh police in each of the Naxal-affected states.
- Raising of CoBRA[4] battalions of the CRPF, and re-orientation training to the CAPF for the envisaged anti-naxal operations.
- Establishment of NATGRID[5] and POLNET.[6]
- Sanctioning the raising of India Reserve Battalions – A total of 37 battalions have been sanctioned in nine affected states, out of which 31 have already been raised (MHA Annual Report 2010–11). They have been raised mainly to strengthen the security apparatus at their level, and to enable the states to provide gainful employment to the youth, particularly in the LWE-affected areas.

- Allocation of funds for setting up 15 Counter-Insurgency and Anti-Terrorist schools in the Naxal-affected states. These have been set up, or are in the process, due to the success achieved through training of the CAPF in similar schools run by the army.
- Allocation of 10 helicopters on lease for SF operations: These helicopters have been stationed at different places in the LWE-affected areas and are on call primarily to provide prompt logistical support to the SF and the people.
- Recruitment into CAPF: Recruitment guidelines have been revised to permit 40% recruitment into the CAPF from the border areas and areas affected by militancy or the LWE.

Development-related measures

It includes the following:

- Implementation of IAP with a focus on strengthening of governance in 83 districts identified as focus areas by the government. This scheme will cover all those areas where the Naxals either have influence or can have influence in future because of development deficit.
- A "Backward Regions Grant Fund" has been constituted to replace the erstwhile Backward District Initiative. Under this scheme, 250 districts will be given Rs. 45 crore each on a non-lapsable basis for developmental works.
- The Ministry of Tribal Affairs has released Rs. 499.99 crore as additional central assistance for the construction of hostels and ashram school buildings.
- Various other developmental schemes aimed at development of critical infrastructure like roads, bridges, schools, and health care services under ongoing central schemes have been provided for the Naxal-affected districts.[7]

Governance-related issues

Some concrete steps have been taken to address the core grievances of the affected areas. One of the foremost steps in this direction has been the enactment of Scheduled Tribes and other Traditional Forest Dwellers (Recognition of Forest Rights) Act, 2006. This seeks to recognize and vest the forest rights and occupation of forestland in forest – dwelling scheduled tribes and other traditional forest dwellers, who have been residing in such forests for generations, but whose rights could not be recorded. The rules have been notified on January 1, 2008. Further, to facilitate social and physical infrastructure in the forest areas, the Ministry of Environment and Forests has issued general approval to allow such infrastructure by utilizing up to 1 hectare of forestland for non-forest purposes. The ministry has also permitted the upgrading of unmetalled (kutcha) roads constructed before 01 September 1980 into metalled (pucca) roads.

To ensure *on-ground implementation* and to carry out effective monitoring of the same, the Management Information System has been, reportedly, monitoring implementation of the various flagship programs in the 35 focus districts, which are affected by the LWE. A number of monitoring and coordination committees have been formed at each level to review not only the security situation but also the progress of the developmental plans and address issues regarding governance.[8] To encourage surrender by the Naxals, incentive awards have been increased, both for surrendering with or without a weapon.[9] The efficiency and effectiveness of these monitoring mechanisms and development plans are still not visible, commensurate with the resources allotted. The surrender incentive scheme too has not shown the desired results so far. Most of these measures look good on paper, but a lot would depend on their execution on the ground.

Categorize development activities

Given the seriousness of the situation – post Darbha Ghati and Dumka district incidents of May and July 2013 respectively – we can, on an optimistic note, expect that a national strategy and CNP will be put in place to fight the Naxal challenge. It may, however, be appreciated that improvements in the security situation are visible much more immediately than development. The development activities have a certain gestation period before the fruits of the same percolate down to the grassroots levels, in order to be clearly visible. From my practical experience of joint civic action programs in the Northeast and J&K, it would be more appropriate to categorize the development projects into immediate/short-term, medium-term, and long-term measures. This would ensure that the results of development initiatives would be visible throughout the year, to build the much-desired trust between the state and the people.

Short-term measures

The aim of the short term initiatives should be to provide basic facilities and services like medical and education facilities; development of social infrastructure; and creation of employment opportunities, in order to offer immediate relief to the local population. Some of these can be achieved by participative development, if the powers are devolved to the local governing bodies. In fact, in a coup of sorts, the Naxals reportedly won panchayat elections in about 30 blocks of Malkangiri and Koraput districts in February 2012.[10] This raises certain reservations regarding judicious utilization of enormous development funds made available to the panchayats. There is, therefore, a need to break such a nexus by improving the security environment, and strengthening the village panchayat system. Basic health services such as immunization, safe deliveries, health checkups, state-sponsored surgeries and treatment for poor, health camps and prevention of communicable diseases would require urgent attention. Coupled with this is the development of educational facilities – there is a need to revitalize school infrastructure and playfields; provide quality teachers and staff; and encourage the parents to educate children, particularly girls.

An effective public distribution system (PDS) and provision of basic civic facilities like safe drinking water through spot sources, sanitation and solid waste disposal would help to build trust with the administration. Food security would be taken care of, if adequate job opportunities are created. Besides effective implementation of MGNREGA, vocational education and training for job- related skills, based on 'skill gap survey', release of additional vacancies would help to wean away the youth from the Naxals. Development of social infrastructure – dredging of ponds, installation of hand pumps, electrification, constructing community centers, connecting major habitats by roads – and economic activities such as small-scale markets, state funding of self-employment schemes would merit concurrent attention. Picking up threads from Tripura state government's efforts, the Naxal-affected states would do well to identify the displaced people and victims of violence to provide relief in terms of shelter/housing and employment opportunities.

Medium-term measures

To carry forward the initiatives, the rural areas need to develop and analyze human resource database. The village panchayats, on being empowered, could undertake obligatory, complementary and regulatory functions, and take ethical steps for governance. Based on a health survey, the states should establish public healthcare centers, and further build the capacity and capability of hospitals. The civic action programs should graduate to providing safe drinking water through piped sources, with necessary safeguards of water testing and purification means. While improving the educational system, vocational training could be planned in ITIs, medical, engineering, law, management and veterinary colleges in high population centers. There is a need to address the employment and economic activities by establishment of mandis, markets and banking services. Construction of ponds, canals, small-scale dams, and community halls are important, as they are visible projects, which affect a large segment of the population.

Long-term measures

The aim should be to gradually assimilate various elements of the affected regions into the main stream of the nation, thus giving them a sense of belonging. In the long term, the human resource data base should graduate to integrated management information system, direct transfer of funds, UID and automation of land records. Simultaneously, land reforms and acquisition of land for poor and distribution to the landless should be pursued. The state would do well to look beyond the horizon so that long term interests of rural population are taken care of by promotion of agro and social forestry; development of water bodies and promotion of fisheries; water and soil conservation and promotion of animal husbandry. These could be further supported by creating opportunities for poor people – household and small-scale industries, self-help groups, promotion of tourism, gender and social equality and vocational training – to send a healthy signal to the masses of the state's seriousness to develop the region.

Assessment: Rural Naxalism 2020

There is an overall decline in the number of deaths in the Naxal-affected areas from 1005 in 2010 to 414 in 2012; i.e. a decline of 58%. This declining trend of the Naxals violence could also be deceptive, as they seem to be operating fearlessly in certain parts even now, and extorting money at will. Therefore, these encouraging figures should not lull the state into a false sense of complacency, as one to two years of improved performance should not be a benchmark to compare results. Yet this trend does reflect, in some small measure, the growing prowess of the SF in combating the Naxals, the effectiveness of the security-related improvements carried out by the central and state governments, and development initiatives on the ground. The specialized CoBRA battalions have been raised by the CRPF on near-similar lines of greyhounds of Andhra Pradesh. They have been successful in keeping up a sustained pressure on the Naxals by carrying out not only the regular counter-insurgency operations but also the surgical strikes based on specific intelligence, which has led to the elimination of their top leaders like Kishenji on November 24, 2011. These successful security actions along with a slew of social, economic, and political measures instituted by the union and state governments, as discussed earlier, reveal a marginal improvement in the overall situation, especially the security situation. So far, it appears that there has been no noticeable change in the Naxals' will to fight and achieve their goals. However, as insurgencies are highly complex and violent, and the root causes and conditions vary from region to region, we must not yearn for simple solutions and quick results. Cut out solutions of El

Salvador (1980s), Malaya (1948–1960), and Sri Lanka (1980–2008) must not be applied blindly, because of the unique and dynamic nature of each type of insurgency.

The central and state governments are becoming increasingly alive to the magnitude of the problem and the broad actions to be taken to manage the conflict. It would, therefore, be possible to control the situation to an acceptable level, if an integrated strategy is executed on the ground. It must be remembered that most of the insurgencies in India since the early 1950s have been controlled, by the effective intervention of the state police (e.g. Punjab, Tripura, Andhra Pradesh), along with other elements of national power. The Naxals would do well to understand that the military wings of none of the insurgencies in India have been able to graduate from guerrilla warfare to mobile/ positional warfare stage due to the mission-oriented actions of the SF and other agencies.

If the central and state governments remain focused on the implementation of all the developmental plans, participative development, and effective perception management, it would be safe to assume that there will be a definite improvement in the overall situation in the Naxal-affected rural areas. It is expected that the levels of Naxal spread and violence will come down to approximately 30% to 35% of the levels witnessed during 2009 and 2010. In other words, we may have pockets of strongholds of Naxals, which would be at different places, with a mix of "ideological-cum-criminals drug cultivators' nexus" to sustain the movement. These islands of resistance would hinge on people involved in extortion, levying taxes, criminal activities, and drug cultivation to generate funds. A few of these may continue to hold, due to the influence of the hardcore ideologues and families that have been the victims of the violence. These general areas could be – with some variations – in and around the "critically affected areas". However, if the policies are not pursued with vigor, and there is also a down-turn in the economy (having an adverse effect on the growth, development and employment opportunities), the Naxals could exploit the opportunity to re-group and consolidate in their bases and re-emerge stronger.

Urban Perspective Plan (UPP)

Large-scale violence along with the brutal killing of a manager at Maruti Suzuki's Manesar plant on July 18, 2012, had set the government seriously thinking whether there was any Maoist influence on the trade unions in the industrial belts in the National Capital Region.[11] Near-similar incidents of violence have taken place in other industrial hubs of the country in the recent years. Notwithstanding the outcome of the investigations, the Maoist urban perspective plan merits an analysis to understand its likely impact.[12]

The "STIR and UPP" documents, drafted by the CPI (Maoist), put forth the strategy for the Naxal revolution in the urban areas. Liberation of urban areas would form the last stage of their revolution, the center of gravity being the urban working class. The Naxals in their grand strategy have enumerated plans for spread of their ideology and movement among the working class in the semi-urban/urban areas. They see the urban areas as the centers of power of the "ruling class" whom they plan to overthrow to capture political power. The working class in the urban areas is identified as a reliable ally in their revolution. Therefore, if properly motivated, the working class would form a major support base for their revolution, once it closes in on the urban areas. A study of their documents reveals that the Naxals consider that the urban movement would be one of the main sources, which would provide cadres and leadership having various types of capabilities essential for the people's war and for the establishment of liberated areas. The responsibility for the provision of supplies, technology expertise, information, and other such things to the people's war is seen to lie on the shoulders of the urban class. Hence, in their perception, the urban revolution has a great significance without which they feel that the growth of the people's war will face limitations and difficulties in its advancement.

The Naxals have laid a great deal of stress on their work in the urban areas. The envisaged role of urban work would be to form close links with the working class and through the class struggle establish the party as a proletarian vanguard; thereby, mobilizing and unifying all other sections (as identified by them to be likely allies) under the proletarian leadership. As part of the long term strategy, they wish to avoid engaging the state in a fight until the conditions turn in their favor. The Naxals feel that the policy should be protecting, preserving, consolidating, and expanding the party forces, while mobilizing and preparing the broad urban masses for revolutionary struggle. Their plan propagates that the party organization within the urban areas must be a secret, whereas the mass organizations should be open to have a wide base. However, they maintain that the link between the two must be kept in utmost secrecy. The work in the cities and towns has been combined under four broad objectives.

Building the united front

It envisages the mobilization of the basic class in the urban areas, i.e. the working class, as well as other classes and sections like the semi-proletariat, students, middle-class employees, self-employed persons, and intellectuals. It also aims at dealing with the problems of special social groups like women, dalits, and religious minorities, and mobilizing them for the revolutionary movement. The goal is to form a working class unity (e.g., trade unions), industry-based unity (formation of coordination committees of unions within a particular industry), issue-based unity (joint front of various unions and political organizations to oppose government policies or take up socio-political issues), and area-based unity, also called ghettoization (common front for a particular industrial area/locality/community-related problems like water, electricity, transport, etc.). Thus, they aim at absorbing these classes into the party fold once they are suitably politicized and then build an alliance between the working and the peasant classes.

Military tasks

They have put forth the military plans for the urban areas. They seek complementary roles for the urban class as far as military tasks are concerned. These involve sending the cadre to the countryside, infiltration into the enemy (implying state) ranks, organizing activities in key industries, sabotage actions in coordination with the rural armed struggle, logistical support, etc.[13] Formation of the Urban Militia is envisaged only at an advanced stage of the movement.[14]

All India perspective plan

To put their urban plan into action, they have carried out extensive research to identify and prioritize the main target areas and their inter-se importance in helping and strengthening base areas and guerrilla zones set up by them.[15] It is under this plan that they have, according to reports, set up a "Golden Corridor Committee" to build its base in hitherto untouched areas of Maharashtra and Gujarat, stretching from Pune to Ahmedabad. These areas are one of the most industrialized belts in India and include commercial hubs like Mumbai, Pune, Nashik, Surat, Ahmedabad and Vadodara.[16]

Hit the towns

The seriousness of urban plan is evident from Ganapathy's statement after the Unity Party meet, "*No more hit and run. Now time has come to spread in the towns and identify specific targets, hit them precisely and with impunity.*"

Assessment

Long term perspective

The Naxals have correctly assessed that the urban population in India today is greater than what was available in urban China at the time of the Chinese Revolution. Therefore, the importance that they attach to the urban revolution can be gauged by the fact that they have published a separate document giving details of their ideology and strategy to be followed for the urban areas. The "urban area perspective", however, is the last stage of the Naxal revolution and definitely not the end state. The document is biased in its approach towards appreciating the Indian fact file. The assumptions of the urban profile appear to be largely correct. However, it does not cater for the ever-evolving nature and awareness of the working class, which may be a critical factor in the movement. The future perspectives have probably been deliberately ignored to retain an apparent upper hand in portraying the background information. They are looking at the urban areas to supply them with literate cadres, who would form the base of their leadership in the rural areas. In short, they, however, do not intend targeting the urban areas with guerrilla warfare-style attacks, as they fear that it may dissuade the literate urban class from supporting them, thus eroding their mass base.[17] The document thus points to a long-term approach of the Naxals towards the urban areas. This would include consolidating their existing bases in urban areas, trying to penetrate the industrial worker class, white-collar employees, youth bodies, and NGOs. They have also discussed the use of cyber warfare, which is intended to be used more in the urban environment due to higher penetration of the internet in the urban areas. Though not given out in detail, it probably intends to target vital installations; crucial networks like financial networks, security networks, and essential services, which today function on the internet; and social networks to profess their ideology and spread their propaganda.

Rich and poor divide

The Naxals intend to exploit the economic divide in the urban society. The widening disparity between the rich and the poor is the main vulnerability of the society. The tacit support being given to various types of mass organizations like trade unions, associations, and NGOs for furtherance and deeper penetration of their agenda in the government organizations/industries must be guarded against by proactive checks and preventive countermeasures. However, they have underestimated the capability of established private industry, which is today forming a large part of our services and manufacturing industry, in preventing the activism of the trade unions. Retention of a skilled work force is one of the major challenges faced by industry today. Most of the established private industries are sensitive to the aspirations of their work force. Industry is also under tremendous pressure to contribute towards social and environmental responsibilities. However, a lot more needs to be done to improve the working conditions of the workers, their pay, and facilities; terms and conditions of service; opportunities to improve their skills or professional knowledge; and progression of their careers.

Other areas of concern

The Naxals are enthusiastic to take advantage of the religious divide between the Hindus and the Muslims, by proclaiming the Muslims as the oppressed class by "fascist" Hindus.[18] This is an alarming proposition, as it tends to fuel a decade-old perceived simmering feud between the two communities, which is not true and must be guarded against at all levels through proactive measures by the government. The 'All India Perspective Plan' drawn up by the Naxals does not appear to be pragmatic since it lacks credible direction and vision. The document is vague and does not indicate clear-cut objectives, tasks, task analysis, timelines, logistics, finances, training, propaganda, communications, futuristic leadership, or a credible action plan. While the document appears to have been circulated only to appease the masses by selling a popular dream, it could actually gain ground if we do not address the serious issue of uncontrolled urbanization, huge unemployment among the youth and lack of basic facilities for the increased urban population. Extension of urban support for the armed struggle in the rural areas should also be of prime concern; thus, the state must take immediate actions to cut off all the intellectual, moral, psychological, financial, and logistics support emanating from the urban areas.

Urban Naxalism: 2020 and Beyond

> *The final objective of the revolution is the capture of the cities, the enemy's main bases, and this objective cannot be achieved without adequate work in the cities.*
>
> – Mao Tse-Tung

Based on a survey done by the Naxals, they are seriously concerned that they have failed to penetrate into the urban areas and the industrial hubs of the country, as per their plan. Their fears and apprehensions are correct. In addition to the fundamental flaws in their basic documents STIR and UPP, as brought out, spread of urban Naxalism is restricted by a few other prominent constraints. Therefore, urban movement has been discussed in three sub-parts; first, the reasons due to which the Naxals could not penetrate the urban areas, as planned (only limited presence has been observed); second, historical perspective of critical urban movements, their likely impact and lessons for India; third, measures to counter the potential threat.

Functional democratic system

Any insurgency, whether rural or urban, requires certain favorable conditions to grow and sustain itself. These conditions are an inspiring and motivating ideology that is based on a common cause, achievable goals and objectives, presence of a charismatic and popular leader(s) with a large following, suitable terrain, availability of resources, and external support. To appeal to the masses, the cause should be based on the suffering of the people. It could dwell on socio-economic divide, unprecedented corruption, voids in governance, poor law and order situation, lack of basic amenities, or a combination of such grievances. A close look at these conditions would suggest that the Naxals, at present, do not fulfill most of the pre-requisites to initiate an urban movement. People in urban areas do have fair interaction with the government functionaries to resolve their problems. Because of this, the middle class of the country is generally not supportive of the movement and its ideology, without whose support the Naxals may not acquire the desired critical mass. They have, as of now, failed to appeal and penetrate into the urban/semi-urban areas, as per their plan, over the last few years. It is undisputed that the developing countries will witness an increase in the middle class and urban population, in terms of both absolute numbers and percentage of the population. We must not forget that the mass protests in Greece, Turkey, Spain, Egypt and Brazil, in recent times, are an expression of anger of the middle class and the youth against their governments. The moot point, however, remains whether rapid urbanization in India can keep pace with development of matching infrastructures, provision of basic amenities, and employment opportunities. Kapadia expresses his concern that nearly 75% of the urban settlements of the country are growing without any spatial plan or planned intervention.[19]

Leadership

The Naxals do not have any national-level charismatic leader(s) to carry forward the movement in a synergized manner across the country's urban areas. At present, small trade unions are initiating action at the local levels, where they have local influence. It would not be possible for a number of splintered trade unions or labor unions or segments of a society to put up a joint front at the national level. Even within a large city, the industrial areas and residential-cum-slum areas are spread out in a number of pockets at different places. It would, therefore, be difficult to achieve harmonized response to a particular situation. Even in the current context, there is infighting among the leaders based on differences in their perception, or the leadership issues. Sabyasachi

Panda, Secretary of the CPI (Maoist) State (Odisha) Organizing Committee, admitted that there was lack of unity among the division that he was heading.[20] Panda, the Maoist commander in Odisha, was expelled from the party in August 2012, for allegedly shifting towards democratic reforms. Clashes between the CPI (Maoist) and its splintered group in Chatra district in Jharkhand on March 28, 2013, where 10 Maoists were killed in a gun battle, is a case in point.

Inadequate support

The Maoists are losing their traditional support base (e.g. Telangana), and are not getting sufficient volunteers to join the movement either. It appears that the unemployed youth or the dissatisfied industrial trade union workers could join the movement on specific issues that hurt them the most, but not on a permanent basis. The working class in the urban areas does not wish to pick up weapons against the state. However, the Naxals would endeavor to penetrate the urban areas and build a nucleus in the industrial corridors and slums/ghettos to exploit the sentiments of the vulnerable population. There is also the burning issue of large-scale unemployment and crime. Considering the "threat in being", we have to be watchful of the events, lest non-availability of basic amenities and unemployment of youth act as catalyst, and results in the scales tipping in Naxals' favor. It underscores the requirement of a strong and effective intelligence system at the national level to monitor the related activities of the Naxals, and the response of various communities and organizations. It is the joint responsibility of the center and state to effectively combat insurgency and terrorism. Although the constraints have been brought out objectively, it must not lull the state into a sense of complacency. Going by the experience of conflicts the world over, the country must remain sensitized to the threats in being and the new developments, which could cause a conflict, if not addressed on time.

Naxals' presence in urban areas

Despite the constraints, the Naxals have been able to exert some influence in the urban areas and the industrial hubs of the country, which is evident by their activities. During 2007 to 2012, a few of their prominent leaders and cadres have been arrested from cities like Pune, Thane, Mumbai, Nashik, Delhi, Hyderabad, Nagpur, Kolkata and Ranchi. Ramana observed, "Maoists presence in Delhi has been detected quite some time back."[21] As per another report, the Naxal showed their presence in Pune when a number of posters were seen, demanding release of their comrades, including Kobad Ghandy, Angela, Vikram and Vijay.[22] Kobad Ghandy is known to be the head of the sub-committee on urban

Naxalism. Through the medium of their front organizations, they have established links with social groups, intelligentsia, media, and academic community in the urban areas, to espouse their cause. Further, if the rebels join hands with the terrorist or crime organizations, it could pose a security challenge to the state.

As their aim is to connect with the urban masses, they would like to support the grievances of urban masses by way of protests against the state, by political and social pressures – including militant tactics, whenever required – to achieve their objectives. A case in point is the support provided to the teachers' strike in Raipur in December 2012,[23] and calls for all India level bandhs in support of issues like price rise, terror state, among other. Concerns have been raised over the likely hand of the left wing extremists in the strikes in Maruti Suzuki at Manesar in July 2012. A senior Andhra Pradesh-based cadre of Maoists, named Kopa, is known to have taken charge of their urban networks in Maharashtra. He has been entrusted to improve the Naxal base in the urban centers, around the guerrillas' command areas in jungles and remote places[24]. Although the Naxals have established nucleus cells in some of the important urban areas, they would avoid direct confrontation with the government agencies at this stage. While they would continue to provide support to the rural insurgents, they would, concurrently, consolidate their positions, subvert various organizations, support urban mass movements, and identify critical targets for the future. Although the situation in the urban areas is well under control at present, there is a need to be sensitive to the latest developments – happening the world over – to take preventive actions.

Historical perspective: Urban insurgencies

History provides us enough cases where rapid urbanization coupled with huge migration from rural areas leading to high degree of stress on the economic and social fabric of the urban society have led to terrorism and insurgency. Although the Turkish Insurgency from 1976 to 1980 is an apt example of the same, it must be viewed in the light of the differences in the political, economic, social, and cultural dynamics of the country.[25] Before drawing any major deductions, an objective analysis of the class character of their society, effectiveness of governance, and economic unevenness should also be done. Sabri Sayari and Bruce Hoffman have analyzed the Turkey's insurgency in detail. Between 1976 and 1980, Turkey experienced one of the bloodiest terrorist campaigns of the 1970s.[26] Nearly 4500 Turks, who were killed during the period, witnessed the intensity of terrorist violence that erupted in Turkey. It is well documented that the terrorist groups mostly concentrated their activities in large urban areas. Analysts of Turkish society and politics tend to see a close relationship between the hyper-urbanization of cities and the growth of political terrorism during the 1970s, among other factors. The predominantly rural society in Turkey had increasingly transformed into an urban one with the urban population almost doubling from a mere 18.5% in 1950 to 41% in 1970.[27] The unprecedented flow of villagers to the urban areas had led to striking changes in Turkey's major cities. More than three-fourth of these migrants were settled in squatter settlements in five of their largest cities. This not only led to overcrowding but also led to increase in unemployment and lack of basic civic amenities. To aggravate the situation, the Turkish economy, at that time, was facing a great turmoil; thus, it could not manage this problem. This became a source of social and economic unrest in the cities. Coupled with this, an environment of social, economic, and human insecurity dominated the migration from Turkey to Europe and, in particular, Germany.[28] The Turkish government failed to establish their complete authority in the squatter settlements, which further allowed the terrorist groups to function with impunity. These factors, along with the large proportion of young able-bodied youth among the migrants, created an environment ideal for nurturing the type of insurgency campaign waged by the extremist groups.[29] There were other contributory factors too which resulted in the situation becoming worst.

The rapid urbanization of Nepal is another case in point. Kathmandu district – the largest urban center of Nepal – has one of the highest population growth rates in the world at 4.71% per year. This rate of population growth has increased the area under urbanization to grow at the rate of 24.6% per year during the period 1984–2001.[30] It is also during this very time that Nepal was a witness to large-scale Maoists armed violence that peaked in 2002. From 2000 to September 2012, the total casualties have been 13,289; civilians (1,360), SF personnel (2,260), and Maoist insurgents (9,669).[31] A study carried out by the Harvard Business School based researchers Lakshmi Iyer and Quy-Toan-Do – published in February 2009 – states that poverty was a major cause of civil war in Nepal and it initially affected the rural areas. As the conflict progressed and became more intense, it spread to relatively better off areas, meaning the urban areas.[32]

A study of conflicts in various countries – including the recent popular uprisings in North Africa in Tunisia, Egypt, Morocco, Algeria, Jordan and Libya – suggests that three common factors that were instrumental in initiating the conflicts were the "human security concerns, power of the youth and high level of unemployment" among the working age population. Some of the other major reasons in the North African uprisings have been the political oppression, poor governance, and disregard for the well-being of the people. (The political systems, economic, social and cultural dynamics of these countries are vastly different from India's systems.) If the 'youth power' crosses the threshold of critical levels, more importantly due to lack of employment opportunities and poor response of the government or political leaders towards the problems of the society, it may throw up complex security challenges. With other contributory factors also playing their role in conflict situations, the data on the youth profile of some of the present day conflict zones like Egypt, Syria and Libya, is given in the Table 9.1. Another glaring example is Tunisia, where the youth unemployment, with other socio-economic conditions, played a prominent role in the uprising in January 2011.[34]

Table 9.1: Age Profile of Youth[33]

Conflict Zone	*Below 25 Years (%)*	*Below 35 Years (%)*	*Below 40 Years (%)*
Egypt	51.2	68.8	74.8
Syria	55.6	72.6	78.7
Libya	50.3	68.0	75.2

Nigeria is on the brink of a revolution for near-similar reasons, as given in, *Revolution: Warning from Strange Quarters.* It underscores, "In Nigeria, unemployment and socio-economic problems are slowly but surely edging the people and the nation towards a precipice."[35]

South Asian and neighboring countries – Nepal, Pakistan, Sri Lanka, Bangladesh, Afghanistan and Myanmar – also have young population with high levels of unemployment. According to the "World Factbook", the percentage of total population 'below 25 years age' in South Asian region is: Afghanistan – 64.5%, Pakistan – 55.6%, Nepal – 56%, Myanmar – 45%, Bangladesh – 52%, Maldives – 45.3% and Sri Lanka – 40%. These countries have continued to witness a large number of internal movements/conflicts. As regards Pakistan, Joshua concludes – though not surprisingly – that most Lashkar-e-Taiba (LeT) operatives were young, educated, and belonged to densely populated and urbanized districts of Pakistan, not necessarily the tribal areas. The studies also point towards "growing urban terrorism".[36] The concerns of the Nobel laureate Aung San Suu Kyi are worth taking a note of, particularly in the case of Myanmar that has a population of 54.58 millions,[37] just about 4.5% of India's population, "*I'm extremely worried about the youth employment in Myanmar, a time bomb! ... The youth have little to do in life and not much hope.*"[38] She listed Myanmar's most essential needs as basic education and vocational training to foster political reforms, and jobs to end high unemployment among the youth. In India, this problem is far more serious. Youth power has played a significant role in controlling the societies and the governments in power. While the trigger point for a movement may be an incident affecting a large segment of the society, the major causes of discontent have to be monitored and action taken well in time. Countries with weak political institutions are most vulnerable to youth-bulge-related violence and social unrest.[39]

Other contributory factors

It would be wrong to conclude that the youth power alone is the reason for initiation of civil conflicts; there are a number of other contributory factors too. Factors such as poor governance, corruption, ethno-religious tensions, poverty, large-scale unemployment, non-availability of basic amenities, and poor political institutions also throw up complex security challenges, and thus play significant contributory roles towards conflicts.

Explosion in Urban Population

Demographic growth

One of the key drivers of the national security process is the aspect of "demographic growth and demographic transition". India's population has increased from 846 million in 1991 to 1210 million in 2011.[40] It means an increase of 364 million (30.1% increase in population in two decades). While comparing the population figures of the two decades, i.e. 1991 and 2011, the rural population has increased by 204 million (an increase of 32%) and the urban population by 160 million (74%). It shows that there has been a quantum increase in the urban population over the last two decades. During the past decade also, the urban population has grown by as much as 31.2% as compared to the rural growth rate of 12.18%.[41] The Census 2011 shows us that for the first time in 90 years, urban India (91 million) has added more people than rural India (90.6 million). This explosive rise of population in urban areas is attributed to three major reasons – growth of new urban centers, natural increase, and migration from rural to urban areas. A large number of illegal migrants have also moved into the urban areas over the last few years. Since 1991, India has added 160 million to its urban population, i.e. roughly close to the present population of Pakistan, the sixth most populous country in the world. If the present growth rate were any indicator to go by, then the projected population in the year 2031 in the urban areas would be close to a figure of 590 million.[42] Thus, India would have added close to 373 million to its urban landscape since 1991, which is 60 million more than the present population of the United States (refer Figure 9.1, p. 186).

Youth bulge theory

To examine the theory of the youth bulge, the views of different research scholars and organizations have been studied, to see their relevance to the Indian environment. The term "Youth Bulge" was coined by a German social scientist and economist Gunnar Heinsohn[43] in the mid-1990s. In his book, *Sons and World Power* published in 2003, he states, "when 15 to

29 year olds make up more than 30 per cent of the population, violence tends to happen; when large percentages are under 15, violence is often imminent. There are 67 countries in the world with such 'youth bulges' now and 60 of them are undergoing some kind of civil war or mass killing." He draws particular reference to the young male population. This theory has gained greater currency in recent years, thanks to the work of American political scientist Jack A. Goldstone,[44] and the Population Action International, a Washington-based private advocacy group.[45] Youth bulges are not necessarily counterproductive. With the right focus towards education, discipline, values, vocational training for job-related skills, and adequate employment opportunities, the youth can make positive contribution to the development and growth of the country. However, this remains a million dollar question!

Youth profile: LWE-affected areas

The District Collector of the newly formed district of Sukma, Chhattisgarh, Alex Paul Menon, who spent 13 days in the Maoists' captivity revealed, after his release in May 2012 that 80% of the rebels (meaning Naxals) were illiterate and all were in the age group of 16–22 years. They carried various small arms, from which they drew a great sense of power to fight for the poor. What does it mean? First of all, there is no doubt that India is a young nation, where, as per Census 2011, the average ages of 49% of the Indian population is below 25 years, 67% below 35 years, and 72% below 40 years. Commenting on the Indian youth bulge, *The Economist* observed, "*Indian youth is one of the biggest, and potentially scariest demographic bulges the world has seen.*"[46] Surprisingly, what is most striking is that the average age of the population of the majority of Naxal-affected states is even much lower than the national average (see Table 9.2).

Table 9.2: Youth Population as Percentage of Total Population of LWE-affected States

Age in Years	*Chhattis-garh*	*Jharkhand*	*Odisha*	*Bihar*	*West Bengal*	*Maha-rashtra*	*Madhya Pradesh*	*Uttar Pradesh*	*Andhra Pradesh*
Below 25Years	51.4%	53%	46.2%	55.9%	45.1%	45.8%	53.5%	56.3%	44.6%
Below 35Years	66.4%	68%	62.5%	69.7%	61.7%	62.9%	68.7%	70.6%	61.6%

Source: Census of India, 2011. *National average age: 49% below 25 years, 65% below 35 Years.

How does the youth bulge theory affect India? Essentially, this needs to be examined in two parts; first, the statistical data of the youth, particularly in the Naxal-affected areas; and second, analysis of the resources, opportunities available to engage them in a positive manner. In the case of India, one must take into account the fact that

India accounts for a meager 2.4% of the world's surface area, whereas it supports about 17.5% of the world's population (Census of India, 2011). It would mean that a rather large population base, more importantly the youth, would contest for the limited resources of the country. Let us now look at some of the figures pertaining to youth population of India, from the point of view of Gunnar Hiensohn's theory.[47]

- As per Census of India, 2001, the youth population in the age group of 15–29 years was 284 million,[48] which constituted 27.6% of the total population of 1.028 billion.[49] This proportion is close to the 30% theory that precludes conflicts as propounded by Gunnar Heinsohn. However, even with 27.6% figure, we have seen overall high levels of insurgent activities and mass movements in the country from the late 1990s up until 2010.[50] The second set of figures suggested that nearly 32.9% of the population aged less than 15 years. As they advanced in their age profiles (15-29 years), the country continued to witness various forms of violence since then.
- The latest census (March 2011) shows that the population in the age group of 15–29 years constitutes 26.1% (316 million) of the total population of 1.21 billion.[51] The population below 15 years of age constitutes 29% of the total population, which still points to an imminent threat of violence in the future.
- By 2020, India's population is projected to be 1.32 billion. Approximately, 17.1% of this population (230 million people) would be the youths in the age group of 15-24 years. The working age population (25–59 years) would be approximately 631 million.[52] If the two are totaled up, i.e. 15 to 59 years, we come to an astounding figure of 861 million.[53] This translates into a need for creating huge number of jobs, which could otherwise lead to large-scale unemployment, and consequent internal instability. Historically, a large proportion of able-bodied youth facing uncertain future and large-scale unemployment have invariably caused the onset of mass movements/revolutions. Unemployment among the youth remains a major problem in the country, more so in the Naxal-affected areas.

According to the "UN's 2011 Revision of the World Urbanization Prospects", India will add another 477 million to the urban population between 2010 and 2050. In 2025, Delhi and Mumbai with 33 million and 27 million respectively, will be the second and third most populous cities of the world , with Tokyo (39 millions) being the most populous urban city. While providing new opportunities to improve education and public services, the urbanization trend would also pose new challenges of providing basic jobs, housing, energy, and infrastructure to mitigate poverty, expansion of slums, and deterioration of the urban environment.[54] The essence of the youth bulge of India is that it has a young population, which needs to be channelled in a positive direction – correct education, morals, values, discipline, and vocational training for jobs – to harness their full potential.

Fact file: Ground realities

India's growth has not been inclusive and has largely benefited some 250 to 300 million urban middle-class people. A meaningful trickledown effect has not been visible so far. Inequality in earnings has doubled in India over the last two decades, making it a poor performer on this count in comparison to the other emerging economies. The top 10% of wage earners now make 12 times more than the bottom 10%, up from a ratio of six in the 1990s.[55] The country's growth story should take into account its demographic structure; otherwise, it could lead to internal security turbulence. What can, however, be the tipping point and could lead to instability is the massive urbanization, which had started after 2000 due to economic revival and growth in India. The agricultural sector has grown at an average pace of 3% in the last few decades, whereas the rural population, which is mostly dependant on it, has grown at 12.18% during the last decade, which is far more than the agricultural growth. This excess population has moved out of the rural areas, as fewer people are required for agricultural work due to slow growth in the agricultural sector. Thus, there has been a rapid growth of urban population to the tune of 74% (160 million), during the last two decades.[56] Illegal migration from neighboring countries has also added to the increase in the urban population.

Additionally, rural migrants usually do not have skills appropriate for urban settings and can only find unqualified and low-paid jobs, which causes growing discontent among them. The situation is aggravated by the fact that most of the rural-urban migrants are usually young. Thus, not only will the most radically inclined part of population grow numerically, it will also become concentrated near the centers of political and economic system, presenting a potential danger to stability. This could translate into a rural-urban fault line of serious dimensions. The first manifestation of this fault line in India has taken the form of Maoism.[57]

The formulation of an urban perspective plan, specifically targeting the urban areas, is a proof of the fact that the Naxals are acutely aware that a conflict situation can be developed in India, due to the prevailing inadequacies and fault-lines. It would be prudent to understand that as of today, India's urban areas continue to remain the centers of financial hubs and economic growth. It is these areas, which form the hub of the services and industrial sectors, and, currently contribute 57% and

20% to the GDP of our country, respectively.[58] Faced with sustained counter-insurgency operations and waning mass support in rural areas due to the likely success of governmental efforts, the Naxals would, as already discussed, face a threat to their movement in rural areas in the years ahead. In the emerging geo-strategic-cum-economic environment, the mode of warfare has changed to target the economic growth of the country, by sub-conventional or irregular means. Thus, by looking at the urban areas, the Naxals would actually be targeting the very basis of our country's emerging global power – its economy – and would, therefore, be able to hit where it hurts the most. Looking at the Maoists' scheme of urban plan, Ramana wrote, "there are eight strategic areas, one of which is the 'Golden Corridor', that extends from the region around Pune and stretches to Ahmedabad and includes Mumbai, Nashik, Surat and Vadodara."[59] The Naxals are known to have formed an "urban sub-committee", that was tasked to prepare the blue print for the urban perspective plan. They have chosen the economic-cum-industrial hubs of the country to attack the growth story of the country. In the light of this, let us now look at the impact of accelerated urbanization in the Indian scenario.

Increased Risk of Conflict

Reasons for urbanization and its impact

Migration is not a problem in itself. Migration from rural to urban areas is one of the natural outcomes of economic development. Megacities provide better employment opportunities, modern life, education, industry, culture, and trade. Economic growth, especially when it is driven by services and industry, is labor intensive (both skilled and unskilled, though the proportion of skilled labor required is much more). Therefore, migration of people from rural to urban areas in search of better jobs, lifestyle, and education is a natural outcome. Coupled with this, urbanization is also driven by a lack of adequate physical, economical, and governmental infrastructure, and few job opportunities in the rural areas, which result in poverty, food insecurity, hunger, and lack of basic amenities. Environmental degradation, poor quality of life, and increased crime in the rural areas are also some of the factors for urbanization. Thus, having lost their only source of income in rural areas, they come to urban areas only to end up in slums,[60] which severely lack these basic amenities. Hence, they find themselves at the receiving end of corruption, social and economic exploitation, and an inefficient administration. Inefficient planning and poor governance have already resulted in an infrastructure deficit[61] and a lack of basic amenities for this ever-increasing population. Increasing awareness and greater visibility due to proliferation of media and revolution in communications will allow the underprivileged rural migrants and the urban poor to compare their deprived situation with the communities that have all these facilities, even though they live side by side in the same city/town. This great divide or inequality[62] is likely to create disgruntlement in the minds of the deprived people. This dissatisfaction could then develop into a conflict situation, which could be fully exploited by the urban Naxal organizations and cells. Although the democratic system does give adequate opportunities to all individuals and groups to voice their dissent, yet such conflicts cannot be ruled out; particularly when the urban resources are stretched, and there is large-scale unemployment and poor governance.

India's urban areas are much more developed than the rural areas. The much visible lop-sided development and poor delivery of essential services in the urban areas[63] is a source of great frustration to a large proportion of the urban poor. More than 60 million people (16%) of the 377 million urban population who live in 429 cities are housed in slums, and struggle for the most basic civic amenities.[64] This type of anger due to perception of deliberate unfairness and inequality in the distribution of national resources is the key factor for extreme violence and crime that we see in the Kenyan urban society today.[65] Uncontrolled migration on an ever-increasing scale is only putting more strain on the already stressed resources and enormous environmental degradation of the urban landscape. It is no surprise that as per a report by international experts, none of India's cities figured in the first 200 ranks of the global urban competitiveness report.[66] It is due to the cumulative effect of a number of reasons. Rural areas apart, our urban areas are highly short of energy, due to the high growth rate of urban population.[67] A case in point is that with rapid urbanization and massive construction work in Gurgaon, there is a serious depletion of the ground water at the rate of 1.5 meters per year (the underground water level has reached an all time low of 51 meters).[68] Similarly, the important cities of the country are increasingly becoming a victim of unplanned urbanization, industrialization, inadequate job opportunities, and cost-effective sustainable development. The urban poor, who today form a large portion of the working class in the urban landscape and settled in slums or ghettos, are, therefore, likely to be exploited by the Naxals or the anti-national elements.

Urbanization, crime, and terrorism

Historically high rates of unemployment due to lack of essential skills (which are much needed for the services and industry sector) have always served as a catalyst to drive a few of these able-bodied young men and women to a world of quick money (read crime). The media and information explosion expose the youth to an unprecedented high degree of materialistic desire. They are also considered gullible to join mass movements, strikes, demonstrations, and indulge in unlawful activities like arson, rioting, violence, and sabotage to project their annoyance and grievances. If unchecked, these could further manifest themselves in the form of organized crimes, subversion, cyber crimes, armed conflicts, and terrorism. It may, therefore, lead to some percentage of this section of the society to enter the world of crime for earning easy money.[69] This kind of crime is already on the increase and is all too visible every day. High population density and poor law enforcement are factors that further encourage crime. This is because high population density makes it easy for a criminal to be faceless in the cities. Similarly, poor law enforcement and delayed justice makes it easier for him to escape the clutches of the law.

One thing is certain that megacities with a high density of population are lucrative targets of criminals, mafias, drug cartels, and the terrorists, because of which the cities face complex socio-economic-security challenges. We have been witness to a large number of terrorist attacks in high-density populated cities like Delhi, Mumbai, Bengaluru, Pune, Ahmedabad, Jammu, Srinagar, Hyderabad, Guwahati, and Lucknow; thus the terrorists achieved publicity and higher results in terms of striking at high-value targets. The terrorists/insurgents are well aware that most of the populous megacities have inadequacies in terms of effective surveillance and intelligence systems, responsive trained police force to tackle attacks of large magnitude, surface connectivity and traffic system to facilitate quick mobilization of SF, communications, and monitoring systems to check infiltration. Due to different service providers and agencies in the cities, there is no single organization that is responsible for directing, controlling and coordinating all the resources to respond effectively against a terrorist attack.

According to various research and findings carried out across the globe, rapid urbanization has a direct link to increases in crime and conflict.[70] I entirely agree with Gautam Bhatia that "Urban planning holds the key to safer cities".[71] The developing countries give the highest priority to economic growth, with much lesser concern for environment and sustainable development. Additional population growth and density could lead to, among others, scarcity of renewable natural resources such as productive agricultural land, fresh water, and forests. With such underpinnings, the Naxals could exploit the sensitivities of the population.

Cyber warfare is another important emerging threat, to be used against the economic structures.[72] Criminal activities, especially organized crimes are funded mostly through drug trafficking. Historically, it is this network which has been used by anti-national elements to transport and finance arms smuggling. Collation of data on terrorist attacks on high-value targets in the past decade indicate that most of these attacks have been targeted at urban cities and towns, with greater frequency at densely populated cities. Therefore, though we may not see the kind of guerrilla warfare being enacted by the Naxals presently in the rural areas to take place in the urban areas; an increase in such crime-related activities may allow the sleeper cells of the Naxals to permeate into the urban landscape, to carry on with their agenda in an unobtrusive manner. They could mobilize masses, students, and workforce intensive organizations against the government machinery and build up their offensive forces through easier access to weapons and money, taking advantage of the breakdown of law and order.

Preparing for the Future: Countering Urban Naxalism

Urban movement – different manifestations

According to the Maoists' urban perspective plan, they aim to achieve their objectives in the urban areas by forging unity among the working class, industrial class, and joint fronts on common socio-economic and policy issues of the government. By subverting organizations such as industrial workers and labor unions, community organizations, slum resident unions, etc., the Naxals could exploit a weak situation to generate a local movement, to begin with. It can subsequently snow ball into something larger. With increase in operations by the SF in the rural areas, the Naxals may attack soft targets, political leaders and urban centers. The manifestations of urban movements would be much different from the rural insurgency.

Having foreseen the urban conditions, Maoist leader Kishenji had stated that they had aimed to establish an armed movement in Calcutta (Kolkata) by 2011, which did not succeed. As Naxals shift focus from rural to urban and semi-urban areas, it was reported that the rebels have started concentrating on students' hostels and slums in towns and cities, including Mumbai. They have been recruiting mainly teenagers – from the SC and ST – into their dalams (squads). They are first inducted into front organizations, and then slowly indoctrinated before recruiting into dalams.[73] In pursuance of their urban aims, they had called for nationwide bandh to protest against "price rise, scams and state terror" in February 2012.[74] The CPI (Maoist) backed the teachers' strike in Raipur, the capital of Chhattisgarh, during mid-December 2012. As per reports, more than 50,000 teachers and families were protesting against low wages. They have also been calling for nationwide bandhs on issues that affect the masses, with the added aims to show their strength and to unite the divided factions of the party. The country is likely to witness such incidents involving the support of the Maoists more often in the urban areas.

Though there is no specific data available, it has generally been observed that more than 80% of the people participating in anti-corruption movements in 2011 and 2012 were the youth, between the age group of 18 and 35 years. A brutal gang rape in December 2012 awakened India's collective conscience. The youth, with similar age profile particularly from the middle class, took to the streets – supported by the social media – to challenge the security of women, inadequate law enforcement, and the criminal justice delivery system. Naxals, besides recruiting teenagers, may make efforts to subvert certain organizations of the youth, from the middle class, to support popular protests against the action of the government – be it against corruption, lack of basic amenities like potable water or electricity, non-clearance of garbage, wage hike, improvement in the working conditions of the workers, etc. Even these peaceful movements and nationwide protests, as discussed earlier, send three serious messages. The first pertains to the quality of leadership at various levels and the response mechanism of the government. The mindset of the leaders, at all levels, has to change according to evolutionary changes in the society and people's aspirations. There is a generation gap in the current lot of leaders and the youth of the country. Second, with the growing middle-class population and their aspirations, the movements in the urban areas are not likely to be based on ideology, but on specific issues: corruption, governance, safety, public goods and services, price rise, land acquisition, etc.[75] Third, the country is likely to witness such incidents involving the support of the Maoists more often in the urban areas and in the industrial hubs of the country. Hence, it is time that we seriously start thinking on issues related to urban development, governance, and security. We do have major plans focused on urban development like the Jawaharlal Nehru National Urban Renewal Mission (JNNURM), which was inaugurated in 2005. However, what has always been lacking is the proper on-ground implementation of the same. The success, therefore, hinges on effective implementation of projects along with all-inclusive growth of our economy, to benefit all.

Given the major problems, the government needs to promote awareness about the aims and the modus operandi of the Naxals, and methods to counter the spread of Naxal threat to urban areas. The following are the areas which need to be worked upon and suggested ways to fight the potential threat:

- **Uncontrolled migration and job opportunities:** There has been an unprecedented rate of population explosion in the urban centers, particularly the metros. It is an area of immediate concern. How can uncontrolled migration to cities that are already over-stretched in provisioning of basic amenities be rationalized or controlled? This will partially be controlled by social and economic development underway in the rural areas. Kerala is perhaps one state that has developed and empowered its rural areas, having made available the basic amenities, connectivity and better quality of life. The aim should be to develop the rural economy, improve education, medical facilities, provide training for job-related skills to the youth, and create employment opportunities closer to the rural areas. However, the gestation period for this development is large and by that time, the Naxal spread would have permeated the urban areas. Therefore, we cannot wait for the rural development to bear fruit. Simultaneous focus must be applied to improving our urban and semi-urban infrastructure to absorb the migrant population. Most of our urban areas are today overflowing with population and are at the brink of saturating their resources. Hence, new planned settlements close to these urban areas and planned development of semi-urban areas, close to rural areas, must be the focus of our planners. Creation of jobs and job-related skills among the rural youth, with a combination of incentives for shifting of select services and other industries to rural areas will prevent migration of rural youth in search of greener avenues to the urban areas. The British administration, which fought the Malayan insurgency successfully, had initiated in early 1950s, the "rural industrial development projects" to empower the rural economy. At the same time, the focus must also be not lost for the urban youth, especially the poor who have already migrated and are settled in "ghettos" or slums. Creation of jobs and setting up of training infrastructure for job-related skills in the urban areas must happen side by side of the development taking place in the rural areas.
- **System of governance:** One of the weakest and the most crucial links in the system is the governance. Urban local governments in India are among the weakest in the world, in terms of both capacity to raise resources and financial autonomy.[76] Although the governments plan projects with good intentions, their execution and implementation is poor due to corruption at all levels. In the coming decades, the urban sector will play a critical role in the structural transformation of the Indian economy and in sustaining the high rates of economic growth. The availability of primary services like water supply, electricity, sanitation, sewage disposal, education,

healthcare services, and roads in most of the towns and cities of the country, having a direct impact on quality of life, are under severe stress, leading to agitations, traffic blockages, and mass movements. The gap between the aspirations of the people and the availability of goods and services on the ground is widening day by day, which must be attended to.

- **Effective intelligence and security system:** The dense urban areas make it easy for a criminal or insurgent to hide and operate. Therefore, the law-and-order machinery has to be strengthened and criminal networks and syndicates already existing in the urban areas must be targeted and broken down. These networks are likely to be used by the Naxals to spread their organized crime and terror network.[77] As per a think tank of the US, "This movement (Naxalism) in the urban areas could manifest in the form of terrorism".[78] Preventive laws have to be made harsher and implemented to reduce the activities of criminal gangs. The intelligence agencies functioning in the urban areas must be alert to the activities taking place in labor unions, social NGOs, unemployed youth, and industrial workers who overtly support Naxals' ideology or sympathize with them, and educational institutions, which have become the hub of over-ground front of the Naxals. It is equally important to monitor all the workforce-intensive organizations of essential services like conservancy and water management boards, water bodies, electricity boards, solid waste management, etc. Ideally, adequate surveillance, monitoring, and pre-emptive mechanism must be put in place, particularly during the preparatory and the subversive stages – the most vulnerable period – of any such movement in the urban areas. To counter any threat to urban areas, a specialized and responsive police force – with a good intelligence mechanism, that provides specific and real time details – would be required. The activities of the recognized front organizations of the Naxals, indulging in anti-national activities, must be closely watched, including their financial transactions. The creation of a national-level intelligence organization with close links to state intelligence, specifically tasked to maintain data bank, monitor urban Naxalism-related activities, sharing of data on-line, coordination with police authorities that will help mitigate the threat in being, assumes importance. In addition to training the nominated SF, there is a need to comprehensively analyze the envisaged threats, develop a workable strategy without causing alarm and create training infrastructures to combat threat to urban areas.
- **Investment and development:** The number of metropolitan cities with population of 1 million and above has increased from 35 in 2001 to 50

in 2011 and is expected to increase further to 87 by 2031, as noted in the report on Indian Urban Infrastructure and Services, submitted under the Chairperson, Dr. Ahluwalia; and by Kapadia, an urban expert.[79] This massive increase in population in urban areas and the subsequent rapid urbanization is putting a tremendous strain on the resources available for provision of basic amenities and livelihood. "The present investment in urban infrastructure is only 0.7% of our GDP. The investment required for improving urban infrastructure is estimated at Rs 39.2 lakh crores at 2009-10 prices. The backlog for this sector is very large, ranging from 50% to 80% across cities in India."[80] Urban local governments in India are among the weakest in the world, in terms of capacity to both raise resources and financial autonomy. Therefore, the challenge of managing urbanization will have to be addressed through a combination of decongesting the main cities, increased investment in urban areas, strengthening of the framework of governance and financing, and a comprehensive capacity-building program at all levels of the government. The recommendations put forward by expert committees constituted to deliver reports on the urban infrastructure and services like the one mentioned earlier must not only remain on paper, but must be implemented on the ground. One important aspect, which can be considered, is that the slums which have become home to a large proportion of migrant and poor population in the urban areas should be selectively legalized, so that the funds can be allotted officially and essential services like water, electricity, and sanitation can be planned or resettlement ensured for such areas. It is only then that these areas can be developed. Considering the backlog for creation of infrastructure and the requirement of investments, public-private partnership (PPP) should be bolstered to expedite the process.

- **Prevention of cyber crime:** Today most of our economic, financial, trade, transportation, communication, command and control, and educational activities are totally dependent upon information technology. The Naxals therefore have specifically mentioned tactics to use the cyber space to derail our economy and carry out propaganda against the nation state. It is a live problem as there have been numerous reports of hacking of websites by the cyber criminals. Therefore, specialized cyber crime units must be set up within the police or separate organizations in the urban areas, especially the metros, to tackle the cyber crimes. Ethical hackers can be recruited to carry out safety checks of all networks and report on any vulnerability. Proactive measures must be put in place to prevent morphed images, inflammatory material, and provocative messages being posted on the social networking sites, to incite people for mass mobilization. In addition to the US, the Chinese too have taken proactive measures to tighten its grip over the internet to monitor various social sites and anti-national activities. Rather than reacting to situations, India must proactively protect its economic, business, security, social cohesion and harmony, and cultural interests from cyber attacks or from social networking sites.

- **Urbanizing small towns:** The migration to urban areas and development of infrastructure must complement each other to ensure harmonious living. Urbanizing the villages and small towns, in a planned manner, will also help arrest the trend of uncontrolled migration to cities. The need of the hour is to empower the rural economy and to create job opportunities for the youth closer to the villages. The need to create newer semi-urban areas near rural areas or on the outskirts of large urban areas or tier-2 and tier-3 cities that can absorb the migrant population must be viewed seriously.
- **Optimum sustainable population:** A large number of metros and urban areas are already experiencing acute problems pertaining to water shortage, woefully inadequate supply of electricity, public transport system, sewerage problems, etc. A study needs to ascertain the optimum level of sustainable population in each of the present, upcoming, or planned semi-urban/urban area, based on availability of infrastructure, economic activities envisaged, basic amenities, and resources, up to next 25 to 30 years. This can be a precursor for planning development of such areas. In addition, the people can be made aware of such issues through a massive awareness campaign highlighting the drawbacks of the uncontrolled migration to urban areas and the resultant problems.

Role of industry

Industry will have to play a more positive and larger role in the nation building and ensure that the workers within their organizations are not exploited by the Naxals. Corporate leadership needs to be educated on the Naxals' Urban Perspective Plan, their strategy, modus-operandi, and the potential threats. The industrial workers aspirations must be given due consideration. The management must be fair, transparent, and must know the pulse of their workforce to prevent Naxals exploiting them. Best practices must be applied with reference to the selection, recruitment of personnel, terms and conditions, working environment, relationship between the management and the workers, opportunities for professional/career progression of the work force and pay. As the Naxals have identified the industrial hubs as their next objectives, these organizations would have to exercise greater caution and monitor the activities of their trade unions and associations. Simultaneously, the industries must genuinely contribute to the society and the environment as part of their social responsibility. Corporate found wanting in discharging their CSR, and indulging in degradation of the environment – particularly land, water, air and vegetation – must be heavily penalized, to drive home the correct message.

Community policing: New challenges

Community policing initiative in urban cities is a holistic and proactive approach that not only helps in detection and prevention of crime and crime-related activities, but also lends a psychological approach to policing. Therefore, the police must develop close relationship with the community. Trojanowicz and Bucqueroux suggest that community policing helps improve quality of life.[81]

In the Indian context, which has a diverse demographic profile and has perpetual threats from terrorist and insurgent organizations, the concept of community policing would require a few modifications, to assist in meeting new threats and challenges to national security as well. This concept needs to also factor that security of the country is every citizen's responsibility. With rapid increase in population, hyper-urbanization, and fair percentage living in slums, it is extremely difficult to monitor unlawful and anti-national activities. A case in point is that the population of Delhi (national capital territory) is 16,753,235, with an exceptionally high density of 11,297 persons per sq km.[82] In such populous cities, community policing allows the public to become a stakeholder in the safety and security of the community, the city, and brings the police in close contact with the public; thus, giving them a more humane and public face. It facilitates effective monitoring of real-time problems affecting the population, in general. Any anti-national or security-related issues or misuse of social networking sites to incite the population may also be known in advance to take proactive measures. To ensure effective implementation of the concept, the scope and the mandate have to be defined clearly, with checks and balances to prevent misuse of authority. This type of initiative must be encouraged as an institutionalized measure by city police department. Ordinary citizens, who have no criminal records, should be co-opted in this program to provide useful inputs to solve and prevent crimes, among others. However, adequate training and incentives would have to be provided to the volunteers. The program should also aim at preventing abuse of power by the citizens, who are part of this program to report such events. The nucleus of the organization should, as a concept, train the youth in the schools and colleges by conducting outdoor camps, leadership

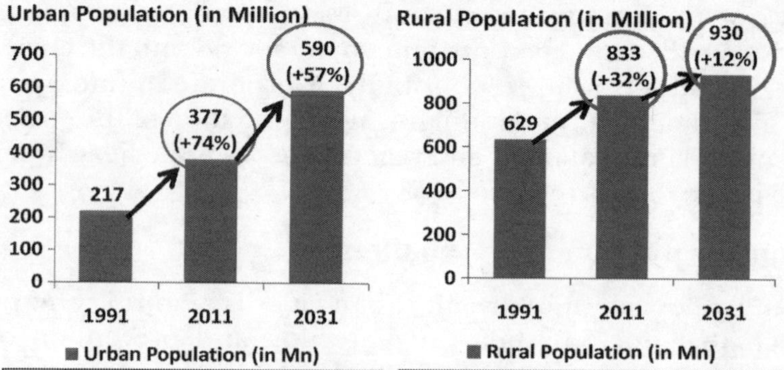

Year	Total Population	Urban Population	% of Total Population
1991	846	217	25.6 %
2011	1210	377	31.2 %
2031	1520	590	38.8 %

Year	Total Population	Rural Population	% of Total Population
1991	846	629	74.4 %
2011	1210	833	68.8 %
2031	1520	930	61.2 %

Figure 9.1: Rise in Urban versus Rural Population: Threats

Source: The Census of India 2011 and http://www.census.gov/population/www/popclockus.html, Accessed on December 20, 2011.

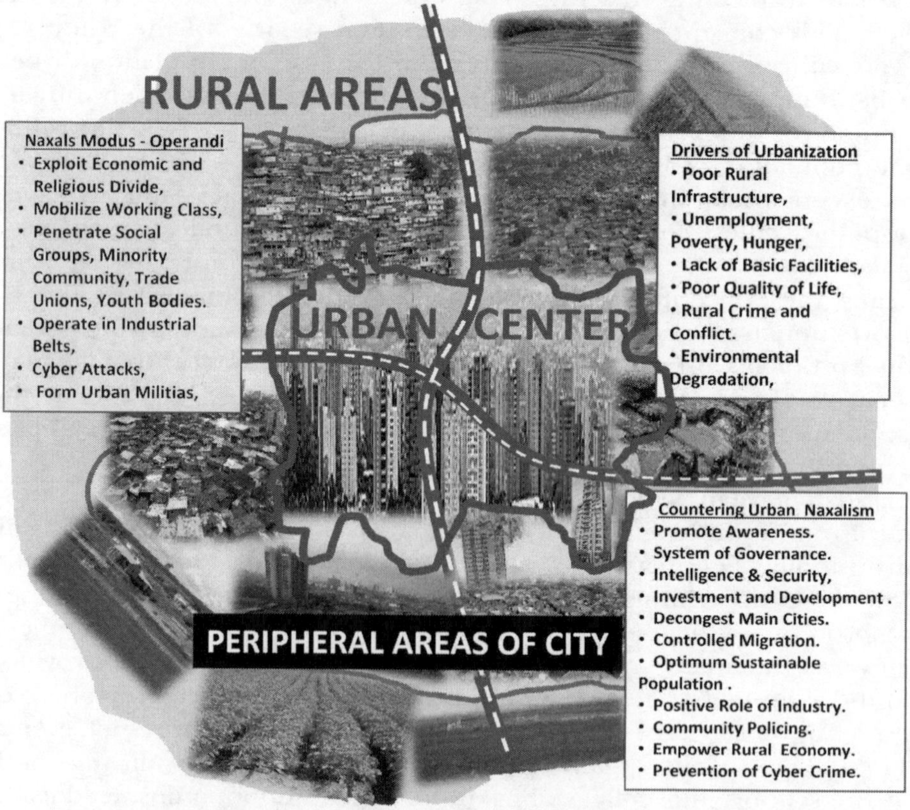

Figure 9.2: Countering Naxals' Threats to Urban and Industrial Areas

capsules and case studies. They should also help prevent crime against women and the weaker sections of the society. The center and the states need to work together to make it a success.Numerous examples of such fairly successful initiatives are available in other countries, and in India like Students Police Cadet model of Kerala,[83] Friends of Police in Tamil Nadu, Samarth Yojna Community Policing, Coimbatore, and "Prahari" program in Assam. The "Home Guards" of Kenya helped defeat Mau Mau, and the "civilian defense committees (comite's de autodefensa)" of Peru, and "sons of Iraq" are some of the examples of irregular civilian guardsmen that have made positive contribution towards providing security to communities.[84]

Summarized overview

As the threat of spread of Naxalism is no longer confined to the rural areas only, preventive actions must be taken to counter its spread to urban areas, with a sense of urgency. A brief overview of essential features of countering threats to urban and industrial areas is given at Figure 9.2 (p. 186).

Notes

1. Ipsita Pati, "Maoists Blow up MP's House in Jharkhand", *The Hindu*, May 12, 2011.
2. Bharti Jain, "J'khand records highest Naxal violence this year", *The Times of India*, April 20, 2013. [As per reports, CPI (Maoist) and People's Liberation Front of India (PLFI) have been engaged in bloody local wars in a few districts of Jharkhand. More than 6-8 Maoist organizations are active and locked in the battle for supremacy.]
3. Ministry of Home Affairs Web site. Accessed October 03, 2012, http://mha.nic.in/uniquepage.asp?Id_Pk=540.
4. Commando Battalion for Resolute Action (CoBRA) is a specialized unit raised specially for anti-Naxal operations. They are commanded and controlled by the CRPF and form part of its organization. They are highly trained in jungle and guerrilla warfare, and are equipped with the latest weapons.
5. The project, known as the National Intelligence Grid (NATGRID), is an information database grid designed to consolidate and make searchable data gathered by existing security and law enforcement agencies to prevent terrorist activity within the country. It was formed after the terrorist attack on India's financial capital Mumbai in November 2008, which raised concerns about India's intelligence infrastructure.
6. The GoI has embarked upon a modernization plan by way of communication through satellite. It is one of the most reliable modes of communication as the satellite is accessible from any place in the country. This has now become feasible on account of the indigenous availability of satellite transponders and the relevant ground equipment, such as HUB, V-SAT

(very small aperture terminal), which are capable of providing connectivity on voice/DATA/FAX.

7. The schemes include Pradhan Mantri Gram Sadak Yojna, Indira Awas Yojna, and Mahatma Gandhi National Rural Employment Guarantee Scheme (MGNREGS), National Rural Drinking Water Programme, Rajiv Gandhi Grameen Vidyutikaran Yojana, National Rural Health Mission, and the Sarva Shikha Abhyan.
8. Primary among these are the Coordination Center under the Union Home Secretary constituted in 1998, the Standing Committee of Chief Ministers under the Union Home Minister, constituted in 2005, and the creation of a separate Naxal Management Division (NMD) within the MHA for monitoring the Naxal situation within the country.
9. Vishwas Mohan, "Surrender sop for Maoists up 25 times", *The Times of India*, July 14, 2012.
10. Prabhu Dhal Samanta, "Naxals Win 30 Blocks in Orissa Panchayat Polls", *The Indian Express*, February 16, 2012.
11. "Extreme Left-wing May Have Triggered Maruti Violence", *The Times of India*, August 02, 2012.
12. V.K. Ahluwalia, "Urban Perspective Plan – An Analysis of Maoist Perspective and Assessment", Quarterly Journal, *USI*, July-September, 2012: 367–377. Parts of this article have been cited in this book.
13. "Dangerous Shift in Naxal Strategy: IB", *The Asian Age*, October 06, 2011.
14. Setting up of self-defense teams and formation of an urban militia are their major military tasks for the urban areas. Formation of the Urban Militia is envisaged only at an advanced stage of the movement.
15. Key industries, towns and cities of military, and economic significance from their document "Urban Perspective Plan.
16. Vishwa Mohan, "Red Octopus Spreads Tentacles in West India", *The Times of India*, December 14, 2011.
17. Such a similar situation had happened with the movement in 1971 when Charu Majumdar tried to usher in such dramatic attacks and violence in urban areas of West Bengal, which did not go down well with the urban middle class, thus, leading to a loss of support for the movement leading to easy subjugation by the SF.
18. CPI (Maoist) *Urban Perspective Plan*. Chapter 2, sub para 2.2.4: 14.
19. Kavas Kapadia, a professor of urban planning, "The myth of sustainable cities", *India Today*, April 08, 2013. He also mentions that the number of towns has increased from 5161 in 2001 to 7935 in 2011, an increase of 54%.
20. Special Correspondent, "There's Disunity, Admits CPI (Maoist) Leader", *The Hindu*, March 26, 2012.
21. P.V. Ramana, "Naxals spread activities in urban India", Mumbai Mirror, Sept. 20, 2012. Further, around March 2008, it was reported that an organization known as "Delhi Safai Karamchari Sangathan" which is essentially the association of sanitation workers in Delhi has been infiltrated by the Maoists.
22. "The Naxal Urban Culture", accessed on March 19, 2013, http://www.indianexpress.com/news/the-naxal-urban-culture/937567.
23. Suvojit Bagchi, "Maoists Backing Chhattisgarh Teachers' Stir", *The Hindu*,

December 17, 2012, CPI (Maoist) backed the strike in which more than 50,000 teachers and their families participated.

24. "Kopa heading Naxals' urban network in state", accessed on March 19, 2013.http://articles.timesofindia.indiatimes.com/2013-01-17/nagpur/36393822_1_naxals-security-agencies-cadre.
25. "Turkish Hizballah: A Case Study of Radical Terrorism", *The Journal of Turkish Weekly*, March 04, 2013. Accessed on March 21, 2013,http://www.turkishweekly.net/article/181/turkish-hizballah-hizbullah-a-case-study-of-radical-terrorism.html.
26. For more details, see Sabri Sayari and Bruce Hoffman, "Urbanization and Insurgency: The Turkish Case, 1976–1980" (A RAND corporation note).
27. Sabri Sayari and Bruce Hoffman, "Urbanization and Insurgency: The Turkish Case, 1976–1980" (A RAND corporation note).
28. Jeffrey H. Cohen. "Turkish culture of migration: Flows between Turkey and Germany, socio-economic development and conflict." 2012. Accessed March 06, 2013, http://www.academia.edu/937582/Turkish_culture_of_migration_Flows_between_Turkey_and_Germany_socio-economic_development_and_conflict.
29. For more details, see Sabri Sayari and Bruce Hoffman, "Urbanisation and Insurgency: The Turkish Case, 1976–1980" (A RAND corporation note).
30. Nirjal Dhakal, "Urban Management of Kathmandu Valley". Accessed February 16, 2012, http://nirjaldhakal.hubpages.com/hub/Urban-Management-of-Kathmandu-Valley.
31. Casualty Figures: Nepalese Civil War. Accessed December 03, 2011, www.satp.org.
32. Lakshmi Iyer and Quy-Toan-Do, "Geography, Poverty and Conflict in Nepal". *Working Paper 07-065*, Harvard Business School, February 2009.
33. Data Source – US Census Bureau, Feb 2012, International Database. All figures in percentage.
34. J. Shola Omotola, "Legitimacy Crisis and Popular Uprising in North Africa", *Strategic Analysis* 36, no. 5 (September–October 2012): 714. Shola observes, "Despite its claim to microeconomic achievements, the country (meaning Tunisia) has one of the highest levels of unemployment in the region.
35. For more details, see Wale Sakunbi, "Revolution: Warning from Strange Quarters", accessed October 27, 2012, http://transparencyng.com/index.php/contributions/60-guest/5986-revolution-warnings-from-strange-quarters.
36. Anita Joshua, "Young, educated and dangerous", Indian Strategic Studies, April 10, 2013, accessed April 11, 2013, http://www.thehindu.com/opinion/op-ed. An analysis of 900 biographies of Lashkar-e-Taiba (LeT) killed between 1989 and 2008 chips at the argument that youngsters take to terrorism out of poverty and deprivation alone. LeT operatives were well- educated compared to Pakistani men, and bulk of recruitment was from Punjab. Maximum terrorists were from the densely populated areas of Gujranwala, Faislabad and Lahore.
37. CIA World Facebook, estimated population as on July, 2012. China People's daily reported the population in 2009 as 59.2 million.
38. Nobel Laureate, Aung San Suu Kyi addresses the participants at the World Economic Forum on East Asia on June 1, 2012.

39. Lionel Behneer, "The Effects of Youth Bulge on Civil Conflicts", April 27, 2007, accessed December 21, 2011, http://www.cfr.org/society-and-culture/effects-youth-bulge-civil-conflicts/p13093.
40. GoI, MHA, Census of India – 2011, http://mha.nic.in/pdfs/AR(E)1011.pdf.
41. GoI, MHA, The Census of India – 2011, http://mha.nic.in/pdfs/AR(E)1011.pdf.
42. U.S. POPClock Projection. Accessed December 20, 2011, http://www.census.gov/population/www/popclockus.html. Population Census Organization, Government of Pakistan. The present population of Pakistan is 178.13 million. Accessed December 20, 2011, www.census.gov.pk.
43. Gunnar Heinsohn is a German sociologist and economist. He is known most widely for his theory of the Youth Bulge, which was propounded first by him in early 1990s and subsequently published as part of his book, *Sons and World Power* in 2003.
44. Jack A. Goldstone argues that the rapid growth of youth can undermine existing political coalitions and can create instability. Most major revolutions, including most 20th century revolutions in the developing countries, have occurred where exceptionally large youth bulges were present.
45. Lionel Behneer, "The effects of Youth Bulge on civil conflicts". Published April 27, 2007. While analyzing the period between 1970 and 1999, it states that 80% of civil conflicts occurred in countries where 60% of the population or more were under the age of 30 years. In 2007, there were 67 countries with such youth bulges, of which 60 were experiencing social unrest and violence.
46. "Farewell to Incredible India", *The Economist*, June 09, 2012 (India will be the youngest nation in 2020, with average age as 26 years).
47. US Census Bureau. International Database. Accessed January 31, 2012, http://www.census.gov/population/international/data/idb/country.php on
48. Ibid., calculated from Table 1.
49. GoI, MHA, Census of India 2001.
50. Given the youth profile of India, with multi-faceted problems such as large-scale unemployment, huge inequality in wealth, resources and opportunities, the earlier theories would merit a relook. In India, the potential threat for social unrest could persist even when "people with 15 to 29 years of age make up around 25 to 30% of the population, along with other contributory factors". This is visible on ground even today, i.e. in 2012 and 2013.
51. GoI, MHA, Census of India 2011. Calculated from Table 1.
52. Population Projections for the research have been calculated based on projection percentages given in the "Report of the Technical Group on Population Projections Constituted by the National Commission on Population", May 2006.
53. Projected population in 2020 has been calculated based on the document: Census of India, 2001, "Population Projections for India and States, 2001–2026", Tables 8, 16, and 19 (Report of the Technical Group on Population Projections constituted by the National Commission on Population, May 2006).

54. "UN's 2011 Revision of the World Urbanization Prospects", *The Times of India,* April 07, 2012.
55. For more details, see Special Correspondent, "India's Income Inequality has Doubled in 20 Years", *The Times of India,* December 07, 2011.
56. Census of India – 2011, Provisional Population Totals, Paper 2, Vol. 1 of 2011, p. v.
57. G.D. Bakshi, "Left Wing Extremism in India: Context, Implications and Response Options", *Manekshaw Paper,* November 2009.
58. The Agricultural sector only contributes 3% to 4% to our GDP.
59. P.V. Ramana, "India's 'Golden Corridor' Turning Into Maoist Hub – Analysis", *IDSA,* May 20, 2011.
60. On an average, 25% of the population in many Indian cities lives in slums; in Greater Mumbai, slum dwellers account for 54% of the total population. *Source:* Isher Judge Ahluwalia, *Report for Indian Urban Infrastructure and Services,* March 2011.
61. Mahmoud Mohieldin and Apurva Sanghi, "Growing Pains or Growing Gains?" *Mint,* December 19, 2011. (The 12th Five Year Plan starting 2012 identifies the need for USD 1 trillion in infrastructure spending to cover the gap between existing infrastructure and rapidly growing demand.)
62. Mahua Venkatesh, "The Great Indian Divide", *The Hindustan Times,* December 18, 2011.
63. Isher Judge Ahluwalia, "Report on Urban Indian Infrastructure and Services". The High Powered Expert Committee (HPEC) for Estimating the Investment Requirements for Urban Infrastructure Services, March 2011. Accessed March 06, 2013, http://urbanindia.nic.in/programme/uwss/FinalReport_hpec.pdf.
64. Mahua Venkatesh, "The Great Indian Divide", *The Hindustan Times,* December 18, 2011.
65. Development Policy Management Forum, "A Brief General Profile on Inequality in Kenya", accessed January 07, 2012, http://www.dpmf.org/dpmf/index.php?option=com_content&view=article&id=97:a-brief-general-profile-on-inequality-in-kenya.
66. For more details, see "Making cities livable", Editorial, *The Hindu,* November 03, 2012.
67. Rolland Simon and Patel Aneri, "Rural Electrification in India: Challenges and Successes", accessed January 10, 2012, http://india.carbon-outlook. In 2000, the population grew at a rate of over 6 per cent, which required a rate of 9 per cent of energy growth . In the past 20 years alone, urbanization has driven a 208% growth in India's energy consumption .
68. Ajay Sura and T. Roy Chowdhury, "New Contraction in Gurgaon Put on Hold to Tackle Water Problem", *The Times of India,* July 17, 2012.
69. Kapil Dixit, "Youths Entering World of Crime to Live Life King-size", *The Times of India,* December 3, 2011.
70. Celia V. Sanidad-Leones, "The Current Situation of Crime Associated with Urbanization: Problems Experienced and Countermeasures Initiated in the Philippines" (Tokyo, Japan: UNAFEI, 2006) and Hafiz Hanzla Jalil and Muhammad Mazhar Iqbal, "Urbanization and Crime: A Case Study of Pakistan", *The Pakistan Development Review* 49, no. 49 (2010): 741–55.

71. Gautam Bhatia, "Urban planning holds the key to safer cities", *Times of India,* March 24, 2013. "60 years of freedom has seen manifold increase in different forms of crimes."
72. Cyber Warfare in the context of Maoist movement would be associated with hacking highly sensitive strategic servers of the government carrying financial, military, and administrative data, which can lead to complete breakdown of these services and cripple the government or use of the internet as a tool for carrying out extensive propaganda and psychological warfare.
73. Indian Social Institute, *Naxal/Maoists – 2011* (January to December 2011). Human Rights Documentation (New Delhi: Indian Social Institute), accessed on March 21, 2013, http://www.isidelhi.org.in/hrnews/HR_THEMATIC_ISSUES/Naxals/Naxals-2011.pdf.
74. Ibid.
75. India already has around 250 million middle-class people*, which is expected to double by 2025.
76. Isher Judge Ahluwalia, "Report on Urban Indian Infrastructure and Services", The High Powered Expert Committee (HPEC) for Estimating the Investment Requirements for Urban Infrastructure Services, March 2011.
77. While the goals and objectives of the insurgents, terrorists, criminals, cyber criminals and drug mafias may be different, they all – seen from the examples of LTTE, Afghanistan, Pakistan, Philippines, J&K, northeastern and LWE affected states of India – apparently have certain common linkages and overlapping interests. These need to be identified and their vulnerabilities tackled in a planned manner.
78. US think tank, IANS, Washington, July 09, 2010, accessed on March 18, 2013, http://www.hindustantimes.com/News-Feed/India/Naxals-may-take-to-urban-terrorism-says-US-think-tank/Article1-569675.aspx.
79. Kavas Kapadia, "The myth of sustainable cities", *India Today,* April 08, 2013. "The sheer pace of urbanization is astounding...."
80. Isher Judge Ahluwalia, "Report on Urban Indian Infrastructure and Services", The High Powered Expert Committee (HPEC) for Estimating the Investment Requirements for Urban Infrastructure Services, March 2011.
81. David L. Carter, "Measuring Quality: The Scope of Community Policing" (School of Criminal Justice, Michigan State University). (A new philosophy of policing, based on the concept that police officers and private citizens working together in creative ways can help solve contemporary community problems related to crime, fear of crime, social and physical disorder, and neighborhood decay.... An important goal of community policing is improving the quality of life.) Accessed on January 17, 2013, http://www.cj.msu.edu/~people/cp/cpmeasure.
82. Census of India – 2011.
83. Vishwa Mohan, "Nod for community policing budget hike", *The Times of India,* April 25, 2013. The concept "provides training to students through various camps and classrooms".
84. Joe Quinn, and Mario A. Fumerton, *Counterinsurgency from Below: The Afghan Local Police in Theoretical and Comparative Perspective.* Discussion Paper, November 2010.

Chapter 10

Way Ahead

Let all bear in mind that a society is judged not so much by the standards attained by its more affluent and privileged members as by the quality of life which it is able to assure for its weakest members.

– H.E. Javier Perez de Cuellar
(Fifth Secretary General of the UN)

With the uneven socio-economic growth, large-scale unemployment, rise of fundamentalism, wide diversity, and poverty, India continues to face a number of internal security challenges. Although Naxalism was crushed to a large extent in 1971, it has grown in strength – in terms of both geographical spread and intensity of violence – due to gross underestimation of the magnitude of the problem and the lack of political will to resolve the conflict. Despite India's good growth story for the last two decades, the inequality continues to persist in distribution of wealth, resources, and opportunities. The Naxals have exploited the vacuum in governance, administration, lack of development, and unavailability of job opportunities, by establishing secure bases and strengthening the three magic bands: "the party, the people's army, and the united front." This chapter deals with formulation of the national strategy and the sub-strategies to resolve the conflict. It further highlights the importance of committed involvement and synergistic application of all the elements of national power.

Evolution of National Strategy

One size fits all

When an insurgency like the LWE spreads over a very large geographical area and affects a huge population base, it is certain that each region would have peculiar set of problems and the insurgency is likely to manifest in different phases and forms. Each region has unique and distinctive characteristics, traits, and dynamics rooted in the history of the conflict. A "one size fits all" solution cannot be applied to all the areas. Empathy to see the issues raised from the Naxals' point of view would also facilitate better comprehension of the problem and the solutions thereof. In past, the governments, at both the center and the state levels, had put in place a large number of social welfare schemes and other ambitious plans to tackle the Naxalism, some of which have borne fruit in the short term. To resolve the conflict, the first and foremost requirement is to comprehend the complexity of the entire problem, more importantly, the human dimension aspects. Therefore, it calls for having a grand strategy at the national level and different sub-strategies related to different set of on-ground conditions. The national strategy must focus on a number of dimensions – the political, social, economic, psychological, and cultural domains – to simultaneously address the root causes and solve the multi-faceted problems.

National strategy

The basic tenets of the national strategy must include the following:

- A grand strategy needs to be formulated because it determines the most appropriate pressures and influences to be brought to bear upon the Naxals in the prevalent conditions. To remove any ambiguity, it must spell the broad mandates and roles of each element of national power, the time frame, and various contingencies in which they would be required to play their part in the counter-insurgency campaign. Such an action would ensure that each element of national power/influence knows its specific role and would therefore prepare for it, and deliver the goods on the ground.
- Sub-strategies that constitute the basic framework for implementation of the grand strategy – based on the ground realities and the genuine aspirations of the people – need to be defined. These must spell out the directives/guidelines to various ministries, different departments of central and state governments, public and private institutions, NGOs, and the SF.
- Capacity building in administration, local governance institutions, infrastructure development, state police forces, vocational education, and institutions for job related skills must form part of the sub-strategies. Resources must be allocated accordingly to the stakeholders for implementation of the sub-strategies. For instance, besides providing better security environment, the poor people of the remote areas of the Naxal-affected states would require a focus on implementation of land reforms (redistribution of land to the landless), forest rights, right on selling minor forest produce, and strengthening of the grassroots level self-government organizations like the panchayats and gram sabhas.

- Development of an advantageous strategic situation to make the Naxals realize that the conflict is likely to bring about their certain defeat; thereby, forcing them to capitulate without an open struggle. It should be incorporated in the national strategy. This will only be possible if the Naxal's strategy and tactics are studied comprehensively, particularly their organization, leadership, command and control structure, popular base, cadre strength and their capabilities. The dependency of the rebels must be studied carefully to exploit their vulnerabilities. In this case, they depend on the funds, weapons, equipment, logistics support, recruits for their cadres, and safe sanctuaries, which need to be targeted. These are also closely related to the ideological propagation and the leadership of the Naxals. Simultaneously, the country's response must be based on the realistic examination of the capabilities and capacity of the states to combat Naxalism. A SWOT analysis would bring forth the answers to key questions, and facilitate preparation of security strategy, which would flow out of the "grand strategy".
- Clausewitz's thought, "Guerrilla war is the extension of politics by means of armed conflict", still holds good, particularly in the developing countries. However, the essential features of counter -terrorism should also form part of the counter-insurgency doctrine so that terrorism, which is a critical part of the four stages of a classical insurgency, viz., subversion stage, terrorism stage, guerrilla warfare stage, and mobile warfare stage, gets addressed as and when required. It is known that whenever the government response becomes effective, insurgency may fall back to the terrorism stage. While the Naxals have also been indulging in sporadic acts of terrorism, using force and violence, it complements the protracted people's war to achieve their political goals and objectives. A mix of insurgency and terrorism, therefore, tends to sustain the movement and allows it to grow stronger. This possibility has been amply exhibited by acts of terrorism, subversion, and organized crime that the Naxalites are currently indulging in. It was also true for the LTTE, where insurgency and terrorism complemented each other to further strengthen their movement.

Architecture of success

There are four important aspects to comprehension, formulation, and implementation of strategies. First, the architecture of a grand strategy rests on achieving "political will and improvement in center-state synergy" to resolve the conflict at the earliest. Refer Figure 10.1.Unfortunately, due to widely differing perceptions in the center and states, even subjects like terrorism and insurgency, having a direct impact on country's security

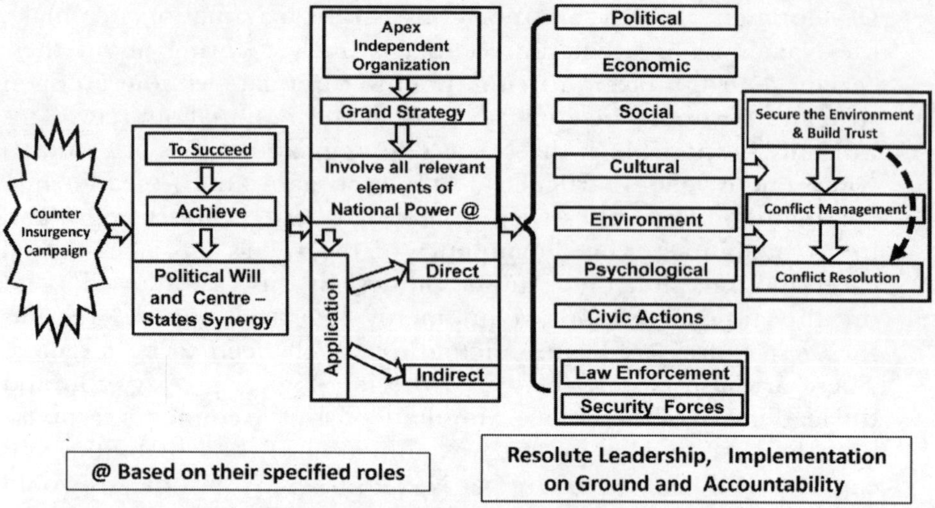

Figure 10.1: Grand Strategy for Conflict Resolution

and economic growth, have not been addressed with a sense of urgency. A case in point is the establishment of National Counter Terrorism Center (NCTC) and the necessity to adopt uniform anti-naxal policies. Second, there are six basic pillars to uplift each region and its people; namely, governance, development, empowerment, continuous dialogue and negotiations, perception management, and security, that merit attention of all the stakeholders. Of these, governance is the lynchpin that would move the wheels of other pillars. Refer Figure 10.2. Third, to strengthen each of these pillars, sub-strategies must necessarily address the political, economic, social, psychological, environmental, cultural, and security-related issues, as applicable to each region. Fourth, the aim should be to secure the environment and bridge the trust with the civil population. Although the wire diagram at Figure 10.1 shows all actions taking place in a sequence, they would invariably be concurrent.

Figure 10.2: Six Basic Pillars to Uplift Each Region and its People

Political Strategy

One of the biggest road blocks to the evolution of a comprehensive national plan and grand strategy at the national level is the lack of unity of thought at the political level. By adopting crisis management techniques, we may, at best, suppress the movement, for it to resurface again, e.g. Naxalism itself. To cite an example, the government of the Philippines had defeated the communist insurgency during the 1950s, but a decade later, another Marxist-inspired insurgency flared up. Thereafter, the Philippine leaders continued to struggle against Marxist and Muslim separatist groups.[3] As per the latest initiatives and reports, the conflict may end soon.

Political strategy is one of the most important strategies without implementation of which other sub-strategies cannot be expected to bear fruit. According to the research by Craig Charney, political will is a combination of three factors: opinion, intensity, and salience.[4] In the current phase of LWE conflict in India, "opinion" merits greater attention. Mobilization of the political will would mean finding a way to work through the dangerous and multifaceted problem like Naxalism. One of the ways to mobilize political will is to assign targets, action plans, and areas of excellence to each stakeholder. For instance, the political component of the nexus with the Naxals could be attacked by making the political executives responsible and accountable for enforcing the pro-people legislations and empowerment of the local governance bodies on ground. The Naxals' violence component can be minimized by a successful anti-naxal campaign by the SF; the bureaucratic component through performance audit; and the industry component by resorting to bringing transparency in business transactions. Collective impact of nudging the centers of gravity of individual components of the various stakeholders will be as good as mobilization of political will. Once the political will is evolved, there is a need to mobilize the opinion of different stakeholders so that political consensus is achieved. Measures that can help mobilize the political will are the effective use of modern media means, laying down the norms of responsibility for the center as well as the states. Wide-ranging debates, wherein the views of all the stakeholders, including the views of the tribal groups of the Naxal-affected states, would result in national consensus. Government must then express it to the nation by documenting national vision, national aim, national interests, and national objectives. These expressions of political consensus – assigning specific responsibilities to various elements of national power – must then be promulgated by adopting them on the floor of the House. Core areas of concern like safety and security of the citizens and their well-being must be treated as national obligations for the central as well as the state governments.

National consensus

Based on the analysis of the statistics and diverse views of experts on the subject, I feel that the rural spread of Naxal movement has apparently reached a plateau. Now on, it could spread to semi-urban and urban areas, if not checked in time. By moving into the urban areas, they would be able to divert the attention of the state from their traditional strongholds in rural areas, to recoup and refit themselves. With the mix of urban-rural movement and the inroads that the rebels are making into northeastern areas, they are not only attempting to create conditions for the revolution to sustain itself, but also trying to take the insurgency to the threshold level of the ultimate victory.

Achieving national consensus across the seats of power and party lines is a precursor to formulating the national strategy to counter Naxalism. Non-implementation of the comprehensive 14 Point Policy of the union home minister to the desired levels, points towards lack of political will and consensus, at both the center and the states. National consensus can be achieved through a sustained and vibrant campaign involving all the tools of information age to educate and sensitize the masses about the nature, depth, and enormity of the Naxal problem and the potential threats. This would trigger a debate under a very positive framework involving politicians, think tanks, bureaucrats (serving and retired), social reformers, experts on different aspects of governance, economy, industry, security, and the people from the Naxal-affected areas. A deliberate effort by the government to cover all probable areas of policymaking, ways and means to ensure implementation of schemes on ground, structured organization for performance audit, and fixing accountability would help in decision making and resolving the conflict. This would also help raise the issue on the national conscience; thereby, ensuring commitment of various stakeholders including the political parties. The political will, should then translate this consensus into the national grand strategy and enunciation of the widely accepted principles and guidelines for formulating various sub-strategies as the subsets of national strategy. A good example that merits emulation is the Malayan counter-insurgency campaign. In fact, in the first 3 to 4 years, the British administration had not achieved much success on ground. The British political leadership and the administration analyzed the situation on ground, evolved a consensus, and thereafter developed a campaign strategy.

Improvement in center-state relations

Historically, India has always remained federal because of ethnic, religious, linguistic, and cultural aspirations of the people. Lately, with the advent of strong regional parties and complex political scenario, there has been less-than-desired understanding of the national-level requirements. To achieve synergized actions towards national security issues in particular, notwithstanding the diversities within the country, the center and the states have to be on the same page. While it may sound indulging in "idealism", it is vital that our political leadership, across the party lines, should accord top priority to national interests over their political agendas and personal ambitions. The Naxals understand the weaknesses of the federal structure, and they continue to take advantage of this complex political scenario. If the violence crosses the threshold of the critical mass, we can expect certain hostile foreign powers to exploit the situation to further destabilize the heartland and target the economic growth of the country.

- Leading the initiative for counter-insurgency is a job that can be best done by the state governments, particularly when there is no overt external involvement. The central government cannot substitute the state governments with respect to any of the six pillars of regional strategy (Figure 10.2), as the latter have direct control over numerous agencies operating in the state, with accurate real-time knowledge of the people, sympathizers, underground workers, over ground workers, changes in terrain and surface communications, and the likely sensitive areas.
- In a scenario where insurgency or acts of terrorism have engulfed a number of states and are posing a danger to the unity of the country, and safety of its people, the center and the states need to synergize their efforts to defeat such designs. Under such conditions, the central government must issue directives to all the stakeholders, which should be implemented uniformly across all, without regard for political affiliations. This would be in consonance with our fundamental rights of "right to life" and responsibilities of the central government, as enshrined in our Constitution. Another method would be to move towards a "cooperative model" of internal security, which hinges on close inter-state cooperation. It is unlikely to be achieved to the desired levels, due to the prevalent complex political structure, inter-state and the center-state relationship in the country.
- The central and the state governments have announced a number of people-centric welfare schemes – with good intentions, for the right purposes, and with huge allocation of funds – to improve the socio-economic conditions of the poor people. Sadly, the delivery mechanism is poor on ground. To ensure implementation of the projects on ground, the answer lies in carrying out "performance audit" rather than the financial audit, to be undertaken by a suitably structured statutory body, based on consensus. Briefly, performance audit would mean achieving "value for money". It would mean delivery of ultimate benefits to the people on ground; in terms

of the quality of completed projects, adherence to the time lines, any cost overruns involved, and planned method of its subsequent maintenance. The statutory body could consist of representatives from the center, affected states, society, local stakeholders and field/area experts. This body should be empowered to assist the states in carrying out performance audit of the implementation of various development programs, which will enable the state to judge their effectiveness and reach.

- Continuity of policy affecting national security is the true measure of the national consensus and seriousness of pursuit of national objectives. Other than extraordinary changes in the circumstances, the long-term policy decisions must generally be adhered to, irrespective of the political party in power at the center or the state. Policies on subjects such as coordination of security operations on the inter-state borders, sharing of intelligence, surrender, and rehabilitation of surrendered people, which have a direct bearing on the security and safety of its people, must invariably be uniform – with built in flexibility to review dynamic situations – across all states. These should not be changed at will to suit the political agendas. For instance, the surrenders and rehabilitation policy needs to be backed by suitable legal provisions, catering to the long-term safety needs of the surrendered person and his family.

Intelligence: Strengthen existing organization

In the Malayan Campaign, Sir Templar realized the significance of developing intelligence capabilities to win the war. Therefore, he also assumed the responsibilities of director of intelligence to ensure timely acquisition, analysis, coordination, and dissemination of intelligence. Lt. Col. Julian Paget, a British Army officer, is highly acknowledged for his painstaking work on the subject, "Counter-Insurgency Campaign", in which he has listed six principles to win a campaign. Interestingly, in the insurgency/terrorism-affected countries like Malaya, Kenya, Cyprus, Rhodesia, Northern Ireland, West Germany, and Italy, Paget's first two principles – having an effective intelligence organization in advance of the insurgency and knowing the enemy before the insurgency begins – were not applied by any of them.[1] Because of this, it is evident that all these countries had to put in much greater efforts, commit larger number of resources and, in some cases, take harsh measures to put down the insurgencies. Still, not all of them were successful. It is equally true for the multiple insurgencies in India, including Naxalism. While some intelligence systems have been put in place in the country, they are woefully inadequate to provide the kind of intelligence required to take pre-emptive actions against the insurgents or against a rising new insurgency, or corrective measures to improve the "trust" between the people and the state. A case in point is the Naxal's urban perspective plan and the efforts being made by them to penetrate the urban areas and the industrial hubs of the country. Given the persistent threats to India from terrorist and insurgent groups, there is an urgent need to comprehensively analyze the threats due to "irregular warfare", to varied institutions of the country, not just internal security alone. It is well known that the intelligence mechanism has remained an inherent weakness in our system.

With regard to the threat of urban movement and as a part of the preventive strategy, it would be prudent to follow the Paget's principle of putting in place an effective intelligence organization to gain intelligence and prevent its spread to the urban centers and industrial hubs. It would be expedient to further strengthen the existing organizations like NATGRID and NIA – both at national level – to make them effective, efficient and accountable. It would then facilitate early detection, seamless dissemination of intelligence to the states, and result in an appropriate response to an emerging situation

In the prevailing geo-strategic environment, with a nuclear overhang, the probability of an "all out war" to resolve conflicts is remote. However, the probability of limited wars/conflicts remains reasonably high. In addition to soft power being utilized as a geo-strategic tool, the aim of the adversaries would be to target the economic growth of the country, by destabilizing it by sub-conventional means or 'irregular warfare', as the Chinese call it. They may, along with the support of the Naxals, attempt to exploit the innumerable vulnerabilities of the country. Therefore, the country requires an effective and efficient intelligence organization at the national and the state-level, to be proactive in its mandatory roles. This organization must look at all the aspects of internal security in general, insurgency and terrorism in particular.[2] With the passage of time, an insurgency tends to mutate and manifest itself in the form of terrorism, among others. A large number of terrorist and insurgent organizations in Latin America and the Middle East – on not achieving much success in their declared political goals – have turned to drug and narcotics cultivation and trafficking. Naxals are also known to be indulging in extensive cultivation of opium, drug trafficking, organized crime, and acts of terrorism.

The primary role of the intelligence organizations should be to gain information about multi-faceted aspects of insurgents such as their organizations, command and control, leaders, front organizations, changes in doctrinal and strategy/tactics, infighting, spread to urban areas, linkages with external powers and militant organizations and state of morale. It should analyze the Maoists' documents, their capabilities, their activities towards urban areas, nexus with various labor-cum-industrial workers organizations, proceedings of their periodic meetings, and the decisions taken thereof. At the national level, an online data bank – with all intelligence inputs about the terrorists and insurgents – should be maintained and made available to various stakeholders on a need-to-know basis. Simultaneously, they must gain information regarding vacuum in different regions due to political, economic, social, and governance reasons to prompt the state to take timely actions. The difficulties and grievances of the poor people must be known through various channels. The intelligence agencies must also provide inputs to the teams entrusted with the task of negotiations and dialogue, so that the critical issues that affect the people are addressed.

Eradication of corruption: "Zero tolerance"

One of the reasons for lack of political will – in a fair number of cases – is unprecedented corruption, due to the dangerous Maoist – politician – civil servant – business – police nexus. A number of politicians own swathes of land beyond the ceiling limits prescribed by the law. Apparently, grant of licenses for mining and industrial projects in the affected regions is a major source of income for such corrupt politicians and colluding officials. Johnson observes that some of the politicians and their families have a large stake in illegal mining businesses running into crores of rupees.[5] Most of the contractors of forest produce or timber provide "commissions" to corrupt officials of the forest, revenue, and police departments to run their businesses. Funds pumped in by the center for number of infrastructure development and social welfare schemes in backward districts are diverted into the coffers of the corrupt, because of the lack of accountability. In a few cases, the politicians have taken the support of the Naxals to fight their elections or the rebels have shown open support to political parties. Thus, for these reasons, the lack of political will would continue to block the efforts towards building of national consensus. In case of the nexus with the Naxals, the individual players share power and have different perceptions, priorities and preferences, based largely on their stakes. Hence, the way out of such a mess is to set the goals to be achieved by each individual stakeholder, to be followed up by an extensive awareness campaign, and by improving the public visibility of the response of each one, through performance audits. This will not only expose the erring components to public, but also create pressure on them to act in the desired fashion. Simultaneously, a quick, time bound investigation should be completed to punish the defaulters. This in turn will help move towards "zero tolerance" with regard to corruption, inefficiency, and poor delivery mechanism.

Negotiations and dialogue

Resolution of the Naxal problem could come through conciliation, compromise, negotiations, dialogue, and confidence building measures, only if the government comes out with a realistic option creating a win-win situation and appeals the common sense of humanity, for the genuine good of the people. Until as late as 2009, the central government approach to the negotiations with the Naxal groups was rather rigid. It was stated that there would be no talks or negotiations with the Naxals until they abjure violence and lay down their arms. The strategy should be based on the comprehensive understanding of the situation, i.e. level of insurgency, number of incidents, intensity of Naxal violence, material capability of the rebels, their morale, mass base support, the status of their leaders, reasons for surrenders; and the success achieved by the development and security agencies, and the impact of perception management. Similarly, the timing for offering the negotiations is equally important. Around December 2011, when a large number of the Naxal leaders were either killed or arrested by the SF, and there was a general decline in the levels of violence, that was one such opportunity. Naxal outfits were facing a great deal of pressure due to sustained operations by the government machinery and organizational turmoil such as split in the Odisha state leadership (Sabyasachi Panda's ideological differences with the party and the disunity[6]) and acceptance of democratic process[7] by the cadres (four ex-Maoists joining the All Jharkhand Students' Union). Thus, in such regions where the Naxals were not so firmly entrenched, the prevailing weak situation among their cadres and the lack of charismatic leadership could have served as a good platform to commence negotiation towards conflict management.

It can be further argued that clear superiority of the SF in India as a nation, and the temptation among local Naxal leadership to explore routes other than violence to salvage some of their objectives, provided an opportunity to the government to initiate genuine efforts for peace. Government could have – without any bargaining – adopted measures to restore human dignity and rights, set some rebel cadres (with lesser culpability) free, acknowledged the sufferings of the people, and then asked them to come to the negotiating table. It must continue its amnesty programs towards the Naxals, and reassure them of its resolve to reintegrate them into the society. Such initiatives would have served well to signal government's commitment and exposed the fallacies of their leadership with respect to their avowed cause. These initiatives do not in any way suggest that anti-naxal operations against "the hard core rebels, their leaders or their secure bases" must cease.

Incidents such as successive arrests or killing of Naxal leaders and reverses faced by them – in two or more operations in quick succession – must not be treated as opportunities to exploit them or to submit them to negotiations, but as a chance to maintain dialogue and give to the people what they deserve. More importantly, the Naxals are the citizens of the country, who are fighting for their rights to improve their socio-economic status. The methods adopted by them are unconstitutional. The states must not be soft against the hard core rebels and criminals indulging in inhuman and brutal tactics. Security operations must be pursued vigorously against them. However, as part of its long term strategy, they must be heard and their genuine grievances addressed. When all this is done, the government will have the authority to demand from them the shunning of all the activities that are unconstitutional. Among the affected population, the tribal groups – constituting about 8.2% of population of the country – are the worst affected, as they have poor representation among the political leadership or at the government's administrative hierarchy. Hence, the government has an added responsibility for identification and cultivation of suitable leaders from among the tribal groups to voice and represent their genuine concerns at the panchayat and sub-regional level. A few of these recommended steps would empower the tribal people, and isolate them from their central leadership. Hardikar was categorical when he said that, over the years, a social and political vacuum has existed in Central India, with the demise of the local Rajas,[8] which must be corrected. The bottom line is that the government must be seen to be accommodative, flexible, and genuinely concerned to resolve the armed conflict.

Devolution of power: Effective panchayats

The panchayats have continued to remain marginalized constitutional bodies[9] due to political reasons. For participation in governance and holistic development, there is a need to devolve power to the local level, by legitimate local elections at the earliest opportunity. In the final analysis, the gram panchayats and gram sabhas have to be empowered – by the political leaders and civil servants – to play their full part in not just implementation, but more importantly in the planning of various socio-economic welfare schemes of the government and other organizations. The village panchayats must also be revitalized, trained, and be empowered to settle local disputes, including land disputes. The people's institutions at the village panchayats must be strengthened in terms of their authority, organization, responsibilities, and resources. This is closely related to improving the education levels of the people, especially the females. Kerala has led the way in both planning and implementation of MGNREGA, and raising the literacy levels of the state.[10]

It should be mandatory to have 50% women as directly elected members in the panchayats (Panchayati Raj Institutions), as the Union Cabinet had approved the amendment of Article 243 D of the Constitution on August 27, 2009.[11] The sarpanch should necessarily be living in the same village to plan and implement the welfare schemes. Political alienation of the population in the affected areas must be reduced through greater representation in panchayats, municipal elections, and state assembly/parliament elections, especially women, who are locals from such areas.

Malik Ahmad Jalal, has observed that, in the short term, authoritarian regimes are better equipped to fight insurgencies due to unity of command. However, in the long term, democratic systems are more effective in managing the tensions generated by internal conflict and to bring disparate groups on board.[12] Therefore, innovative solutions are required to empower the gram sabhas, panchayats, and blocks for a long-term solution, which will further weaken the hold of the rebels. A soft and inconsistent approach of the government will continue to be exploited by the Naxals.

Socio-economic legislations

Provisions of Part IV of the constitution titled "Directive Principles" must be given the due focus, particularly in the adivasis and dalits habitation areas, so that these people can live an honorable life at the place that belongs to them. Laws should be enacted keeping in view the interest of the tribal people, forest dwellers, poor peasantry, and other marginalized sections of the society. Existing acts and policies such as Rehabilitation and Resettlement Policy, 2007; Chhattisgarh Special Public Securities Act, 2006; Forest Rights Act, 2006; Unlawful Activities Prevention Act; PESA Act; etc., must be implemented on the ground. While monetary awards may incentivize surrender by the rebels, an assured rehabilitation is far more important for a long-term solution. Generally, the functionaries take credit for the 'surrenders' to further their career interests, but rehabilitation and resettlement of the surrendered Naxals remains neglected. Fayyaz empathically states that "absence of a comprehensive rehabilitation policy for the surrendered militants (in J&K)[13] has made life hellish for those who had surrendered." The case of the surrendered Naxals needs to be managed correctly.

Unfortunately, there is a lack of urgency to debate these vital issues in the Parliament. The much-awaited land acquisition bill, meant for good of the common person, has continued to be pushed back to the later sessions. The anxiety, anguish, aspirations, and hopes of millions of people and their families, because of such delays, cannot really be quantified. Violation of the laws that have direct impact on security of people must be punishable by the law.

People-centric measures

Boots on the ground – T.E. Lawrence, a British Army officer, based on his vast experience of the Palestinian Campaign and the Arab Revolt against Ottoman Turks (1916–18), states, "Rebellions can be made by 2 percent active in a striking force, and 98 percent passively sympathetic (of the total population)". Contrary to this, the insurgencies in China and Vietnam had much higher percentage of 'active supporters'. Therefore, the percentage of three broad categories of population – in active support, against and passive neutral to the insurgents – would vary for different regions and phases of an insurgency. Mao notably said, "*Historical experience suggests that there is very little hope of destroying a revolutionary guerrilla movement after it has acquired the sympathetic support of a significant segment of the population (15 to 25%).*" It is, therefore, important to understand the behavior pattern of the "neutral" category. It is predominantly governed by the effectiveness of the SF to create a safe and secure environment. In the Kenyan and Malayan campaigns, the British had learnt that whenever it was able to protect the population from the insurgents' reprisals, it received the community's assistance and support.[14] From my personal experience of service in J&K and the northeastern region, it was evident that the passive neutral population would support the government and the SF, provided they felt safe, and were convinced of their (the SF and the government) success. On a number of occasions, the locals of the area provided valuable information about the terrorists, their strength, and movement profile; and even accompanied the SF to lead to their bases, caches or hideouts. Therefore, to win the support of the population, the civil administration and the SF must have their "boots on the ground", meaning that the civil administrators and functionaries must also have the government on the ground, to maintain close contact with the people.

In near-similar conditions, while highlighting the essential principle of colonial administration, Crawshaw referred to "getting government on the ground."[15] Besides certain obvious advantages, it restores the trust and the confidence of the people. Good military commanders follow this dictum, "boots on the ground", seriously to fully understand the ground realities, own strengths, weaknesses, critical areas affecting operational preparedness, etc. By maintaining contact with the people, the administrators also remain abreast with the ground realities and are able to strategize the future course of action. Much before the Naxals exploit the situation and take credit, the administration must fix the "minimum support price (MSP)" of the minor minerals and forest produce. Similarly, they must institutionalize the procurement system to prevent exploitation of the poor people. Political expediency on matters that are crucial for governance, law and order, justice, and provision of essential services should be enshrined in the work ethics of the governments, both at the center and the state levels. To build trust and confidence with the people, it may be prudent to extend political and economic concessions to the affected population like the adivasis, dalits, and the displaced people. All the victims of violence – by the Naxals or the SF, or on account of relocation of the people – should be provided compensation and shelter as a priority.

Legitimacy and accountability are central to the success of people-centric welfare schemes. Coupled with this is the credibility of the officials and agencies tasked to fill the vacuum in governance, administration, and development. As part of the feedback mechanism, legitimate popularity of these agencies – those indulging in corruption, high handedness, and misuse of authority – must be sought. There is an urgent need to provide people-centric administration, co-opting credible NGOs at functional level to boost state initiatives on development, and making the justice mechanism responsive. The central government had initiated the scheme in 2011, to enroll IIM graduates, IT professionals, social workers, etc., to work in the critical Naxal-affected areas. The aim is to win back the confidence of the people, create a perception change among the youth, and contribute to the cultural and social process to bring the region back on the development agenda. It is an excellent scheme, but would require much larger numbers than just 156, as reported in the newspapers.[16] Secondly, these young professionals should be subjected to intense training so that they are confident to undertake the challenging assignment. These "fellows", along with the state administration, must aim to improve the delivery mechanism on the ground, which has been the bane of our system. In addition, appointment of fearless administrators, posting of motivated and experienced short-service commissioned officers, on retirement from the army – as fellows under the Prime Ministers Rural Development Fellow (PMRDF)[17] scheme, especially in critically affected areas – will facilitate the improvement of delivery mechanism at the grassroots level. To achieve this, selection of honest and committed leaders should be the main criteria. Herbert had correctly observed, "*Good governance never depends upon laws, but upon the personal qualities of those who govern. The machinery of government is always subordinate to the will of those who administer that machinery. The most important element of government, therefore, is the method of choosing leaders.*"[18]

Diplomatic initiatives

There is also a very strong case for all the political parties to speak in one voice on the international forum against Naxalism and other internal armed conflicts in the country, and facilitate the government's efforts to curb any form of external support to them. Diplomatic efforts must highlight the crimes being committed by the rebels in the name of revolution, and international support must be garnered against the banned outfits. Our diplomatic missions and intelligence organizations must be co-opted to continuously monitor the situations and provide concrete proofs on the external forces providing support to the Naxals and other militant organizations. Political and diplomatic officials should proactively engage the concerned foreign powers and seek assurances, particularly our neighboring countries, that their soil would not be used by the Naxal sympathizers to provide any support to the Naxals, overtly or covertly. Links of the Naxals with the organizations in Nepal, Bangladesh, Pakistan, China, and Sri Lanka must be monitored by the diplomatic and the intelligence agencies to take appropriate pre-emptive actions.

Economic-cum-Development Strategy

The economic-cum-development strategy must aim towards the economic development of the regions, communities, and individuals. India has achieved a phenomenal 5% to 9% annual economic growth after 1990s. In the absence of all-inclusive growth, the rich have become richer and the poor, poorer.[20] This has widened the gap between the "haves" and the "have not", leading to a great amount of dissent, and a feeling of alienation as a natural outcome. This gap has to be narrowed considerably, especially in the affected areas. This can be done only if the local people are made stakeholders in the developmental process. The MGNREGA is a shining example of one such plan that aims at generation of employment through participative community development. However, corruption and inadequate implementation have ensured that such a wonderfully drafted and conceived plan has not been able to bring about the desired degree of development as was envisaged.[21] The prime minister of India has also asked the rural development ministry to fix the issue of delayed payments for workers of MGNREGA, as it was denting its appeal.[22] The state and central governments must seek accountability from the block and district development officers, based on performance of such schemes in the affected areas. Perhaps, the government's scheme to improve the PDS (meaning food security) and to transfer cash directly to the accounts of the respective workers would help mitigate such problems, if implemented correctly. While the growth needs to be inclusive, performance budgeting rather than financial budgeting must be the key for all centrally funded schemes.

Merely allocating the large chunks of funds for development of the affected areas is not the solution. The solution lies in getting those funds to reach the grassroots. It would be prudent if the funds were allocated as per the necessity of the region through careful study and analysis of the requirements by a think tank or body of experts. While carrying out this study, the security situation must also be assessed, to ascertain whether these funds can be fully utilized or not. In some of the critically affected areas, the conflict-prone environment is not conducive for implementation of economic or social developmental schemes. These areas must therefore be allocated fewer funds than other areas, where it is possible to implement various schemes. Therefore, allocation must be based on categorization of areas as mentioned earlier, and not on a uniform basis to all the critically affected districts. Andrew Natsios, American civil servant and an author, has aptly suggested, "*If you put too much aid too quickly into weak institutions, where there isn't capacity, you have corruption and programs don't work.*" It is true for our system of allocation of funds. Despite the announcement of numerous welfare schemes and reforms, and funds allotted, the situation on the ground does not show improvements commensurate with the resources allotted. The success of these schemes would hinge on three important factors: *ensuring implementation of projects on the ground, performance audit, and accountability of functionaries.*

Job opportunities for youth

Given the huge youth bulge in the country, with approximately 460 million people between 13 and 35 years of age, empowerment of youth, training on job-related skills, and creation of job opportunities should be an important listed goal of the 12th plan of the Government. To meet this challenge, there is a need to identify committed local partners, expand capacities, and impart quality training. During 2010 and 2011, a large number of army recruitment rallies were organized in the Naxal-affected areas of Chhattisgarh, Jharkhand, Odisha, Bihar, Uttar Pradesh, and Madhya Pradesh. It was amazing to see the number of youth, particularly the tribal youth, who turned up to be recruited into the army. At the recruitment rally at Jagdalpur in Chhattisgarh in September 2011, the results of tribal boys were impressive. The results of recruitment were even better when the army gave them pre-recruitment training. It means the youth; even the adivasis from the remote areas in particular, are looking forward to a decent life, provided they are empowered with the requisite vocational skills, and adequate job opportunities are made available. We should synergize our efforts to wean away the youth from the Naxals. A coordinated special drive should be launched to recruit youth into the armed forces, police forces, public sector undertakings, other central and state services, and the industry at large. Simultaneously, training on job-related skills – as per local demands – should be explored, for both men and women. National Rural Livelihood Mission should aim at providing training and jobs to the unemployed youth in the service sector, with added focus towards the 83 IAP districts.

Just as the Indian Army has tribal boys from various northeastern states recruited into the Assam and Naga regiments, the feasibility of raising a regiment – a 'mixed class composition regiment' on an all India basis with boys predominantly from the Naxal-affected belt of Chhattisgarh, Jharkhand, Odisha, Andhra Pradesh, Maharashtra, Madhya Pradesh, West Bengal – could be assessed. Alternatively, there should be a quantum jump in the vacancies for recruitment into the armed forces and the CAPF, from the affected areas.[19] The latter proposal can be implemented immediately, for both the armed forces and the CAPF. Relaxation in the educational qualifications could also be considered. If required, special pre-recruitment training could be conducted in the affected areas to promote awareness and to select suitable candidates, without compromising the quality of intake into the military or the CAPF. In addition, there is a need to allocate additional vacancies in government organizations, to the Naxal-affected areas for the next 10 to15 years, particularly at lower levels/grades in the initial stages.

Considering the literacy levels in the country, particularly the Naxal-affected states, there is a need to create jobs taking into account the literacy state of the people in different categories – purely illiterate, 5th dropouts, 8th dropouts, and so on. Based on data compilation of literacy levels, it should aim at conducting vocational training in the skills that are in demand locally. Simultaneously, jobs should be created based on youth population-cum-literacy demography. In other words, innovative methods need to be applied for different set on conditions arising on ground.

Electrification as a priority

More than 18,000 villages live without electricity in India. According to the International Energy Agency, 404.5 million people do not have access to power[23] (Refer Figure 2.5, p. 18). Rural electrification is an important facet of economic development to which not much attention has been paid to by successive governments. The worst affected areas in the country are also the ones affected by Naxalism, e.g. rural areas face serious problems with the reliability of power supply. The regions which are worst affected by Naxal activities are also the regions which have abundant natural resources that are used to produce electricity. However, administrative apathy has ensured that the very regions that provide the resources for generation of electricity are themselves devoid of the same. Electrification brings about greater productivity in agriculture, small-scale, and medium-scale industries. It also brings about social changes as it aids education, promotes awareness about agriculture, live stock, cattle rearing issues, and spread of media, entertainment programs which can be utilized to shape the public perception. Therefore, well-conceived schemes like the Rajiv Gandhi Grammin Vidyuthikaran Yojna (rural electrification plan), which commenced in 1995 and is specially meant for rural electrification, must be fully implemented in these areas. It was required to provide electric power to one substation in each block, and one transformer in each village. At the same time, alternate sources of energy must be tapped and provided to these rural areas. India's climatic conditions make it a very suitable place to rely on renewable energy; with very high level of solar radiation and wind capacity, renewable energy business growth has much potential.[24] As most of the states are rich in coal reserves, additional thermal power plants should be sanctioned to improve the electricity situation in the region. Renewable energy holds lots of promise in this regard and some investments in this direction can be made for areas which are very remote and where laying of new transmission lines is likely to have a large gestation period. Further, the aim should be to incentivize private investment, and rationalize the regulatory structure.

Encourage cash crops

The tribal and poor people of the remote Naxal-affected areas generally live on barter economy, subsistence farming, shifting agriculture, forest produce, and hunting of animals. These areas do not grow any meaningful cash crops, due to which they find that "illegal growth of opium and cannabis" provides them the much-needed easy money. India is one of the major drug transit or illegal drug-producing countries.[25] It is spread over 10 provinces, and most of the opium is grown upon explicit instructions from the Naxals.[26] Experience of most of the insurgencies of the world suggests that drug and narcotics trade flourishes simultaneously to provide an easy source of funds. Areas affected by insurgency in the northeastern states and LWE are known to indulge in drug trafficking extensively. Any changes to the existing practice of easy money is likely to meet stiff resistance. Given the prevalent state, cash crops must be introduced gradually, seeds and technology made available and necessary guidance given to facilitate better yield and returns. In addition, to empower the rural economy, institutions must focus on modern agricultural methods, animal husbandry and vegetable farming.

District versus block system of development

During 2011, there was a debate among the policymakers whether the development of the Naxal-affected areas should be planned based on district or block system. The existing system is district based. There are also some merits in looking at block-level development rather than at district level. Suggestions and measures regarding these, put up by the union rural development minister merit serious debate.[27] He has suggested the implementation of the IAP by identifying blocks that are affected and not the districts, which is currently the norm. This is because there are a large number of districts, which are not critically affected as a whole, but some blocks in them are critically affected. However, due to the rule regarding implementation of the IAP only for critically affected districts, the affected blocks may not get full attention, and therefore this suggestion is worth assessing. Another measure suggested by him is to allow the participation of the elected representatives of the blocks in the decision-making process regarding the type of works to be executed in the blocks.[28] In the federal system of governance, it is the responsibility of the federal government to make available funds for various important socio-economic developmental projects, but the implementation is the responsibility of the respective state government. The state governments, through the districts administrations, implement various development schemes.

- **District-based system:** Some of the factors that favor the existing system of district administration are that the districts are organized, designed, staffed, and equipped to plan, implement, and monitor the development schemes. The meager staff at the block level, to date, has not been exposed to such planning activity and may not have the capability to take on major projects independently. Infrastructure, especially roads, electricity, and bridges, has to be planned, technically examined, and implemented at the appropriate level only. With due consideration to difficulties at the grassroots, the Chhattisgarh government – and many other states – had earlier increased the number of districts from 16 to 18, and on 01 January 2012, the districts increased by 9 more. It would also be easier to implement and monitor various schemes and would provide employment opportunities to skilled personnel at the district level due to the availability of ITIs and factories, and maintenance of data bank.
- **Block-based system:** In this case, only the blocks affected by Naxalism will be provided with the much-needed resources. Certain blocks will be excluded while some will be added. A clearer picture will emerge, at the national level, regarding the effect and impact of

Naxalism. It would be easier to provide unskilled and semi-skilled employment opportunities at the block level. This would be in the form of self-help groups, local cooperatives, tribal artifacts, etc. Development of security-related infrastructure like police stations and outposts may be sharply focused upon getting quick results. Roads in the villages and towns, water supply, medical facilities, and school buildings may stand to benefit. Minor irrigation projects like check dams and ponds may be developed faster. Issues pertaining to UID, ration cards, PDS, and MGNREGA schemes may be better taken care of due to the focus of the civil administration and panchayats. The institutionalized involvement of "panchayats" and lower-level civil administration functionaries will go a long way in ensuring success of the development model at the block level. The all-important caveat to implement this scheme is that the blocks would have to be organized, staffed, equipped, and trained to undertake major development tasks, and establish additional law and order organizations, to maintain a secure environment.

Private sector as partners in progress

Private and public corporations, which operate mines, thermal electric stations, major industries, large infrastructure projects, and transportation systems, have a huge responsibility towards the nation, society, and the environment. They must play their full part towards corporate social responsibility (CSR), and be accountable to audit. The private companies contribution towards CSR must be made transparent. While granting them projects, clauses must be built in to ensure that they will offset certain percentage of the project value awarded by the government or the net profit in the developmental projects aimed at local communities in the affected areas. It may be more appropriate for the government to identify critical sectors and projects, regionally to enable private/corporates to undertake them as part of their CSR. The projects could be improving the PHCs, adoption of schools and villages, electrification of villages, construction of roads, tracks, culverts, and organizing training for job-related skills. Encouraging young and willing entrepreneurs to come and set up innovative industries in the rural areas will strengthen the rural economy.[29] Land and infrastructure must be made available to them at suitable rates to set up units in rural areas, which will provide employment to the locals. These industries must be the ones that require low level of technical skills, which are available in these areas.[30] The services sector can become a major player in this arena. In their pursuit to generate profits, the mining and industrial companies tend to neglect conservation of the environment. Government and the local bodies must prevent environmental degradation that manifests in the form of destruction of "land, water and vegetation resources".

Local art and craft

The locals in the rural areas have large amount of expertise in areas like arts and craft, food processing, cattle and poultry rearing, dairy farming, beekeeping, sericulture, aquaculture, floriculture and bamboo craft, which can be promoted widely to provide employment to them.[31] During my interaction with locals of Bastar region, they showed me their iron craft products like unique iron sculptures, which have distinctive rustic appeal. It shows that the local artisans have matchless expertise, imagination, and creativity, which needs to be further refined and marketed the world over. The tradition of iron craft in Bastar has been passed down from generation to generation. The artisans create iron sculptures with themes that include local deities, armed tribal soldiers, animals, birds, and ritual ceremonies. With the advent of modern technology in the rural areas, the youth artisans have the potential, with the assistance from the government to provide the infrastructure, artisan hubs, funds, guidance and access to markets, to display the artisanal work of their region to the world. The banks should provide interest-free credit loan to the artisans unto Rs. 3–5 lakhs, without harassment. Artisanal works such as stone craft, metal craft, iron craft, wood work, bamboo craft, local paintings, embroidery, leather work, silk industry, mithila painting, marble works, and lacquer industry could be promoted by establishing "artisan development centers" at district or block level, with their subsidiaries at the panchayat level. Each state should explore ways and means to gradually shift the artisans from unorganized sector to organized sector. It requires dedicated teams to motivate and help the rural folks with the necessary guidance until the entire project becomes self-sustainable. As part of their CSR, the industry/corporates could be given specific responsibilities to create artisan development centers, and guide the locals to become self-sustaining.

Willing entrepreneurs, who set up their projects in these areas, can innovatively optimize the available skills. There are numerous examples of such entrepreneurship in India and abroad, which can be emulated and promoted in the Naxal-affected areas. Lower attrition rates and lower infrastructure costs would make these areas more attractive to the entrepreneurs. The challenges, however, would be four fold. First, to psychologically prepare the tribal people and the poor farmers to move forward progressively from their areas of expertise to other small-scale ventures; second, to develop the requisite infrastructure in these areas; third, to provide the requisite training in close proximity; and fourth, to ensure availability of funds at the grassroots levels by strengthening the micro-credit structure. The remote areas require banks in close proximity to provide requisite loans to the needy people. The post offices have a wide network spread over the entire country. With reduction in the post office jobs due to internet, social sites, and revolution in communications, and pending establishment of banks in rural areas, post offices should start undertaking limited banking jobs to facilitate the people in the rural areas.

A "dedicated team" – part of the government or private organizations – empowered with responsibility, authority, and accountability, can achieve excellent results to uplift and empower the tribal people. Most important aspect is creation of artisan development centers and markets for the products. We need to gradually exploit the technology to empower the rural economy, provide recognition, and the best value for the goods. Web-based global initiatives, whereby, the products could be put on the web sites and demands/orders could be generated. This would enhance the market for the products, ensure global exposure, and fetch good returns.

Skills gap survey

Unemployment has acquired alarming dimensions. There are two significant aspects to unemployment. First, there is a need for creation of job-related skills among the locals, which is a major challenge and which warrants high priority. Before that, there is a requirement to carry out, on a time-bound basis, a detailed survey of the "skills gap" in the affected areas. The sectors, which can provide large-scale employment, must also be identified. Second, gender imbalance in the work force must be minimized. Poverty reduction will be much faster with empowerment of women, particularly in the rural areas. Massive unemployment among rural youth, particularly the male population, has led to unprecedented migration to urban areas as discussed earlier. Not finding any suitable jobs in the rural areas, due to lack of job-related skills, leads to disillusionment with the system; thereby making these able-bodied people perfect targets for insurgent organizations like the Naxals. The creation of National Skill Development Corporation in 2009, with the aim of developing skills in 21 identified core sectors, including in the unorganized sector, is an excellent step. The existing ITIs were set up to provide such skills to the youth, but their performance, functioning, and results have not been up to the desired level.

Public and private industries must be encouraged to recruit people from these areas. Such industries should be given incentives by way of tax breaks or allotted additional funds, depending on number of locals trained and recruited. The government must look at methods wherein the private industries or welfare foundations are encouraged to set up training infrastructure for creation of job-related skills. In addition, organizations like the Chamber of Indian Industry, the Federation of Indian Chamber of Commerce, and the Associated Chambers of Commerce and Industry of India must play a significant role towards the youth on job-related skills. Part funding by the government (while seeking a laid-down percentage of absorption in the industry) can also be considered. Greater focus should be on imparting training to youth to make them proficient tradesmen, such as plumbers, electricians, carpenters, masons, blacksmiths, tinsmiths, scooter, and cycle repairers. In addition, training on poultry management, animal husbandry, modern agricultural, honey collection methods, sericulture, aquaculture, etc., could help empower the rural economy. Therefore, pending improvement in the educational levels, we should be prepared to accept youth with lesser academic qualifications – bare reading and writing should be enough in a few trades.

Participative development

As for the development process, I had interacted with a few locals of Naxal-affected areas, and with the army troops belonging to those areas. Two issues stood out clearly: firstly, inadequate awareness of the pro-poor welfare schemes and reforms at the grassroots level; secondly, non-implementation of the schemes on the ground in real earnest, due to widespread corruption, siphoning of allotted development funds, and lack of commitment among the functionaries responsible. Non-payment of salaries to the workers of MGNREGA on time is a case in point. An effective perception management campaign and participative development programs in smaller projects in concert with devolution of power at lower levels, to begin with, will help improve the situation. Participative development will ensure that the government's welfare schemes will get the desired publicity, and the panchayats will feel secure, satisfied and empowered to undertake various projects.

Social Strategy

The Social Development Theory as put forward by renowned social scientists Gray Jacobs and Harland Cleveland in November 1999 states:

> *Social development has been defined in its broadest social terms as an upward directional movement of society from lesser to greater levels of energy, efficiency, quality, productivity, complexity, comprehension, creativity, choice, mastery, enjoyment and accomplishment.*

In view of this theory, we must understand that in the areas affected by Naxalism, the true needs of the people are recognition of their tribal rights over land, forest, and mineral wealth, law and order, self-sufficiency in food and shelter, and vocational training. The social strategy must therefore aim to address the social issues like tribal welfare, individual and community rights, education, empowerment of local communities especially women, caste and gender-based exploitation, health and sanitation, child abuse, and poverty. The strategy must ensure sustainable and equitable development of the society so that the aspirations of the individuals and the communities are addressed.

Education

One of the principal focus of this strategy must be greater thrust on primary and secondary education, with special spotlight on the education of the girl child.[32] Teachers are the most vital segments for nation building. Education will help to uplift the social status of the tribal and the poor people, and thus prevent exploitation by the powerful and the upper castes. The major challenges are the lack of quality teachers, and drop out from the school by girl children. Willing and enthusiastic teachers must be sent into these remote areas, provided adequate security and incentives to function in such remote areas are made available as compared to their similar counterparts in semi-urban/urban areas. The state must provide incentives to deliver primary education to all, and progressively expand enrolment in secondary education.

During the visits to the Naxal-affected areas in 2010 and 2011, I observed that there were instances, where two or three teachers were handling four to five classes in schools in villages in the remote Naxal-affected areas. There is a need for the states to review their policy for having schools within 1 to 2 km of the villages they are meant to service. If two or three schools are merged together, the number of teachers will increase, which will also improve the teacher-student ratio. Thus, the government will be able to provide more funds to one school, provide better infrastructure and facilities, and will be able to appoint more permanent teachers at lesser cost. It will also be possible to monitor the education system and other allied facilities like midday meals to students. The strength of ad-hoc teachers is much more than those who are employed on the permanent basis. The permanent employed teachers get full pay scale and emoluments, whereas the temporary or the ad-hoc teachers are paid on a lower pay scale. The huge pay disparity is a major factor of discontentment, which also affects the motivation of the teachers.[33] To overcome such problems, as part of their social responsibility, it will be apt to post the newly appointed young teachers to the remote areas first, considering it as their probation period. Such teachers should be provided with adequate incentives, recognition, and career progression in the future. Considering the security requirements, the teachers should move into the interior Naxal-affected areas in a progressive and gradual manner, in consonance with the security strategy for that region. Social groups and NGOs must be involved in educating the locals about the benefits of education and encourage the families to send their girl child to schools. Individuals who belong to these ST or SC and who have climbed high in the society must be enrolled to become role models. Such individuals must be identified and given the due recognition in public, particularly among the ST and SC.

Employment and education to women will provide a greater social standing to them. The BDOs and SDOs must focus on these issues. The MGNREGA scheme must have special provisions for the Naxal-affected areas, e.g. for women like childcare facilities and more percentage of reservation. Works other than manual labor like artisan, handicraft, and tailoring (garment enterprises) works must also be brought under the provisions of the MGNREGA scheme.[34] This will encourage more women to participate in this scheme and will increase their bargaining power in the society, thus lifting their status. The scheme should be made more popular by ensuring payment of wages on time and by increasing the scope of work profiles. Micro-credit institutions will have to be strengthened in these areas to provide credit to women for self-employment. Bangladesh has achieved huge success in micro-credit financing to uplift their poor people, the women in particular.

Social equality and justice

Land reforms

Social equality and justice for all are enshrined in our constitution. The Naxal movement began primarily as an agrarian movement with the demand to provide land to the tillers and the landless. All governments had recognized this problem since independence. However, due to vested interests, corruption at various levels within the government as well as the administrative machinery, lack of adequately trained revenue staff for carrying out survey on the ground, and general apathy in the administration, meaningful actions were not taken. Even though the Land Reforms Act was passed by the Parliament in 1955, until now the majority of states have not taken any action to implement it on the ground. There are three main problems related to land in India: large number of poor possessing little or no land, concentration of land in the hands of few, and large number of legal disputes due to lack of proper revenue records. Availability of land with the government is not a problem as the states have a large amount of land which they had acquired subsequent to the passing of the Land Reforms Act of 1955. The act laid down the ceiling of holdings. However, the lack of adequately trained revenue officials and the enormity of the task to update ownership records and title deeds are hampering the recognition of the landless.[35] All the 83 districts under the IAP should be covered under National Land Records Modernization Programs, at priority.

Therefore, there exists a case for increasing the number of trained staff for the same. As a priority for the areas critically affected by Naxalism, this can be done by mobilizing specialists in the field of land survey and recording. Besides training and employing the youth of the area, retired ex-servicemen from the artillery, engineering branches of the army/armed forces (who specialize in land survey), the CAPF, and civil departments can be called upon to augment the revenue staff at the district level to carry out survey and recording with a sense of urgency. Accomplishment of such tasks by the nominated team would require, what the army would call, "mission-oriented" approach. Settling of title disputes can be fast tracked by setting up fast track courts especially for this purpose (though these courts would require revenue records to be updated to pass judgments).

Another area of concern with respect to land that has not been addressed adequately is the issue of leasing of land. To improve productivity of agriculture and reduce insecurity among small and marginal farmers, who rely on leased land, ground-breaking solutions like creation of Public Land Banks (PLBs) managed by Panchayati Raj Institutions[36] in the affected regions can be thought of and deliberated upon. These PLBs would take "deposits" of land parcels from owners wanting to lease out their land, with full freedom to withdraw their deposit after a fixed period. These in turn would be leased out to needy farmers at calibrated rates based on land quality. This would benefit both the sections, the ones who deposit, as they would get a small payment depending upon the period of deposit (analogous to short-term or long-term deposits in a financial bank) and the ones who lease in the land as they get tenure security and lower transaction costs.

Forest rights

Another area of concern is the restoration of the Right to Forests to the Tribals. This has been a cause of disagreement for decades in the largely tribal inhabited areas of Chhattisgarh, Jharkhand, Madhya Pradesh, and Odisha. The Indian Forest Act, 1927, India's main forest law, was created primarily to serve the British need for timber. The law destroyed all the community management and regulation systems that had existed before, forcing people to choose either abandoning the forest entirely or living as a "criminal" within or near it. Corrupt forest officials were known to exploit the simple tribal people, giving rise to angst among them. This has largely been addressed by the government through the ST and Other Traditional Forest Dwellers (Recognition of Forest Rights) Act, 2006, that was passed on December 18, 2006 and has been in force from December 31, 2007. It has been supplemented by a notification framed by the Ministry of Tribal Affairs on procedural aspects of the act on January 1, 2008. Besides implicit implementation of this act to benefit the grassroots levels, speedy documentation and updating the record of rights will also play a major role in successful restoration of forest rights through the medium of this act.

Panchayats Extension to Scheduled Areas (PESA) Act

Implementation of PESA Act of 1996 enables the powers of managing the forest in the hands of the panchayats run by the tribes, who live there. Among the districts affected by Naxalism, 32 are PESA districts.[37] To be fair, the Forest Rights Act of 2006 and the Panchayat (Extension to the Scheduled Areas) Act should be applied to all the 83 districts under the IAP. However, this act has not been fully implemented by the various state governments as it overrules all land acquisition acts. It would put an end to the hegemony of mining and other powerful industrial lobbies. Some of the state governments still apply the Central Land Acquisition Act of 1894 vintage, to acquire tribal lands. The implementation of PESA Act would provide the much-needed boost to the feeling of being part of the nation to these communities, who have been separated from the mainstream. A social audit must be carried out by an independent body of experts, appointed by the government, from time to time of all the plans implemented to review their impact on the society and the requirement of midcourse correction, if any.

Perception Management Strategy

A perception management campaign should aim to establish credible rapport and relationship of the government with the masses, as also convey the right message to the insurgents. It means the state and perception management agencies must complement each other. While discussing Tripura's case of successful counter-insurgency campaign, Sahaya aptly describes that the psychological operations were focused on correcting the tribal person's negative perception about the state and the mainland, and inducing confidence in and credibility about the state's intentions.[38] In various ways, perception management combines truth projection, ground realities, security operations, cover and deception, and psychological operations. To apply on ground, a critical part of perception management effort is to understand others' perceptions and the rationale for those perceptions.

Target the ideology and strategy

It is the men's mind that wars of subversion have to be fought and decided.[39]
– Kitson

Due to the prolonged nature and the casualties being suffered by the SF, anti-naxal campaigns could degenerate into killing insurgents (Naxalites) rather than addressing the root cause of the problem. The primary aim of a perception management campaign would be to target the ideology and the strategy of the Naxals, and thus deny them achieving their objectives. Wisdom has it that it should be our endeavor to neutralize them rather than kill them (insurgents) and focus on the "Number Game." SF must, however, continue to conduct operations against the hard core Naxals. A perception management campaign has to be pitched at different levels to achieve the stated aims.[40] The difference would be in objectives of the perception management campaign at each of these levels. When designing a perception management plan, it is important to analyze the insurgents' ideology, beliefs, mass following, capabilities, leaders, decision-making capabilities, and ability to propagate their beliefs. Detailed research would facilitate formulation of strategic goals and objectives of perception management. To do so, there is a need to analyze in detail the Maoists' ideological documents, historic eight documents, STIR, UPP, party program, and record of discussions during various meetings and interviews, and the method of indoctrination at the grassroots level. Two of their documents – STIR and UPP – have been analyzed in detail in this book to formulate the perception management strategy. A few themes can be chosen from the Maoist documents and proved to be unrealistic and impossible to achieve. Atrocities by the Naxals; killing of civilians; kidnappings; using women, children, and innocent civilians as human shield during operations; targeting passenger trains and helicopters; destruction of socio-economic infrastructures; etc., could also become a very useful theme, with accurate statistical data. The prevailing fear psychosis and sentiment of the local population should be part of the perception management campaign.

Acknowledge state's inadequacies

During the Malayan counter-insurgency campaign, the British worked on a detailed perception management and propaganda plan to build trust with the population, and to discredit the insurgents. They acknowledged the voids in their administration. In formulating their strategy, they gave higher priority to human intelligence, to get accurate information about the "people." Chatterji emphasizes that perception management requires a vast and unique information database, and highly trained analytical skills to shape an information campaign, which is hard hitting and far reaching. The information campaign can be won only if the government has a clear political plan and a grand strategy in place. Otherwise, it may lead to an inconsistent plan of action. To maintain the credibility of the organization and build trust, the campaign must be based on truthful statements and commitments. It would be more appropriate to acknowledge, with tact, the existing inadequacies and fault lines in the system of governance than to hide them. The areas of deficit in governance and administration must be acknowledged and the remedial measures being instituted be given adequate publicity. By so doing, the concerned official functionaries and the stakeholders would at least try to address the fault lines. If a commitment is made, it must be honored. This approach is likely to result in the establishment of a good rapport and relationship with the population at large.

Morals, ethics and discipline

The image of the government and its functionaries is a soft and fragile asset, and hence, it has to be protected and preserved by exhibiting the utmost regard for ethical conduct and disposition. Negative features that will turn a population against government functionaries are ill-trained forces employed in critical areas, resorting to unethical practices, corruption and moral turpitude. Worse, we will end up creating more number of rebels. Therefore, there should be zero tolerance for cases of sexual assaults, rapes, custodial deaths, and extortion by the SF and the police.

For morals, ethics, tolerance and discipline, the youth generally tend to follow the benchmarks set by their elected representatives and leaders, which is the bane of our system, particularly in a pluralistic society. One of the measures in psychological warfare, besides empowering the youth with vocational skills is to instill good values and moral ethics through the education system. This will lead to a better state of discipline and code of conduct, thereby reducing many ills of the society that aid the insurgency environment and many more threats that are non-conventional. The National Cadet Corps (NCC) is one such institution, already functional, which is capable of carrying out this task of infusing patriotism, leadership, good morals, ethics, and discipline in the youth of the present and the future. This institution must be further expanded, strengthened and invigorated in the newly created states like Chhattisgarh and Jharkhand. Joining the NCC could be made compulsory in senior-level schools and colleges, both government and private. Ex-service members and eligible youth must be trained and recruited in large numbers as instructors and staff to carry out this mission. The initiative of the Kalinga Institute of Social Sciences at Bhubaneswar, where 16,500 students from the tribal areas are being educated, is an excellent method of combating Naxalism.[41] More institutions of this kind will help wean the youth away from the clutches of the Naxals. Besides educating the youth of the future, the "fertile recruitment catchment areas" will automatically start disappearing.

Cultural, religious and language sensitivities

Cultural sensitivities, faith, leanings, aspirations, and customs will serve as the themes for the perception management. It would require common themes at national level and sub-themes to target specific requirements and sensitivities of different regions. A great amount of stress was laid by the US forces and the ISAF, also called the coalition forces, in Afghanistan to understand the local customs, practices and traditions, so that they are "culturally sensitive." Also having a few soldiers fluent in local languages like Pashto or Dari languages helped greatly to establish rapport with the locals. As understanding of human behavioral science is an important facet of a counter-insurgency environment, the SF must also induct officers and junior leaders, who have studied sociology, psychology, political science, and law to analyze the people's aspirations and human behavior to bridge the gap of trust deficit with the state. The junior leaders also must understand the need to work within the framework of law. Although there is wide diversity in languages, customs, and culture, the troops should be sensitive to, and respect the customs and culture of the local population, to win their trust and social space. In the case of Vedanta (bauxite mining project),the Supreme Court protected the community as well as cultural and religious claims of the Dongria and Kutia Kondh tribes of Odisha, and directed the gram sabhas to take the final decision on the subject.[42] More examples of this nature – under the authority of the civil administration – will help to empower the local bodies.

The tribes and communities have a very vibrant culture with unique dance forms, folk lore, and artisan works. Their culture, arts, craft, and language should be promoted using all resources available at the state and the national levels. Cultural festivals, advertising of culture through electronic media, promotion of artisan work through special exhibitions, introduction of aspects of their culture in school curriculum of respective states are some of the measures that can be successfully employed to promote their culture. It is quite common to see traditional dance forms, cultural festivals, and exhibitions of arts and craft being organized at Delhi and state capitals. Sometimes, it gives an impression that such functions – patronized with a view to draw political mileage – end up merely as photo opportunities for politicians. It does not achieve the desired impact at the affected grassroots levels. Such events and their scope need to be expanded to larger areas, so that the population of the affected areas gets the message about the seriousness of the government to promote language, culture, and traditional arts and crafts.

Mass communication technique: Themes and slogans

The communication technique advocates use of themes, slogans, media, audio-visuals, music, rumors, etc., to convey messages to the target audience. In complex insurgencies that are marked by volatility, fear, uncertainty, and ambiguity, a good theme or slogan helps convey the emotions and positive message to the masses, more quickly. Another important facet for perception management is the presentation of the communication plan, innovativeness of promotional strategies, creative ideas, and the work experience of the agencies that are likely to be involved in the entire effort to counter-Naxalism. In the Philippines, the Aquino administration announced their proposals under the theme "Food and Freedom", "Jobs and Justice" as the key to peace. In Tripura, the slogan, "Forest for Environment and Forest for Livelihood", targeted to generate 60% of its total revenue from forests. It was a huge success.[43]

The villagers of Menda Lekha (Gadchiroli district, Maharashtra state) coined the slogan, "Mere gaon mein meri sarkar", (My government in my village), to regain the community forest rights (CFR) for their produce.[44] Similarly, symbols and mascots can also be used effectively to communicate an ideology or strategy and its objectives. They are effective means to convey ideas, concepts, and themes on variety of issues like participative development, education for all, against violence, human nature, jobs for school dropouts, against recruitment of child soldiers, etc. A combination of slogans, symbols, mascots, and themes could be extremely effective in conveying meaningful messages. Based on the comprehensive analysis of fears, apprehensions, and aspirations of the people, specialists should create them.

- To connect with the masses, the language in which themes need to be communicated has to be the local language/dialect. It should further be aimed at the specific strata of the audience, which is the most critical target. During one of my visits to the army's formation, conducting training in the Naxal-affected areas of Kondagaon-Narayanpur (Chhattisgarh) in July 2011, I visited a battalion of the Bihar regiment. They had a few adivasi soldiers belonging to the same area. When the locals met their own kith and kin (adivasis), there was a visible sense of happiness, satisfaction, and confidence building between the army and the local population. The locals listened to the adivasi boys (soldiers) with rapt attention, with some disbelief, and there was an 'instantaneous connect' between the locals and the army. Imparting training to the youth – before the recruitment rallies of the army and the presence of a female medical officer in the section hospital – further helped cement the trust, rapport, and confidence between the army and the civil population. It was an exhibition of genuine interest towards the welfare of the tribal and poor people. The locals started visiting and using the medical facilities and camps of the army in larger numbers. Despite the fact that the army has been conducting training in the Naxal-affected areas, there has been no violence or attack against it in any form. In the overall plan, perception management played a very important role in changing the mindset of the Naxals, the people, the media, and the local population. Careful thought was given to perception management before moving the army for training into Kondagaon-Narayanpur and it worked. The message conveyed by the tribal boys of the army was well received and the response of the local populace showed a positive change. The credibility and acceptance of the message would be further enhanced if the spokesperson is one who is trusted by the Naxals. He should be fully conversant with the customs, traditions, culture, language, and local dialect.

- Messages against the Naxals should be bold and loud, but conveyed in a gradual manner. Multiple modes such as audio, visual, pamphlets, plays, art groups, interactive seminars, workshops, and discussions should support it, so that lasting impressions are created. Such impressions are best reinforced by another run through by different agency and different media. Media is a very important tool, especially if it is a vernacular media with good repute. Popular local newspapers, folk shows, radio, and TV channels that enjoy great credibility among the locals should be used for the perception management campaign. During the earlier times, leaflets were used extensively, as part of psychological warfare and propaganda. Although the importance and usage of leaflets for propaganda or psychological warfare has reduced over the years, it continues to play an important role in the remote areas of Chhattisgarh, Jharkhand, Odisha, eastern Maharashtra, and northern Andhra Pradesh.

Creation of apex-level synergy

Synergy in perception management could only be achieved by creating an organization starting from apex level and percolating to the functional level. It will exhibit a "genuine unity of thought" in the country's fight against Naxalism. While at the top level, the role should be in terms of formulating strategy, coordinating, and allocating resources for perception management, the lower echelons should be entrusted with the task of managing and executing the efforts. Aspects such as civic action, psychological operations, propaganda, and counter-propaganda need to be planned and controlled at different levels of functioning. The central government, the state government, the SF, and the district-level administration need to have structured organizations manned by personnel trained to undertake such tasks and equipped to execute them in the desired manner. The vehicles for perception management such as print media, electronic media, and the web-based social media are very crucial for implementation of the strategy. Internet and social networking sites can play havoc as well as help positively, depending on who controls and who is using it. Internet and social networking sites accessed through cell phones have become the norms for generating and directing mass movements. Examples of North African revolutions in 2011 and 2012, and the eruption of violence in Assam in 2012 are live examples indicating the necessity to hone the skills and the abilities as a nation to harness their true potential. J&K is another example where separatist organizations are exploiting the potential of these tools for managing bandhs, protests, and violent activities.

Negotiations, dialogue, and consensus – building measures are as much a part of perception management as any other strategy. The persons nominated for such tasks should be scientifically trained, as it is specialized work. It helps the counter-insurgents to understand the problems and hardships of the rebels. While the state should be willing to talk to the Naxals without any conditions, track II diplomacy should work alongside. For instance, in an adverse situation for the rebels, wherein they have suffered large casualties or their leaders have been killed/arrested, track II could be utilized to discuss and negotiate with a genuine desire to bring normalcy. It would be prudent to discuss less contentious issues first, to begin the process of sustained dialogue. Rather than trying to bargain, the state should try to meet their legitimate requirements to provide a better quality of life. In addition, the state must make constant efforts to maintain sustained dialogue with the tribal communities, as they have remained marginalized. However, the state must not be soft against hard core insurgents and their leaders.

It is common to hear statements being made by the political leaders and ministers on Maoists issues to improve the situation, while also seeking political mileage. It would be most appropriate to brief the concerned leaders of the state's efforts towards policy issues and perception management, so that conflicting views are not expressed on policy matters conveying a wrong message. The population at the grassroots gets more confused than inspired by such statements. It also compromises the genuineness of the spirit of government's initiatives. A wide reaching campaign must be mounted by constituting a special task force, with experts from all fields, who will be able to analyze the problems and perceptions, regionally. They will thus provide guidance on every issue being raised not only by the rebels but also by the affected people, and the people enamored by the ideology of the Naxalites. They would, thus, be responsible not only for projecting the good work being done by the government, issuing rebuttals for any hollow claims or opinions made by the Naxals and the intelligentsia, but also carrying out critical analysis of governmental work and policies. However, to ensure security of perception management plans, the organization of the task force must be small with direct reporting channels. For instance, news items such as "Maoists in Jharkhand join the democratic process" and "Reverse sterilization procedure to surrendered Naxals, to return to normal family life", in 2012, are positive indicators, which could get adequate publicity in vernacular press as well. Therefore, media has a responsible role in providing balanced news to highlight the difficulties of the people and also projecting the initiatives of the government towards improving the overall situation.

Medak model: Rural radio services

An excellent and successful experiment carried out in Medak district of Andhra Pradesh using mass media is the adoption of low-cost, low-power "Rural Radio" services, which dealt specifically with local issues like agriculture, animal husbandry, government schemes, educational schemes, opportunities for vocational training, cropping patterns, education, health and medical services, and awareness of individual and community rights.[45] To enhance the effectiveness and its reach, this was transmitted in the local language/dialect, and through songs composed on folk tunes. It is the most popular means to reach the tribal people. It was an extremely successful and effective experiment. A similar means could be adopted in other states, by using the funds made available through IAP.

Security Strategy

A comprehensive security strategy should aim to provide a secure environment, to facilitate governance and development initiatives come to fruition. It should help in not only reducing and curbing violence by the Naxals, but also in preventing activities like linkages with other militant organizations, recruitment of cadres, drug trafficking, gun running, illegal money transactions, and cyber crimes, which directly supplement their activities. For optimum results, close coordination is required between different forces of the CAPF, state police, intelligence services, forest department, civil administration, and logistics services. A broad categorization of the regions – according to the degree of Naxal activities recorded and the security situation prevailing – would help to develop an appropriate response to specific problems. The areas can be broadly divided into four categories.

- **Category I, Areas under Naxal control:** These are those limited areas, which are presumably under the control of the Naxals, as the writ of the state is not effective in the remote areas. According to reports and assessments, these areas include certain inner forested parts of Dandkaranya, Abhujmadh and adjoining areas (Bijapur, Sukma, Bastar, Dantewada, Narayanpur, Gadchiroli, Malkangiri, Koraput), Latehar, Palamu, Gumla, Lohardaga, Simdega and Dumka in Jharkhand.[46] Parts of about 13 districts fall under the purview of category I. Earlier, certain segments of these areas were perceived as "liberated zones", primarily due to absence of effective form of government machinery and security apparatus. This had occurred due to three major reasons – remoteness of the areas and difficult terrain, the high degree of violence by the Naxals resulting in massive fatalities to government functionaries, and the lack of political will of the respective state governments to send their authorities, backed by adequate SF into these areas to re-establish their control. Besides the requirement of a large contingent of trained SF personnel, the fact that massive security operations could result in collateral damage and casualties to the civilians, had also dissuaded some of the affected state governments to conduct anti-naxal operations. It had actually boiled down to creating a void by the political, governance, administrative, or law and order agencies, which was filled up by the rebels to provide relief to the people. Given the large geographical spread and inadequate troops to deploy, the inter-se-distances of the company operating bases of the SF is rather large to provide any operational or logistic mutual support to each other or to provide a secure environment to the local population. It makes the SF extremely vulnerable, from both operational and logistics points of view. These are some of the major constraints in achieving effectiveness.
- **Category II, Critically affected areas:** These are the areas in which the levels of Naxal activities are high; although there is government machinery, it has been rendered ineffective due to the threat and fear of the Naxals. According to the Naxal management division

(NMD) of the MHA, this category has a total of 83 districts, including districts that form part of Category I areas (refer Appendix F for state-wise details of the districts). However, going by the statistical data and the ground realities, total number of critically affected districts would be around 40 spread over nine states, including category I. Lately, Naxals seem to have increased their areas of influence to western Odisha, particularly Nuapada, Navrangpura, Balangir and Kandhamal.

- **Category III, Moderately affected areas:** These areas are under moderate influence of the Naxals. The government machinery is functional and effective, though it routinely faces hindrances in its functions due to intermittent violent activities.
- **Category IV, Potential/targeted areas:** These are the areas that are likely to be targeted by the Naxals due to the low levels of development or their potential to provide mass support/logistical support to their movement in the future. It not only includes rural areas but also includes certain semi-urban/urban areas and industrial hubs of the country.

Thus, the national strategy to tackle the Naxal problem should be applied according to the categorization of the areas. Broadly, they will be considered under two broad groups with over lapping areas, namely, "Security-led Development" and "Development-led Security" groups. Security and development are interdependent and are complementary to each other. For the development process to be effective on the ground, the environment should be secure enough to facilitate a preliminary survey, planning, and execution on the ground.

Security-led development

Category I

The strategy should aim at providing a secure environment, and at establishing the state authority in the area by progressively squeezing the operational space of the Naxals. By such an action, they would be forced to move away to another area, during which they expose themselves to the SF, surveillance, and intelligence agencies. In addition, they would be required to re-establish their writ, command and control, and the logistics in a relatively new area, which would take a long time. It would then be possible to provide physical, political, social, and economic security to the people, and for the development process to begin.[47] The initial requirement in these areas would be for the government to mobilize the SF at its disposal and carry out security operations in a "gradual and progressive" manner. Simultaneously, civil administration should move to consolidate and initiate their development projects. It is vital for each region to identify the critical infrastructures required by the people that will show immediate results in terms of improving the quality of life.[48] These may be in the form of providing critical roads, bridges, culverts, provision of electricity to a block or a remote region, medical facilities in terms of a bigger hospital to cater for specific prevalent diseases, improvement of schools, cellular communication facilities and establishment of ITIs to provide job-related skills in various categories. The resources of the nation should be mobilized to complete the major infrastructural projects. These schemes would also provide employment to the locals, besides fulfilling the immediate aspirations of the people. In so doing, the rebels would start losing their control in their so-called "strong holds".

The aim should be to "Clear, Hold, Develop, Consolidate, and Move Forward." How would these actions translate on ground, i.e. creating a secure environment for the development to take place and for basic facilities to be provided?

- The counter-insurgency operations should aim to *clear* the area bit by bit, moving from secure areas to difficult areas and by restricting the critical escape routes of the insurgents. However, in such difficult forested tracts, it is virtually impossible to plug all the escape routes.
- Then *hold* the cleared area with adequate forces and protect the population from reprisals by the Naxals. Simultaneously, success by the SF or the military needs to ensure two aspects; first, carry out a de novo appreciation of the threats to the area thus cleared, and second pertains to building the functional institutions of the state administration, bringing in the officials, and improving the governance.
- Simultaneously, *develop* the area economically and socially, by encouraging participative development. Depending upon the state of surface connectivity, it may be prudent to repair and upgrade the tracks, culverts, and bridges. Coupled with this, the mobile phone towers should be made fully functional. Functional health centers, up gradation of schools, provisions for drinking water, and efficient functioning of the PDS would help restore normalcy. This can happen only if the SF and civil administration can build confidence among the masses. However, it would be one of the most challenging tasks to move the local populace.
- *Consolidation* phase requires continuous political dialogue and implementation of self-governance by local communities. The stages "hold-develop-consolidate" must start taking place concurrently. Tripura practiced this philosophy with vigor and achieved good measure of success.

- Thereafter, the SF could *move* on to areas in the depth. During the final part of consolidation phase, the thinning out of SF must take place to facilitate the state administration, the local governance bodies and the police to carry out their functions effectively. It would, however, take considerable time to reach the consolidation phase.

Development Task Force (DTF) – Just as the army had developed the concept of the Army Development Group (ADG) in 1960s, which had successfully worked in the remote under-developed rural regions of the northeastern states, the government could consider a comparable civil organization called, "DTF" to carry out near-similar tasks. The ADG was a composite task force consisting of a security team and a composite development force, with a judicious mix of teams of combat engineers, communication personnel, medical and veterinary representatives, and electrical and mechanical engineers. Similarly, the DTF could be the lead agency that can carry out low-level rural developmental works within the security umbrella of the SF company operating bases. Close security would be provided by the in-built security team forming part of the DTF. In this way, some of the short-term tangible projects – providing basic amenities – would start come to fruition.

Category II

The strategy in these areas must aim at re-establishing the control through sustained counter-insurgency operations by deploying the SF on an operational grid. In these areas, due to the nature of the Naxal activities, simultaneous application of development programs along with security operations would be possible. The DTFs must be employed to carry out developmental tasks, as described in Category I earlier.

Development-led security

Category III

These areas could be given higher priority for allocation of development funds initially, in comparison to those under category I or II. This is because the situation in these areas is presently conducive for carrying out the developmental activities, without much hindrance from the rebels. The SF may not be deployed in these areas but should be highly mobile with failsafe communications, located in bases within an acceptable reaction time. Maximum effort should be put in by both the state and the center to develop these areas socially and economically, as these areas are within "visible reach" of the population residing in category I and II areas. Therefore, good governance and development of these areas can serve as a massive force multiplier in psychological and perception management campaigns.

Category IV

These areas are those that have been identified by the Naxals as possible future targets of their movements. These would include semi-urban/urban areas and industrial hubs, which are likely to be targeted by the Naxals in due course. Some activities of the Naxals – mostly through front organizations – are already functional in these areas. Thus, these areas need to be looked at as a priority for implementation of action plans for curbing its spread. With the focus of the government being on development and security, it would also reduce uncontrolled migration from rural to urban areas, by empowering the rural economy, and by providing basic modern facilities and job opportunities.

National Counter-Insurgency and Counter-Terrorism Institution

India is located in one of the most unstable regions of the world. The Global Peace Index (GPI) 2013 has ranked India among the 25 least peaceful nations to live in, having lost more than two lives a day – or a staggering 799 persons – to internal conflicts in 2012. Due to a number of reasons, India is highly vulnerable to violent protests, subversion, insurgency, crime, and terrorism. In addition, any movement or insurgency in such a backdrop would be different and unique in its character. Statistical data suggests that both insurgency and terrorism have shown an upward trend in its spread and intensity, the world over. Given the ground realities, India is also likely to continue to experience internal armed conflicts or terrorism in the future too. The Naxals have also been indulging in huge acts of terror. If this is accepted in principle, then the country must take concrete measures to address the envisaged internal security problems. Rather than always reacting to situations, the country should plan, among others, a national level institution, "National Counter-Insurgency and Counter-Terrorism Institution", which must be the center of excellence to deal with both the subjects. It should aim at training the nucleus of military, CAPF, NSG and the state police forces, by shedding 'turf warfare' in the national interest. The political leaders, civil servants, intelligence agencies and other elements of national power should also be integrated into national security aspects, by participation in specially structured capsules. The institution should be organized to not only conduct training, but also carry out research, in-depth analysis and doctrine development, leading to the formulation of a grand strategy for the country. Subsequently, it should expand its scope to comprehensively analyzing all types of sub-conventional threats, with close interaction with world's leading think tank organizations. Some of the weaknesses pertaining to threat assessment, modus operandi, effective surveillance, intelligence aspects, human rights, psychological reassurance & perception management, cyber warfare, training for negotiations and legal aspects would receive the much-desired attention. This institution could work in close coordination with the Indian National Defense University (INDU) and the leading institutions of the world in the future.

Capacity Building of Police Forces

Cultural shift

Insurgency (Naxalism) is not a conventional war. While the insurgents are asymmetric and the weaker force in their combat strength, they are extremely motivated, committed, physically fit, and are adept in guerrilla warfare tactics. There is a great difference between normal policing duties and fighting insurgents and terrorists. The police forces (CAPF and state police), by nature of their mandated roles and tasks are tuned to a defensive-cum-protective mindset. Their orientation is mostly towards protective duties, their primary role being maintenance of law and order, public order, protection of installations, riot control, election duties, road opening, airport security, and protection of VVIPs/ VIPs. However, fighting the Naxals in guerrilla warfare in alien terrain requires a different mindset. There has to be a cultural shift from conventional policing role to an unconventional and guerrilla method of operation. To defeat an insurgent, the SF must think to fight better than a guerrilla – with speed, stealth, surprise, and intelligence. Maoists have laid out a comprehensive plan to penetrate into the semi-urban/ urban areas in the future. A study of recent insurgencies suggests that long-drawn insurgencies, including Naxalism, tend to move away from their pure ideology and take recourse to criminal activities, kidnappings, subversion, and acts of terrorism. They start indulging in extortion, racketeering, drug cultivation, and its trade to make easy money. Their leaders start leading a life of comfort and are not connected to the grassroots. Therefore, there has to be a cultural shift from conventional military thinking or routine policing tasks to an unconventional and innovative method of tackling different manifestations of insurgency, by the civil administration, society, police, CAPF and the military.

Cardinal issues

Due to their ideological motivation, proficiency in guerrilla warfare, detailed knowledge of terrain, an effective intelligence system, and the will to win, the Naxals have been successful in a number of operations against the state. The central and state governments have also instituted a number of measures on the security front. A massive modernization and expansion drive of the CAPF is already underway. Therefore, capacity building of the CAPF, the state police forces, and the intelligence system would be the most important facets of the security strategy. There are five main pillars to this capacity and capability building; namely, re-orientation training from defensive to the envisaged offensive role for counter-insurgency operations;[49] enhancing leadership skills; modernization of weapons, equipment, and infrastructure; strengthening of intelligence setup; and implementation of police reforms.

The country already has a plethora of paramilitary forces and intelligence setups. Although there is a need to have a "separate force" for counter-insurgency operations – suitably organized and structured along with a specialized intelligence wing – it may not find favor due to major organizational changes, restructuring and enormous costs involved. The blueprint of the Naxal scenario 2020 and beyond, being what it could be, the CAPF must essentially remember the following for operations in the counter-insurgency environment:

- Restructure the force into small units, with small operation teams (SOTs). To succeed, they should be fully trained in guerrilla tactics – "fight a guerrilla better than a guerrilla", innovatively and by giving away the conventional jargons and standard operating procedures (SOP). The SOT of 10 men should receive extensive specialized training in jungle warfare, explosives, counter-IED drills, communications, and first-aid treatment so that they can penetrate deep into the Naxal dominated areas and carryout specific intelligence based operations. When a number of SOTs operate and spread over a large area, in a coordinated manner, it has a profound psychological impact on the Naxal cadre and the movement of their leaders gets restricted; thus, severely restricting their ability to lead and guide their cadres. Dog squads are force multipliers in counter-insurgency operations.
- Considering the future trends, the CAPF should also be trained to tackle criminal activities, drug-related crimes, extortions, and kidnappings, along with the civil police. It should be prepared to tackle situations arising in the semi-urban/urban areas, slums, ghettos, and the industrial belts. The activities of trade unions and sangathans dealing with essential services require to be monitored by specialized intelligence organizations, and the information shared appropriately.
- Operations based on actionable intelligence should remain the key

criteria, lest the troops conduct operations aimlessly and become tired and complacent. Such operations also cause tremendous hardships to the local population. As a cardinal principle, the local population must be supported, protected, and all precautionary actions taken to prevent any casualties to innocent civilians.[50] Once the situation starts improving, it would be prudent for the state police to progressively start playing the dominant role to bring the situation under control.

- The IR battalions, on being raised, could be restructured and trained somewhat similar to the RR battalions – to be staffed and officered by their own cadres – to improve their operational effectiveness.

Besides an alarming rise in voluntary retirements among the personnel of the CAPF, there have been a fair number of cases of suicides and attrition of the force due to fratricides, stress in an intense and uncertain operational environment, fear, and administrative-cum-domestic reasons. To de-stress the CAPF, particularly those operating in anti-naxal operations, it would be expedient to rationalize the tenures of the units on field and peace profile system. It is undesirable to move units from one operational assignment to another, as a matter of routine. Such moves would be acceptable to meet an emergent operational requirement. The exact structure of the force would, however, entail a comprehensive examination to meet the requirements of the country's internal security needs beyond 2020. Coupled with this, the units need to follow the ethos of combat units, wherein officers and inspector level ranks are affiliated to one unit or a group of 3 to 4 units in which they would serve, if feasible. It would give a sense of belonging to a unit, regimentation, camaraderie, and team spirit. Such an action would facilitate better officers – men relationships, which is extremely important for combating an invisible Naxal or an insurgent.

In a counter-insurgency environment, troops are required to be emotionally and psychologically strong, even when a colleague is injured or killed due to an IED blast or violent action(s) by the insurgents. Therefore, training is one of the most important facets – professional, physical, mental, and psychological subjects – to withstand the pressures of operations. There should be no compromise on quality of training. On the operational aspects, the commanders would do well to analyze the threat from the Naxals in detail and then decide their own concept of operations and deployment of troops, along with a responsive logistic system. Rather than losing troops due to avoidable management and administrative reasons, it would be desirable to put into place measures to address the physical, mental, emotional, psychological requirements of troops serving in difficult conditions. Facilities like leave entitlements, additional allowances, monetary benefits, rest and relief system, quality of accommodation, food, medical, communications and transport, and a fair system of awards and punishments would help further enhance their motivation, morale, and combat effectiveness. The troops are extremely sensitive to promotions, just like the senior ranks. They need to be provided equal opportunities to improve their professional standards and appear in promotion tests, to further their careers.

Counter-insurgency and anti-terrorist (CIAT) schools

The central government has sanctioned a number of CIAT schools for imparting quality training to the police forces. The police forces passing out through them are beginning to show results. These CIAT schools should become centers of excellence and must keep updating their training curriculum according to the tactics adopted/changed by the Naxals. Elite specialized forces on the pattern of greyhounds of the Andhra Pradesh police, in small numbers, need to be set up in each state. These forces need to be given the offensive capability to carry out surgical and precision strikes, and to carry out other specialized tasks of raiding the Naxal hideouts, bases, and laying ambushes based on specific intelligence inputs. The CoBRA battalions of the CRPF have managed such success in the past; a case in point being the elimination of Kishenji on November 24, 2011 in Burisole forest of West Midnapore district. They should be highly mobile so that they can have longer reach, and a faster response time. For this, light- and medium-lift capability helicopter of the Mi-17/ALH class must be requisitioned, and kept on call for these forces. Special incentives may be provided for the personnel of these forces to serve in harsh operational environments. The incentives can be in the form of better postings, monetary, career enhancing schemes, and honors and awards.

While attending a number of seminars and questions posed by the participants, I got an impression that there is an extraordinary emphasis on the creation of a large number of commando forces or the special forces in the CAPF and the state police forces. Greyhounds or special forces should be limited in numbers, lest we end up training the entire force into commando forces like the Greyhounds/CoBRA/Jharkhand Jaguars/C-60 commandos, etc. Creation of such elite forces – the force multipliers – require special efforts and resources to train and sustain them. Additional efforts would be in terms of selection of personnel, multi-faceted specialized training, equipping, additional funds, logistics, creation of infrastructure for training, qualified instructional staff, and air effort. In addition, these forces must have "refresher training" periodically. Therefore, raising such special forces, in each state, should be based on a comprehensive analysis of the envisaged threat perception. Quality of force requires greater focus than mere numbers. The exact quantum would, of course, depend on a number of variables like the intensity of Naxal violence, nature of incidents, number of strategic-cum-economic high-value objectives in the state and the threat to them, the training capacities available, and the envisaged future threat perception.

Leadership

> *One of the most valuable qualities of a commander is flair for putting himself in the right place at the vital time.*
>
> – Field Marshal Viscount Slim (Unofficial History, 1957)

Another grey area that needs to be addressed as a priority is the quality of frontline leadership. Unlike the armed forces, where leadership is seen as a key element, the leadership in the police forces, by virtue of their routine policing tasks, generally carries out managerial-cum-administrative tasks. The leaders, both junior and senior, of the nominated counter-insurgency forces must train together with their units and sub-units to form integrated homogenous teams to take to field. During my interaction with some of the senior officials of the CRPF, I learnt that due to organizational constraints, it is not possible to have a system like an infantry battalion of the regular army. In the army, the officers continue to be a part of the same permanent combat unit from the rank of lieutenant (young officer) to colonel (commanding officer), even with a few "out of the battalion professional assignments", during which the officers gain experience on staff, instructional and foreign deputations. This system, where officers spend the bulk of their tenure with their unit, definitely has certain obvious advantages, particularly as the officers and the men go to war or counter-insurgency operations together as a well-knit team. It is a similar case even with the junior leadership. Though it may not be possible to retain a strict regimentation-type scenario for the officer cadre in the police forces due to the constraints of the organization and the nature of their role, at least the junior-level leadership (inspectors, sub-inspectors) may be retained, if feasible, in the same unit and a military – like ethos built into them. The morale and the enthusiasm of the SF remain high when they see their leaders with them in difficult operational conditions. Selected junior leadership in the CAPF must be made to carry out on-the-job training with specialized units like the RR and Assam Rifles (AR). If feasible, the police forces operating in the Naxal areas need to be of a younger age profile, so that they can match the physical and mental agility of the rebels. In the famous book, "Crisis in Command", perhaps the most important lessons from the military's performance of the United States in Vietnam, "*One factor virtually guaranteeing poor military performance is bad leadership and its destructive effect on group cohesion*",[51] must not be forgotten.

Police reforms: Modernization of police

"State police forces are the foundation on which the entire internal security apparatus of the nation must rest."[52] Non-implementation of police reforms has been the bane of our police forces. After waiting for years to implement them, the Supreme Court, in a response to a petition filed by Mr. Prakash Singh, IPS, delivered a historic judgment on September 22, 2006, instructing central and state governments to comply with a set of directives, laying down practical mechanisms to kick-start the police reforms. The courts directive seeks to achieve two main objectives – functional autonomy and enhanced police accountability. Until guidelines for issues like streamlined procedure for postings, appointments, tenures, and accountability, both for organizational performance and individual misconduct, are not put in place, police officers will be handicapped in terms of improving their overall efficiency and effectiveness. This in turn has long-term implications on the internal security situation of our nation. In addition, modern weaponry, equipment, mobility, communication, and the surveillance capabilities need to be improved. Attacks by the Naxalites on police posts and armories can be prevented only if the infrastructure of the existing police stations is strengthened, surveillance enhanced, failsafe communications provided, and the defenses beefed up.[53] A lot has been done regarding this aspect, and as a result attacks on police/SF posts have reduced considerably.

Expansion of the police forces is underway in a substantial manner to counter the threat of Naxalism. It would be worthwhile to adopt the 'sons of the soil concept' and carry out large-scale recruitment from the affected areas, but their employment should not be restricted to local areas only. This will ensure that not only is employment generated, but also people familiar with the terrain, local language/dialect, local customs and traditions and their issues, are inducted into the SF. Personal interaction with the tribal people in these areas has brought out that the local tribes, e.g., the Munda, Kol, Oraons, Ho, Santhal, Korwa, etc., have good potential and possess military-like qualities. They have good aptitude for military skills and possess the requisite "ferocity" required in a fighting soldier. Thus, given the right amount of education, training, and orientation, such individuals will make excellent soldiers, both in regular forces and in the CAPF. These men can also provide invaluable inputs for successful counter-insurgency operations in the affected areas and can project a local friendly face to the SF.

Actionable intelligence

This refers to the intelligence requirements at the operational and tactical levels, without which no tangible success can be achieved in counter-insurgency operations. Accurate, timely, and actionable intelligence is the key to any successful counter-insurgency operation, and the absence of this has been the bane of most of our anti-naxal operations. In contrast, the Naxals have a simple but effective intelligence network. Most of their operations have been successful, based on actionable intelligence. Therefore, mere collection, collation, analysis, and coordination of intelligence is just not good enough. Actionable intelligence must be disseminated to the operational force in time to achieve success. Generally, the local police is credited with having a good intelligence network because of their knowledge of the area, local language, and their proximity to the locals. This is, however, not effectively utilized due to lack of coordination, turf wars, and insufficient analysis. Over-reliance on technical intelligence should be avoided in anti-naxal operations, as the Naxals are firmly rooted to the ground and are well merged with the locals. Therefore, greater reliance must be placed on traditional human intelligence. Inter-state coordination must be carried out for every security operation being conducted along the fringes of the state boundaries. This is because most of the critically affected areas are those that share borders among two or more states. It is widely believed that one of the reasons for the spread of Naxalism in Chhattisgarh, Odisha, Maharashtra, and Madhya Pradesh is the escape of erstwhile PWG cadres from Andhra Pradesh into these states due to lack of coordinated action among various state governments.

Increase footprint

Since the British Raj, i.e. both before and after independence, some of the LWE-affected states/areas remained highly neglected and under-developed for a number of reasons. In comparison to other parts of the country, these areas have limited presence of establishments of the central government including the armed forces and the paramilitary. It is time to increase the footprint of the armed forces, CAPF, central government organizations and establishments by locating PSUs, training institutions, training areas, military schools, sports centers, regional headquarters, research units, support organizations of the CAPF, so as to enhance the inherent security due to their presence. Such initiatives will also provide job opportunities to the local population and boost the economy of the area.

The current system has three major flaws. First, there is a lack of coordination among various central organizations and between the central and state organizations. This, in turn, has a detrimental effect on contribution by other elements like the industry, NGOs, social activists, and the media. Second, there is lack of sense of urgency and commitment to improve the region. It manifests itself in the form of inordinate delays in decision-making, not pursuing cases to their logical conclusion, and unwillingness on part of functionaries to see the actual situation on the ground. A case in point is the installation of mobile phone towers in the Naxal-affected areas. More than 200 towers were blown up by the rebels during the last four years in the nine states, as the Naxals claim that police were being tipped off about their movements and locations by informers through mobile phones.[54] These are required to facilitate development-cum-security-related projects, a fact acknowledged by everyone. Joshi, an expert on Naxalism, laments that despite the government's decision, in early 2012, to install 2200 mobile towers in nine Maoists – hit states, the ambitious project is yet to take off, over cost-estimates of installing mobile towers.[55] Third, between 2001 and 2012, 5714 civilians and 2045 SF personnel have been killed in the LWE-affected states. The majority of the civilians killed were tribals. Despite such large number of killings in the LWE-affected areas, timely corrective measures and initiatives were not taken to reduce the pain and sufferings of the people. The situation has started improving – though marginally – after 2011.

A number of organizations and agencies are working in the naxal-affected areas, but without adequate coordination and unity of purpose. Their contribution is predominantly based on their own perception of the problem. Such an approach has its own obvious pitfalls. Generally, the actions taken based on individual perceptions result in sub-optimal outcome and the conflict getting prolonged, as has happened in the case of Naxalism. The formation of an independent central organization would be able to achieve better synergy and coordination between various elements of national power and to implement the approved plan. As the number of retired soldiers living in the Naxal-affected states is limited, it may be worthwhile to utilize their expertise – as has been done in Bihar – in security related duties, close to their native places. Such an initiative will keep them away from the coercive tactics of the Naxals to train their cadres and to produce their training literature.

Employment of Armed Forces

"Police" and "public order" are state subjects. The maintenance of law and order is the primary responsibility of the state governments, according to the provisions of the constitution. It has, however, been observed that most of the anti-insurgency campaigns have always had some commitment of the army to control the situation; e.g., Malaya, Kenya, Northern Ireland, Sri Lanka, northeastern states in India and J&K. Initially, the army is required to create a secure environment to enable the government and its administration to carry out their routine functions, and socio-economic development work. Given the root cause of Naxalism – an indigenous movement in the heartland of the country – and the force required to combat it, the security element is supposed to be the state police forces, suitably reinforced by the CAPF, as required.

The Indian armed forces must always be fully prepared to take on the challenges being posed to the sovereignty of our borders by these external threats, which is their primary mandate. However, as per the provisions of Article 355 of the Indian Constitution, it is the duty of the Union to protect the states against external aggression and internal disturbance. Therefore, as part of their secondary mandate, the armed forces in general and the army in particular have been deployed for countering a large number of internal security threats to the country since independence. In J&K and the northeastern states, which have approximately 70 districts, affected by terrorism and insurgency, India has a fair complement of its army already deployed for counter-insurgency operations, where it, along with other SF, has brought the situation under reasonable control.

According to Katoch, Director, Centre for Land Warfare Studies (CLAWS), New Delhi, there is a requirement to raise six additional infantry divisions of the army alone to combat Naxalism.[56] Bakshi, in his article, "Countering LWE: A Role for the Army?" mentions about the requirement of raising up to six additional RR force/infantry divisions to secure the Red Base areas. I partially agree with both the views. Firstly, Naxalism is an insurgency in the heartland of the country that has no direct involvement of foreign powers, except linkages with certain militant and anti-national elements. As it is neither a separatist nor secessionist movement, it should ideally be tackled by the police forces, which are also in the process of substantial expansion and modernization. Therefore, the government should make efforts to improve their capability and capacity to undertake such tasks. Secondly, at present, there is an acute shortage of officers in the army, in particular. Milking junior officers from units will adversely affect the combat potential of the army. Thirdly, given the geographical spread and the intensity of violence over the years and the current capabilities of the CAPF, I agree with them that there is a requirement for additional trained forces to tackle the critically affected areas, which needs to be analysed comprehensively.

A few analysts had suggested that , as a onetime measure, army should be employed to carry out an offensive sweep of the Naxal- affected areas, for a limited period. As mentioned earlier, deployment of the army in internal security duties requires special provisions to protect the rights of the operatives and these special provisions are given through the AFSPA of 1958, amended in 1972. To apply this act, the area has to be declared as disturbed by the government. Such a situation has an undesirable effect on the security status of the country, its image, investment, and economic growth. In case of the Naxal problem, this is not a viable solution; the repercussions for doing so for 83 critically affected districts spread over a large landmass of the country have already been discussed. Going by the experience of other insurgencies (Nagaland, J&K, Assam, etc.) in India, it can be safely assumed that any deployment of the army in counter-insurgency operations will be for a prolonged duration. Excessive reliance on the army also shows lack of faith and trust in the CAPF and the police forces, which may be detrimental to their motivation and morale. With the current commitments at hand, the role of the army should be to advice, to provide maximum support to improve their (CAPF) capability, and to boost their morale to take on internal security problems.

Another aspect that must not be missed is that the Maoists would claim a moral victory in front of the local population, having forced the government to deploy its armed forces. It would simultaneously evoke support from the neighboring countries, militant organizations, and non-state actors, inimical to India's interests. Interestingly, after the situation in the disturbed areas, e.g., J&K and northeastern states, stabilizes to a reasonable degree, there are a fair number of political and local leaders who raise questions on the army's counter-insurgency role, mandate, and the need to do away with AFSPA. While it is perfectly in order to review the situation and relevance of AFSPA, it must be appreciated that semblance of law and order in such insurgency environments is achieved with huge sacrifice and commitment of the SF, over a number of years. Such decisions should be taken on the basis of a comprehensive examination. Views of the army and the CAPF merit due consideration, lest the insurgents are buying time to re-emerge stronger.

We have to learn a few lessons from the insurgency in southern Thailand. It was hoped that the insurgency that flourished in southern Thailand in 1970s and 1980s, had melted away, with the amnesty in 1990s. "With the consolidation that ensued among various factions in the next decade, the conflict in southern Thailand has escalated to previously unseen levels – the death toll continues to escalate. Instead, it has come back in a more powerful and threatening manner, with effect from 2004."[57] Caution needs to be exercised to prevent an insurgency or a controlled insurgency resurfacing with greater strength, due to poor governance or premature pulling out of troops or revoking the

"Disturbed Area Act." The government must carry out a comprehensive analysis of the security situation and the envisaged threats.

The CAPF today is under a great amount of expansion and modernization program. In the coming years, this will increase its capability and capacity to deal with insurgencies of the level that we are experiencing today. 37 India Reserve battalions and 10 Specialized India Reserve Battalions were sanctioned for the seriously Naxal affected states. In addition, Chhattisgarh alone has 22 battalions of CRPF, besides five and three battalions of the ITBP and BSF respectively. The strength of the Chhattisgarh's state forces has also increased manifold. Therefore, it should be capable of handling internal security problems, provided its capacities and capabilities are built to the desired levels. Focus should shift to a high quality counter-insurgency force, with military ethos and effective leadership.

If the situation becomes critical or has the potential to become critical to the national security, then, in consonance with the spirit of Article 355, it would be in order to provide the army's special forces or regular army support for surgical operations or to restore an adverse situation, and then move out of the area after handing over the situation to the police forces. Under such circumstances and to achieve "unity of effort", all the troops involved in anti-naxal operations should ideally be placed under the operational control of the army. These security operations should not be carried out in isolation, but must be a part of the overall national security plan drawn up at the highest level or a plan for that specific region. These endeavors of the army would be in concert with its secondary role, i.e. to provide impetus to the primary role of the CAPF and facilitate the army to remain operationally fit to meet its primary role. The air force must continue to provide administrative and logistical support to the Naxal-affected states. UAVs, including mini-UAVs, are the 'eyes in the sky' provided they are fitted with foliage penetration radars or devices. They need to be optimally and imaginatively utilized. Therefore, the armed forces must always keep themselves fully abreast with the emerging situations and carry out an in-depth analysis, as part of the evolving threats to national security.

Organization for Conflict Resolution

Considering the complex nature of conflict and large geographical spread affecting huge population base, it would be appropriate either to reinforce an existing organization or create an effective additional government organization with the powers to formulate strategy, plan, allocate resources, and coordinate civil and security efforts towards the counter-insurgency campaign. In Thailand, the government established the "Internal Security Operational Command (ISOC)" to coordinate and integrate counter-insurgency efforts of various government agencies.[58] Likewise, the British created a separate organization during the Malayan insurgency for similar purposes, as discussed earlier. In the Malayan and Kenyan counter-insurgency campaigns, a director of operations was appointed, who was responsible to oversee the entire conduct of the counter-insurgency campaign – security, governance, development, intelligence, perception management, rehabilitation and resettlement. The system of 'Unified HQ' – both in Srinagar and Jammu regions – was not found to be fully effective to deliver the desired results. While India's size, federal system of government, and the nature and spread of the insurgency are far different from the examples quoted, it would be prudent to create an apex organization at the center, with a clear-cut mandate, powers, responsibility, and accountability. While it should aim to be effective with constitutional powers and be able to achieve "unity of effort" of all elements of national influence, the reorganization must be accompanied by minimum turbulence. The Naxal-affected states could consider the Malayan campaign model, suitably modified to local conditions, to ensure that a single dedicated authority is responsible for the entire spectrum of anti-naxal campaign. Coordination with the central apex body would also be more effective.

Roles and responsibilities

Before discussing the options available to the government, it is essential to briefly look at the "envisaged roles and responsibilities" to resolve such conflicts.

- Analyze the overall internal security environment, and the envisaged future threats.
- Prepare grand strategy, sub-strategies, and a comprehensive national plan (CNP) – in conjunction with the stakeholders – allocating roles and responsibilities to the relevant elements of national power: union ministries, state governments, local governance bodies, industry, social activists, NGOs, media, the people.[59]
- Ensure judicious allotment of resources and funds for welfare schemes and essential infrastructure, based on a comprehensive analysis of deficits on ground.
- Identify the districts under IAP/SRE/backward development grant, etc., to monitor expenditure of funds and carry out performance audit.
- Coordinate and monitor the implementation of various projects, and suggest measures for mid-course corrections. Raise and train DTFs to undertake development works in critically affected areas.

- Recommend policy reforms in the areas of land acquisition, land distribution/holding, forest rights, tribal affairs, resettlement and rehabilitation of displaced people, industry, mining, health care, education and PDS.
- Propose measures for mitigation of hardship of the underprivileged and those who have suffered, including provision for compensations to victims of Naxal violence, actions of the SF or the Salwa Judam.
- Recommend changes in national strategy or sub-strategies, due to changes in the intensity and spread of violence, and the response of Naxalites towards peace making.
- Coordinate inter-state actions pertaining to security and development, resolve disputes between states and other stakeholders.
- Analyze the drivers and causes that could lead to spread of Naxalism to urban areas and industrial hubs; and its impact on economic growth, security, and other related aspects.

Options

The MHA has multifarious responsibilities such as internal security, border management, management of CAPF, center-state relations, disaster management, etc. Article 355 of the Constitution enjoins the Union to protect every state against external aggression and internal disturbance. The government has previously created sub-organizations or separate appointments to deal with various insurgencies/armed conflicts. Nanavatty points out that they apparently did not prove to be useful.[60] The MHA already has a Department of Internal Security, which deals with all type of threats to internal security, anti-national and anti-subversive activities, terrorist funding, narcotics, drugs, national security act, among others. In principle, our endeavor should be to strengthen the existing set up, by making it more effective and efficient. However, given the nature and number of internal armed conflicts in the country, some of which have direct intervention and support of foreign powers, it is extremely difficult for the said department in the MHA to analyze and comprehend each type of threat/conflict, and take actions to resolve them. Under such circumstances, and in the absence of a concrete national plan, it is difficult to even manage a conflict effectively, leave alone resolve it.

To effectively deal with Naxalism, four broad options of "apex organizations" could be considered.

- First, create an independent body of experts and specialists to formulate strategy, plan, allocate resources, and monitor the implementation of the approved plans on ground.
- Second, create an organization "National Counter Naxal Authority

(NCNA)", on similar lines – but more elaborate with a larger mandate – as the National Disaster Management Authority (NDMA).[61]
- Third, create a sub-ministry of internal security within the MHA.
- Fourth, create an independent ministry to deal with Naxalism.

With the complex political arrangements and federal structure of the government, the first option – though created with least amount of turbulence – is not likely to be effective due to the lack of constitutional authority. It is unlikely to succeed in prevailing upon the concerned ministries, the states, and other stakeholders to adhere to the directives issued, and thus, not optimally achieve the laid-down mandate. The second option is comprehensive enough – formed with least amount of turbulence – to basically oversee the functioning and progress of work in the Naxal-affected states. Much like the first option, it also lacks executive powers to prevail upon the states to follow the directives of the authority. However, the organization is adequate to fulfill most of the responsibilities, if it is given the necessary constitutional authority and political patronage to succeed. The third option is also not likely to be fully effective, primarily because of the heavy workload (dealing with all the internal security issues), inadequate freedom of action, and the state government may not be fully responsive to a sub-ministry's directives. The sub-ministry thus created may get consumed in the mammoth ministry that MHA is. The creation of a separate ministry – particularly for an insurgency like Naxalism – would help plan, direct, allocate resources, coordinate, and closely monitor the progress of work in each critically affected state. A minister of the cabinet rank should head it, with senior representatives from all ministries that are directly involved in improving the political, social, and economic conditions in the affected states. To implement the mandate, a balanced professional organization is proposed, to be assisted by experts, specialists, knowledge, technology, and skills. While creating organizations at the state and the district levels, establishment of a central authority – with the principle of civilian supremacy – needs to be maintained to ensure unity of effort and seamless coordination among all agencies. For the Indian conditions, Nanavatty has suggested a broad organization of a separate ministry, which could deliver the goods to resolve the conflict.[62] For a burning issue like Naxalism, a separate ministry, with a cabinet-rank minister, would perhaps be the best option to resolve the conflict, with the NCNA as the next in the order of priority.

Critical areas to be addressed

There are numerous examples where strong political will and visionary leadership have played a vital role in taking bold decisions to defeat insurgencies. Naxalism poses a huge challenge to the nation as a whole, and not to any single state alone. All elements of national power have a role to perform at different stages of insurgency, either directly or indirectly. These roles need to be documented and their progress monitored periodically. The critical areas that need to be addressed, by the apex organization, lie predominantly in the political, social, economic, cultural, environmental, security and public perception management domains. The national strategy must necessarily endeavor to first make the environment secure, to build the trust with the people (see Figure 10.1). The success of anti-naxal campaign would hinge on mobilization of the political will, formulation of a CNP with clearly defined roles and responsibilities of each element of national power, tight governance and on the ground implementation of pro-people legislations. This is closely linked with taking concrete measures to devolve powers to the panchayats and gram sabhas, to ensure participative development. To enable security and developmental initiatives to be implemented on the ground, a comprehensive national security strategy be put in place at the national level, that must also address the concerns of the affected states.

While India may boast of being among the leading and fastest growing economies of the world, the growth must necessarily aim to provide the basic needs of poor people – education, health, employment opportunities, food security, potable water, hygiene and sanitation, connectivity, electricity and rural infrastructure. Despite a number of well intentioned welfare schemes and projects to uplift the lives of tribal and backward people, the Naxal-affected areas continue to remain the worst affected on most counts. Therefore, it would be prudent to give added impetus to surface and telephone connectivity, social infrastructure and renewable energy projects.

The Naxal-affected areas have much higher youth population than the national average. Therefore, empowerment of the youth and providing adequate job opportunities to the youth – based on a skills survey done in each region – is a huge challenge, which must be addressed as a priority. Special drive to recruit youth in various central and state services – with additional vacancies and relaxation in educational qualifications – will pay handsome dividend. As per official reports, Naxals have recruited nearly 4,000 children, including girls, as part of a recruitment drive to strengthen their depleted cadre base. It shows that the traditional support base to the movement may be reducing, forcing the organizations to indoctrinate children instead. Education of children, in particular, must receive the right focus to empower them, and to dissuade them from being coerced into 'Bal Sangthans' by the Naxals. Coupled with this, pro-active measures are required to be put in place to thwart the urban perspective plans of the Naxals.

Recently, the 'Global Peace Index (GPI) 2013' has ranked India among the 25 least peaceful nations to live in, due to internal conflicts in 2012.Considering an increase in the sub-conventional threats the world over, an effective and efficient national level intelligence system – fully integrated with the states – would help to address security requirements of the country. While modernizing the police forces, emphasis should be on capacity and capability building, and creation of a quality force – well trained and well led. As internal armed conflicts are likely to persist in the years ahead due to variety of reasons, it may be desirable to create a 'central counter- insurgency force', with military like ethos to meet the future challenges. Besides the traditional human intelligence, seamless coordination and synergy – particularly among the CAPF and the state police, and at the inter-state boundaries – would actually assist to turn the tide in favor of the SF. While the armed forces of the country should focus on their primary roles, they should keep themselves fully abreast with the emerging internal security situation. In comparison to 2009 and 2010, the period 2011-2013 has seen an overall decline in the number of incidents and violence. During this period, there was a need to give a huge boost to governance, development works, public perception management and psychological reassurance campaign, to capitalize on the gains. Though delayed, these need to be pursued vigorously. Issues pertaining to legal aspects, human rights, environment and culture merit equal attention. Finally, implementation of planned schemes on the ground would be the key to successful resolution of the conflict.

NOTES

1. Refer to Paget's principles in a tabulated form in Bruce Hoffman and Jennifer Morrison Taw, "*A Strategic Framework for Countering Terrorism and Insurgency", RAND Corporation Note, 1992: 119.*
2. In the Malayan counter-insurgency campaign (1948–60), the British administration had decided to further strengthen the existing Police Special Branch, rather than raising a new organization. In the case of Naxalism, the geographical spread is rather large. There is a need to not only strengthen the state police and their intelligence machinery, but also to collect, collate, analyze, and coordinate the intelligence at the national level.
3. For more details, read James D. Kiras. "Irregular Warfare: Terrorism and Insurgency", Oxford University, accessed December 23, 2012, http://www.oup.com/uk/orc/bin/9780199548873/baylis3e_ch09.pdf.
4. Published by Charney Research, accessed on December 12, 2012, www.charneyresearch.com. Opinion is an outcome of awareness as well as debate among stakeholders and public. It is shaped by policy frameworks and indicates the direction of the political will. Intensity, the second factor, determines the strength with which the political will is connected to the public and its proof lies in the polarization generated on the policies. Finally, salience is the measure of the importance that government and

public attach to the issues and decisions.(In Indian context, 'opinion' needs to be addressed first).

5. T.A. Johnson, "In Bellary, Illegal Mining and Gun Permits Hit Simultaneous High", *The Indian Express,* September 26, 2011.
6. "There Is Disunity, Admits CPI (Maoist) Leader", Prafulla Das, *The Hindu,* March 26, 2012.
7. Sanjay Ojha, "4 ex Maoists Join Jharkhand party", *The Times of India,* September 24, 2012.
8. Jaideep Hardikar, Special Correspondent, during the National Conference at New Delhi on September 26, 2012, explained how there has been a breakdown in communication and dialogue with the tribal people.
9. The panchayats got their constitutional status by the 73rd Constitution Amendment Bill, passed by the Parliament on December 23, 1992.
10. "Putting Kerala to Work", Reetika Khera, *The Hindu,* August 01, 2012.
11. Amendment to article 243D of the Constitution of India for enhancing reservation for women in Panchayats to 50%.
12. Ahmad Malik Jalal, "Think Like a Guerilla: Counterinsurgency Lessons from Sri Lanka", *Harvard Kennedy School Review.*
13. Ahmed Ali Fayyaz, "Promise of paradise that didn't come true", *The Hindu,* April 6, 2013.
14. Bruce Hoffman and Jennifer Morrison Taw, "*A Strategic Framework for Countering Terrorism and Insurgency", RAND Note, 1992: 38.*
15. Michael Crawshaw, "Running a Country: The British Colonial Experience and its Relevance to Present Day Concerns", *The Shrivenham Papers,* no. 3 (April 2007).
16. "156 Professionals Set to Join PM Scheme in LWE Districts", K Balchand, *The Hindu,* April 05, 2012.
17. The GoI had launched a special program in 83 critically affected districts called Integrated Action Plan (IAP). On 13 September 2011, it announced a scheme of PM's Rural Development Fellows for deploying young professionals in each of the IAP districts to assist the district collector in resource planning, budgeting, process implementation, and innovations in delivery mechanisms.
18. Franklin Patrick Herbert Jr., "An author on religion, politics and power", accessed on March 21, 2013, http://www.goodreads.com/quotes/23099-good-governance-never-depends-upon-laws.
19. Although there are some proportion of tribal boys from the naxal-affected areas in the armed forces and the CAPF, there is a need to provide additional vacancies to wean away the youth from the Naxals' influence.
20. Mahua Venkatesh, "The Great Indian Divide", *The Hindustan Times,* December 18, 2011. (According to an OECD report, "Divided We Stand: Why Inequality Keeps Rising", published on December 05, 2011, India and China have witnessed widening inequality even though the two most populous nations drove economic growth.)
21. "Study Finds Massive Corruption in Govt's Flagship NREGA", *Rediff News,* accessed January 14, 2012, http://news.rediff.com/report/2010/may/23/study-finds-massive-corruption-in-govts-flagship-nrega.htm.
22. "PM Seeks Quick Fix for Delayed NREGS Payment", TNN, *Times of India,* July 15, 2012.

23. Rolland Simon and Patel Aneri, "Rural Electrification in India: Challenges and Successes", accessed January 10, 2012, http://india.carbon-outlook.com/content/rural-electrification-india-challenges-and-successes.
24. Ibid.
25. Lalit K. Jha, "Afghanistan World's Largest Opium Producer", accessed March 09, 2012, http://www.rawa.org/temp/runews/2011/09/16/afghanistan-world-s-largest-opium-producer-2.html.
26. Mahadevan Prem, "The Naxal Insurgency in India: Between Crime and Resolution", *Small Wars and Insurgencies* 23, no. 2 (May 2012): 216.
27. ET Bureau, "Rural Development Minister Jairam Ramesh Favours Block-based IAP to Curb Maoists Influence", *The Economic Times*, February 1, 2012.
28. At present, the District Collector, Superintendent of Police, and the District Forest Officer are doing this job.
29. Industries, which specifically take advantage of existing skill sets of the local tribal communities or which can develop skill sets based on the ability of the locals, would come under this category.
30. The local tribal population has a poor representation in the various modern sectors/industries. This is due to lack of education and job-related skills. Therefore, such innovative industries/services sector can help build up the representation of the local tribal population.
31. During the interaction with local population, the author learnt that the locals prefer government jobs, which are very few in number. This trend/mindset must change and the people of the area must be encouraged to seek self-employment also.
32. The state has been, to an extent, successful in encouraging children to join schools, but it is failing to retain them. Parents want their children to assist them in earning their livelihood and to help in their domestic activities, which has resulted in high dropout rates. This is more prominent with the girl children.
33. Suvojit Bagchi, "Maoist Backing Chhattisgarh Teachers' Strike", *The Hindu*, December 17, 2012.
34. MGNREGA will be effective provided it is flexible to accommodate the requirements of the Naxal-affected areas, and appointed functionaries are accountable to ensure its implementation.
35. P.K. Agarwal, "Naxalism: Causes and Cure" (New Delhi: Manas Publication, 2010), 200. (The work for updating record-of-rights would take anywhere up to 10 to 20 years, if undertaken seriously).
36. For an insightful account, see Bina Agrawal and Pravesh Sharma, "An Idea to Bank On", *The Times of India*, January 12, 2012.
37. "Left Wing Extremism: An Internal Security Challenge and Response Strategy for SF 2015", *CLAWS* report, 146.
38. For more details and the actions taken by the state government, read D.N. Sahaya, "How Tripura Overcame Insurgency", *The Hindu*, September 16, 2011.
39. Kitson, premier military strategist, who authored the counter insurgency bible, "Low Intensity Conflict", Britain laid great emphasis on psychological warfare operations to defeat the IRA insurgency. Also, Art Ryan L. Seachon, "Insurgencies in History: A Blueprint for Future Strategy", *OG5 Digest* (October–December 2004): 16(4/5).

40. S.K. Chatterji, "Perception Management in Conflict Zones", accessed November 11, 2012, http://www.au.af.mil/info-ops/iosphere/10winter/iosphere_win10_chatterji.pdf.
41. For more details read, "Education Is the Best Weapon to Combat Naxalism", *Millennium Post,* October 15, 2012.
42. Dhananjay Mahapatra, "Tribal rights supreme in Vedanta case", *The Times of India,* April 19, 2013.
43. Other cases that are well known are: Lenin's revolutionary slogan was "Land, Bread, Peace", to get the support of the masses. In Zimbabwe, the Movement for Democratic Change adopted the slogan, "ENOUGH", against the regime of Robert Mugabe. . "Share no more blood", movement by the Naga Mothers Association has been able to nurture and sustain a ceasefire between the Naga underground groups and the government, among other aims.
44. Jaideep Hardikar, "Central India: Towards Conflict Resolution" presentation at the National Conference on 26-27 September 2012 at Jamia Millia Islamia University, New Delhi, September 27, 2012.
45. PTI, "Community Radio Empowers Women in Andhra Pradesh", *The Hindu,* April 16, 2010. (Established in 2008 as one of the first community radios in the country and managed by a team of dalit women, "Sangham Radio" in Manchoor village of Medak district carved a place in the lives of nearly 10,000 listeners spread over 100 villages in the region.)
46. Sanjay Ojha, "Maoist threat in Jharkhand forces government redesign of official buildings", *The Times of India,* March 21, 2013. This news item suggests that the Naxals remain in control of some of the areas.
47. Rostum K. Nanavatty, "Internal Armed Conflict in India: Forging a Joint Civil-Military Approach" (New Delhi, Pentagon Press, 2013), 16. (Nanavatty deduces from Galula's four laws to gain the support and participation of the people, that "effective military and police operations must precede political, social and economic actions: and the counter-insurgents must always negotiate from a position of strength". This technique would be appropriate for security-led development.)
48. For instance, during an interaction, the medical officers at Kondagaon informed that the most common diseases or ailments affecting the local population are tuberculosis (more due to malnutrition), anemia, skin diseases, and malaria. Therefore, region-based study can identify the critical areas and thus help provide immediate relief to the people.
49. Envisaged offensive role means reorientation of training "to fight a guerrilla better than a guerrilla".
50. In an uncertain and ambiguous operational condition, particularly at night and during poor visibility, it is extremely difficult to differentiate between a rebel and an innocent civilian. Coupled with this, inaction by the SF could result in heavy casualties to its own forces.
51. Richard A. Gabriel and Paul L. Savage, "Crisis in Command: Management in the Army" (New York: Hill and Wang, 1978), 49.
52. Rostum K. Nanavatty, "Internal Armed Conflict in India: Forging a Joint Civil-Military Approach" (New Delhi: Pentagon Press, 2013), 78.
53. "Need for Intel-based Ops in Naxal-hit States: PC", *Express News Service, Indian Express,* December 2, 2011.

54. PTI, "Govt to Set Up 2,200 Mobile Towers in Nine Maoist-Hit States", *DNA*, April 29, 2012.
55. Sandeep Joshi, "Mobile Tower Project in 9 Maoist Hit States Stuck Over Cost Issues", *The Hindu*, January 18, 2013.
56. Gurmeet Kanwal and Dhruv Katoch, "Naxal Violence: The Threat Within", KW Publishers Pvt Ltd, 2012, 243.
57. For more details, see Joseph Chinyong Liow and Don Pathan, "Confronting Ghosts: Thailand's Shapeless Southern Insurgency" (Sydney, NSW: Lowy Institute for International Policy, 2010).
58. Art Ryan L. Seachon, "Insurgencies in History: A Blueprint for Future Strategy", *OG5 Digest,* October-December 2004, 17. (Internal Security Operational Command [ISOC] had proved to be effective, as it had to a smaller geographical area and population base.)
59. Preparation of strategy and the NCP should be by a committee comprising experts – with on ground knowledge and experience – including representatives/members of judiciary, human rights, economists, sociologists, environment, military, police, industry, local governance bodies, NGOs, and media. Some of them may not be part of the core group.
60. Rostum K. Nanavatty, "Internal Armed Conflict in India: Forging a Joint Civil-Military Approach" (New Delhi: Pentagon Press, 2013), 201. [The government has experimented with having a Minister of State for IS within the ministry (meaning MHA) and it has established a Ministry for the Development of the Northeast Region (DONER). Apparently, none of these initiatives have proved to be useful.]
61. The NCNA – an apex body for countering Naxalism – should be mandated by the President of India to lay down policies, plans, and guidelines based on the national strategy and the sub-strategies, as given out by the GoI. The vice chairperson would be a nominated expert, with the status of a cabinet minister. Deputy minister level specialists to head various departments: (a) Policy, planning, reforms and feedback, (b) Intelligence, perception management and public information, (c) Resource allocation, coordination, inter-state dispute settlement and project management, (d) Infrastructure development, industry and environment, (e) Health and social department, (f) Education, employment and empowerment, (g) Security, policies, modernization, coordination, and human rights. All the affected states will have the State Counter Naxal Authority (SCNA) organization that will be the mirror image of the NCNA. However, the SCNA will have representation from adjoining states at appropriate levels. In case of critically affected districts bordering other states, the SCNAs of states could mutually appoint one of the districts-level functionaries as the chief coordinator so that there are no gaps at the ground level.
62. For insightful details, read Rostum K. Nanavatty, "Internal Armed Conflict in India: Forging a Joint Civil-Military Approach" (New Delhi: Pentagon Press, 2013), 204. (While proposing a separate ministry, the structure and organization for management of internal armed conflict at the national level essentially includes departments such as political affairs, external affairs, civil affairs, security affairs, information affairs, among other national agencies.)

Conclusion

From a mere agrarian movement, the armed revolution became central to the Naxal strategy to seize power. By adopting guerrilla warfare tactics, one of their aims has been to tie down the SF over a large geographical area, wear them out and the government machinery; thus, showing the helplessness and legitimacy of the government. While it may be reasonable to think that the government alone could have remedied the situation before it attained such an ominous scale, I cannot help but think that a part of responsibility does fall in the hands of the citizens and other pressure groups of the country. They too have failed to make it a part of the national agenda of the relevant political parties, to resolve the conflict.

If the government fails to offer peace with freedom and social justice, the Naxals will continue to fuel insurgency and maintain popular support of people by promising them the dream of freedom from oppression, brutalities and injustice. They will retain the strategic advantages of moral and psychological ascendency over the government. This will further be augmented by the tactical successes achieved by the Naxals against the SF and government machinery. This gives them a sense of invincibility and moral legitimacy in the eyes of the people, overcoming the apprehensions about their ability to ever attain final victory against the might of Indian SF. Hence, whether it is a matter of legitimacy of government authority, maintaining control over human resources and material, intangible factors that ensure following by the people hinges on the genuine support of people.

There are a large number of key strategic challenges, as discussed in the book, which merit early action and resolution. Though land reforms are a state subject, the central government needs to give adequate publicity and prevail upon the states to take suitable actions. The grassroots-level organizations like block development, panchayats, gram sabhas must be empowered and made accountable. Resettlement of the already displaced people remains a huge challenge with the government. The basic requirement, therefore, is to ensure that all reforms and welfare schemes pertaining to *Jal, Jungle, Jamin, and Khanij* are properly implemented on the ground, to provide relief to the tribal and the affected population. Uncontrolled migration to the urban areas, without matching infrastructure and facilities, could act as a catalyst to the Naxals to activate their urban cells to create crisis, and allow urban Naxalism to grow in strength. We must not ignore the "threat in being" and, therefore, take pro-active measures to prevent their urban perspective plan to take roots, which is already moving at a fair pace in a few select cities and industrial hubs of the country. 'Human security' is one of the most important responsibility of the government. Besides physical security, the other relevant aspects of human security like protection of human rights, freedom to conduct economic activity, public safety and public health also require equal and urgent attention of the government, to restore confidence of the local populace.

There are a few cases where an otherwise suppressed insurgency has resurfaced much more potent and stronger due to complacency and neglect by the state. It is imperative that the state takes proactive corrective measures to prevent such cases. While it remains the primary responsibility of the state to combat Naxalism through the least violent means possible, the government and non-governmental actors should focus on promoting a debate and creating awareness to remove information asymmetry in this field and assist in the development of a national strategy for resolution of the conflict. As Naxalism is the biggest challenge to the national security, it is the duty of all elements of the national power and influence to work collectively, with the aim of synergizing and harmonizing our efforts towards conflict resolution.

> *The arrow shot by the archer may or may not kill a single person. But stratagems devised by wise men can kill even babes in the womb.*
>
> – Kautilya

Appendices

Appendix A

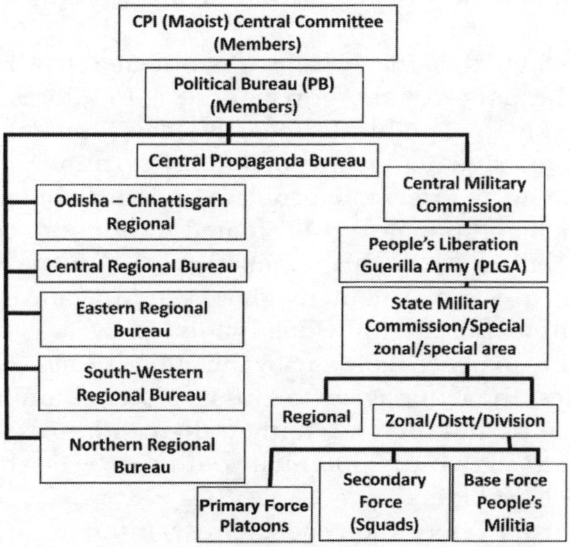

Flow Chart of CPI (Maoist) Central Committee

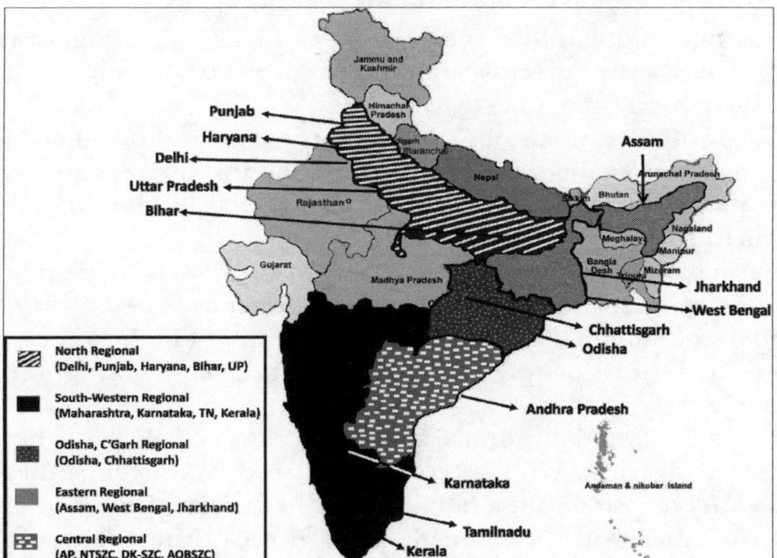

Regional Bureaus of CPI (Maoist)

Appendix B

14-Point Policy: MHA Document and Assessment

The then union home minister announced in the Lok Sabha, on March 13, 2006, the 14-point of the union government to deal with Naxalism.

- The government will deal sternly with the Naxalites indulging in violence.
- Keeping in view that the Naxalism is not merely a law and order problem, the policy of the government is to address this menace simultaneously on political, security, development, and public perception management fronts in a holistic manner.
- Naxalism being an inter-state problem, the states will adopt a collective approach and pursue a coordinated response to counter it.
- The states will need to further improve the police response and pursue effective and sustained police action against the Naxalites and their infrastructure individually and jointly.
- There will be no peace dialogue by the affected states with the Naxal groups unless the latter agree to give up violence and arms.
- The political parties must strengthen their cadre base in the Naxal-affected areas so that the potential youth can be weaned away from the path of Naxal ideology.
- The states from where the Naxal activity/influence, and not Naxal violence, is reported should have a different approach with special focus–accelerated socio-economic development of the backward areas and regular interaction with the NGOs, intelligentsia, and the civil liberties groups to minimize over ground support for the Naxalite ideology and activity.
- Efforts will continue to be made to promote local resistance groups against the Naxalites but in a manner that the villagers are provided adequate security cover and the area is effectively dominated by the security forces.
- The mass media should also be extensively used to highlight the futility of Naxal violence and loss of life and property caused by it and developmental schemes of the government in the affected areas so as to restore people's faith and confidence in the government machinery.
- The states should announce a suitable transfer policy for the Naxal-affected districts. Willing, committed, and competent officers will need to be posted with a stable tenure in the Naxal-affected districts. These officers will also need to be given greater delegation and flexibility to deliver better and set up government presence in these areas.

- The government of Andhra Pradesh has an effective surrender and rehabilitation policy for the Naxalites and has produced good results over the years. The other states should adopt a similar policy.
- The state governments will need to accord a higher priority in their annual plans to ensure faster socio-economic development of the Naxal-affected areas. The focus areas should be to distribute land to the landless poor as part of the speedy implementation of the land reforms, ensure development of physical infrastructure like roads, communication, power, etc., and provide employment opportunities to the youth in these areas.
- Another related issue is that the development activities are not undertaken in some of the Naxal-affected areas mainly due to extortion, threat, or fear from the Naxalite cadres. In these areas, even contractors are not coming forward to take up the developmental work. Adequate security and other measures are needed to be taken to facilitate the uninterrupted developmental activities in the Naxal-affected areas.
- The central government will continue to supplement the efforts and resources of the affected states on both security and development fronts and brings greater coordination among the states to successfully tackle the problem.

Assessment

The government had, for the first time, accepted that the Naxal problem was not merely a law and order problem, but a grave threat to national security. It acknowledged the requirement to deal with it in a holistic manner. However, its directive on improving the "police response" was not comprehensive enough, and skirted the basic issue of capacity and capability building of the police forces, to fight well trained guerrillas. It also did not address the issues of police reforms.

Considering the spatial spread, the central government had recognized that the Naxal problem is an inter-state problem, as a number of states were affected by it. Thus, it had recommended that the states should adopt a collective approach and a coordinated response to conduct counter-insurgency operations. It had recommended a number of multi-dimensional and multi-faceted measures required to be undertaken by the states in its policy directive. However, it seems to have undermined its role, by relegating itself to the supplementary role, as implied in the policy. Though law and order is a state subject, it must be understood that when such senseless violence is perpetuated by the Naxals and it encompasses a number of states, the intervention of the center with a firm hand is definitely required. It must not only act as the policy maker, but also must enforce and ensure implementation of the same in all the states afflicted by the Naxalism. To this extent, it should have defined its role in the policy directive, the constraints of federal structure notwithstanding.

The governments had put in correct perspective the need to have a different approach to the problem in areas affected in varying degrees. Therefore, rather than having a uniform solution to the problem, a thorough study should have been carried out in each area with respect to the levels of Naxal activity/influence, the demography of the area, the socio-economic conditions, and the impact of terrain on counter-insurgency operations. This would have given out the area-wise strategy required to be followed to deal with the issue. The government had propagated a rather rigid stance in establishing a dialogue or negotiations with the Naxals. The conditions laid down were that they should have given up violence and arms. It did not yield much result. The government should be more flexible to bring them to negotiating table.

The government had, with good intentions, promoted the idea of establishing local resistance groups. However, some of the local resistance groups themselves became the perpetrators of mindless violence. The case of Salwa Judum has been covered in detail in the book. The government had laid emphasis on psychological operations and perception management, as it was evident in its policy directives urging the states to co-opt mass media and adopt a model surrender and rehabilitation policy. This approach had worked well in both Tripura and Andhra Pradesh. The directive by the government, to post committed and competent officers in all departments of the administration with greater delegation and flexibility, was good. While efforts were made to improve governance and to shape the perception of the public, it lacked unity of effort due to the lack of national level strategy.

Addressing the need for developmental actions in the Naxal-affected areas, the government had rightly identified the focus areas for speedy implementations of land reforms, distribution of land to the landless labors, development of physical infrastructure, and employment to the youth in the affected areas. However, the critical areas like rehabilitation of the displaced tribal groups and ensuring forest rights to the tribal people were not addressed. Due to the prevailing insecure environment, the policy had rightly identified the problem of implementation of developmental works due to hesitation of contractors to carry out these works in the areas. Resultantly, Border Roads Organization was detailed to ensure construction of roads and developmental works in conflict ridden areas. The 14-Point Policy was a welcome step to tackle the Naxal challenge. Unfortunately, the policy was not implemented in an effective manner on ground, both by the central and state governments.

Appendix C

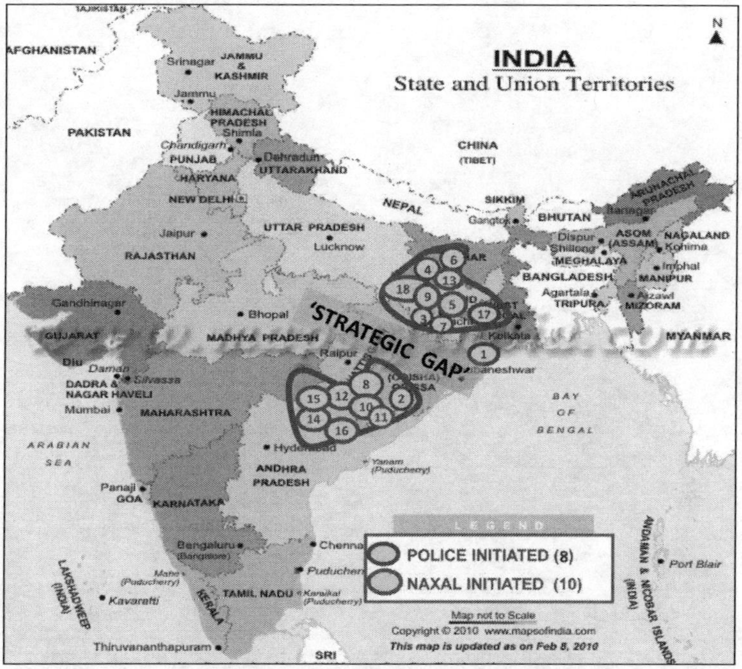

Major Naxal Related Incidents: 2011

Source: Compiled from SATP, MHA web site and Open Sources

NAXAL INITIATED (10)

CHATRA, JHARKHAND 2 MAR 11 (5)
- AMBUSH
- SF KILLED - 03, SF MISSING - 03
- LOOTED – 01 INSAS, 02 X .303 BORE RIF

LOHARDAGA, JHARKHAND 3 MAY 11 (9)
- IED BLAST
- SF KILLED - 11

DANTEWARA, C' GARH 17 May 11 (10)
- ENCOUNTER, LANDMINE BLAST
- CPO KILLED – 05, INJURED – 02

NUAPADA, ODISHA 24 MAY 11 (11)
- ENCOUNTER
- SF KILLED - 09

NARAINPUR, C' GARH 9 JUNE 11 (12)
- ATTACK ON CAMP
- CPO KILLED – 05, ARMS LOOTED – 02

MUNGER, BIHAR 2 JUL 11 (13)
- KILLING
- CIV KILLED – 06

DANTEWARA, C' GARH 10/11 JUNE 11 (14)
- IED BLAST, ENCOUNTER
- CPO KILLED – 13,
- NAXAL KILLED – 10

BIJAPUR, C' GARH 19 AUG 11 (15)
- AMBUSH , ENCOUNTER
- SPF KILLED – 12,
- NAXAL KILLED – 04, CIV - 01

JAGDALPUR, C' GARH 21 OCT 11 (16)
- AMBUSH
- SPF KILLED – 06
- SPF INJURED -04

LATEHAR, JHARKHAND 3 DEC 11 (18)
- IED BLAST / AMBUSH - MP CVY
- SF KILLED – 10
- SF INJURED – 02
- CIV INJURED - 01

POLICE INITIATED (8)

JAJPUR, ODISHA 1 JAN 11 (1)
- ENCOUNTER
- NAXAL KILLED - 05
- REC – COUNTRY MADE GUN & RIFS - 10

RAYAGADA, ODISHA 10 JAN 11 (2)
- ENCOUNTER
- NAXAL KILLED - 09
- REC - .315 BORE RIF - 09

LATEHAR, JHARKHAND 28 JAN 11 (3)
- ENCOUNTER
- NAXAL KILLED - 09
- REC – 01 SLR, 05 X .315, 3 X PISTOLS

BANKA, BIHAR 26 FEB 11 (4) (12)
- ENCOUNTER
- NAXAL KILLED – 06
- NAXAL INJURED - 01

EAST CHAMPARAN, BIHAR 13 MAR 11 (6)
- ENCOUNTER
- NAXAL KILLED – 06
- NAXAL INJURED - 10

KHUNTI, JHARKHAND 15 MAR 11 (7)
- ENCOUNTER
- NAXAL KILLED - 05

DANTEWARA, C' GARH 17 MAR 11 (8)
- ENCOUNTER
- CPO KILLED – 03, INJURED – 03
- NAXAL KILLED – 30, NAXAL APPRE - 10

BURISOLE FORESTS, WB, 24 NOV 2011 (17)
- KISHENJI KILLED

Major Naxal Related Incidents: 2011

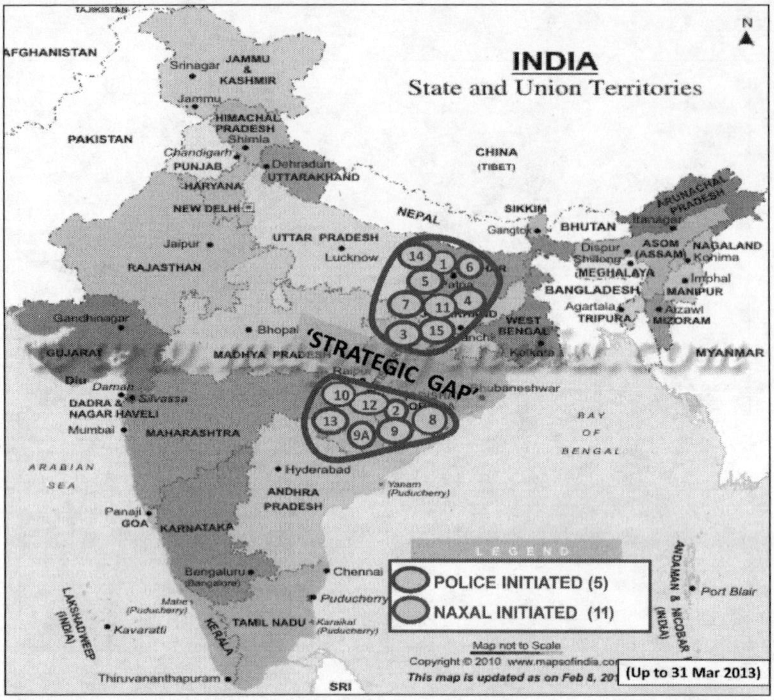

Major Naxal Related Incidents: 2012-2013 (Up to 31 March 2013)

Source: Compiled from SATP, MHA web site and Open Sources

NAXAL INITIATED (11)

(2) KANDHAMAL, ODISHA 5 JAN 12
- LANDMINE BLAST
- SF KILLED - 03
- SF INJURED - 03

(3) LATEHAR, JHARKHAND, 07 JAN 2013
- IED AND AMBUSH
- SF KILLED - 07
- CIVS KILLED - 04
- SF INJURED - 09

(4) BOKARO, JHARKHAND, 17 JAN 2013
- IED
- SF INJURED - 11

(5) GARHWA, JHARKHAND 21 JAN 12
- AMBUSH
- SF KILLED - 13
- LOOTED – 11 X INSAS, 02 X AK47, 01 X SLR

(6) JAMUI, BIHAR, 27 JAN 2013
- KIDNAPPED
- CIVILIANS- 11

(7) LATEHAR, JHARKHAND 1 FEB 12
- LANDMINE BLAST
- SF KILLED - 03
- SF INJURED - 02

(9) (9A) MALKANGIRI, ODISHA, MAR AND APR 12
- KIDNAPPING INCIDENTS - 02
- SF KILLED - 02

(13) DANTEWADA, CHHATTISGARH06 AUG 12
- LANDMINE BLAST
- SF KILLED - 01
- SF INJURED - 05

(14) GAYA, BIHAR 18 OCT 12
- IED
- SF KILLED - 06
- SF INJURED - 09

(15) GIRIDIH, JHARKHAND 9 NOV 12
- AMBUSHED POLICE VAN
- SF KILLED - 03
- CIVILIAN - 01

POLICE INITIATED (5)

(1) ROHTAS, BIHAR 02 JAN 12
- ENCOUNTER
- NAXAL KILLED – 03
- NAXAL INJURED - 01

(8) KORAPUT, ODISHA, 04 FEB 2013
- NAXALS ARRESTED - 07

(10) NARAYANPUR, CHHATTISGARH, 24 MAR 13
- NAXALS ARRESTED - 06

(11) CHATRA, JHARKHAND , 28 MAR 13
- NAXALS KILLED - 10

(12) BIJAPUR, 29 JUN 12
- ENCOUNTER
- NAXAL KILLED – 07 ?
- CIVILIANS KILLED - 10 ?
- SF INJURED - 06

Major Naxal Related Incidents: 2012-2013 (Up to 31 March 2013)

Appendix D

Counter-Measures against IEDs

Passive Measures	*Active Measures*
• Doctrine development, Research and Development on IEDs, improving counter-measure technologies and counter – IED action plan. • Promote better awareness and IED consciousness. Counter-IED training and up gradation of IED and communication equipment; i.e., deep search mine detectors, robotic arm for bomb disposal, bomb disposal suits, mobile phone locaters and surveillance systems, latest equipment based on information and communication technology, etc. • Counter-IED teams, along with sniffer dogs, be created and located in high-threat areas. • Deny easy availability of explosives material and detonators to individuals. Periodic audit of explosives and stores. Ensure fail-safe physical security of explosives and accessories being held. Vendors of material should be made accountable for their actions. Ammonium Nitrate Rules, 2012, be effectively enforced. • Secrecy of movement plans be ensured. Do not follow any established pattern. • Black top roads ensure easy detection of IEDs being planted. • Proper analysis of IED attacks and early dissemination to troops on the ground.	• Detect and neutralize IEDs. • Road opening drills be followed meticulously. The electronic functioning of detonators and command activation system be neutralized by jamming the systems selectively. • Develop effective surveillance and intelligence network. Surveillance by UAVs and, in near future, by satellites. • Avoid establishing a set pattern of operations. • Effective area domination to prevent planting of IEDs. • Neutralize IED activation network by physical checks on ground. • Monitor sale and consumption of locally available material that can be used for fabricating IEDs. • Conduct raids on storage dumps of IED and related equipment.

Clay Wilson, "Countering Improvised Explosive Devices (IEDs)" and "IEDs in Iraq and Afghanistan: Effects and Counter-measures". IED Menace, Defence and Security Alert, Vol. 2, Issue 5, February 2011.

APPENDIX E

Naxal Propaganda Leaflet

भारतीय सेना वापस जाओ ! बस्तर नहीं, जगं मत लड़ो !
आदिवासी विदेशी नहीं, देश के मूलवासी हैं !
उनके हक की लड़ाई का समर्थन करो !

भारतीय सेना के जवानों,

भारतीय सेना ने बस्तर की धरती पर कदम रखा है । 3000 जवानों का जंगल वारफंर ट्रेनिगं शुरु हो गया है । नारायणपुर जिले के माड इलाके की 649 वर्ग किलोमीटर जमीन सेना को दी गयी है ।

आखिर भारत सरकार ने अपनी सेना को बस्तर क्यों भेजी ?

… … … … … … …

दण्डकारण्य स्पेशल जोनल कमेटी
भारत की कम्यूनिस्ट पार्टी (माओवादी)

(English-translated Version of the Entire Document)
Go Back Indian Army! No Bastar, Don't Fight War!
Tribes Are Not Alien, Are Natives of the Country!
Support Their fight for Right!

Soldiers of Indian Army

The Indian Army has stepped into the land of Bastar. 3000 soldiers have started their jungle warfare training. 649 square kilometers land of Maand area of Narayanpur district has been allotted to the army.

After all, why has Indian government sent army to Bastar?

Bastar does not share border with any foreign country, here there is no foreign enemy. Here, only the natives live. In Maand, one of the oldest tribes, Maandiya tribe lives. Indian government considers the residents of Bastar as its enemy. The Indian Army is being sent to fight against the residents of Bastar. Why the soldiers who are trained to fight against foreign invaders and to defend the country are now being given jungle warfare training?

Because the tribes of Bastar are struggling to protect their water, forests, and land. The residents of Bastar are bravely fighting in collaboration with Maoist Party's Army, Jan Mukti Chhaapamar Sena (Peoples Liberation Guerilla Army), against their displacement from forestland, for their genuine development, and against exploitative rule to finally form a People's Government. The army is continuing with jungle warfare training to eliminate the struggling people and CPI (Maoist), which is leading them. The army is being deployed here to handover water, forest, land, and natural resources of the people of Bastar to Multi-national companies (MNCs) and big industrialists.

The ruling classes of India are feudal and inimical to the people. Capitalist, brokers, and central and state governments representing them are anti-national, anti-people, and inimical to the interest of the people because they are selling the water, forest, land, the natural resources, and other valuable assets of the people to MNCs and to the big industrialist houses on very cheap rates. Both national and foreign capitalists are being given concessions to exploit the laborers and to set up the special economic zones. Anti-labor policies, capitalist favoring industrial policy, and anti-farmer agricultural policies are being formulated in favor of both national and foreign capitalists.

Tens of thousands acres of tribal land particularly from Bastar is being forcefully snatched and given to Tata, Jindal, Mittal, Essar, and MNCs like TPG. These are all being done by violating the self-made laws like the 5th schedules, PESA, Forest Laws, etc. Not only this, big dams are being constructed and quarries being opened forcefully to favor the capitalists.

To crush the public, the black laws like UAPA, Chhattisgarh Special Public Security Act, MCOCA, etc., are being framed and various state-sponsored gangs like Salwa Judum, Sentra Village Circling, Tandya Liberation Federation, Civil Defence Committee, etc., are being promulgated. People are deprived of basic amenities like food, clothes, house, education, health, and employment.

Lakhs and crores of black money is being deposited in foreign banks by the corrupt people. Instead of resolving the problems of poverty, hunger, unemployment, illiteracy, poor, health, lack of housing, etc., they are responding with bullets, jail, caning, etc. Hence, people have only the option of Peoples War of Independence. Maoists are the real patriots because they are fighting against the feudal capitalists, brokers, and all other imperialist forces including USA for the national sovereignty and true independence. We are fighting to save the valuable resources of the country from being looted by the MNCs and capitalists. People's war is dedicated to setting up a society based on equality against the rule of the exploitative ruler class.

Who are the soldiers of Indian Army?

Soldiers of army belong to the low middle-class farmers, labor, and tribal families of the country. Poverty and unemployment have compelled them to become soldiers. No soldier comes from a family of landlords, capitalists, leaders/bureaucrats. If at all anyone does, he joins as an officer. Personally, army men are not our enemies. We believe that it is a part of suppressive rule policy of the exploitative ruling class. The ruling class raises army to save their government, to protect life and property, and to sustain their exploitation. The class which is exploited, suppressed is enrolled in the army after falling bribes. This is a policy which is akin to putting fingers in one's own eyes.

The Indian Army is not an army to secure or serve the people. It is hired army of rulers. Patriotism, security of country, and love for country are only in rhetoric. Actually, the real duty of the Indian Army should be to save the life and property of people from enemies and invaders. It is pertinent to ask what are BSF, deployed in Kanker district and ITBP located at Rajnandgaon district doing in Bastar, when both of them were raised to defend the borders of the country.

The army is deployed to suppress the struggling masses, facilitating establishment of factories and allotting mines to the capitalists, looting property and depriving the tribes from the water, forests, and land, and to harm their culture and existence. The residents of Bastar are freedom and nature lovers. They are full of courage and bravery. They are accustomed to fight against the corrupt rulers and exploiters. They have chosen the path of civil war for their existence, self-esteem, self-rule, and real development. The CPI (Maoist) is working with public and leading them since 30 years.

The "Jan Mukti Mar Sena" is struggling for the liberation of people and to establish the people's rule. To crush the revolutionary movement of people, schemes like Salwa Judum were initiated, which were defeated by the people of Bastar. The people of Bastar, through civil war, will also defeat the army.

The Soldiers and Junior Officers of Army

- Being trained soldiers of army, which is raised to fight against foreign invaders, do not use gun against the people of the country.
- Recognize the anti-national and anti-people character of the central and state governments, which started war against its own people.
- Your loyalty should be towards the people of the country and not towards the corrupt, scam ridden, traitors, characterless leaders, officers and industrialists, anti-nationals, who have deposited lakhs and crores in foreign banks, MNCs, and especially against America, the leading terrorist state and number one enemy of the world.
- Identify your root class.
- In the continuing class struggle, do not use gun against your own class, your own people.
- Do not work as an instrument of exploitive ruling class.
- Support the just and courageous war of people of Bastar.
- Oppose the unjust war of the government against the people.
- Demand the return of Indian Army from Bastar.

Dandkaranya Special Zonal Committee
Forest Zonal Special Committee [CPI (M)]

APPENDIX F

List of 83 Left Wing Extremist affected districts included under SRE scheme

Andhra Pradesh (SRE = 16, focus districts = 01) 1. Anantapur 2. Adilabad 3. East Godavari 4. Guntur 5. Karimnagar **6. Khammam** 7. Kurnool 8. Medak 9. Mehboobnagar 10. Nalgonda 11. Prakasam 12. Srikakulam 13. Visakhapatnam 14. Vizianagaram 15. Warangal 16. Nizamabad **Bihar** (SRE – 15, focus districts – 06) **1. Arwal** **2. Aurangabad** 3. Bhojpur 4. East Champaran **5. Gaya** **6. Jamui** **7. Jehanabad** 8. Kaimur 9. Munger 10. Nalanda 11. Nawada 12. Patna **13. Rohtas** 14. Sitamarhi 15. West Champaran	**Chhattisgarh** (SRE = 09, focus districts = 07) **1. Bastar** **2. Bijapur** **3. Dantewada** 4. Jashpur **5. Kanker** 6. Korea (Baikunthpur) **7. Narayanpur** **8. Rajnandgaon** **9. Sarguja** **Jharkhand** (SRE = 18, focus districts = 11) **1. Bokaro** **2. Chatra** 3. Dhanbad **4. East Singhbhum** **5. Garhwa** 6. Giridih **7. Gumla** **8. Hazaribagh** 9. Koderma **10. Latehar** **11. Lohardagga** **12. Palamu** 13. Ranchi 14. Simdega 15. Saraikela-Kharaswan **16. West Singhbhum** 17. Khunti **18. Ramgarh** **Madhya Pradesh** (SRE = 01, focus districts = 01) **1. Balaghat**	**Maharashtra** (SRE – 03, focus districts = 02) 1. Chandrapur **2. Gadchiroli** **3. Gondia** **Odisha** (SRE = 15, focus districts = 05) **1. Gajapati** 2. Ganjam 3. Keonjhar 4. Koraput **5. Malkangiri** 6. Mayubhanj 7. Navrangpur **8. Rayagada** **9. Sambhalpur** 10. Sundargarh 11. Nayagarh 12. Kondhamal **13. Deogarh** 14. Jajpur 15. Dhenkanal **Uttar Pradesh** (SRE = 03, focus districts – 01) 1. Chandauli 2. Mirzapur **3. Sonbhadra** **West Bengal** (SRE = 03, focus districts = 01) 1. Bankura **2. Midnapore** 3. Purulia

Note: The districts shown in bold are 35 worst affected districts taken up for focused development.
Source: http://mha.nic.in/pdfs/LWE-aftdDist-131210.pdf, accessed on March 04, 2013.

Bibliography

Aarti Dhar, "De-notified Tribes to Get Better Deal in 12th Plan", *The Hindu*, December 19, 2012.

Age Correspondent, "NE-Maoist – J&K Mega Rebel Plan Revealed", *The Asian Age*, October 08, 2011.

Ahmad Malik Jalal, "Think Like a Guerrilla: Counterinsurgency Lessons from Sri Lanka", *Harvard Kennedy School Review*.

Ajay Sura and T. Roy Chowdhury, "New Constructions in Gurgaon Put on Hold to Tackle Water Problem", *Times of India*, July 17, 2012.

Ajit Kumar singh, "Maoists look at North - East", Pioneer, November 5, 2011.

Amarnath K. Menon, "A Deadly Ambush", *India Today*, July 03, 2008.

Anahita Mukherjee, "India uproots most people for progress", Times of India, June 04, 2012.

Annual Report 2007-08, MHA, GoI, and "Naxals Surge Ahead – The Nation under Siege", Martyrs' Memorial Research Institute (MMRI), 29 June 2011.

Annual Report 2010-11, Ministry of Tribal Affairs, Government of India.

Annual Reports 2010-11, 2011-12, Ministry of Home Affairs, Government of India.

Anumeha Yadav, "Belly Bomb Sewn into Soldier's Body", *The Hindu*, January 11, 2013.

Art Ryan L Seachon, "Insurgencies in History: A Blueprint for Future Strategy", *OGS Digest*, October–December 2004.

Aung San Suu Kye, "World Economic Forum on East Asia", June 01, 2012.

Bajpai Kanti, "Parliament Fiddles While India Burns", *Times of India*, September 15, 2012.

Basu Durga, "Shorter Constitution of India" (Nagpur: Wadhwa and Company Law Publishers, 2004).

Bina Agrawal and Pravesh Sharma, "An Idea to Bank On", *The Times of India*, January 12, 2012.

Brahma Chellany, "Regional Security Challenges: Indian State in Asia", Manas Publications, 2010.

SK Chatterji "Perception Management in Conflict Zones", http://www.au.af.mil/info-ops/iosphere/10winter/iosphere_win10_chatterji.pdaccessed on November 11, 2012.

Bruce Hoffman and Jennifer Morrison Taw, "A Strategic Framework for Countering Terrorism and Insurgency", *RAND Note, 1992.*

Bureau of Police Research and Development, Conducted by Centre for Development And Peace Studies, Guwahati.

Census of India 2011, Provisional Population Totals, Paper 2, Vol. 1, 2011, p. v.

Chakraborty Sujit, "No Leeway Any More for Militants", *The Hindu*, September 30, 2012.

Chandrashekar and Jayati Ghosh, "Employment under New Growth Trajectory 2010.

Deeptiman Tiwary, "Manipur Rebels Supplying Arms to Maoists, Says NIA", *Times of India*, December 19, 2012.

Dilip Kumar Mekala, "Few Lessons Learnt, Revisiting the Horrors of Chintalnar Massacre", http://forceindia.net/FewLessonsLearnt.aspx, Force magazine.

Dixit Kapil, "Youths Entering World of Crime to Live Life King-size", *The Times of India*, December 3, 2011.

DN Sahaya, Governor Tripura (2003–2009), How Tripura Overcame Insurgency, *The Hindu*, September 16, 2011.

Dr P.K. Agrawal, "Naxalism Causes and Cure", Manas Publications, 2010.

Dr N.C. Asthana and Dr. Anjali Nirmal, "Terrorism, Insurgencies and Counterinsurgency Operations", Pointer Publishers, 2001.

E.N. Rammohan, "The Naxalite Maoist Insurgency in India – The Root Causes and a Possible Solution", *USI Journal*, July-September 2012.

Galula David, "Counter-Insurgency Warfare: Theory and Practice" (New Delhi: Pentagon Press, 2008).

GD Bakshi – "Left Wing Extremism in India: Context, Implications and Response Options", Manekshaw Papers, November 2009.

Ghosh Avijit, "Reds Aiming at High Value Targets', Say Analysts", *Times of India*, April 26, 2012.

Goepner Eric, "An Enduring Argument against Counterinsurgency", *Small Wars Journal Article*, September 27, 2012.

GoI, Ministry of Home Affairs, Census of India, 2011.

Gurmeet Kanwal and Dhruv C. Katoch, "Naxal Violence: The Threat Within", KW Publishers Pvt Ltd, 2012.

Hsu Long-hsuen, "History of the Sino-Japanese War (1937–1945)", Taipei, 1972.

Human Development Index Report 2011, Planning Commission, GoI, Oxford University Press.

Ishar Judge Ahluwalia, "Report on Urban Indian Infrastructure and Services", March 2011.

James D Kiras, "Irregular Warfare: Terrorism and Insurgency", Oxford University.

Jawaid Sohail, "The Maoist Movement in India", New Delhi Associated Publishing House 1979.

Jennifer Lynn Cucchisi, "The Causes and Effects of the Chinese Civil War, 1927–1949".

Joshi Sandeep, "Abondon Operations if Maoists Use Human Shields', Security Forces Told", *The Hindu*, July 07, 2012.

Jyoti Basu Memoirs, So Far as I can Remember, Chapter VII, Tebhaga Movement, accessed via http://jyotibasumemoirs.wordpress.com/page/2/ on December 12, 2011.

Kilcullen David, "Influential Counterinsurgency", Oxford University Press, 2010.

Kitson Frank, "Low Intensity Operations: Sub-version Insurgency & Peacekeeping" (Harrisburg: Stackpole Books, 1971).

Kujur Rajat Kumar, "Violent Revolution: The Naxal War Zone in Odisha", IPCS, July 08, 2008.

Leung, Edwin Pak-wah Leung, "Historical Dictionary of Revolutionary China, 1839–1976", New York: Greenwood Press.

L.N. Rangarajan, "Kautilya: The Arthashastra", New Delhi, Penguin Books, 1992.

Louise Chipley Slavicek, "Mao Zedong", Library of Congress Cataloguing-in-Publication Data, 2004.

Manpreet Sethi, "Land Reforms in India – Issues and Challenges", Manas Publications.

Marwah Ved, "India in Turmoil: Jammu & Kashmir, the Northeast and Left Extremism (New Delhi: Rupa & Co, 2009).

Menon Meena, "Forest Versus Forest Talk", *The Hindu*, August 05, 2012.

Michael Crawshaw, "Running a Country: The British Colonial Experience and its Relevance to Present Day Concerns", The Shrivenham Papers, Number 3, April 2007.

Ministry of Rural Development, "GOI – 2009: Report of the Committee on State Agrarian Relations and the Unfinished Task in Land Reforms Commission".

Ministry of Telecommunications, GoI, "Annual Report 2010-11".

Mockaitis Thomas R., "Resolving Insurgencies", Strategic Studies Institute (SSI), June 17, 2011.

Monitorable Targets & Milestones for 2010-11 infrastructure sectors: Planning Commission.

N. Manoharan, "No More 'Indigenous': External Linkages of Left Wing Extremism", Article 1508, July 17, 2010.

Namrata Goswami, "Counter-Insurgency Best Practices: Applicability to Northeast India, *Small Wars Journal*, December 06, 2012.

Nayak Girdhari, "Neo-Naxal Challenge, Issues and options", Pentagon Press, 2011.

Olugbile O.B. and Coker A.O., "Conflict in the Niger-Delta of Nigeria:

An Analysis of the Problem", *African Journal of Traumatic Stress,* Volume 1, Number 2, December 2010.

Paget Julian, "Counter Insurgency Operations: Techniques of Guerrilla Warfare" (New York: Walker and Co, 1967).

Prakash Singh, "The Naxalite Movement in India", Rupa Publications, 2010.

R W Kromer, "The Malayan Emergency in Retrospect: Organization of a Successful Counterinsurgency Effort", a 1972 RAND study.

R. Radha Krishna and Shovan Ray (2005), "Handbook of Poverty in India: Perspectives, Policies, and Programmers", Oxford Press.

Rajnish Sharma, "New ISI Strategy to Equip Naxals", *The Asian Age,* October 24, 2011.

Rakhi Chakrabarty, "Welcomed by Reds, Harassed by Cops", *Times of India,* July12, 2012.

Ramana P.V., "The Naxal Challenge: Causes, Linkages and Policy Options (New Delhi: Pearson Longman, 2008).

Ramprastha Primera, "Orissa Industrial Dream Mired in Delays", *Indian Express,* October 29, 2012.

Ranjit Kumar Gupta, "The Crimson Agenda: Maoist Protest and Terror", Arthur Monteiro Publications, 2004.

Report of the Expert Group lead by D. Bandhopaday titled "Development Challenges in Extremist Affected Areas", Planning Commission, 2008.

Richard A. Gabriel and Paul L. Savage, "Crisis in Command: Mismanagement in the Army", Library of Congress Cataloguing Publication Data, 1990.

Robin M. Williams Jr., "The Wars Within, The People and States in Conflict", Manas Publications, 2004.

Rostum K. Nanavatty, "Internal Armed Conflict in India, Forging a Joint Civil-Military Approach", Pentagon Press, 2013.

Sahaya D.N., Governor Tripura (2003–2009), "How Tripura Overcame Insurgency", *The Hindu,* September 16, 2011.

Satish Kumar, "India's National Security Annual Review 2006", KW Publisher, 2006.

SGM Herbert A. Friedman (Ret), "Psychological Warfare of the Malayan Emergency, 1948–1960".

Srinivasan Rukmini, "At 217m, India Houses Largest No. of Malnourished", *The Times of India* October 10, 2012.

Sudeep Chakravarti, "Red Sun: Travels in Naxalite Country", Published by the Penguin Groups, 2008.

Suniti Kumar Ghosh, "Naxalbari Before and After: Reminiscences and Appraisal", New Age Publishers Ltd, 2009.

Suvojit Bagchi, "Maoist Backing Chhattisgarh Teachers' Strike", *The Hindu,* December 17, 2012.

Thompson Roger, "Defeating Communist Insurgency: The Lessons of Malaya and Vietnam" (New York: Praeger Publishers, 1970).

TRAI, "Measures to Improve Telecom Penetration in India – The Next 100 Million Subscribers", 2008.

Trinquier Roger, "Modern Warfare: A French view of Counter-insurgency" (New Delhi: Pentagon Press, 2008).

Vinaya Deshpande, "Engage, don't Encroach", *The Hindu,* June 22, 2012.

Williams Robin M. Jr., "The Wars Within: Peoples and States in Conflict", (New Delhi: Manas Publications, 20041).

Zhang, Chunhou. Vaughan, C. Edwin. [2002] (2002), "Mao Zedong as Poet and Revolutionary Leader: Social and Historical Perspectives.' Lexington books.

Papers by the Author

Ahluwalia VK, "Strategy and Tactics of the Indian Maoists: An Analysis", Strategic Analysis, IDSA, September-October 2012.

Ahluwalia VK, "Urban Perspective Plan – An Analysis of Maoist Perspective and Assessment", *U.S.I. Journal,* July–September 2012.

Ahluwalia VK, "Bloodiest Years of Naxal Violence: Strategic Challenges", Defence and Security Alert, November 2012.

Ahluwalia VK, "Reds Use Brutal Tactics to Create Fear Psychosis", *The Times of India,* New Delhi, January 19, 2013.

Ahluwalia VK, "India–China Relations: Implications for Regional Peace and Security", National Defence College, Dhaka, September 06, 2003.

Ahluwalia VK, "Status of Naxalism: Strategic Options", Defence and Security Alert, May 2013.

Subject Index

About the Author

Lieutenant General Vijay Kumar Ahluwalia retired from the Army on February 29, 2012 as the General Officer Commanding-in-Chief, Central Command. He is a graduate of Staff Course, Wellington, Higher Command Course, Mhow and National Defence Course, Dhaka (Bangladesh). He has had a wide experience of command and staff in the Northeast and Jammu and Kashmir. He served as a regimental officer in the Northeast (1982-83 and 1986-89), and commanded his Artillery Regiment in Rajouri Sector (J&K) and in Rajasthan. He commanded an Infantry Brigade in the Valley (J&K) (2001-02) and a Mountain Division in Kargil Sector (2005-06), both in an intense operational environment. After an eventful tenure as Director General Military Training (DGMT) at the Army HQ, he commanded the Corps in Leh-Ladakh region in 2008-09. As a colonel, he served on important staff duties in Manipur-Nagaland and J&K from 1995 to 1998.

As the Army Commander Central Command (2010-12), he was involved in analyzing the problem of Naxalism, ground realities, and strategic challenges for conflict resolution. Out of the large number of states that form part of the area of responsibility of the Central Command, four states, namely Jharkhand, Chhattisgarh, Bihar, and Odisha, are critically affected by Naxalism. He has authored a number of essays and articles on Naxalism. Highly decorated, he is a recipient of the Param Vishisht Seva Medal, Ati Vishisht Seva Medal and bar, Yudh Seva Medal and Vishisht Seva Medal for his distinguished services, predominantly in active operational environments. As the General Officer Commanding of the Division in Kargil, he received the Bombay Natural History Society (BNHS) green governance award for initiating the unique concept called "Operation Green Kargil", which was awarded by the Prime Minister of India on November 10, 2005. Currently, he is a member of the Armed Forces Tribunal, Jaipur; and is pursuing PhD in "Internal Security and Naxalism".